Politics in

CHINA

The Little, Brown Series
in Comparative Politics

Under the Editorship of

GABRIEL A. ALMOND

LUCIAN W. PYE

A COUNTRY STUDY

Politics in

CHINA

Third Edition

James R. Townsend
University of Washington

Brantly Womack

Northern Illinois University

Boston   Toronto
LITTLE, BROWN AND COMPANY

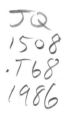

Library of Congress Cataloging-in-Publication Data

Townsend, James R. (James Roger)
  Politics in China.

  Little, Brown series in comparative politics. A
country study.
  Includes index.
  1. China—Politics and government—1949–1976.
2. China—Politics and government—1976–
I. Womack, Brantly, 1947–   . II. Title. III. Series:
Little, Brown series in comparative politics. Country
study.
JQ1508.T68 1986   320.951   85-19873
ISBN 0-316-85132-9

Library of Congress Catalog Card No. 85–19873

ISBN 0-316-85132-9

9 8 7 6 5 4 3 2 1

ALP

Published simultaneously in Canada
by Little, Brown & Company (Canada) Limited
Printed in the United States of America

ACKNOWLEDGMENTS

Table III, Growth of the Chinese Communist Party, 1921–1982 (Figures for years 1927–1961).

From John Wilson Lewis, *Leadership in Communist China.*
© 1963 by Cornell University. Used by permission of the publisher, Cornell University Press.

Table V, Communist Youth League Membership, 1949–1959
Reprinted by permission of the author and the publisher from Klaus H. Pringsheim, "The Functions of the Chinese Communist Youth Leagues (1920–1949)," *China Quarterly*, no. 12 (October–December 1962), pp. 90–91.

Table VIII, Continuity Between the Eleventh and Twelfth CCs
From Hong Yung Lee, "China's 12th Central Committee: Rehabilitated Cadres and Technocrats." © 1983 by The Regents of the University of California. Reprinted from *Asian Survey*, Vol. 23, No. 6, June 1983, p. 680, by permission of The Regents.

To Sandy and Ann

Preface to the Third Edition

In the mid-1980s the People's Republic of China has moved beyond the revolutionary concerns of its founding generation. To be sure, there are still active leaders whose careers have spanned over half a century of China's modern history. Deng Xiaoping, the most powerful Chinese leader of the post-Mao period, was a member of one of the earliest Chinese communist groups, worked closely with Mao Zedong before Mao gained control of the party in 1935, and made the legendary Long March. But the surviving older leaders, especially Deng Xiaoping, are preoccupied with increasing China's prosperity within a stable domestic and international political environment. As a victim of the Cultural Revolution, Deng attaches special importance to strengthening institutions and insuring a smooth transfer of power. He is using his remaining years and his personal authority to promote the rule of law, to protect state institutions from arbitrary party control, and to require the party to serve the needs of modernization. His commitment to a smooth transfer of power can be seen in the promotion of Hu Yaobang and Zhao Ziyang to the top party and state positions and, more generally, in the encouragement of younger and better-trained cadres throughout the system.

Under the patronage of Deng Xiaoping, the new leadership has been increasingly bold in its efforts to reform the economic and political structure and thereby promote modernization. A general relaxation of central control can be seen. Private economic activity has revived after near extinction in the Cultural Revolution, enterprises have been given much more autonomy, and life on the streets of China is proof that earlier revolutionary puritanism has softened. Important exceptions to relaxation are population policy, internal party discipline, and criminal sanctions. Moreover, institutions and procedures have been reformed and revitalized. Chinese leadership is attempting to guarantee that current reforms will continue indefinitely. At the highest level this concern can be seen in the promotion of the 1982 Constitution and the development of the legal profession, but it also affects daily life in the form of long-term production contracts for households. Finally, the policy change most obvious to a foreign audience is the new commitment to international openness, which has brought hundreds of thousands of tourists and rapidly increasing amounts of foreign investment to China as well as thousands of Chinese students to Western countries.

Paradoxically, the very stability of post-Mao politics and the normalcy (by Western standards) of its policy concerns create difficulties for the understanding of PRC politics as a whole. What are the continuities between the post-Mao period and the Cultural Revolution? To what extent are current policies a return to the politics of socialist construction of the 1950s? Are current decollectivization policies in rural areas a fundamental and permanent rejection of rural policy since land reform in the early 1950s? The attempt to answer such questions requires a well-balanced understanding of past and current phases of Chinese politics.

It is easy to assume that the current phase of Chinese politics is politically self-contained and does not require a serious investigation of earlier phases. This assumption is encouraged by Chinese political rhetoric, which emphasizes the total rejection of the Cultural Revolution on the one hand and the arrival of a new era of modernization on the other. It should be remembered, however, that the Cultural Revolution also claimed to be a total rejection of the previous period and promised a new era of permanent revolution. In retrospect, interpretations of Chinese politics that simply accepted the rhetoric of the Cultural Revolution appeared dated and naive. The basic inadequacy of only taking current politics into account is not that the phase may change and make one's analysis irrelevant, but that the starting point of any new phase is the experience, political behavior, and ideas of previous phases. The differences between the Cultural Revolution and the post-Mao era are undeniable, but the significance of these differences can be understood only in historical context. For Chinese political actors, this context is a matter of personal experience and requires little explicit analysis, but external observers must constantly ask themselves how the historical context structures and gives meaning to political action. Hence, the primary task of the third edition of *Politics in China* is to seek an overall understanding of Chinese politics that is sensitive to its historical continuities as well as to its post-1976 changes.

Understanding a changing Chinese political system requires changes on the part of the analyst as well. A major change in this edition of *Politics in China* is the addition of Brantly Womack as co-author. We believe that our fresh look at the subject has improved this book in several ways. The first and most obvious area of innovation is the inclusion of new political material up to mid-1985. We have reconsidered issues in every chapter and have restructured some of them in the light of developments in the first decade of post-Mao politics. For example, the discussion of political organization not only takes into account the new party and state constitutions of 1982 but also gives greater attention, in Chapter Three and elsewhere, to the post-Mao emphasis on institutionalization, law, and socialist democracy. Secondly, a general book of this kind relies heavily on the quality of scholarship in the field, and we have incorporated in our analysis many important advances by our scholarly colleagues. A name index has been added to facilitate the reader's use of our references to the impressive body of scholarship available on various topics of interest. A third improvement results from much better data and opinion from China. There has been a significant quantitative and qualitative development of China's informational resources in recent years, which has greatly strengthened the data base of the third edition. This can be seen in the appendices, for example, and in the discussion in Chapter Five of the communications media.

This edition of *Politics in China* has benefitted greatly from comments on the second edition by students and colleagues, and we invite readers to continue to send their comments and suggestions for the improvement of future editions. We are especially grateful to Lowell Dittmer fo his extensive comments on an earlier draft, and we acknowledge with thanks John Frankenstein's "Note on the Romanization of Chinese," which we have retained from the second edition. We are indebted to Cheryl Fuller for her very able word-processing. Finally, we extend our thanks to several other people whose support and assistance helped bring the manuscript to completion: Lucian Pye, the academic editor for this volume in the Series in Comparative Politics; John Covell and Barbara Breese of Little, Brown and Company; and Terri Gitler and Cathy Lockman of Publication Services. All errors and shortcomings, are of course, our own.

A Note on the Romanization of Chinese

There are several systems, all of them unsatisfactory in some way, for rendering Chinese words in the Roman alphabet. The two most widespread today are the *pinyin* system, used in the People's Republic of China, and the older Wade-Giles system, which until recently was almost universally used in English-language scholarly work on China. This book uses, except as noted, the official *pinyin* system; the more familiar Wade-Giles transcription follows the *pinyin* rendering in parentheses at the first occurrence.

There are, however, a number of cases where familiarity, custom, sheer recognizability, and ease of scholarly access argue for retention of older romanizations, especially in a textbook such as this. Thus, in this book, Peking [Beijing], Canton [Guangzhou], Yangtze [Changjiang], Manchuria [Dongbei], Tibet [Xizang], and Inner Mongolia [Nei Monggul] are given in their non-*pinyin* versions; brackets denote *pinyin* versions of older usages. The names of some individuals (Chiang Kai-shek, Sun Yat-sen) and organizations (the Kuomintang, referred to throughout this text by the standard initials KMT) are not changed.

Finally, we should note that we have retained that word of most uncertain origin, China. Otherwise, the name of this book would be *Politics in Zhongguo*.

Contents

Figures and Tables

People's Republic of China

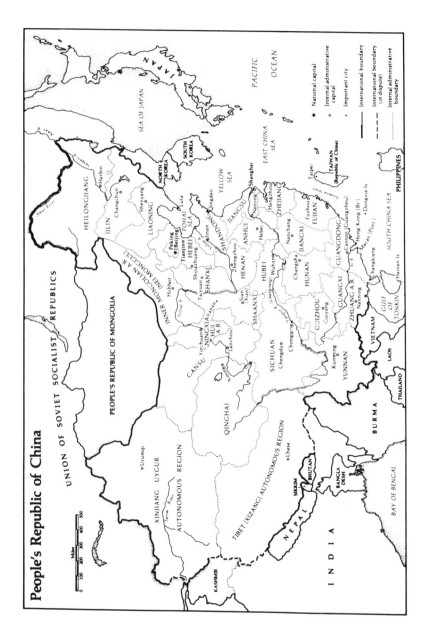

CHAPTER I

The Study of Chinese Politics

THE SETTING OF CHINESE POLITICS

The Revolutionary Setting. POLITICS IN CHINA are the product of a prolonged revolutionary era, spanning at least the period between 1911 and 1949 and including not one but three forceful overthrows of the political system. The first revolution in 1911 displaced an imperial system that had endured for centuries. The second, culminating in 1928 with the establishment of a new central government under the control of the Kuomintang (KMT), replaced the disunited "warlord" rule of early republican China with a more vigorous, organized, and centralized system of single-party domination. The third revolution of 1949 brought the Chinese Communist Party (CCP) to power, inaugurating the present Communist system.

Even this delineation, broad as it is, does not define the scope of China's revolutionary era. Successful efforts to overthrow national political institutions and elites establish the decisive peaks of a revolutionary process, but they do not necessarily mark the limits of the process itself. In the case of the Chinese revolution, it is probably best to date the initiation of the process from the Taiping Rebellion (1850–1864), an upheaval so disruptive in its impact and goals that it may be regarded as "revolutionary in character" and "the beginning of the end of Confucian China."[1] Moreover, despite the Communist victory

[1] Franz Michael, in collaboration with Chung-li Chang, *The Taiping Rebellion, Volume I: History* (Seattle: University of Washington Press, 1966), p. 199.

1

of 1949, the revolutionary era lasted until the death of Mao Zedong in 1976. The Great Proletarian Cultural Revolution, which erupted in 1966 and dominated the subsequent decade, was clear evidence of continuing revolutionary features in Chinese politics. Mao and his supporters insisted that this campaign was truly a "revolution"; indeed, their propagandists called it "the greatest of revolutionary mass movements," one which "has no parallel in the history of mankind."[2] Without necessarily accepting the accuracy of this claim, it is testimony to Chinese perceptions that their times are revolutionary.[3]

The revolutionary setting of Chinese politics is, for the external observer, a source of both fascination and frustration. The richness and power of Chinese civilization have long held a peculiar fascination for outsiders. To that attraction is now added the recognition that one of the most dramatic events of human history has occurred, and is still unfolding, in modern China. The politics of revolution defy easy understanding or generalization, however, regardless of the student's interest and enthusiasm. Later in this chapter, we discuss some debates about how to interpret the Chinese revolution, but a few more concrete problems deserve mention here.

Political upheaval and social change, are, of course, the essence of revolution. It is obvious that modern Chinese politics have been unstable, that political and social changes have come so rapidly during the course of the revolution that descriptions at one point in time have seldom held true for long. It is not so obvious, perhaps, to recognize how often these changes have violated preconceptions about what was "possible" in China. Consider only a few examples of propositions seriously held by at least some observers during recent decades. At various times it was thought that Communism could never triumph in a family-dominated society like China; that China after World War II

---

[2] *Peking Review*, no. 42 (October 18, 1968): 26, 31.

[3] Indeed, Deng Xiaoping has described the post-1978 reforms as a "second revolution"; see *Beijing Review*, vol. 28, no. 14 (April 8, 1985): 6. However, we view the death of Mao as the end of the revolutionary era because Deng's reforms do not have the anti-institutional, critical and disruptive features normally associated with a revolution. For insightful analysis of the postrevolutionary character of post-Mao politics, see Lowell Dittmer, "Ideology and Organization in Post-Mao China," *Asian Survey*, vol. 24, no. 3 (March 1984): 349–369.

would be a firm American ally; that ideological bonds made the Sino-Soviet alliance unbreakable; that the authority of the CCP could not be seriously threatened from within; that the conflict that developed between the United States and China in the 1950s was irreconcilable; that China would never again welcome foreign economic activity within its borders. All of these propositions were plausible at one time, but all proved false. The lesson is that analysis of a revolutionary era calls for special care in evaluating the conventional wisdom of the times.

Second, a revolutionary setting raises the stakes of political competition, transforming many differences into struggles for political and human survival. The "agreement to disagree" is not impossible in such a setting, but it may be a luxury and a risk. When the outcome of political struggle is seen as decisive for both personal careers and long-term structuring of society, participants who hold firmly to their ambitions and ideals will not hesitate to extend the "rules" of the game. The use or threatened use of armed force then becomes central in the political process, as it was in China throughout the 1911–1949 period. The army's declining role in Chinese politics between 1949 and 1958 was a concrete sign of the decline of revolutionary politics. Its rising political role after 1959 and into the Cultural Revolution—first symbolic, then as a threat, and ultimately in deployment against other organized political groups—was equally concrete evidence of a revolutionary revival. By the mid-1980s the army's political role was at its lowest ebb since 1949, perhaps since the mid-nineteenth century, as China entered its postrevolutionary era.

Finally, the prosaic yet unavoidable problem of source material and corroborative evidence must be raised. It is not easy to acquire knowledge about the dynamics of Chinese politics. Data on contemporary China are drawn largely, although by no means exclusively, from official Communist sources that are subject to severe limitations and restrictions. This is not simply a post-1949 problem that flows from the CCP's effort to maintain a closed communications system. The production and preservation of reliable source material probably suffers in any revolutionary situation. Archives may be lost, destroyed, or sealed; key participants may be silenced; independent sources may be suppressed while official sources become overtly propagandistic;

the acquisition of data generally, whether by scholars or officials, assumes a low priority and becomes immensely difficult in a society disrupted by internal war and revolution.

Chinese publications and data have risen in both quantity and quality since 1976. Coupled with the greater openness to foreign travelers and residents and the opportunities for foreign research in China, this trend produces much more information about China from a variety of sources and perspectives. Nonetheless, there are still many gaps and contradictions in sources on modern Chinese politics, raising important methodological issues about how to use the raw data that comes to us from Chinese publications, emigrants from the Chinese mainland, foreign journalists, and other sources.[4] The student of Chinese politics must remain conscious of source limitations and how they affect interpretations of the subject.

The Historical Setting. The Chinese revolution occurred in a society reknowned for the quality and longevity of its culture and political tradition. In Chapter 2, we will consider how some important characteristics of the Chinese political tradition influenced revolutionary history, while noting here the expectations of greatness that this tradition has left in the minds of Chinese and foreigners alike. Historically derived images have an intangible quality, but their importance with regard to China is unmistakable. Indeed, in modern times they have led repeatedly to exaggerated estimates of China's influence and capabilities. They appeared in a dangerous complacency with which the Manchu emperors responded to intensified Western pressures beginning in the late eighteenth century. Perhaps equally misguided were the Western traders and missionaries on the other side, who foresaw a commercial or religious conquest of China that would alter the shape of world history. The United States in World War II nourished what were at that time illusory visions of China's world status. Cold war American fears about China's

---

[4]See Michel Oksenberg, "Sources and Methodological Problems in the Study of Contemporary China," in A. Doak Barnett, ed., *Chinese Communist Politics in Action* (Seattle: University of Washington Press, 1969), pp. 577–606; and Amy Auerbacher Wilson, ed., *Methodological Issues in Chinese Studies* (New York: Praeger, 1983).

domination of Southeast Asia, its influence in Africa, or its military threat to the North American continent drew more on the image than the reality of Chinese power. The Chinese, too, have tended to attach global significance to their actions, as in the earlier quote about the Cultural Revolution. Although political rhetoric naturally exaggerates hopes and fears, China's tradition is an important influence on expectations about the nation's future.

In more practical terms, the student of Chinese politics must grapple with historical references simply because they pervade Chinese political discourse. The Chinese frame of reference is strikingly self-centered and historical. Comparisons are mainly with the past—with the empire, with the KMT, with "before Liberation" or "before the Cultural Revolution" or "since the Gang of Four"—rather than with other systems. Well-known figures from the past provide analogues for contemporary heroes and villains. Examples and metaphorical images draw heavily from the historical and literary traditions.

This tendency to load contemporary political discourse with references to the past is partly a cultural characteristic, partly a function of the closeness and relevance of the traditional system. Many of the leaders who governed the People's Republic of China (PRC) until recently were born before the fall of the empire in 1911. Mao and his senior colleagues knew imperial society firsthand and received part of their education in the traditional style. Younger leaders were recruited into politics before 1949 and are well aware of traditional ideas and social patterns that persisted after 1911. In short, the historical setting continues to serve as a reference point for evaluating contemporary programs and goals.

The International Setting. The international setting provides a third vantage point for introducing the study of Chinese politics. The PRC's area of 9.6 million square kilometers (about 3.7 million square miles, a bit larger than the United States) makes it the world's third largest state; its population—1.036 billion at the end of 1984—is by far the world's largest, comprising over one-fifth of the global total (see Appendix B.2). Economic growth since 1949 has been cumulatively strong despite a severe economic crisis in the early 1960s. Official Chinese statistics record the following average annual growth rates for 1952 through 1982, in percentages: national income 6.0; population 1.9; total social product 7.9; industrial output 10.7; agricultural output 3.8 (see Appendix B.1). Because of pricing and accounting differences, foreign observers usually deflate industrial output, thereby lowering the overall growth rate. Nonetheless, the Chinese economy more than quadrupled between 1952 and 1980. By the early 1980s, it was the largest economy in the Third World and the ninth largest in the world as a whole, exceeded only by the seven largest industrial market economies and the Soviet economy.[5] We might think of the PRC economy, one scholar has suggested, as roughly comparable to those of Japan and the USSR twenty years earlier.[6] The PRC's current level of development, great north-south extent across temperate zones, varied topography, and rich mineral and energy resources, give it the potential to become a major force in the world economy within a few decades. Projections are hazardous, but there is good reason to believe it will realize this potential.[7]

The territory of China dominates the East Asian area, sharing borders with the Soviet Union, Pakistan, India, Vietnam, Korea, and other countries and in proximity to Japan and Southeast Asia. It occupies the center of a region of great strategic importance where much of the world's population is concentrated. Diplomatically, the PRC has been a member of the United Nations and its Security Council since 1971; in 1983 it had diplomatic relations with over 120 countries, compared with 25 countries which maintained formal ties with the Republic of China (ROC) on Taiwan. PRC armed forces exceed 4 million, with over 3 million in the army. China detonated its first nuclear

[5] World Bank, *World Development Report 1983* (New York: Oxford University Press, 1983), pp. 152–153. Some higher estimates of China's GNP indicate it is above Canada, Italy, and the United Kingdom, making it the world's sixth largest economy. See Appendix B for more detail on PRC economic growth.

[6] Dwight H. Perkins, "The International Consequences of China's Economic Development," in Richard H. Solomon, ed., *The China Factor* (Englewood Cliffs, N.J.: Prentice-Hall, 1981), pp. 115–117.

[7] See *ibid*; and Joint Economic Committee, Congress of the United States, *China Under the Four Modernizations, Part I* (Washington: GPO, 1982), especially Robert F. Dernberger, "The Chinese Search for the Path of Self-Sustained Growth in the 1980s: An Assessment," pp. 19–76; and Arthur G. Ashbrook, Jr., "China: Economic Modernization and Long-Term Performance," pp. 99–118.

device in 1964, orbited its first space satellite in 1970; missile delivery capabilities are growing, although they remain far behind those of the superpowers. The PRC is a major regional power, a potential global power, and an important actor in international politics. Its diplomatic recognition by the United States in January 1979 removed the last formal barrier to full international participation.

This is an exceedingly simplified view of China's international setting, one that stresses the country's weight in the global scales. It must be qualified by several points. First, the PRC's economic power reflects its size, not its level of development. Despite a strong growth record and three decades of rapid industrialization, China remains unevenly developed and still heavily dependent on its agricultural sector. In terms of per capita GNP (about $400), it is among the poorer countries of the world. More to the point, it has a precarious food-population balance that complicates growth strategies. The basic problem is that only about 15 percent of the land is suitable for agricultural use, with most of the rural population–which is about 80 percent of the total population–concentrated on the cultivated one-sixth of China's land surface. Chinese officials observe that their economy must support over one-fifth of the world's population with only 7 percent of its cultivated land. To support industrialization and feed its population, China must keep agricultural growth ahead of population growth. It has done so, but with little surplus. Grain production per capita fell far below peak levels of the 1950s during the crisis of the early 1960s and failed to reach new highs until the late 1970s (see Appendix B). Reduced population growth in recent years—approximately 1 percent in 1983 and 1984—has helped, as has a surge in agricultural production brought about by new agricultural policies (the "responsibility system") adopted after 1976. These trends have alleviated the food-population problem, although serious food shortages could still arise as a result of successive harvest failures or another severe economic crisis. In any event, China's long-term economic development requires a technical revolution in agriculture. Current efforts to promote agricultural growth by increasing material incentives for rural households have not settled arguments about how to combine technical transformation with socialist principles.

There are other trouble spots in future PRC development. Rising consumer demands may disrupt a development pattern that assumes a large-scale investment under state control. Transportation and housing have lagged behind other sectors, and there are persistent energy shortages despite China's impressive potential in this area. Scientific and technological backwardness is a major obstacle to future economic and military development. The growth strategy of the 1980s places increasing reliance on foreign trade, technology, and capital, which poses delicate political issues for Chinese elites. An unwieldy bureaucracy tends to perpetuate inefficiencies and resist reforms. In short, China's growing importance in the world does not mean development will be easy, automatic, or free from serious internal strains and conflicts.

Second, China's current cooperative involvement with the international system contrasts with the international conflicts and insecurities that have characterized most of the PRC's existence. Throughout the 1950s and 1960s, it perceived the United States as a major threat to its security because of American intervention in the Korean War in 1950–1953 and Vietnam in the 1960s, U.S. military security treaties with Japan, South Korea, Taiwan, and the SEATO and ANZUS countries, and diverse American efforts to contain and isolate China. American support enabled the ROC to hold the China seat in the UN and to receive diplomatic recognition from a majority of UN members until 1971. A serious territorial dispute with India led to a brief border war in 1962, followed by years of strained relations between these two Asian powers. Chinese fears of Japanese rearmament were strong in the 1960s. Above all, the intensification of the Sino-Soviet conflict after 1960 made China the potential target of both the nuclear superpowers. Border fighting with the Soviet Union in 1969 underscored the USSR's emergence as China's major enemy and was a major factor leading to Sino-American rapprochement in the 1970s. Since then, and especially since Mao's death in 1976, China's foreign relations have been more peaceful (the major exception being fighting on the Sino-Vietnamese border), with a steady growth in international contacts and trade, primarily with capitalist countries (see Appendix D).

The earlier period of relative isolation and insecurity remains important, however, partly because it combined with themes of self-reliance and revolutionary militancy to influence a political generation, partly because some specific issues remain unresolved. The PRC still has unsettled territorial claims to Taiwan, to Indian and Soviet border areas, and to island groups in the East and South China seas. Military action on these issues is currently unlikely but cannot be excluded from long-range forecasting. As a militarily backward power trying to catch up, China is suspicious of international agreements to limit armaments and nuclear tests. Its foreign trade is still relatively weak, as evidenced by estimated trade figures for 1983 of $40 billion (in U.S. dollars), compared to an estimated $45 billion for Taiwan and $35 billion for Hong Kong. Most significantly, perhaps, improved Sino-Soviet relations have not ended the security threat on China's northern frontier. The PRC is seriously inferior to the USSR in both conventional and strategic capabilities and must continue to give this issue high priority in both domestic and foreign policies.

Finally, to think of the PRC as having "joined the club" is to invert the image of China as a revolutionary force in global politics, an image that dominated both Chinese and foreign views in the 1950s and 1960s. Increasingly over those years, the PRC presented itself as a self-conscious opponent of the world power structure, as a champion of Third World countries and national liberation movements. The ascendancy of the Maoist model within China, especially in the Cultural Revolution, attracted great interest as an alternative to both Western and Soviet developmental models. This is not the place to assess the actual distinctiveness of the Maoist model,[8] but it is essential to note that the Chinese themselves, and many foreign observers, are accustomed to thinking of the PRC as an opponent of and an explicit alternative to the world of the superpowers—a force for

[8]For a sample of the debate about the distinctiveness and possible transferability of the Maoist developmental model, see John G. Gurley, *China's Economy and the Maoist Strategy* (New York: Monthly Review, 1976); Michel Oksenberg, ed., *China's Developmental Experience* (New York: Praeger, 1973); Ross Terrill, ed., *The China Difference* (New York: Harper and Row, 1979); and Dick Wilson, ed., *Mao Tse-tung in the Scales of History* (Cambridge: Cambridge University Press, 1977).

radical change that would necessarily challenge rather than accommodate the existing order. This image complicates the position of current PRC leaders who have, since the death of Mao Zedong in September 1976, intensified China's global interactions in their pursuit of national security and access to the foreign trade, technology, and capital necessary for continued development.

The revolutionary, historical, and international settings pose formidable challenges to the student of Chinese politics—whether beginner or old hand. The student must try to understand the breadth and rapidity of change in China's revolutionary era, while acknowledging the relevance of patterns rooted in an imperial order two milennia old; must take account of the partisanship that pervades both Chinese and foreign sources on the revolution, while making use of this substantial and valuable body of literature; must grasp the uneven character of China's development, in which intractable problems and backward sectors coexist with impressive social and economic advances; must puzzle over China's efforts to find security and support within the international order, even as it struggles to transform that order and escape its restraints; and must comprehend the dialectics of the PRC's movement toward and away from Maoist, Soviet, and Western concepts of development. These challenges enhance the fascination of the subject and also help to explain why foreign observers have argued so much about what issues and models students of Chinese politics should emphasize. Let us more closely examine how this debate over issues and models has kept shifting as students have tried to keep up with the changing realities of revolutionary and postrevolutionary China.

ISSUES IN THE HISTORY OF CHINESE COMMUNISM

For some time after 1949 the major debates and generalizations about Chinese Communism revolved around questions relating to its historical background, seeking thereby to identify the essence of the new regime. There were many reasons for this historical orientation. History and historians held a special place in Chinese studies, while political scientists in the field were relatively few. The newness of the Communist government and the inadequacy of information about it discouraged a thorough examination of post-1949 events. So far as Americans were concerned, political considerations intruded by eliminating contact with the mainland and riveting American attention on the question of why China fell to the Communists. In time, all these considerations lost some of their force, and studies based directly on post-1949 politics began to grow rapidly. Nonetheless, debate on the character of the Communist Revolution, relying heavily on pre-1949 data for proof and documentation, dominated early efforts to generalize about the Communist system. This debate divides roughly into three major themes or controversies: Maoist independence versus Marxist-Leninist orthodoxy; Chinese versus foreign influences; the sources of Communist victory in 1949.

Maoism Versus Orthodoxy. The controversy over "Maoism" is the most explicit, controversial, and enduring debate about Chinese Communist politics. When the *China Quarterly*—the foremost Western journal of contemporary Chinese affairs—began publication in 1960, Maoism was the subject of lead articles in the first two issues;[9] the choice was an accurate indication of what seemed to be the most important controversy in the field. Without attempting to present the views of particular writers, the general thrust of the argument can be stated simply. Supporters of Maoism argued that Chinese Communism, as shaped by Mao Zedong's leadership and represented by his writings, contained distinctive, deviant, or heretical forms of Marxism-Leninism and hence was politically and ideologically independent of Moscow. Those who argued for Chinese "orthodoxy" and rejected the "Maoism" label found no significant deviations by Mao from Marxist-Leninist doctrine and strategy, and they saw the Communist Revolution in China as politically and ideologically dependent on Moscow. In reality, of course, the argument has been an exceedingly sophisticated and tortuous one. Still, as suggested by the simplified version stated above, it posed a fundamental political question that was crucial to an understanding of the post-1949 regime: were the Chinese Communists independent revolutionaries who were

[9] Karl A. Wittfogel, "The Legend of 'Maoism,'" *China Quarterly*, nos. 1, 2 (January–March, April–June 1960): 72–86, 16–34; and Benjamin Schwartz, "The Legend of the 'Legend of "Maoism,"'" *China Quarterly*, no. 2 (April–June 1960): 35–42.

not tied to Moscow, or were they simply the leaders of the Chinese branch of a movement centered in Moscow?

The Sino-Soviet conflict resolved the question of China's political independence in favor of the "Maoist" position. Despite substantial Russian influence in China during the 1950s, the CCP soon demonstrated its political and ideological autonomy, with Maoism gaining wide acceptance in the West (the word *Maoism* is seldom used in China) as the most appropriate term for the distinctive Chinese brand of Marxism-Leninism. The post-1949 triumph of Maoism naturally strengthened the arguments of those who had emphasized its pre-1949 roots.[10] The Maoism debate continues on two broad fronts, however. First, the exact timing and extent of Mao's early deviation from Soviet doctrine remains in dispute, with arguments focusing on the intricacies of revolutionary strategy and CCP-Comintern relationships in the 1927–1935 period.[11]

Second, and of more current interest, has been an ongoing discussion about who are the orthodox Marxist-Leninists. Granted that a significant doctrinal gap exists between Chinese and Russian Communists—the earlier denials of the gap having been silenced—is it Maoism or Soviet socialism that is most true to the parent doctrine? The Russians and some Western analysts, although far from agreement, see Soviet socialism as more orthodox and Maoism as a deviation tending toward some variant of anarchism, subjectivism, bourgeois nationalism, or Trotskyism. The Chinese and other Western analysts—again not in agreement—see Maoism as closer to Marxist values and Leninist revolutionary themes, with the Soviet Union exhibiting

[10]For an excellent survey of Mao's thought, especially his "sinification" of Marxism-Leninism, see Stuart R. Schram, *The Political Thought of Mao Tse-tung*, rev. and enl. ed. (New York: Praeger, 1969). See also Brantly Womack, *The Foundations of Mao Zedong's Political Thought, 1917–1935* (Honolulu: University Press of Hawaii, 1982).

[11]See, for example, Hsiao Tso-liang, *Power Relations Within the Chinese Communist Movement, 1930–1934* (Seattle: University of Washington Press, 1961); Ilpyong J. Kim, *The Politics of Chinese Communism: Kiangsi under the Soviets* (Berkeley: University of California Press, 1973); John E. Rue, *Mao Tse-tung in Opposition, 1927–1935* (Stanford, Cal.: Stanford University Press, 1966); Shanti Swarup, *A Study of the Chinese Communist Movement, 1927–1934* (London: Oxford University Press, 1966); and Richard C. Thornton, *The Comintern and the Chinese Communists, 1928–1931* (Seattle: University of Washington Press, 1969).

a heretical tendency toward bureaucratism, imperialism, and all-around revisionism or capitalist restoration.[12] This is a fascinating debate, infinitely more complicated than these remarks suggest, and now further complicated by post-Mao reversals of some of the Cultural Revolution policies believed to be at the core of Maoism. In this context, earlier assertions about the essential similarlity of Chinese and Soviet socialism have revived, although the distinction between the two when China was under Mao's leadership seems secure.

Chinese Versus Foreign Influence. As the Sino-Soviet split cooled the controversy about the CCP's relationship with the Soviet party, a related but more subtle question came to the fore: did the victory of Chinese Communism represent a conquest by foreign ideas (Western if not Russian) that would destroy the Chinese tradition, or did it represent the beginning of a new "dynasty," foreign in some aspects of its style but faithful to traditional patterns of rule? Despite occasional allusions to a CCP "dynasty" or to Mao as "emperor," serious discussion of this theme has avoided polarization around a literal acceptance of either of the two positions. The view that the Communist Revolution is essentially antitraditional and a vehicle for spreading values foreign to China is more common, although it seldom appears without qualifications; it has strong support, of course, in the self-image that the Chinese Communists project. Arguments on the other side have been presented succinctly by C. P. Fitzgerald, who has pointed out strong similarities between Communist and traditional Chinese patterns of rule. He has emphasized in particular the idea of a "world sovereign authority," state management of a balanced economy, and the establishment of an orthodox doctrine to order society and provide a standard for recruiting elites.[13]

Obviously, contemporary Chinese politics show a mixture of indigenous and foreign influences. The real value of this debate

[12]See Wilson, ed., *Mao Tse-tung in the Scales of History*; and "Symposium on Mao and Marx," *Modern China*, vol. 2, no. 4 (October 1976), and vol. 3, nos. 1, 2, 4 (January, April, October 1977). This "symposium" contains articles and comments by several scholars holding different views on the question.

[13]C. P. Fitzgerald, *The Birth of Communist China* (Baltimore, Md.: Penguin, 1964), pp. 41–42 passim.

is not to prove one perspective right and the other wrong but to establish what the mixture is. Since the prevailing tendency is to focus on the changes accomplished and sought by CCP elites, it is healthy to heed the reminders of those who assert the "Chineseness" of China. John Fairbank has been a temperate but persistent spokesman for this view, urging caution in concluding that the tradition is weakened or destroyed, despite what ideology and official directives might imply, and insisting that Chinese history still provides some explanations for Chinese behavior.[14] The analysis in later chapters will identify many areas in which the influence of the Chinese past is still evident.

It is worth noting that debate over the proper role of Chinese and foreign influences is not simply a Western intellectual gloss of no interest to the Chinese themselves. To the contrary, China's intellectuals and politicians have addressed this question explicitly ever since the late nineteenth century, offering different formulae on how to use things foreign and Chinese in the reconstruction of their system.[15] Recent Chinese diatribes against the Gang of Four for irrationally praising things Chinese and opposing things foreign are a striking resurrection of this theme. Chinese efforts to explain their difficulty in building socialism by reference to a long tradition of "feudal authoritarianism" and a very short exposure to capitalism and modern democracy, and their assertions about China's need to learn from advanced countries in achieving modernization, are other examples of a renewal of interest in the positive aspects of foreign influence on modern China. It seems that Chinese as well as Western views are shifting toward a more complex assessment that sees mixed benefits and liabilities in both Chinese and foreign influences on the revolution.

Sources of Communist Victory. The third major controversy about the history of the Communist Revolution involves the sources of the CCP success in its struggle with the KMT. What

---

[14] John K. Fairbank, *China: The People's Middle Kingdom and the U.S.A.* (Cambridge, Mass.: Belknap Press, 1967).

[15] For analysis of Mao's position on this question, see Stuart R. Schram, "Introduction: The Cultural Revolution in Historical Perspective," in Schram, ed., *Authority, Participation and Cultural Change in China* (Cambridge: Cambridge University Press, 1973), pp. 3–27.

conditions and appeals gave the CCP the strength for victory, and what kind of revolution did it lead? The most provocative thesis has been Chalmers Johnson's study of Communist growth during the Sino-Japanese War (1937–1945).[16] Johnson argues that the CCP's leadership of nationalist peasant resistance to the Japanese invader was responsible for the party's emergence as a contender for national power; the Communist Revolution derived its main strength from nationalist appeals, not from a program for socioeconomic change. It is clear that the Japanese invasion permitted the CCP to strengthen greatly its position relative to the KMT; the nationalist legitimacy that the party acquired during the war was indispensable for the attraction of popular support and neutralization of opposition that led to ultimate victory. Japanese actions and Communist response were probably decisive in the timing and staging of the CCP's conquest of the mainland.

However, there are other factors to be considered in defining the basis of Communist victory. KMT weakness as well as CCP strength, especially the mix of political and military capabilities on both sides, influenced the final outcome. The Communist's commitment to social and economic change, particularly their promise of land redistribution, was a source of popular support and revolutionary recruitment during many periods of party history. Organizational skills and personal behavior of CCP members played a major role in expanding the party's influence, regardless of the specific issues that made a locality vulnerable to Communist penetration. The CCP's ability to address more traditional peasant economic needs and concepts of social justice illuminates the seeming paradox of a Communist revolution based more on peasantry than proletariat. And because of its peasant base, the movement interacted with and was influenced by many traditional forms of rural organization and protest.[17]

[16]Chalmers A. Johnson, *Peasant Nationalism and Communist Power: The Emergence of Revolutionary China, 1937–1945* (Stanford, Cal.: Stanford University Press, 1962). Criticism of Johnson's thesis is summarized in Elinor Lerner, "The Chinese Peasantry and Imperialism: A Critique of Chalmers Johnson's *Peasant Nationalism and Communist Power*," *Bulletin of Concerned Asian Scholars*, vol. 6, no. 2 (April–August 1974): 43–56. Johnson responds to his critics in "Peasant Nationalism Revisited: The Biography of a Book," in *China Quarterly*, no. 72 (December 1977): 766–85.

[17]For a sample of diverse interpretations of the Communist Revolution, see Lucien Bianco, *Origins of the Chinese Revolution, 1915–1949* (Stanford, Cal.:

None of these factors denies the importance of the Japanese presence and the CCP's nationalist appeals to resist it, but they show that the Communist Revolution was a multifaceted phenomenon that cannot be labeled neatly as either a "national" revolution or a "social" revolution. The same can be said of the post-1949 period, in which themes of national independence and reconstruction have continued to blend with themes of radical social and economic change.

These debates about the essence of Chinese Communism have raised important questions about the post-1949 system without providing definitive answers. Neither the questions nor the difficulty of answering them is unique to China, of course; students of the Bolshevik Revolution have grappled with similar issues, without notable success in resolving them. The problem, as suggested in this chapter's introductory paragraphs, is that the essence of revolution defies simple definitions. In the Chinese case, the initial "either-or" questions have yielded, as scholarly studies have multiplied, to recognition of the complexity of the questions posed. This is probably a healthy development. In any case, it helps to explain the inconclusiveness of efforts to classify the PRC's political system, a topic to which we now turn.

MODELS FOR THE CHINESE POLITICAL SYSTEM

During the 1960s, controversy over historical issues began to wane, and a substantial body of literature on post-1949 politics emerged. One striking characteristic of this literature was the

---

Stanford University Press, 1971); Lloyd E. Eastman, *Seeds of Destruction: Nationalist China in War and Revolution, 1937–1949* (Stanford, Cal.: Stanford University Press, 1984); William Hinton, *Fanshen: A Documentary of Revolution in a Chinese Village* (New York: Monthly Review Press, 1966); Roy Hofheinz, Jr., *The Broken Wave* (Cambridge, Mass.: Harvard University Press, 1977), and "The Ecology of Chinese Communist Success: Rural Influence Patterns, 1923–1945," in Barnett, ed., *Chinese Communist Politics in Action*, pp. 3–77; Tetsuya Kataoka, *Resistance and Revolution in China: The Communists and the Second United Front* (Berkeley: University of California Press, 1974); Suzanne Pepper, *Civil War in China* (Berkeley: University of California Press, 1978); Elizabeth J. Perry, *Rebels and Revolutionaries in North China, 1845–1945* (Stanford, Cal.: Stanford University Press, 1980); Mark Selden, *The Yenan Way in Revolutionary China* (Cambridge, Mass.: Harvard University Press, 1971); and Ralph Thaxton, "On Peasant Revolution and National Resistance: Toward a Theory of Peasant Mobilization and Revolutionary War with Special Reference to Modern China," *World Politics*, vol. 30, no. 1 (October 1977): 24–57.

absence of a dominant model as a guide for analysis and the considerable diversity in efforts to classify the system. Initially, there was an inclination to call the PRC a totalitarian system or at least to group it with other Communist systems. This gave way to greater interest in treating China as a "developing" system, shifting away from European-centered models and emphasizing China's similarities to Third World countries. There has also been a pronounced tendency to classify the system on its own terms, to identify a Chinese or Maoist model that might stand alone as a type.

The Totalitarian Model. It is not surprising that theories of totalitarianism were attractive to students of Communist China. The theories developed largely from studies of Nazi Germany and Stalinist Russia, leaving the Soviet Union as the principal model of totalitarianism in the postwar years. When China proclaimed its intention of following the Soviet model—while Stalin was still alive—there was a natural tendency to assume that China had incorporated the totalitarian model. Moreover, Chinese Communist political behavior and institutions displayed sufficient "fit" with the model, particularly in the drive for ideological conformity and the monopoly of power by a single party, to defend its assumed applicability. Despite wide acceptance of the term and implicit use of the model, no full-scale analysis of "Chinese totalitarianism" appeared. There was reluctance to apply the totalitarian model systematically to all aspects of the Chinese system.

One reason for this reluctance was the emergence of important discrepancies between the People's Republic and the model. The clearest and most representative statement of the totalitarian model laid out six "basic features" of the "totalitarian dictatorship": an official ideology; a single mass party led typically by one man; a system of terroristic police controls; a technologically conditioned monopoly of communications; a similar monopoly of all means of effective armed combat; and central control and direction of the entire economy through bureaucratic coordination.[18] However, in China it seemed that Mao Zedong's leadership

---

[18] Carl J. Friedrich and Zbigniew K. Brzezinski, *Totalitarian Dictatorship and Autocracy* (New York: Praeger, 1961), pp. 9–10.

of the CCP was not comparable to the dictatorships of Hitler or Stalin; controls rested much more on psychological pressures of indoctrination and persuasion and on close personal supervision by cadres rather than on police terror; central bureaucratic planning and controls were less salient, especially after 1957, than in the Soviet Union. Moreover, theorists of totalitarianism had identified the phenomenon as a reaction against or perversion of the modern Western state, one that "could have arisen only within the context of mass democracy and modern technology."[19] While the Chinese revolution occurred in such a context in the global sense, it was not directly aligned with this particular historical pattern.

The totalitarian model's application to China was also inhibited by questions about its inherent validity that came to the fore in the 1960s. Working mainly from developments in the Soviet bloc following de-Stalinization, critics argued that the model had been overly influenced by the excesses of particular personalities (e.g., Hitler and Stalin); that it could not account for pluralistic phenomena within the assumed "monolithic" totalitarian state; and that it failed to differentiate adequately among different types of systems (e.g., fascist and Communist states) that might display some of its characteristics. As alternatives, they suggested abandonment of the model, limitation of its application to the few historical examples that approximated it, or major revisions to accommodate variations within highly ideological and authoritarian single-party states.[20] In any case, the growing challenge to the model's credentials made it progressively less attractive as a guide for rigorous analysis of the Chinese system.

As the totalitarian model lost ground, the comparative study of Communist systems began to attract students of China. Although this approach is now common in studies of Soviet and East European politics, it has not acquired a dominant place in the China field. Very few scholars have the skills and inclination

[19]Ibid., p. 3; and Hannah Arendt, *The Origins of Totalitarianism* (New York: Meridian, 1958).

[20]For a summary discussion of the totalitarian model and its critics, see Robert Burrowes, "Totalitarianism: The Revised Standard Version," *World Politics*, vol. 21, no. 2 (January 1969): 272–94. See also contributions to a "Symposium on Comparative Politics and Communist Systems" in *Slavic Review*, vol. 26, no. 1 (March 1967).

to carry out a rigorous comparison of European and Chinese Communist systems. Moreover, the Sino-Soviet conflict and the debate over totalitarianism have left a reservoir of skepticism about assumptions of similarities between the two great Communist powers. There is great value in including China in comparisons of Communist systems, but much of that value lies in demonstrating the extent of variations within the category.[21]

"Developing Country" Models. The intensification of the Sino-Soviet conflict in the 1960s coincided with the growth in Western academic circles of a vast literature dealing with problems of development. While neither China nor any other country is typical of what are so loosely called "developing" or "under-developed" areas, it is understandable that students of China began to explore this literature for conceptual guidance and possible models. Modern China's credentials for inclusion in this group are substantial. Its experience with Western (and Eastern) imperialism, its preindustrial agrarian economy, and its revolutionary confrontation with traditional institutions have generated most of the problems broadly associated with the developmental process. Of course, there is no single model for a developing political system, nor even agreement on the definition of terms like *development* and *modernization*, but the literature suggests several categories of systems with which China might be grouped and which illuminate important features of Chinese politics.

One category derives from broad historical outlines of the modern era and groups China with a relatively small number of other countries that began modernization under the influence of the Western example but without direct foreign control. Their traditional governments were sufficiently effective to resist overt colonization and hence embarked on modernization with significant continuities of national tradition, territory, and population.[22] This continuity provides protection against the crises of personal

[21] See, for example, Chalmers Johnson, ed., *Change in Communist Systems* (Stanford, Cal.: Stanford University Press, 1970).

[22] C. E. Black, *The Dynamics of Modernization: A Study in Comparative History* (New York: Harper, 1966), pp. 119–23. The other countries that Black places in this "pattern" are Russia, Japan, Iran, Turkey, Afghanistan, Ethiopia, and Thailand. Black is, of course, aware of the truly formidable differences among these countries in their experiences with modernization.

and national identity that have occurred in other transitional societies but may produce an "authority crisis" when modernizing elites eventually destroy the traditional authority system.[23] Another perspective emphasizes the level of economic development, indicating that China is most appropriately grouped with countries of roughly equivalent economic circumstances. Some proponents of this approach argue that "Communism is a phenomenon of underdevelopment" and that Communist movements "share numerous characteristics with non-Communist modernizing movements."[24] This category, then, includes both Communist and non-Communist systems whose politics reflect similarities derived from common economic problems.

China also corresponds to a system that appears in nearly all typologies of developing countries, variously referred to as mobilization system, movement regime, neo-Leninist mass party system, or radical or totalitarian single-party system.[25] The type varies in its definition by different writers but contains the following core elements: a single political party that monopolizes political power and penetrates all other politically significant organizations; an explicit official ideology that legitimizes and sanctifies revolutionary goals; a determination to politicize and mobilize the citizenry, characteristically through party-led mass movements. The mobilization system, to use David Apter's phrase, clearly has something in common with the totalitarian model, but it places the dominant political party in a significantly different context. Whereas the totalitarian model projects an image of an impenetrable, monolithic, bureaucratic, and technologically competent regime, the mobilization system operates

---

[23] Lucian Pye, *The Spirit of Chinese Politics: A Psychocultural Study of the Authority Crisis in Political Development* (Cambridge, Mass.: MIT Press, 1968), esp. chap. 1.

[24] John H. Kautsky, *Communism and the Politics of Development: Persistent Myths and Changing Behavior* (New York: Wiley, 1968), pp. 1, 3–4.

[25] On the mobilization system, see David E. Apter, *The Politics of Modernization* (Chicago: University of Chicago Press, 1965), esp. chap. 10. On the movement-regime, see Robert C. Tucker, "Towards a Comparative Politics of Movement-Regimes," *The American Political Science Review*, vol. 55, no. 2 (June 1961): 281–89. On the neo-Leninist mass party, see Clement Henry Moore, *Tunisia Since Independence: The Dynamics of One-Party Government* (Berkeley: University of California Press, 1965), esp. the introduction. *Radical* or *totalitarian single-party system* are phrases that fall in the public domain, with predictable variation in their meaning.

in a fluid, unresolved struggle to transform a "transitional" society. The latter seems closer to Chinese reality, identifying the social context more accurately and emphasizing the open struggle to mobilize the population behind the radical, futuristic goals of elites.

The modernization and development literature, like the totalitarian model, has nourished certain assumptions about Chinese politics and development. In terms of specific models, however, it has had little impact. China scholars have gone window-shopping in it—citing a reference here, testing a hypothesis there—but few have adopted any of the general approaches within it. For one thing, the literature itself is too loose and sprawling to be of much help; by the 1970s, it was also the target of much criticism for its ethnocentric biases and empirical weaknesses.[26] Moreover, despite Chinese departures from Soviet Communism, the role of ideology and party in the PRC and its revolutionary origins set it apart from the great majority of non-Communist Third World countries.

One response to this dilemma is to combine the two general perspectives discussed thus far, that is, to classify the PRC with other Communist systems in terms of basic structures, while noting that the developmental issues with which it must deal are closer to those of the Third World. Generally, this is the approach followed in the core volume of the series to which this book belongs.[27] Almond and Powell label China and other Communist systems as "penetrative-radical-authoritarian" systems, thereby distinguishing them from both democratic systems and various nondemocratic systems that have not attained the level of mobilization and penetration that Communist systems have. They also group China with a few other Communist and non-Communist Third World countries that pursue an "authoritarian-technocratic-mobilizational" developmental strategy. Labels like these are a loose fit because, as we will emphasize in

[26]For a sample of this criticism, see Richard Sandbrook, "The 'Crisis' in Political Development Theory," *Journal of Development Studies*, vol. 12, no. 2 (January 1976): 165–85; and Dean C. Tipps, "Modernization Theory and the Comparative Study of Societies: A Critical Perspective," *Comparative Studies in Society and History*, vol. 15, no. 2 (March 1973): 199–226.

[27]Gabriel A. Almond and G. Bingham Powell, Jr., *Comparative Politics: System, Process, and Policy*, 2nd ed. (Boston: Little, Brown, 1978), pp. 71–76, 381–87.

chapters 3 and 4, the PRC has experienced periods of more or less intensive application of the variables cited; that is, it displays these characteristics sequentially or cumulatively rather than all at once over its entire history. Nonetheless, the basic point is well taken: China share many systemic features with Communist countries and many developmental strategies and problems with Third World countries.

The Chinese Model. In the absence of consensus on the applicability to China of totalitarian, Communist, or developing country models, most China scholars in practice have treated the Chinese political system as *sui generis.* They have included in their works many references to other bodies of literature, but they have assumed that the system they study is sufficiently distinctive to provide the basis for a separate model. The tendency is a natural one in the China field, encouraged by the sinological tradition to look upon the study of China as a discipline unto itself. Indeed, there has been some resistance among China scholars to the intrusion of social science or comparative concepts, so much so that others have suggested that some of the problems of the field lie in its lack of receptivity to external conceptual guidance.[28]

However, the most vigorous criticism in the 1970s of Western studies of Chinese politics was that they failed to take the Chinese model seriously, that they had imposed their own ethnocentric assumptions and values on Chinese reality, thereby misunderstanding and misinterpreting the Chinese revolution and the Maoist system emerging from it.[29] What are we to make of these seemingly contradictory points? Have Western scholars assumed the validity and utility of a Chinese model or not?

The issue stems largely from Maoist policies that dominated Chinese politics from the mid-1950s through 1976. These policies

[28]"Symposium on Chinese Studies and the Disciplines," *Journal of Asian Studies,* vol. 23, no. 4 (August 1964): 505–38; Chalmers Johnson, "The Role of Social Science in China Scholarship," *World Politics,* vol. 17, no. 2 (January 1965): 256–71; and Richard W. Wilson, "Chinese Studies in Crisis," *World Politics,* vol. 23, no. 2 (January 1971): 295–317.

[29]For a thorough presentation of this theme, see James Peck, "Revolution Versus Modernization and Revisionism: A Two-Front Struggle," in Victor Nee and Peck, eds., *China's Uninterrupted Revolution from 1840 to the Present* (New York: Pantheon, 1973), pp. 57–217.

seemed to pull the PRC away from totalitarian, Soviet, and various developing country models and defined the guidelines for an alternative in the form of a Maoist developmental model. As used in the debate, then, the "Chinese model" really meant a "Maoist model" that was thought to have the following elements. First, it aims at national independence and self-reliance, veering toward autarky in its avoidance of economic or political dependence on other states. Second, it seeks all-around development, emphasizing the agricultural sector, which is most likely to be left behind in rapid development; it favors decentralization to stimulate local growth and initiative and to direct transferral of resources (personnel, services, facilities, and funds) from urban to rural areas. Third, it emphasizes mass mobilization and participation as techniques for achieving social, economic, and political goals; the destabilizing effects of mass campaigns on bureaucratic procedures and institutions are regarded as healthy or at least acceptable, as is the downgrading of intellectual and technical skills that accompanies this glorification of mass efforts. Fourth, it insists on continuing the revolution, arguing that repeated and possibly violent struggles are necessary to avoid restoration of capitalism, tendencies toward which can arise even within the Communist party. Correct ideology—absolute commitment to the collectivist, egalitarian, participatory society—is the key to revolutionary success; it must be practiced in daily life and must be the primary criterion for evaluating people, their performance, and their social and cultural expression.

This summary identifies some important themes that Western scholars attributed to Maoism as it was articulated in the two decades before Mao's death, especially during the Cultural Revolution decade of 1966–76. This list of general principles and goals had sufficient practical impact under Mao's leadership to become a starting point for analysis of the Chinese political system. However, if there was considerable agreement that such ideas were serving as a model for China, why was there continuing debate about whether or not Western biases were blocking or distorting our understanding of Chinese reality? The answer is that observers disagreed about the function, effectiveness, and value of the model even as they agreed that it was, at some level, a distinct alternative to other developmental strategies.

Those who regarded the model with reservations or hostility did so for a variety of reasons. Some argued it served largely as rhetoric or window dressing that concealed the harsh realities of Chinese life and politics. In this view the model was basically myth even though some policies flowed from it and some idealists seemed to believe it. Others thought Maoism was both believed and practiced but that it could not produce long-run development. They believed the model was utopian in espousing that self-reliance with emphasis on populism and ideology over planning and expertise could achieve development in an increasingly technological, interdependent world. Still others observed the model starting to achieve some of its goals but disagreed sharply with the value of those goals. They insisted that Maoism demanded too high a price in human terms for whatever gains—either ideological or economic—it might achieve.

On the other side were those who admitted varying degrees of uncertainty about the real function of Maoist rhetoric, the thoroughness of the model's implementation, the effectiveness of Cultural Revolution policies in achieving their goals, or the normative value of the model, but who sympathized with the spirit of the model and believed it was achieving some positive results. In this view, the critics displayed ethnocentric or ideological biases that led to willful or unconscious distortion of Maoism precisely because it challenged the orthodoxy of liberalism, Western or Soviet-style development, or the ethics of a materialistic, industrialized civilization. Those critics in turn regarded the sympathizers as naïve or poorly informed at best, willing tools of Maoist propaganda at worst. Of course, most students of Chinese affairs did not take rigid positions for or. against the model but distributed themselves somewhere along the spectrum suggested, sometimes changing their views as the politics of the Maoist period unfolded. Nonetheless, it is clear that the Chinese political passions unleased by the Cultural Revolution had their counterparts among foreign observers, most of whom accepted the premise that China was following a path of its own and could be understood only on its own terms, even as they disagreed about which foreigners were able to pierce their cultural blinders and see China as it really was.

In the years following Mao's death, new perspectives have changed the terms of debate about the Chinese or Maoist model.

Retrospect suggests the model was less clearcut than adversaries implied, partly because Mao took many different positions over the course of his career—making some major changes even during the Cultural Revolution decade—and partly because Cultural Revolution Maoism was never sufficiently institutionalized to make China a test case for the model. The Maoist model remains theoretically interesting as an alternative to more conventional ones, and its political influence in China and elsewhere was substantial for a time, but it does not represent the actual workings of the Chinese political system for a sustained portion of PRC history. Moreover, post-Mao policies have moved China away from self-reliance toward greater independence, strengthened certain similarities between Chinese and Soviet political systems, and emphasized science, technology, and rational planning in what seems to be a much more conventional development strategy. In other words, it seems there is no longer a distinct "Chinese model"—Maoist or otherwise—except in the sense that all independent systems display certain distinctive national features. Finally, recent policies have included an opening to foreign travel and residence, the collection of better statistical data, and a more liberal editorial policy in Chinese publications, so that students of China now have access to better data and a wider variety of sources than at any time since 1949. Due to this improved knowledge of both current and past performance, foreign observers now seem more cautious about the kind of generalizations that provided much of the ammunition for earlier debates.

One lesson to be learned from these constant shifts in arguments about issues and models is that much of the change is in the eyes of the observers. Many years ago, in the aftermath of the Korean War, Harold Isaacs concluded that fluctuating American images of China and the Chinese were more a reflection of changes in the American relationship to China than in the character of China itself.[30] Recently, another scholar has come to a similar conclusion about a very critical attitude toward China that prevailed in many American assessments of China in the early

---

[30]Harold R. Isaacs, *Images of Asia* (New York: Capricorn Books, 1962); originally published as *Scratches on Our Minds* (Cambridge, Mass.: MIT Press, 1958).

1980s; this emphasis on negative aspects of PRC performance and prospects was not so much a reflection of deterioration in Chinese conditions as a reaction to rose-colored images of Cultural Revolution China or at least an earlier tendency to interpret available data in a favorable way.[31] Paradoxically, these pessimistic reports came at a time when the CCP was trying to correct past abuses and was adopting the kind of development policies favored by many foreign observers. There is no doubt that the new stage in Chinese politics has brought a welcome new realism to foreign studies of China. That realism is most likely to fulfill its promise if it avoids the stereotypical images that frequently intruded on earlier debates.

DIVERSITY AND CHANGE IN CHINESE POLITICS

This survey of the setting of Chinese politics and a few of the issues and models debated by those who study the subject has introduced the reader to some of the change and diversity that characterize the politics of modern China. It would be a mistake to conclude that generalizations about Chinese politics are impossible, that no model fits the system, or that the system defies classification. In Chapter 4, after examining PRC political history, institutions, and ideology, we will suggest how the Chinese system might be classified. We argue that China does not fit easily into any *single* category and that the student must keep several issues and models in mind for the most fruitful exploration of different eras and topics.

One important transition is from revolutionary to postrevolutionary eras, a transition that occurred (if a date is needed for reference) with the death of Mao. CCP politics have taken different forms in the pre-1949 revolutionary movement, in the Maoist effort to "continue the revolution" within the framework of a socialist state after 1949, and in the post-1976 period with its pronouncement that the era of revolutionary mass struggle was basically over. Post-1949 history includes three major periods, each represented by different models reflecting its primary features or goals: a Soviet period and model from 1949–57, in which the CCP set about building socialism under pronounced Soviet

---

[31] Harry Harding, "From China, With Disdain: New Trends in the Study of China," *Asian Survey*, vol. 22, no. 10 (October 1982): 934–58.

influence; a Maoist period and model from 1958–1976, dominated by an attempt to redirect Chinese politics toward revolutionary goals as Mao defined them; and, from 1976 to present, a new period and model defined by a drive for socialist modernization that has reversed many Maoist policies, restored some features of the Soviet period, and taken some fresh initiatives that resemble the externally oriented development strategies adopted by many nonsocialist developing countries. If there is a "Chinese model," it is not synonymous with any one of these periods but must accommodate the range of variation among them.

The setting of Chinese politics is a source of some stability or predictability because it establishes the "givens" or raw materials with which Chinese elites must work, but it does not determine particular political outcomes. The combination of revolutionary, historical, and international forces creates certain transcendental problems or questions that must be addressed over and over again: what is the proper balance between revolutionary progress and institutionalization, between traditional and modern culture, between foreign and native methods, between interdependence and self-reliance, between material and spiritual goals? Answers to such questions never seem wholly original because Chinese statesmen and intellectuals have been grappling with them for over a century. In other words, the setting seems to provide precedents or analogues for almost everything that happens in contemporary politics. Nonetheless, historical development changes the political context, so that debates on these long-standing issues constantly reveal new variations of old arguments.

The student of Chinese politics must also be sensitive to cultural, social, and regional diversity in China. In general, China and the Chinese must be examined as a unit; however, when the politics of this society is viewed more closely, its extraordinary diversity becomes apparent. Culturally, it is divided between Han Chinese, who constitute about 93 percent of the PRC population, and some 55 minorities who total about 67 million people (just under 7 percent of the population) and inhabit roughly half the country's territory. The Han Chinese speak many different dialects or languages, although all are taught a single national language. This linguistic differentiation frequently carries other cultural and social differences as well.

There are important variations between regions, social strata, and urban and rural areas in terms of productivity, wealth, resources, education, demographic patterns, and other indices of social change (Appendices A and C). Within regions there may be sharp differences or conflicts among local communities based on kinship, ethnicity, or other communal ties. Historically, these local communities have usually commanded stronger Chinese loyalties than has the central government, and they have proven very resilient in maintaining their solidarity in the face of official efforts to penetrate or disband them. National policies are seldom applied uniformly throughout the country or, at any rate, seldom produce uniform results. Old associations or customs may survive beneath official pronouncements of change or may influence the social patterns that replace them. The most challenging and rewarding task for the student of Chinese politics is the search for generalizations that recognize and incorporate these multiple elements of diversity and change.

CHAPTER II

The Origins of the Communist Political System

THE PEOPLE'S REPUBLIC OF CHINA, officially proclaimed on October 1, 1949, is still a relatively new political system. Its primary origins lie not in the remote past but in a more recent history in which many of today's political elites were participants. The most direct influences on Chinese Communism—the revolutionary setting, Soviet Communism, and the CCP's own pre-1949 history—are largely twentieth-century phenomena. However, China's premodern political tradition is also directly relevant. Not all agree that the People's Republic is a "nation imprisoned by her history,"[1] but few deny that its origins encompass more than the twentieth-century upheavals that brought Communism to power. Since all societies are in some measure a product of their past, a pertinent question is whether the Chinese political tradition exerts an unusual influence on the present. There is good reason to believe that it does, despite the difficulty of offering comparative judgments on such a question.

The longevity and supreme Sinocentrism of the traditional political system are the primary sources of its impact on the present. No system that prevailed for so long and with such a high degree of autonomy could fail to extend its influence beyond its formal institutional life. Even if new institutions

---

[1] John K. Fairbank, *China: The People's Middle Kingdom and the U.S.A.* (Cambridge, Mass.: Belknap Press, 1967), pp. 3–4 passim.

29

could escape the old patterns, traditional values and behavior would endure for an indefinite period of time. The Sinocentric belief that the best possible society was immanent in Chinese experience, that foreign ways might be absorbed but must never replace the essence of Chinese culture, naturally reinforced the longevity of the traditional order.

Extraordinary concern for the study and writing of their own history is perhaps the most tangible evidence of how the Chinese have perpetuated the influence of their past. In imperial times, the study of history was more than a scholarly enterprise to record and impart information; it was also a means of moral and political instruction, providing statesmen with material to guide and legitimize their political actions. The inclusion of classics of history among the standard texts covered in the examinations (through which officials were chosen and degrees awarded) ensured a common body of historical knowledge among scholars and bureaucrats.[2] Moreover, the tendency to cast political discourse in terms of historical events and personalities did not die with the end of the imperial system in 1911. Despite marked differences in vocabulary and interpretation required by a Marxist approach, the Chinese Communists remain highly sensitive to the political uses and implications of Chinese history and have continued "to find legitimization in China's past for the domestic and external developments of her most recent present."[3] Historical "knowledge," admittedly subject to varying interpretations, was and remains part of the basic framework of Chinese political perception.

The actual closeness in time of the traditional order reinforces this deliberate retention of national historical experience. The

[2] See W. G. Beasley and E. G. Pulleyblank, eds., *Historians of China and Japan* (London: Oxford University Press, 1961), pp. 1–9; and Wm. Theodore de Bary et al., comps., *Sources of Chinese Tradition* (New York: Columbia University Press, 1960), pp. 266–67. An illuminating account of the importance attached to historical studies is found in Harold L. Kahn, "The Education of a Prince: The Emperor learns His Roles," in Albert Feuerwerker et al., eds., *Approaches to Modern Chinese History* (Berkeley: University of California Press, 1967), pp. 25–29, 34–36.

[3] Harold Kahn and Albert Feuerwerker, "The Ideology of Scholarship: China's New Historiography," in Feuerwerker, ed., *History in Communist China* (Cambridge, Mass.: MIT Press, 1968), pp. 1–13; the quotation is from p. 13.

imperial system ended only in 1911 with the collapse of the Qing (Ch'ing or Manchu) dynasty. Of the ninety-seven regular members of the Eighth Central Committee of the CCP, elected in 1956–1958, all but one were born by 1912;[4] some of the most senior Communists, including Mao Zedong, actually served in the military forces that were mobilized against the Manchu government in 1911–1912. For these men, knowledge of the imperial political system included personal memory as well as historical study. Since certain aspects of the traditional social order necessarily survived the fall of the Qing, personal knowledge of it is still held by a significant proportion of the Chinese population or is in any case no more than a generation removed. One might still argue that China is no closer to its traditional past than any number of other non-Western developing countries. That is not quite true, however, since the traditional order for most of these countries was overlaid by a colonial regime that brought significant political alterations. Very few non-Western political elites of the twentieth century have experienced such an intense confrontation with their own tradition.

Finally, we must put to rest the notion that the influence of the past is measured only by the continuation or replication of older patterns. Too often the question of contemporary China's relationship to its political tradition centers only on the extent to which aspects of the former perpetuate or resemble those of the latter. In fact, the influence of historical patterns appears in reactions to them, and even rejection of them, as well as in their continuation. For example, the Communists' hostility toward the bureaucratic style must be understood in the context of the Chinese bureaucratic tradition; the revolt in recent decades of many Chinese intellectuals against the style and substance of their culture is meaningless if considered outside that cultural tradition. These and many other examples show that deviations from the past may nonetheless be in part produced by it and thus represent a link rather than a rupture with Chinese history.

In considering the origins of the present political system, it is not possible to describe adequately the historical background

[4]Chao Kuo-chün, "Leadership in the Chinese Communist Party," *The Annals of the American Academy of Political and Social Science*, vol. 321 (January 1959): 44–46.

and developments that led to its establishment. Instead, four major sources of influence on Chinese Communism will be discussed, not in an attempt to do them historical justice but rather to isolate certain factors that have particular importance for the present. The four sources are the Chinese political tradition, the revolutionary setting, Soviet Communism, and the CCP's pre-1949 history. Needless to say, the origins of the Communist system do not fall neatly into these four categories. The most salient characteristics of contemporary Chinese politics are those that derive from more than one source or have been reinforced by a variety of experiences.

THE CHINESE POLITICAL TRADITION

Few terms of social analysis are more arbitrary or loaded than the word *traditional*. The usage here refers primarily to China of the late Qing period, roughly the nineteenth century. In fact, the imperial system at this time was different from earlier periods. It was certainly not representative of the best of traditional China, since a process of dynastic decline was evident throughout the nineteenth century. One could argue, in short, that late Qing China was no longer traditional. On the other hand, some elements characteristic of this period survived well into the twentieth century, suggesting that *traditional* should not refer exclusively to the era of imperial rule. Moreover, the Chinese political tradition actually contained a variety of traditions; any attempt to discuss it as a unitary phenomenon inevitably slights some of its regional and temporal variations in favor of others. Acknowledgment of these qualifications is sufficient, since discussion here will be at a very general level. We wish only to identify major characteristics of the Qing political system that have an unmistakable connection with both earlier and later periods and hence are central in the Chinese political tradition. They are not necessarily permanent or immutable, but they have in fact shown great endurance.[5]

[5]For general analyses of the Chinese political tradition and its present relevance see Etienne Balazs, *Chinese Civilization and Bureaucracy*, ed. with an introduction by Arthur F. Wright, ed. (New Haven, Conn.: Yale University Press, 1964); Immanuel C. Y. Hsu, *The Rise of Modern China*, 2nd ed. (New York: Oxford University Press, 1975); John King Fairbank, *The United States and China*, 4th ed., rev. and enl. (Cambridge, Mass.: Harvard University Press, 1983); Mark

Elitism and Hierarchy in Political Authority. The imperial poltical system was fundamentally elitist in its structuring of political authority. The distinction between ruler and subject, official and citizen, was sharp in both theory and practice. The theory held that certain men were entitled by their virtue, acquired through education, to wield political authority; those lacking virtue were correctly assigned to the status of subjects. In practice, a two-class polity of elites and masses resulted. The elite included officials of the imperial bureaucracy and the degree-holding scholars or "gentry" from whose ranks officials were chosen. They were identifiable not only by office and degree but also by special forms of address, garments, insignia, and legal privilege.[6] Educational accomplishment, measured by degrees attained in the various levels of official examinations, was the primary means of entrance into the elite, although degrees could also be acquired through purchase or recommendation. The elite-commoner boundary was blurred at the local level by wealth, since large landowners and rich merchants had obvious resources for political influence. However, the fact that wealth permitted a person to purchase a degree or to make the necessary investment in education, or was acquired because of degree-holding relatives, meant that elite status remained intimately associated with the holding of a degree. The number of gentry (referring to degree-holding scholars and officials) increased greatly during the nineteenth century but remained very small relative to the population. Even in the latter part of the century, the gentry and their families constituted less than 2 percent of the population.[7] Broadening the definition of *gentry* to include wealthy families without degree-holding members would raise the absolute number significantly but still include only a few percent of the total population.

Mancall, *China at the Center: 300 Years of Foreign Policy* (New York: Free Press, 1984); Gilbert Rozman, ed., *The Modernization of China* (New York: Free Press, 1981); Richard J. Smith, *China's Cultural Heritage: The Ch'ing Dynasty, 1644–1912* (Boulder, Colo.: Westview Press, 1983); and Frederic Wakeman, Jr., *The Fall of Imperial China* (New York: Free Press, 1975).

[6]Chung-li Chang, *The Chinese Gentry: Studies in Their Role in Nineteenth-Century Chinese Society* (Seattle: University of Washington Press, 1955), pp. 32–43 passim.

[7]Ibid., pp. 137–41.

This sharp distinction between a small elite entitled to authority and the mass population not so entitled was a basic characteristic of traditional Chinese politics. Supplementing it was a hierarchical structure of authority throughout society that created an intricate network of superior-inferior relationships. In general societal terms, the authority structure interacted with other political and economic considerations to produce a relatively complex system of social stratification.[8] Of particular interest here is the way in which it cemented the elite-commoner distinction and ordered political relationships within each of these two general groupings.

Within the political elite, the emperor stood alone at the top of the hierarchy, holding absolute power over all his officials and subjects. Although the actual exercise of imperial power might vary with the ability and personality of the sovereign and his ministers, his real and symbolic status as the ultimate locus of political authority was unchallenged.[9] The bureaucracy was divided by ranks and grades, fixing each official's position in a hierarchy descending from the emperor. Beneath the officials were degree holders not selected for official position, also ranked according to the kind of degree held.

Ordinary subjects, who constituted most of the population, did not fall into the bureaucratic or degree rankings. However, where this explicitly political hierarchy left off, a highly complex structuring of social relationships took over, having profound implications for the political system. Norms governing kinship relations and obligations set the basic pattern of authority.[10] In simplest terms, authority within a family or larger kinship group was held by the eldest male within generational lines; the older generation held sway over younger ones, and elder males were superior to females and younger males of the same genera-

[8]See Ping-ti Ho, *The Ladder of Success in Imperial China* (New York: Columbia University Press, 1962), chap. 1.

[9]Ping-ti Ho, "Salient Aspects of China's Heritage," in Ping-ti Ho and Tang Tsou, eds., *China in Crisis*, vol. 1 (Chicago: University of Chicago Press, 1969), pp. 1–37.

[10]On the political role of Chinese kinship systems, see Hugh D. R. Baker, *Chinese Family and Kinship* (New York: Columbia University Press, 1979); and Maurice Freedman, ed., *Family and Kinship in Chinese Society* (Stanford, Cal.: Stanford University Press, 1970).

tion. In large lineages containing numerous families and several generations, the resulting relationships became incredibly complicated. The point, however, is that the system did locate ultimate authority in a single person within a kinship group and placed all those beneath him in a hierarchy that called for obedience to those above and expectations of deference from those below. Politically, of course, the family or lineage head was subordinate to the hierarchy extending downward from the emperor, thereby bringing those beneath him into an ordered relationship with political authority.

The authority structure in traditional China was neither absolute nor perfect. It was not absolute because it left open some relationships of equality (between nonrelated friends or persons holding the same status, for example) and could not always prevent noncompliance with the norms. It was not perfect because it contained conflicting obligations, by far the most important of which was the conflict between political loyalty to the imperial system and familial obligations. What did one do when official and parental desires were in conflict, or when an official's obligations to kinsmen challenged his duty to the emperor? In theory, imperial absolutism gave a clear political answer, but the norms of familial obligations were strong enough to prevent a final resolution. In practice, then, political authority tried to minimize the conflict by avoiding it. Whenever possible, familial obligations were legitimized and made part of imperial edict. For example, officials were granted leave for observance of mourning rites, and heavy penalties were enacted for crimes against kinsmen. The bureaucracy rotated its officials regularly and assigned them away from their native places to avoid conflict of interests. Perhaps most important, officials tried to co-opt local elites so that directives came to the population through the medium of, rather than in competition with, the local authority structure.

This use of the local structure necessarily diluted the political system's direct impact on the population. Political authority was extremely remote from the ordinary subject; its effects were felt largely through a person's immediate superiors, in whose status nonpolitical determinants were paramount. Nonetheless, the *pattern* of hierarchical authority was dominant at both elite and popular levels; any kind of social action, whether perceived as political or not, had to occur within its framework. As a result, the rupture of authority that came with the collapse of the old political system had a traumatic effect on all social relations, and attempts by the Chinese to reconstruct their political system usually have employed elitist and hierarchical authority structures.[11]

The CCP, too, has held an elitist conception of political leadershsip, and it established, after 1949, a highly structured and authoritarian system. However, authoritarianism in post-1949 China has been in persistent contradiction with populist themes that have challenged and modified its impact. Although modern populism is largely a product of the revolutionary period, it also draws on a traditional tendency to romanticize popular rebellion against political authority.

Autonomy of the Political System. The authority structure of traditional China gave the political system supreme power, since it placed the emperor and his bureaucracy at the apex of the hierarchy. Equally significant was the political system's autonomy or relative independence from external influence or restraint. Theoretically, the imperial system had an organic relationship with Chinese society. Supposedly modeled on the family, it was to serve society by maintaining order, performing religious functions, and preserving the virtues of the past. Nor was it isolated from its environment, since its national and international responsibilities required a wide range of actions and contacts. Nonetheless, there developed over time a set of institutions and attitudes that made the system incapable of recognizing any legitimate external influence on its actions. It was in a very real sense a law unto itself, self-perpetuating and self-regulating, entering into its relationships with domestic and foreign entities only on an assumption of its own recognized superiority. There were, to be sure, violations of its autonomy through domestic resistance and foreign penetration. The Qing government itself was headed by a foreign imperial line imposed

---

[11] See Lucian Pye, *The Spirit of Chinese Politics: A Psychocultural Study of the Authority Crisis in Political Development* (Cambridge, Mass.: MIT Press, 1968), for an extended, provocative discussion of the problem of political authority in modern China.

by the seventeenth-century Manchu conquest of China. Accommodation with outside forces was still the exception rather than the rule for a government that guarded so jealously both the symbols and reality of its autonomy.

One important aspect of the system's self-governing status was its handling of political recruitment and advancement. The imperial bureaucracy set the standards by which political elites were recruited, managed the examinations and dispensation of office that formalized elite status, and decided internally on matters of assignment and promotion. Individuals could prepare the way for a political career by acquisition of knowledge or wealth, but formal certication came only from the government. Once in office, a man had no recognized constituency that might dilute his service to the emperor. There was no concept of political representation, although a quota system in the examinations encouraged a certain distribution of degree holders among the provinces.

Just as it denied external claims to influence or representation, the regime acknowledged no legal or institutional limitations on its actions. Particular interests had no right to be heard or protected, no "constitutional" guarantees against the exercise of imperial power. The government could initiate, manage, regulate, adjudicate, and repress as it saw fit. Elites did admit a moral obligation to provide just and responsive government, but its enforcement depended on the political recruitment process, which allegedly chose only men of superior virtue, or on the bureaucracy's own mechanisms of internal control and supervision; that is, it was an obligation enforceable only by elite self-regulation. In short, the traditional political system was relatively free to accumulate and exercise total power.[12]

Since the present Communist system also maintains a high degree of autonomy in its relations with society, it will be useful for comparative purposes to mention briefly some qualifications on this point. In fact, the government of imperial China did not make the fullest possible use of its potential power. Subject to important conditions, it allowed some local politics in which it

[12]The most thorough and theoretical development of this point is Karl Wittfogel, *Oriental Despotism: A Comparative Study of Total Power* (New Haven, Conn.: Yale University Press, 1957), esp. chap. 4.

did not insist on direct control, and it tolerated some penetration of particular interests into the bureaucratic process. As we noted earlier, official authority did not bear directly on the population but was brought to it through local intermediaries—the gentry and other lower-ranking authority figures. The institutional basis of this situation was the limited extent of the imperial administrative system, which stopped at the *zhou* (*chou*, department) or *xian* (*hsien*, district or county) level.[13] Each of these lowest units—of which there were in late Qing times approximately 1,500 with an average population exceeding 200,000—was the responsibility of a single official known as the magistrate. Although the magistrate had a staff of assistants, the enormity of his job required him to seek formal and informal assistance from prominent local persons and organizations. In effect, he governed his district largely by supervising the actions of the local power structure, intervening with whatever measures seemed appropriate (from informal advice up to and including military force) to maintain order and secure compliance with imperial orders.

The resulting relationship is difficult to categorize. It most assuredly did not produce village democracy, since the local power structure was governed by rigid norms of authority and status. It was not truly administrative decentralization, although the magistrate did have considerable power in a unit of significant size, because all local power was conditional on higher approval; neither the magistrate's authority nor that of lesser figures could stand for a moment against the absolute authority of the center. Nor was it really local autonomy, since the government insisted on its right to intervene at any time and for any reason in local affairs. It was an operating arrangement, undertaken largely for reasons of administrative efficiency and conservatism, in which local authorities were encouraged to control their own areas provided they did so effectively and without violation of imperial requirements. The gentry and other wealthy individuals, large lineages, merchant and craft guilds, sects, and secret societies

[13] The following discussion draws mainly on T'ung-tsu Ch'ü, *Local Government in China Under the Ch'ing* (Cambridge, Mass.: Harvard University Press, 1962); Kung-chuan Hsiao, *Rural China: Imperial Control in the Nineteenth Century* (Seattle: University of Washington Press, 1960); and John R. Watt, *The District Magistrate in Late Imperial China* (New York: Columbia University Press, 1972).

could thus exercise great power over their subordinates and members and possibly some influence with the magistrate. They could do this, however, only as long as the magistrate viewed the results as beneficial and, above all, as long as their power did not become competitive with that of the magistrate. Adminstrative efficiency always yielded before the requirements of imperial control and security.

The penetration of particular interests into the official bureaucracy is probably less significant. To a large extent, we are simply noting and indeed repeating a fairly obvious point. The ideal of government by a disinterested, educated elite, chosen through examinations without reference to class or wealth had a profound practical impact on traditional China. Yet it was never a complete description of reality. Wealth did play a role, since officials as well as official status could be bought. Personal obligations and loyalties, especially to close family members but also to those of the same clan, locality, or school, could subvert an official's impartiality. The system tolerated these discrepancies within bounds because it had little choice; it was, after all, staffed with men who held values that could support such discrepancies. However, in acknowledging that private or particular interests could find their way into official politics, we should also note how the autonomy of the political system affected their expression.

In the first place, the system was emphatically hostile to the expression of such interests. Toleration was not to imply legal or moral acceptance, and pronounced partisan activity carried the risk of repression and severe punishment. The result was a tendency to keep special interest politics out of government, or else to submerge it deeply in the bureaucratic framework. At the local level, individuals and organizations might compete with each other and seek the favor of the magistrate, but heavy pressure on or within the government invited repression. Officials also had opinions and interests that they sought to advance, but again, efforts to organize large numbers in a noticeable party or appeals for support from groups outside the bureaucracy risked the charge of "factionalism."[14] Hence, minor issues were con-

---

[14] For illustrative accounts of how imperial absolutism condemned and repressed "factionalism" without necessarily eliminating it, see W. T. de Bary,

tained at the local, largely nonofficial level, while major issues were expressed in a bureaucratic framework that abhorred organized political competition.

We may refer to the resulting form of competition as *bureaucratic politics*. The first condition of bureaucratic politics is that the protagonists must themselves be officials, the more highly placed the better, who reject or conceal any large-scale organizational backing, although they claim to speak in general terms of popular support for their proposals. Interests lacking influential offical spokesmen are in effect denied expression except at the lowest level. Second, political struggle itself is carried on by maneuvering within the bureaucratic hierarchy, in which questions of rank and personal influence become all-important. The objective is not to gain support from the largest number of colleagues—which may help but which runs the risk of punishment for factionalism—but rather to get a favorable decision from the authoritative office for the case in question. Secrecy and gossip, friendships and enmities, decisions expressed in changes of personnel, and small coalitions competing for the favor of superiors are, then, the stuff of bureaucratic politics.

The relevance of these points for an understanding of the Communist system is unmistakable. Like their imperial predecessors, the Communist elites have followed their own standards in recruitment and policy, rejecting claims to representation or recognition of partial interests within the government. Competing political organizations or factions, at any level, are anathema to them, and bureaucratic politics have been the prevailing mode of competition. The Communist system has gone much further, however, in extending its authority directly to the mass level, thereby reducing sharply even that limited "local autonomy" allowed under the Manchus. At the same time, expansion of the bureaucracy's size and responsibilities has complicated control of officials and their factional activity, which has often

"Chinese Despotism and the Confucian Ideal: A Seventeenth-Century View," in John K. Fairbank, ed., *Chinese Thought and Institutions* (Chicago: University of Chicago Press, 1957), pp. 163–203; and David S. Nivison, "Ho-Shen and His Accusers: Ideology and Political Behavior in the Eighteenth Century," in Nivison and Arthur F. Wright, eds., *Confucianism in Action* (Stanford, Cal.: Stanford University Press, 1959), pp. 209–43.

been a severe problem; and political mobilization of the masses has weakened governmental autonomy in the face of societal pressures and demands.

Ideology as an Integrative Force. From ancient times, the Chinese tradition contained a number of philosophical-religious schools of thought. Confucianism, Taoism, legalism, and Buddhism all left their mark, albeit unevenly, on Chinese culture and society. It was Confucianism, however, that became the official ideology of the imperial system. Based on a written and widely studied body of ideas, it was defined as the supreme standard of morality and thus profoundly influenced behavior in all social relationships. The Confucian ethic was exceptionally significant for the political system, since it was the standard by which qualifications for elite status were judged and by which the behavior of officials was controlled. Officials were appointed mainly on the basis of superior performance in examinations that tested their knowledge of the Confucian classics. Study of the classics and mastery of the Confucian style of thought and expression were normally essential to appointment. Although some might gain office without it, internalization of the ethic was crucial for continued service and promotion.[15]

The legitimacy of political authority was said to rest on observance of this moral doctrine, not on wealth, status, power, or representation of special interests. Confucian ideology thus became an integrative force that justified political rule, defined the purposes of the state, provided the common values of the elite, and harmonized diverse interests in society. To the extent that it was propagated and accepted, it would bring society and officialdom together in common loyalty to rightful imperial authority.

The insistence that political authority was morally derived and was represented by guardians of moral doctrine was basic to the operation of the imperial system. Given the absence of institutionalized checks on government power, what was to

[15]For a general account of the examination system, see Ichisada Miyazaki, *China's Examination Hell: The Civil Service Examinations of Imperial China*, trans. by Conrad Schirokauer (New Haven, Conn.: Yale University Press, 1981), first publ. in Japanese in 1963.

prevent the abuse of power and to guarantee that the government would truly serve society? Confucian ideology provided the answer: good men, not institutional restraints, are the guarantee of good government. This is not to say that rules and regulations were lacking, since the traditional system had highly formalized standards of status and procedure. However, formal regulations were devices for ordering bureaucratic procedures and clarifying imperial wishes; they supported the system's operation but did not in themselves determine the *quality* of rule. To ensure justice and wisdom in political decisions, the Chinese tradition relied on the personal quality of the office holder rather than on regulations or institutional structure.

No Chinese statesman, ancient or modern, assumed that all men were equal in virtue or that officials would invariably follow the doctrine correctly. Quite the contrary, the Confucian ethic held that men developed different levels of virtue and that the ruler's task was to see that the truly virtuous were the ones who governed.[16] It was perfectly appropriate, then, for the highest authorities to test and supervise their subordinates continuously; to expect continued study and self-cultivation; to reprimand the deviants and laggards; and to force "correct" decisions on those who failed to see the light. Since ideological rectitude that legitimized authority was a product of learning, not "given" by class or wealth, the system placed great emphasis on education and indoctrination. Instilling or restoring virtue in the minds of men was the road to a good society.

The extent to which this fundamental principle was realized in the practice of traditional politics is questionable, but belief in its validity and the attempt to implement it through the examination system and other institutions made it basic in Chinese political attitudes. The indispensability of official ideology, carefully defined and studied, remains central to Communist views of government, although the substance of contemporary ideology differs significantly from that of the past. Indeed, the CCP has gone far beyond imperial elites in exploiting the integrative benefits of ideology.

In imperial times, the Confucian ethic exerted its greatest influence on the elites themselves, whose study of it made them

[16]See Kahn, "The Education of a Prince," pp. 40–41.

well aware of their role in the political system. Commoners, however, were poorly integrated into the traditional polity, which was remote and authoritarian. Aware of popular indifference and resentment, Qing authorities tried to indoctrinate the population in what they regarded as the virtues of worthy subjects—filial piety, respect for elders and superiors, peaceful and industrious conduct, and observance of the law. Through lectures, ceremonies, and schools that extolled the tenets of imperial Confucianism, they hoped to bring the masses into their ideological orbit, to instill positive loyalty and obedience to imperial rule. Neither the effort nor the result was impressive, however. The Chinese countryside remained an "ideological vacuum" in which most inhabitants were "neither positively loyal to the existing regime nor opposed to it" but were simply concerned with the problems of their own daily lives.[17] The Communists, on the other hand, have been relentless in the ideological indoctrination of the common people as well as the elite. While acceptance of the substance of Communist ideology appears to be uneven, its vigorous propagation has brought most Chinese into a new consciousness of their membership in the political system.

THE REVOLUTIONARY SETTING

The Communist system has emerged directly from a revolutionary period that was not of its making. The onset of the Chinese revolution antedated the formation of the CCP. It had been in progress for decades before the party became a major force in Chinese politics and began to shape its direction. Any analysis of contemporary politics must emphasize the fact that Communist China is a *product* of the Chinese revolution, not its creator.

The CCP's emergence in the midst of an ongoing revolutionary process brought both assets and liabilities. On the negative side, fragmentation of the political order made it difficult to seize national power at one stroke and even more difficult to consolidate rapidly a new regime. The times prohibited an easy transfer of power, as by a palace coup, requiring instead a prolonged

[17]Hsiao, *Rural China*, chap. 6, quotations from pp. 253–54.

struggle to create power as well as to seize it. The ongoing revolution also meant that the Communist elites could not define the issues wholly as they chose; powerful movements were already in existence, and to some extent the Communists, like their competitors, had to sink or swim with the tide.

On balance, however, and with the advantage of hindsight, the revolutionary setting of modern China was plainly an asset to the Communist cause. The basic condition of this period was a near total collapse of the traditional order. Actually, the imperial system demonstrated remarkable endurance. Already declining in the early nineteenth century, the Manchu dynasty suffered heavily from accelerated Western penetration after 1840 and from the Taiping Rebellion of 1850–1864. Its apparently imminent demise was forestalled, however, by a partial revival in the decade following the rebellion, when a few energetic officials tried to refurbish the old system and gained a measure of Western cooperation for their efforts.[18] Decline soon resumed, with new Western pressures for privileges and concessions, joined now by the first thrusts of Japanese imperialism and the stirring of more radical reformers at home. The last few years of the century were disastrous. A humiliating military defeat by Japan in 1894–1895, vast new leases and cessions to the Western powers in 1897–1899, and foreign suppression of the Boxer Rebellion in 1900, followed by the exaction of yet more indemnities and privileges, left the central government economically, politically, and morally bankrupt. Still it held on, embarking at last on a series of reforms that suggested China might yet enter the modern world through the medium of a revived constitutional monarchy. But the reforms accelerated the rate of change and increased demands on the imperial government. In 1911, a number of provinces rebelled under the banner of republicanism; in 1912, the last Qing monarch yielded to the establishment of a new Republic of China.[19]

---

[18]See Mary C. Wright, *The Last Stand of Chinese Conservatism: The T'ung-Chih Restoration, 1862–1874* (Stanford, Cal.: Stanford University Press, 1957).

[19]For a penetrating survey and analysis of this early period of the Chinese revolution, see Mary Clabaugh Wright, "Introduction: The Rising Tide of Change," in Wright, ed., *China in Revolution: The First Phase, 1900–1913* (New Haven, Conn.: Yale University Press, 1968), pp. 1–63.

It soon became clear that there was no viable replacement for the Manchu government. Unlike Japan, where nineteenth-century political elites had forged a compromise between innovative policies and traditional political symbols, China had rejected the old political order without anything approaching consensus on a new one. The prolonged life of the imperial system had permitted the national crisis to deepen immeasurably even while it restrained and fragmented the counter-elites who promoted new approaches. The Revolution of 1911 left as its legacy a thoroughly discredited political tradition that offered no guidelines for a successor and a political vacuum that encouraged further national disintegration. Nominal national leadership was up for grabs, accessible to any group that could muster more force than its opponents. However, real power and authority required an elite who offered a credible response to the national crisis. In a situation that demanded new leaders and policies, the Chinese Communists' credentials were as good as their competitors, and ultimately better. Organized well after the Qing collapse and totally immersed in the revolutionary setting, the CCP necessarily oriented itself toward the major problems of the times. In the process, it became an agent of the Chinese revolution as well as its future master. It is essential, therefore, to look briefly at three themes that have dominated the revolution from its inception down to and including the present.

National Independence. Nationalism was the "moving force" of the Chinese revolution,[20] a unifying theme that brought diverse objectives together in the concept of national regeneration. Perhaps its clearest manifestation was a desire for national independence from foreign influence and control. No other issue was so easy to define in terms of concrete targets and abstract objectives: struggle against foreign opponents to regain national independence and equality. From 1900 to about 1925, virtually all political movements that generated significant

[20]Ibid., pp. 3–4. See also Michael Gasster, *Chinese Intellectuals and the Revolution of 1911: The Birth of Modern Chinese Radicalism* (Seattle: University of Washington Press, 1969); and Kuang-sheng Liao, *Antiforeignism and Modernization in China, 1860–1980* (Hong Kong: Chinese University Press, 1984).

popular support—the anti-Manchu struggles, the frequent boy-
cotts of foreign goods and enterprises, the great strikes and
demonstrations of May Fourth (1919) and May Thirtieth
(1925)—appealed directly to resentment of the foreign role in
Chinese affairs. National independence remained a prominent
issue in the Nationalist Revolution of 1926–1928 and in the early
years of the KMT government, and with the Japanese invasion
of 1937 it again became the paramount national objective.
Although China largely regained its independent status in the
postwar years, its conflicts with the United States and the Soviet
Union have continued the legacy of earlier anti-imperialist
struggles.

China was never a full-fledged colony, retaining throughout
its modern history formal diplomatic recognition as an independent state. As noted earlier, this fact sets Chinese experience
apart from that of most non-Western countries. Both Chinese
and foreigners recognized, however, that Chinese "independence"
was only nominal. Sun Yat-sen, leader of the early Chinese
nationalist movement, called his country a "hypo-colony," by
which he meant that China was in fact a colony of many
countries rather than of one particular power.[21] Mao Zedong
and others used the term "semi-colony" to describe China's
condition, with the qualification that outright occupation by
foreign powers (e.g., Japanese control of Manchuria after 1931)
had transformed certain sections into full colonial status.[22] Whatever the proper term might be, by the early decades of the twentieth century, China had unquestionably lost a large measure of
its independence and sovereignty.[23]

[21]Sun Yat-sen, *San Min Chu I*, trans. Frank W. Price (Shanghai: Commercial
Press, 1928), p. 39 passim.
[22]*Selected Works of Mao Tse-tung* (Peking: Foreign Languages Press, 1965),
vol. 2, pp. 309–14. Mao's works appear in many English-language editions. In
this book we will rely mainly on the following five-volume set: *Selected Works
of Mao Tse-tung* (Peking: Foreign Languages Press, 1965). vol. 1–4; and
Selected Works of Mao Tsetung (Peking: Foreign Languages Press, 1977), vol.
5. The four-volume 1965 edition included most of Mao's major pre-1949
writings. The fifth volume, published posthumously in 1977 (with a change in
spelling of Mao's name that still avoided *pinyin*), includes works from 1949–1957;
it was edited by a committee under Hua Guofeng's leadership, although his
name does not appear on the title page. Hereafter, all references to these five
volumes will cite *Selected Works*, followed by the volume and page number(s).
[23]For discussion of foreign gains and privileges acquired through treaties and
other arrangements, beginning with the Opium War settlement of 1842–1844,

By the 1920s, the territorial sway of the old Chinese empire was significantly reduced. A number of tributary states that had formerly recognized some degree of political dependence on China (Burma, Vietnam, Korea, and Outer Mongolia) were lost. Outright cessions gave the island of Hong Kong to the British, Macao to the Portuguese, Taiwan and the Ryukyus to Japan, and vast areas on the northern and western frontiers to Russia; Tibet [Xizang] was drawn away from Chinese influence; Manchuria was soon to become a victim of Japanese conquest. Within China, some foreign powers claimed large spheres of influence in which they held special economic and military rights. Scattered along the coast and inland waters in cities opened for trade were numerous concessions, or leases to the powers, which the concessionaires administered as their own territory. In these areas, foreigners were guaranteed the right to live, trade, manufacture, and hold land—rights protected by the principle of extraterritoriality that made foreign residents subject to their own rather than Chinese legal jurisdiction. Christian missionaries had unrestricted rights to propagate their faith anywhere in China. Commercial privileges, particularly a fixed limit on the Chinese tariff schedule, gave foreign businessmen important advantages.

The treaty system that established these conditions was of fundamental importance. Needless to say, the Chinese government entered into these treaties under duress; but once sanctified by treaty, the various privileges could be altered only by the consent of all parties. More importantly, the beneficiaries could, and did, invoke principles of legality and national honor to enforce them. Especially after the Boxer settlement of 1901, the foreign powers maintained military forces in China to defend their citizens and interests. Their instruments of defense were not limited to military force, however. Foreigners controlled collections of Chinese customs and the salt tax, the most stable sources of central revenue, and provided key staff in the postal, telegraph, and railroad systems. Their role in governmental operations helped ensure that China would meet its treaty obli-

see the sources cited in note 5 of this chapter and Albert Feuerwerker, *The Foreign Establishment in China in the Early Twentieth Century* (Ann Arbor: University of Michigan, Center for Chinese Studies, 1976).

gations, including payments on a staggering foreign debt built up through frequent loans and indemnities.

A few major points follow from this all-too-sketchy outline. From 1900 to 1928, the central government of China was too weak and dependent on the foreign powers to take actions against these other nations. The new KMT government established in Nanjing (Nanking) in 1928 was stronger and more vigorous in seeking equalization of its status, but it fell far short of the goal of national independence; the Japanese advance was soon to put more Chinese territory than ever under foreign control. In addition to subverting the government's authority, foreign influence was prominent in the major cities and in the more modernized sectors of the Chinese economy. Imperialism never had a direct impact on all or even most areas of Chinese life, but its effects were highly visible and tangible to urbanized laborers, intellectuals, and businessmen who were influential in defining national political issues. Whether it really damaged the handicrafts and land system of the traditional economy and retarded modern economic development remains open to question. [24] What is not in dispute is that most politically conscious Chinese believed that foreign economic activities had a negative effect on Chinese development, and virtually all Chinese who were exposed to the foreign presence resented its forced and privileged penetration of their country. The leaders of the CCP absorbed the resulting anti-imperialist attitudes, used them in their rise to power, and have continued to nourish them since 1949.

National Unification. A second theme of the Chinese revolution has been national unification under a single, central political authority. In a limited sense, this goal was as obvious as the drive

[24]The economic role of imperialism in China is a controversial issue. For arguments that imperialism's purely economic impact was minimal, mixed, or positive, see Robert F. Dernberger, "The Role of the Foreigner in China's Economic Development, 1840–1949," in Dwight H. Perkins, ed., *China's Modern Economy in Historical Perspective* (Stanford, Cal.: Stanford University Press, 1975), pp. 19–47; Chi-ming Hou, *Foreign Investment and Economic Development in China, 1840–1937* (Cambridge, Mass.: Harvard University Press, 1965); and Albert Feuerwerker, *The Chinese Economy, 1912–1949* (Ann Arbor: University of Michigan, Center for Chinese Studies, 1968). Different views are found

for independence. The problem was simply a division of power among several competing groups; the solution was for one group to attain sufficient power to establish a durable central government and to subdue its rivals. This simplified view was an understandable response to the domestic political situation that emerged in the wake of the Revolution of 1911. The basic condition of the times was *warlordism*, a term that refers most precisely to the years between 1916 and 1928 when control of the central government in Peking [Beijing] shifted frequently from one military leader to another, but which in a broader sense may refer to the chronic political and military disunity that prevailed in China from before 1911 to 1949.

A warlord was a military leader "who established and maintained control over territory by the use of his personal army";[25] that is, he had a territorial base over which he exercised political and military control by virtue of an army loyal to him rather than to some higher leader of government. Warlordism developed when the central government lost its ability to control regional military leaders, leaving a field of warlords who fought among themselves for regional and national supremacy. The seeds of warlordism lay in the regional armies recruited to subdue the Taiping Rebellion. The declining Manchu government never fully regained control over these forces, which grew in numbers and strength. When the last Qing emperor abdicated in 1912, leadership of the new "republican" government passed quickly to Yuan Shikai (Yüan Shih-k'ai), who commanded the loyalty of China's most powerful army and thereby maintained a semblance of unified national control until his death in 1916. Yuan's death opened the gates for the heyday of warlordism, in which no single warlord ever controlled more than a few provinces or

in Frances V. Moulder, *Japan, China, and the Modern World Economy* (Cambridge: Cambridge University Press, 1977); and Stephen C. Thomas, *Foreign Intervention and China's Economic Development, 1870–1911* (Boulder, Colo.: Westview Press, 1984). The general effects of imperialism are debated by Andrew Nathan and Joseph Esherick in *Bulletin of Concerned Asian Scholars*, vol. 4, no. 4 (December 1972): 2–16. See also the sources cited in note 33 of this chapter as the issue is inseparable from broader analysis of the economy of modern China.

[25] James E. Sheridan, *Chinese Warlord: The Career of Feng Yü-hsiang* (Stanford, Cal.: Stanford University Press, 1966), p. 16.

was able to maintain an official government in Peking for more than a brief period. The victory of Chiang Kai-shek's Nationalist forces in 1928 brought a significant change, since the KMT represented a much more broadly based movement with genuine programs for national administration and development. The Nationalist movement, however, had won a military victory by striking alliances with some of the warlords, not by eliminating them. As a result, only a few provinces in the Yangtze [Changjiang] valley of central China were solidly under Chiang's control. In fact, his government faced virtually continuous rebellion or threat of rebellion from the residual warlords until the Japanese invasion. It faced as well an armed Communist movement, which, though militarily weak and quite different in character from the warlord armies, magnified the extent of national disunity.[26]

The evils of warlordism need little elaboration. The existence of multiple and shifting centers of power made a travesty of attempts at national government. Taxes multiplied at the local level to finance the warlords, while the central government was politically and financially impoverished. Foreign powers capitalized on this weakness, trading diplomatic recognition for economic opportunities and supporting those warlords who would favor them or oppose their rivals. Wars and troop movements exacted an enormous cost in lives, military expenditures, looting, and property destruction.[27] For any concerned Chinese, the consequences were simply intolerable, appearing all the more shameful in view of China's tradition of civilian rule under an all-powerful central government. Hence there existed the desire for unification at all costs, with an understanding that military power was absolutely essential to the process. The Chinese revolution would not be complete until one government ruled all of China, having eliminated all possible military resistance.[28]

But forceful establishment of a secure central government could only be a first step toward a genuine national unification.

[26] Ibid., pp. 1–6.
[27] Ibid., pp. 20–30.
[28] C. Martin Wilbur, "Military Separatism and the Process of Reunification under the Nationalist Regime," in Ho and Tsou, eds., *China in Crisis*, pp. 203–04.

Unity and security were essential, however, so were governmental effectiveness and legitimacy; although warlordism highlighted the former needs, it also exposed the latter. Military unification alone could not replace the imperial political system, which had combined with its monopoly of force a national administration operative through the bureaucratic-scholarly-familial hierarchies and a legitimate political authority based on imperial Confucianism. The traditional administrative mechanism and its ideology fell with Manchu reforms, the Revolution of 1911, and subsequent changes in Chinese society and ideas. The reunification of China thus required nothing less than a new polity that could meet the demands of a modern nation-state. In administrative terms, it required a new system of political recruitment and of handling an expanded range of governmental activities at all levels, down to and including the village. In ideological terms, it called for a new doctrine that would not only justify the exercise of political authority but also seek the allegiance of ordinary citizens and integrate them in the political system. The real problem, then, was disintegration rather than simple disunity; the solution was reintegration on new terms of which the traditional political order had never conceived.[29]

In this broader sense, the reunification (i.e., reintegration) of China actually began with those reformers of the late nineteenth century who called for a modernized political structure that would base itself on and claim the support of the Chinese people. Implementation of these proposals began with Manchu reforms that antedated the Revolution of 1911. It was not until the 1920s, however, that the political vehicle for forging a new polity emerged in the mass-based political party. Although never successful at either unification or integration, the KMT government spread new political concepts, institutions, and procedures that clearly foreshadowed much of what was to come under CCP rule. Today, the Chinese Communists' understanding of the real dimensions of national unification, their profound commitment to it, and their relative success in attaining it draw heavily on these earlier efforts and experiences.

[29] See "Comments by Wang Gungwu," ibid., pp. 264–270; and Tang Tsou, "Revolution, Reintegration and Crisis in Communist China: A Framework for Analysis," ibid., pp. 277–81.

Socioeconomic Change. Generalizations about socioeconomic change in a revolutionary era—its causes, extent, and political implications—are always inadequate. No discussion of the Chinese revolution is complete, however, without some reference to this subject. Perhaps the most important point to emphasize is that social and economic conditions in modern China were *potentially* the source of a massive revolution. It was not inevitable that they would *cause* one or that they would provide the dominant basis of any revolutionary mobilization that might occur; it was inevitable that they would inject the question of radical social and economic change into the revolution that did occur. The potential explosiveness of Chinese society stemmed from a gross discrepancy between perceived possibilities and current reality. On the one hand, foreign penetration and imperial collapse had already initiated some change in values and social structure, particularly in the cities and among the upper classes. These changes stimulated demands for an accelerated transformation that would legitimize the new values and classes, eliminate China's economic and social "backwardness," and propel China into full equality—in every sense—with the Western powers. On the other hand, prevailing conditions stood in stark contrast and even opposition to these desires; imperialism, warlordism, the persistence of traditional values among most of the population, and widespread poverty and illiteracy seemed to defy the realization of rapid change. For proponents of socioeconomic reform, this gulf between ambition and reality heightened the attractiveness of revolutionary formulae for attaining it. And although the gulf was an immediate obstacle to revolutionary mobilization of the masses, it also created enormous potential support for any movement that could transmit to the common people an image of how their lives could be improved.

National economic development was a prime concern for all Chinese who hoped for national regeneration, since their economy was so weak and backward relative to that of Japan and the Western powers. Contrary to some impressions, the pre-Communist economy was neither incapable of change nor stagnant in the decades preceding 1949. Historically, China had known periods of great wealth and economic change, although dynastic decline and traditional values had inhibited diffusion of the industrial revolution to China in the modern era. Still, industrialization and modern commercialization did come to China well before the Communist Revolution, particularly after 1895. Industrial growth between 1912 and 1949 averaged over 5 percent annually and was especially impressive in the relatively favorable periods of 1912–1920 and 1931–1936; the gross national product (GNP) was also growing, although not as rapidly as modern industry.[30]

Despite this beginning, however, the Chinese economy in 1949 was still "near the bottom of the world development scale," with a per capita GNP of about fifty dollars.[31] Growth in the modern sectors of the economy, particularly industry, had relatively little impact on the national economic situation simply because they started at such a low level and remained very modest contributors to the national product. The economy was still basically preindustrial and agrarian, and the all-important agricultural sector was characterized by low labor productivity, technological stagnation, and great population pressure on the cultivable land. In short, economic development before 1949 was weak and uneven, being confined mainly to Manchuria and the treaty ports where foreign capital played an important though declining role.[32] Key developmental issues, such as the role of state planning and entrepreneurship, geographic diversification, and agricultural transformation, remained unresolved. The beginnings of economic modernization had underscored the need for a program of national economic development, but its implementation was one of the least advanced of revolutionary objectives.

The human consequences of modern China's economic situation were severe. China's great population explosion came in the eighteenth century, when the population grew from about 150 million to over 300 million and began to strain existing economic resources. Population growth then slowed but did not stop, reaching about 430 million in 1850 and, according to the

[30]See the discussion in Alexander Eckstein, "The Economic Heritage," in Eckstein, Walter Galenson, and Ta-chung Liu, eds., *Economic Trends in Communist China* (Chicago: Aldine, 1968), pp. 64–67. For a provocative survey of imperial economic history, emphasizing the wealth and sophistication of the medieval Chinese economy and analyzing its stagnation in the Qing period, see Mark Elvin, *The Pattern of the Chinese Past: A Social and Economic Interpretation* (Stanford, Cal.: Stanford University Press, 1972).

[31]Eckstein, "Economic Heritage," p. 79.

[32]Ibid., pp. 59–61, 66, 74–80.

first Communist census, 583 million in 1953. In the absence of major increases in cultivable land or change in agricultural technology, there developed from the mid-nineteenth century on a basic condition of overpopulation and mass poverty manifested in chronic misery, famine, rebellion, and population movements.[33] In the early decades of the twentieth century, warlordism and civil war compounded the problems of rural life that left much of the population at a level of marginal existence.[34] No single factor explains the depths and complexity of this economic malaise. High rates of tenancy and the presence of a few large landowners were obvious sources of peasant dissatisfaction and obvious targets for reformers and revolutionaries, although neither was a condition typical of all China. High rents and taxes, usurious credit practices, small and fragmented farms, traditional farming methods, low productivity per man, illiteracy, and external disturbances and exactions all contributed to perpetuating the poverty and vulnerability to ruin of most of the rural population. Life in the cities, where a small industrial proletariat was growing, afforded better opportunities for some but scarcely better conditions in general. Low wages, long hours, unsafe working conditions, inadequate housing, and large pools

[33] Ping-ti Ho, *Studies on the Population of China, 1368–1953* (Cambridge, Mass.: Harvard University Press, 1959), pp. 270–78. The increasing impoverishment thesis, like that of imperialism's impact (see note 24 of this chapter), remains the subject of lively debate. Studies suggesting that the Chinese economy held its own against both imperialism and population growth include Ramon H. Myers, *The Chinese Peasant Economy: Agricultural Development in Hopei and Shantung, 1890–1949* (Cambridge, Mass.: Harvard University Press, 1970); and Dwight H. Perkins, *Agricultural Development in China, 1368–1968* (Chicago: Aldine, 1969). That finding is reviewed critically in Cheryl Payer, "Harvard on China II: Logic, Evidence and Ideology," *Bulletin of Concerned Asian Scholars*, vol. 6, no. 2 (April–August 1974): 62–68. Recent essays exploring these questions in greater depth are found in Dwight H. Perkins, ed., *China's Modern Economy in Historical Perspective* (Stanford, Cal.: Stanford University Press, 1975). For a summary of different views on the economy of modern China, see "Symposium on China's Economic History," *Modern China*, vol. 4, no. 3 (July 1978). Despite all this controversy about the source and precise extent of economic problems in modern China, there is general agreement that the problems were severe and required a new developmental effort to resolve.

[34] For surveys of agricultural and living conditions in this period, see John Lossing Buck, *Land Utilization in China* (New York: Paragon Reprint Corporation, 1964); and R. H. Tawney, *Land and Labour in China* (London: George Allan and Unwin, 1932), pp. 23–108.

of unemployed or irregular workers were the rule in China's emerging factory cities.[35]

If these economic conditions had existed in a stable social and political setting, their revolutionary potentiality might never have been realized. Such stability was lacking, however, for the collapse of the traditional order had already set in motion far-reaching social changes. Basic in this changing social setting was the discrediting of the old elite. The abolition of the examination system of 1905, followed by the end of imperial rule, destroyed the bureaucratic stronghold of the scholar-gentry class, opening the ranks of political elitehood to new claimants and eroding gentry power and status at the local level.[36] As the old criteria of legitimate authority declined, leaving crude military and financial power to fill the vacuum, certain groups experienced significant upward mobility; military leaders and the new Chinese bourgeoisie were perhaps the best examples of those groups that were acquiring new power and status. However, social change encompassed far more than a partial replacement of the old elite by warlords and chambers of commerce. The penetration of Western values that both hastened and fed upon the rejection of tradition pointed toward a sweeping liberation of Chinese society from the restraints of the past. Exemplified by the intellectual ferment of the May Fourth Movement of 1919, this trend promoted the study of "science and democracy," the emancipation of women from their servile status within the family, and the elevation of youth to more independent and responsible roles in society.[37] The vision of new freedoms and opportunities for previously subordinate groups was spreading, supported now by at least a few concrete examples of the vision's attainability.

[35] See Tawney, *Land and Labour*, pp. 121–28, 140–54.

[36] For discussion of the "erosion" of local leadership in modern China, see Hsiao-tung Fei, *China's Gentry: Essays in Rural-Urban Relations*, rev. and ed. by Margaret Park Redfield (Chicago: University of Chicago Press, 1953).

[37] On the May Fourth Movement, see Chow Tse-tsung, *The May Fourth Movement: Intellectual Revolution in Modern China* (Cambridge, Mass.: Harvard University Press, 1960). The emergence of new groups and transformation of old ones is analyzed in Wright, "Introduction: The Rising Tide of Change," pp. 32–44.

The actual extent of social "liberation" was sharply limited, of course. Poverty, illiteracy, and traditional isolation from politics made it difficult to persuade the common people that significant changes in their circumstances were possible. Nonetheless, by the 1920s the banner of socioeconomic reform had passed from scattered intellectuals to organized political parties, with increasing evidence that it could be a basis for popular mobilization. Ultimately, the Nationalist Revolution of 1928 remained oriented toward the proven appeals of national independence and unification, but for at least a brief period in 1925–1927 its radical wing (then including Chinese Communists) was able to organize a worker-peasant movement that brought class struggle within Chinese society to the fore. From this point on, fundamental social and economic reform was an unavoidable issue in Chinese politics. It was also the most painful and divisive of the three main revolutionary themes. The KMT after 1928 did more to advance it than any previous government, but persistently gave it lower priority than independence and unification on its own terms. The CCP, on the other hand, perceived social and economic change as an integral part of its program, as inseparable from its nationalist objectives, and was more successful in tapping this vein of potential popular support.

To summarize this discussion, the revolutionary setting of modern China concentrated political energies on the attainment of national independence, national unification and integration, and socioeconomic change. The Chinese Communist movement, existing wholly within the revolutionary period, necessarily absorbed and responded to these goals. Ultimately, it developed a fuller and more convincing response to them than its great competitor, the KMT. The Chinese Nationalists placed unification first, thereby compromising the struggle for resistance to Japan and postponing a concentrated assault on China's social and economic problems; ironically, the strategy heightened national disunity and weakened the KMT's claim to leadership of the revolution. As an illegal opposition party not bearing responsibility for national government, the CCP could talk in terms of programs rather than priorities and could practice some of these programs in a smaller, more manageable setting. Its victory over the KMT was won by force of arms, but only after it had built up an image of real dedication to the paramount national concerns. Once in power, the CCP demonstrated that its credentials for revolutionary leadership were sound by restoring China to greater independence and unity than at any time in the preceding century and by vigorously promoting its social and economic transformation.

Nonetheless, the Communists' ability to come to grips with these problems was heavily dependent on the efforts of earlier actors in the revolution. The popularization of the drive for national independence was largely the work of the KMT and its forerunners, not the CCP. It was the Nanjing government that secured the first real rollback in Western privileges and began to enter into relations with foreign powers on an equal basis, so that China in 1945—still under KMT rule—had largely regained its formal diplomatic equality. Although the KMT never truly unified the country, it was the Nationalists—and even some of the warlords—who established the first modern governmental structures based on experiments begun in the last years of the imperial system. The CCP was to extend governmental authority to the people in an unprecedented way, but the crucial first steps of replacing traditional institutions and introducing new ones were taken by its predecessors. Change in the marriage and family system was well advanced by 1949, with KMT legislation in this area bearing strong similarities to later Communist enactments. The Nationalists did much to spread, although little to implement, the idea of agrarian reform. Educational reform began in earnest as early as the last decade of Qing, producing by 1949 the modern intellectuals, the educational buildings and facilities, and the increased literacy so crucial to many CCP programs. In these and many other spheres, Chinese Communism must be seen as continuing and benefitting from a revolutionary process that it did not initiate or define.

SOVIET COMMUNISM

The role of Soviet Communism in the Chinese Communist Revolution is one of the most controversial issues in the study of this subject. No simple answer explains adequately the historical relationship between the Russian and Chinese "comrades" or Soviet Communism's influence on the political system developed in China after 1949.[38] It is undeniable, however, that the Soviet Union has had a powerful influence on Chinese Communist politics for over half a century. We introduce this influence by commenting on (1) the initial attraction of Marxism-Leninism, (2) a period of early Soviet control, (3) the importance of the Soviet model, and (4) some broad ideological issues. The analysis in Chapter 4 of the evolution of Chinese Communist ideology puts many of these issues in sharper historical focus.

Attractions of Marxism-Leninism. The attraction of Marxism-Leninism for many Chinese revolutionaries and the enduring influence resulting from their interest in the post-1917 revolutionary government of Russia did not rest on easy acceptance of or total conversion to the Soviet doctrine. Even in the initial contacts, at the time of the founding of the CCP, there were subtle differences in the ways that various elements of Marxism-Leninism penetrated Chinese politics.[39] Some elements carried a distinctly positive attraction. The Chinese intellectuals who were to lead the CCP in its early years committed themselves to Marxism-Leninism largely on the basis of those aspects of it that fit their own understanding of China's needs or that reinforced currents already flowing in the Chinese intellectual stream. Other elements followed as a consequence of this general and in some ways superficial commitment to Marxism-Leninism; they were not necessarily forced on the Chinese, but they nonetheless injected some novel or unsolicited influences into the Chinese revolution.

From party beginnings to the present, CCP leaders have differed in their interpretation of the Marxist-Leninist message and how to apply it in China. At the most general level, one can distinguish between men such as Chen Duxiu (Ch'en Tu-hsiu)

---

[38] A useful survey is O. Edmund Clubb, *China and Russia: The "Great Game"* (New York: Columbia University Press, 1971).

[39] The discussion here focuses on the development of Marxism-Leninism in China after the Bolshevik Revolution in Russia. Marxism was known to a few Chinese intellectuals in advance of that revolution, but anarchism was the most attractive brand of European radicalism in China before 1917. See Martin Bernal, "The Triumph of Anarchism over Marxism, 1906–7," in Wright, ed., *China in Revolution*, pp. 97–142; and Maurice Meisner, *Li Ta-chao and the Origins of Chinese Marxism* (Cambridge, Mass.: Harvard University Press, 1967), pp. 52–57.

and Liu Shaoqi (Liu Shao-ch'i) who tended toward a more "orthodox" or "scientific" use of the doctrine, and those such as Li Dazhao (Li Ta-chao) and Mao Zedong, who displayed more "voluntaristic" and "nationalistic" tendencies.[40] However, during the critical founding years of the party, most soon-to-be Communists in China shared a revolutionary commitment that overshadowed their theoretical commitment to Marxism-Leninism;[41] that is, they identified more with the Bolshevik Revolution's general message of radical change than with the specifics of its ideology. Anti-imperialism was perhaps the strongest element in this message, not so much through the subtleties of Leninist theories as through the basic insistence that foreign oppression must and would be overthrown. The primary catalyst in the growth of Marxist adherents and left-wing activity in China was the May Fourth Movement of 1919, a result of an incident that symbolized upheaval in diverse areas of Chinese life but was in its political focus an ardently nationalistic, anti-imperialist event. The publicity and definition that the May Fourth Movement gave to demands for national independence transformed Marxism-Leninism from an esoteric foreign doctrine to an immediately relevant explanation of a crucial fact of Chinese political life.[42]

The May Fourth Movement, in its broadest sense, also pointed toward another profound attraction in Marxism-Leninism—its claim to science, modernity, and progressive change. At its most fundamental level, the May Fourth Movement represented a growing intellectual revolt against the Chinese tradition, a revolt that was divided in its objectives but was clearly set against China's past. Some Chinese who were determined to promote a revolutionary transformation that would propel their country into the modern era on a basis of full equality with the West were to find inspiration and guidance in Marxism-Leninism. The doctrine not only asserted the inevitability of progressive change that would alter China's inferior international status, but it did so with a claim to science and modernity that had previously

[40] See "Comments by Michel Oksenberg," in Ho and Tsou, eds., *China in Crisis*, pp. 488–90.

[41] See Meisner, *Origins of Chinese Marxism*, pp. 56–57; and Stuart R. Schram, *The Political Thought of Mao Tse-tung*, rev. and enl. ed. (New York: Praeger, 1969), pp. 29–32.

[42] Meisner, *Origins of Chinese Marxism*, pp. 95–104.

seemed to be a monopoly of Western capitalism. Particularly important was the Leninist notion that a small group of intellectual elites could, by organized intervention in the historical process, accelerate and guide the promised revolutionary transformation; to Chinese intellectuals aware of their society's inertia and their own traditional role of political leadership, this idea held a special appeal. To be sure, the early Chinese Communists were not uniformly receptive to these various appeals. Perhaps Mao Zedong alone held a kind of "natural Leninism" that made him uniquely responsive to both the revolutionary and organizational themes.[43] But the ideas noted here were central in Chinese intellectual discourse during and after the May Fourth Movement, and they clearly facilitated a growing interest in and commitment to Marxism-Leninism.[44]

Supplementing Chinese responsiveness to these broad revolutionary appeals was the concrete existence and example of a new Bolshevik government in Russia. As suggested earlier, it was the combination of the October Revolution in Russia and the May Fourth Movement in China that opened the way for Chinese acceptance of Marxism-Leninism. The importance of the Russian example bears special emphasis. Like China, Russia was economically backward relative to the leading Western nations and was faced with the task of providing political alternatives to a discredited imperial system. The success and survival of the Bolshevik movement offered empirical proof that there was a new alternative to both Western capitalism and imperial decadence. Soviet Russia was not so much a model in these formative years of Chinese Communism as it was a symbol and example of how a new system dedicated to revolutionary change could

[43] The phrase is Stuart Schram's from *The Political Thought of Mao Tse-tung*, pp. 35, 55. See also Benjamin I. Schwartz, *Chinese Communism and the Rise of Mao* (Cambridge, Mass.: Harvard University Press, 1958), p. 35.

[44] For general discussions of this point, see Chow Tse-tsong, *The May Fourth Movement: Intellectual Revolution in Modern China* (Cambridge, Mass.: Harvard University Press, 1960), passim, esp. pp. 1–15, 358–68; D. W. Y. Kwok, *Scientism in Chinese Thought, 1900–1950* (New Haven, Conn.: Yale University Press, 1965), pp. 11–20, 59–77, 162–71; and Schwartz, *Chinese Communism and the Rise of Mao*, pp. 7–27. For detailed analysis of the political role of intellectuals in modern China, see Jerome B. Grieder, *Intellectuals and the State in Modern China* (New York: Free Press, 1981).

emerge from the ruins of an old imperial order, despite the opposition of the leading Western powers.

Important though this example was to the radical intellectuals of China, it was by no means the only concrete result of the October Revolution. In July 1919, soon after the May Fourth incident, the Soviet government issued the Karakhan Declaration in which it announced its intention to abrogate all "unequal treaties" between Russia and China and to give up all special Russian interests and privileges in China. Although never wholly implemented, the proposal created a highly favorable response and much interest in the new Russian regime from many Chinese.[45] The possibilities of substantive Soviet support were not lost on Chinese revolutionaries, who became increasingly responsive to contacts with Russian representatives. Within a few years, Comintern agents had brought about the organization of the CCP, and the Soviet government had entered into an agreement with Sun Yat-sen's KMT government in Canton [Guangzhou] that was to provide it with Soviet advisers and military assistance. The details of these activities, which were also to produce the first KMT-CCP United Front of 1923–1927, need not concern us here.[46] The point is that Soviet Russia was a source of organizational and military aid to Chinese Communists and Nationalists alike, at a time when both were in need of support and not likely to secure it from any other source. As in the realm of ideas, Soviet Communism had something to offer that was seen as supporting and reinforcing, not altering, the shape of the Chinese revolution.

The acceptance of Marxism-Leninism by Chinese Communists derived mainly from a significant correspondence of ideas and interests, but it led as well to an acceptance of Soviet ideological and organizational discipline. There was no realistic alternative at that point. Moscow *was* the authoritative center of the movement they had joined. For the Chinese comrades, the strategy of their revolution was not what they found in the Marxist historical tradition but rather the Soviet Communist party's interpretation of it. Most of them were in any case poorly prepared to resist Russian authority, even if they had wished to challenge political

[45] Chow, pp. 209–214.
[46] See the sources cited in note 54 of this chapter.

reality. Their knowledge of Marxism-Leninism was in fact weak, so that they relied heavily on Comintern advisers, directives and materials from Moscow, and study in the Soviet Union for a theoretical grasp of the doctrine they espoused.[47] Necessarily, then, the establishment of the CCP and its formal affiliation (in 1922) with the Comintern quickly transformed the attraction of Marxism-Leninism into political subordination to Moscow.

Soviet Control, 1921–1934. For more than a decade, from the founding of the CCP in July 1921 (the date of the party's First Congress) to the early 1930s, the Soviet Communist party controlled the official line and leadership of the CCP. Through the medium of Russian advisers and Comintern agents in China, backed by the threat of withdrawing assistance and Comintern recognition, Soviet elites formulated the CCP's major policy statements and chose its highest officials. This control began to slip following the 1927 rupture of the first KMT-CCP alliance. In the aftermath of Chiang Kai-shek's purge of Communist elements within the Nationalist movement, the CCP was too fragmented and the political situation too uncertain for directives from Moscow to determine all operations in China. Nonetheless, Soviet leaders continued to define the CCP general line and pass judgment on Chinese conformance with it. In a key test in late 1930 and early 1931, the Comintern reasserted its control by purging the Li Lisan leadership of the CCP, replacing it with the "returned students" (or "twenty-eight Bolsheviks") faction, a group trained in Moscow and loyal to its authority. Through this group, which dominated the CCP Central Committee until 1934, the Comintern maintained its hold over the Chinese Communist leadership.[48]

---

[47] The relative weakness of doctrinal study among Chinese party members, to which we allude frequently, was not overcome until after 1935. It was only during the Yanan (Yenan) Period (1937–1945) of Chinese Communism that CCP leaders found time for serious doctrinal study and writing and that the party set up its own system of schools for party cadres. Even then, standard Soviet study materials occupied a prominent place in the curriculum. See Compton's comments in *Mao's China: Party Reform Documents, 1942–44,* trans. and introduction by Boyd Compton (Seattle: University of Washington Press, 1952), pp. x–xi, xxx–xxxi, xxix–xlv.

[48] On this point and the following summary, see Clubb, *China and Russia,* and the sources cited in notes 10–12 of Chapter 1, this book.

The practical consequences of formal Comintern control over the CCP Central Committee in the 1927–1934 period remain in dispute. For a variety of reasons, this control was certainly less meaningful than in the years between 1921 and 1927. Soviet leadership in the later years was increasingly more concerned with European affairs and less obsessed with the domestic political implications of its China policy. The anti-Communist stance of the new KMT government in Nanjing made communications and the support of the CCP more difficult. Most serious of all were de facto political and geographic divisions within the Chinese Communist movement. The events of 1927 shattered its strength in the cities. In the revival that slowly followed, the bulk of CCP activity shifted to the countryside, to the scattered rural "soviets" of South-Central China where Communist guerrillas were struggling to establish territorial bases and a Red Army. The leaders of these rural soviets acknowledged the formal authority of the Central Committee and the Comintern line, but demands of survival and the autonomy derived from geographic isolation and armed support encouraged them to differ at times with orders from the party center. The foremost political representative of the rural areas was Mao Zedong, whose views were in conflict with both the Li Lisan and "returned students" factions. His differences with the latter group led him into rivalry with them for leadership of the party. The resulting competition limited the Comintern's ability to stay in command of the situation in China. Recognizing that the rural soviets and their armed forces had become the real strength of the Communist movement, the Comintern offered doctrinal pronouncements that legitimized their existence and most of their activities. At the same time, once the loyal "returned students" were installed at the party center, the Comintern could ill afford to compromise their formal authority over the Maoist faction. Hence the Comintern favored the "returned students" in the struggle with Mao; yet in doing so it weakened its claim to guide the main force of the revolution.

In the latter part of 1934, KMT military pressure compelled the Communists to evacuate their principal stronghold in southern Jiangxi [Kiangsi] province and embark on the Long March that was to relocate their major forces in the northwestern province of Shaanxi [Shensi]. Early in the course of this march, at the Zunyi [Tsunyi] Conference in January 1935, Mao Zedong successfully challenged the "returned students" faction and became the leading figure within the CCP.[49] Moscow was not thereafter to wield a controlling hand in Chinese Communist affairs. The question of Soviet direction of CCP policy was to arise on several later occasions, most critically CCP acceptance of the Comintern United Front policy in 1935, the CCP decision to work for Chiang Kai-shek's release following his kidnapping in the Sian [Xian] Incident of December 1936, and Chinese entrance into the Korean War in October–November 1950. In each of these cases, however, current evidence suggests that the CCP acted in line with Moscow's wishes not solely because of Russian pressure but also because Chinese leaders independently concluded that their own interests were served best by such actions.[50] In short, Mao's rise marked the end of CCP submission to the dictates of Soviet Communism.

The important point in this brief discussion is that the Soviet Union lost its power to control and discipline Chinese Communist leaders long before they came to power. Even before 1935, men such as Mao had, at least temporarily, acquired opportunities to experiment with their own responses to the Chinese revolution. After 1935, the CCP embarked on yet another period of growth and expansion. This time, however, control of the movement was in Chinese hands, so that decisions concerning both the revolutionary movement and the political system to emerge from it were made by the Chinese Communists themselves.

The Soviet Model. The imposition of Comintern dominance in the early 1920s required not only Soviet organizational control but also CCP acceptance of the Soviet Union as a model and of the Soviet party as the most advanced and authoritative among all Communist parties. Even after 1935, when Russian elites had lost their control, the CCP continued to acknowledge the primacy

[49]For details, see "Resolutions of the Tsunyi Conference," trans. with a commentary by Jerome Ch'en, *China Quarterly*, no. 40 (October–December 1969): 1–38.

[50]On CCP response to the 1935 United Front and the 1936 Sian Incident, see Lyman P. Van Slyke, *Enemies and Friends: The United Front in Chinese Communist History* (Stanford, Cal.: Stanford University Press, 1967), chaps. 4 and 5. On the Chinese decision to enter the Korean War, see Allen S. Whiting, *China Crosses the Yalu: The Decision to Enter the Korean War* (New York: Macmillan, 1967), pp. 27–30, 152–60.

of Soviet experience and standing. While insisting that their movement was independent and must "sinify" Marxism-Leninism for application in the Chinese context, CCP leaders avoided open disagreement with Soviet positions and paid deference to the USSR as the model socialist state.[51] Ultimately, of course, the Sino-Soviet conflict led to China's rejection of the USSR's primacy within the socialist camp; yet the CCP delayed open delineation of the differences between the two parties. The differences began, according to the Chinese, with Khrushchev's criticism of Stalin at the Soviet Twentieth Party Congress in February 1956, but they did not launch direct public attacks on the Soviet leadership until 1963; as late as February 1963, the Chinese claimed, they were deliberately refraining from a full accounting of the conflict.[52] In November 1957, nearly two years after the identified origins of the conflict, Mao was referring to the Soviet Union as an "outstanding example" and the "head" of the socialist camp.[53]

Were this deference entirely a matter of ritual or protocol—which in part it certainly was—its impact on the Chinese Communist system might have been negligible. In fact, however, it was also a reflection of the genuine importance to China of the Soviet model. The influence of this model has been particularly prominent in the organization of the CCP and its conception of its political role. China has had only two significant mass-based political parties—the KMT and the CCP—and both owe their basic organizational structure to Russian advisers who guided their development during the 1920s.[54] The guidelines came from

[51] Careful balancing of these two themes is evident in the writings of Mao Zedong. See Stuart Schram's comments and the selection of Mao's statements on the subject in Schram, *The Political Thought of Mao Tse-tung*, pp. 415–39. Schram notes (p. 115n) that one editorial principle governing the 1951 publication of Mao's *Selected Works* was the deletion of earlier formulations that might be offensive to the Soviet Union. For detailed analysis of the post-1935 "sinification" of Marxism through the medium of Maoism, see Raymond F. Wylie, *The Emergence of Maoism: Mao Tse-tung, Ch'en Po-ta, and the Search for Chinese Theory* (Stanford, Cal.: Stanford University Press, 1980).

[52] *The Origin and Development of the Differences Between the Leadership of the CPSU and Ourselves*, by the editorial departments of *People's Daily* and *Red Flag* (Peking: Foreign Language Press, 1963), esp. pp. 4–11.

[53] Schram, *The Political Thought of Mao Tse-tung*, pp. 435–36.

[54] For discussion and documentation of the Soviet-sponsored organizational development that occurred in both parties, see C. Martin Wilbur and Julie Lien-ying How, eds., *Documents on Communism, Nationalism and Soviet*

the Soviet Communist Party—a hierarchical, disciplined organization based on the principle of democratic centralism that
concentrated organizational authority in a small elite at the top.
The CCP acquired with this Leninist structure the idea of party
dictatorship, the notion that the revolutionary party must ultimately assume dictatorial political power in the name of the
proletariat, even though cooperation with other political parties
and classes might be necessary at earlier stages of the revolution.
While the KMT formally retained Sun Yat-sen's goal of constitutional government that would limit its monopoly of power, in
practice it too clung to a system of single-party rule. Both party
organization and party system in modern China reveal, therefore,
the force of Bolshevik organizational patterns.

Moreover, Soviet influence on the institutions of Communist
China went far beyond the organization of the CCP itself. It
appeared as well in the state structure and administrative practices
that emerged after 1949, in the "transmission belt" structure and
function of nonparty organizations (primarily those for youth,
workers, and women), and in the intimate guiding relationship
established by the CCP over all other institutions. This is not to
say that the institutionalization of CCP leadership in China has
been a direct or permanent copy of Russian experience;[55] it is
simply to point out that organizational patterns evolved in
Soviet Russia have been the primary model for those constructed
by the CCP.

Ideological Influences. Soviet Communism's impact on CCP
ideology is far more difficult to assess. On the one hand, the basic
ideology is Western in origin and was transmitted to China

Advisers in China, 1918–1927 (New York: Columbia University Press, 1956),
pp. 79–205. Comintern recognition of the Chinese parties' organizational
weaknesses in 1921–1922, before Soviet advisers assumed a prominent role in
China, is described in Allen S. Whiting, *Soviet Policies in China, 1917–1924*
(New York: Columbia University Press, 1954), pp. 87–91.

[55] For example, the 1954 Constitution of the People's Republic of China
contained a number of institutional provisions differing from those in the
Soviet Union. See the analysis in Franklin W. Houn, "Communist China's
New Constitution," *The Western Political Quarterly*, vol. 8, no. 2 (June 1955):
199–233; and H. Arthur Steiner, "Constitutionalism in Communist China,"
American Political Science Review, vol. 49, no. 1 (March 1955): 1–21.

largely via Soviet Russia. The early leaders of the CCP came independently to a revolutionary commitment that made Marxist-Leninist themes of social transformation and anti-imperialism attractive; but they also accepted, with varying degrees of enthusiasm, Russian authority to interpret the doctrine and prescribe its operative implications. Reluctance to challenge this authority endured into the late 1950s and placed limits on the way in which the Chinese were to formulate their own views. On the other hand, the CCP experienced a degree of physical separation from Moscow and a duration of revolutionary practice before coming to power that permitted it to test, absorb, and in some cases "sinify" the doctrine, a process described in greater detail in Chapter 4. As a result, the doctrine acquired an indigenous character, so that its acceptance derived from application to and modification within the Chinese political context, not simply from Russian authority. It is an oversimplification, then, to conclude that Chinese Communism is *either* a creative, indigenous product *or* only an application to China of a foreign doctrine.[56] It is a blending of both; it is foreign in its origins but over time has been handled by the Chinese with sufficient independence to make it their own.

This view permits us to acknowledge that Soviet Communism did introduce significant new concepts into Chinese politics, without our assuming that all of them were to be observed rigidly or permanently by the Chinese Communists. Some of the areas in which the CCP's historical experience led it to its own particular emphasis and constructions will be discussed in the next section, after referring briefly here to a few of the most influential ideas that came with the acceptance of Marxism-Leninism. Foremost among the latter are the concepts of class struggle, class analysis, and the leading role of the proletariat. Although some of the early Chinese Communists, such as Li Dazhao, were quite receptive to the idea of class struggle, the centrality of class conflict in Marxist analysis was generally a notion foreign to the Chinese comrades and simply had to be

[56] Most analysis of this complex issue concentrates on the particular case of Maoism (see the sources cited in footnotes 10–12 of Chapter 1, this book), but the doctrine in question is no longer identified so exclusively with Mao's writings.

learned.[57] Part of the difficulty lay in a political tradition that had emphasized social harmony and restrained social conflict.[58] However, even those Chinese whose revolutionary sentiments had led them from images of "harmony" to those of "struggle" found a strict socioeconomic definition of social groups and conflicts unfamiliar. Particularly troublesome was the exalted political role attributed to the urban working class, a class of very small proportions in early modern China. In time, the Chinese Communists became accustomed to analyzing both national and international politics in terms of struggles and alliances between different classes. They accepted, too, the formal acknowledgment of proletarian leadership in the revolution, and after 1949, they were to grant industrial workers special economic and political privileges. Class analysis is now a fundamental element in Chinese political thinking, although it has clashed frequently with desires for national unity and with the realities of Chinese social structure.

The millennial Marxist vision of a classless society, populated by a new socialist man and based on collective ownership and organization, has also had a profound impact on Chinese Communism. Utopian views of man and society were by no means foreign to China, but this particular utopia contained some novel implications. What Marxism-Leninism foretold was a new society that would be both universal and modern, that is, it would ultimately emerge all over the world and would be based on a postindustrial economy.[59] The doctrine thus broadened the revolutionary struggle to include not only China but all other societies as well. Its acceptance encouraged the Chinese to see their revolution as part of a world revolution, to see that the ultimate resolution of class struggle would be on an international rather than simply Chinese dimension. The universalism transmitted by Soviet Communism has never overshadowed Chinese nationalism, but it has given to the present Chinese political

[57] See Meisner, *Origins of Chinese Marxism*, pp. 140–46, showing that even Li Dazhao's enthusiasm for class struggle fell significantly short of a truly Marxist class analysis.

[58] See Arthur F. Wright, "Struggle vs. Harmony: Symbols of Competing Values in Modern China," *World Politics*, vol. 6, no. 1 (October 1953): 31–44.

[59] Cf. Franz Schurmann, *Ideology and Organization in Communist China*, 2nd ed. enl. (Berkeley: University of California Press, 1968), pp. 40–42.

system a sense of intimate, reciprocal involvement in the international system that was not characteristic of China in the past.

The Marxist vision also led the CCP to adopt more specific guidelines for the reconstruction of China that were not necessarily called for by national traditions or conditions. It is in this area that the Soviet model has been of immense importance. Marxism-Leninism did not foretell the exact nature of the future society; it simply stated that any given society would move through a socialist stage to the communist ideal, with the new forms revealed only after the revolution. Once the first socialist society had emerged in Russia, however, the requirements of the "socialist road" became concrete. If China were to follow this road, how could it stray from the path already mapped by the Soviet Union, which was acknowledged to be the most advanced socialist country? The Soviet model was crucial to CCP elites, not because the Russians could force them to follow it, but rather because the Soviet Union seemed to provide the only example of how to move toward their ultimate objectives. When the CCP came to power, it simply assumed that socialist construction required such policies as rapid industrialization, centralized economic planning and administration, and the collectivization of agriculture. It decided, in short, to follow the Soviet model, despite the fact that China's economic conditions were quite different from those in Russia following the October Revolution.[60]

In the early years of the People's Republic, therefore, Soviet influence was very prominent. Efforts to implement general features of the Soviet developmental model supplemented the strictures on doctrine and organization absorbed in earlier years. Russian advisers, assistance, plans, blueprints, and texts came in; but present in the system, too, and ultimately more powerful, were the influences of the CCP's own past. The way in which the Chinese Communists had blended the lessons of both Soviet Communism and their own unique national experience led to modification and then rejection of the Soviet model.[61] Since the middle 1950s, Soviet influence in China has receded to a more

[60] See Schram, *The Political Thought of Mao Tse-tung*, pp. 75–76.
[61] See Schurmann, *Ideology and Organization in Communist China*, esp. pp. 13–15, 33–45, 239–42.

subtle role reflecting its subordination to the national experience of Chinese Communism.

CCP HISTORY

The historical experience of the CCP is the last topic to be discussed in this survey of the origins of the Chinese political system. As with the previous topics, discussion will be selective, seeking only to identify major trends that have had a pronounced impact on later political patterns and attitudes. After a brief review of key periods in party development,[62] which will be useful for future reference, we will examine some of the elements of CCP political style that grew out of its revolutionary struggles between 1921 and 1949.

The First United Front, 1923–1927. Soon after its First Congress in 1921, the CCP entered into an alliance with the KMT to hasten the conclusion of "national revolution" against imperialism and the northern warlords. This decision, which was imposed on the CCP by the Comintern against the wishes of some Chinese comrades, led to a United Front in which Communists joined the KMT as individuals and accepted its formal leadership of the alliance while retaining membership in a separate Communist party. The United Front was in effect from 1923 through the summer of 1927, when the KMT expelled the Communists and broke off its contacts with Soviet advisers.[63]

During this period of cooperation with the KMT and heavy-handed direction from Moscow, the CCP began to transform itself from a tiny group of Marxist (or proto-Marxist) intellectuals into a mass-based revolutionary organization. Most of its growth and organizational success among workers and peasants came

---

[62]For surveys of pre-1949 CCP history, see Jerome Ch'en, *Mao and the Chinese Revolution* (London: Oxford University Press, 1965); Jacques Guillermaz, *A History of the Chinese Communist Party, 1921–1949* (New York: Random House, 1972); James Pinckney Harrison, *The Long March to Power* (New York: Praeger, 1972); and Richard C. Thornton, *China, The Struggle for Power, 1917–1972* (Bloomington: Indiana University Press, 1973). Many key documents of the 1921–1949 period are translated and analyzed in Conrad Brandt, Benjamin Schwartz, and John K. Fairbank, *A Documentary History of Chinese Communism* (Cambridge, Mass.: Harvard University Press, 1952).

[63]See Conrad Brandt, *Stalin's Failure in China, 1924–27* (Cambridge, Mass.: Harvard University Press, 1958).

after the May Thirtieth Movement of 1925, which launched a wave of strikes and protests in Chinese cities and set the stage for the KMT's Northern Expedition against the Peking government. Party membership grew from about 1,000 in May 1925 to 10,000 at the end of the year and to nearly 58,000 by April 1927.[64] Trade unions and peasant associations expanded rapidly during the same period, with Communists playing a major role in their growth and activities. Despite Comintern efforts to restrain the most radical tendencies of this upsurge, conservative leaders of the KMT became increasingly concerned about the direction of the alliance. A reaction began with Chiang Kai-shek's assault on the Communists in Shanghai in April 1927, and by the summer of that year the KMT had embarked on a thorough suppression of the CCP and its organizational bases. The period ended with a shattering defeat for the United Front policy and a near-catastrophic destruction of Communist supporters.

The Soviet Period, 1928–1934. The rupture of the first United Front left the CCP a fragmented, outlaw party. Its Central Committee continued to operate underground in the cities trying to rebuild the proletarian base, but KMT power easily contained these efforts. The real focus of the movement shifted to the countryside, where small Communist forces survived by virtue of armed support and mobile tactics in relatively isolated areas. Gradually, these forces grew and acquired loose territorial bases referred to as *soviets*. In November 1931, the CCP established the Chinese Soviet Republic, which nominally brought together a number of soviet areas scattered about Central-South China, although one was located in the northwestern province of Shaanxi.[65] The stronghold of the Soviet Republic was the Central Soviet District, consisting of a large block of *xian* in Jiangxi province, where the capital was located and where Mao Zedong was a leading political figure. The fortunes and territories of the CCP shifted frequently during the soviet period. At one point in 1933, party membership had risen to a new high of 300,000.[66]

---

[64] Ch'en, *Mao and the Chinese Revolution*, pp. 100–116.

[65] Ibid., pp. 153–54, 165–66, 171–72.

[66] John Wilson Lewis, *Leadership in Communist China* (Ithaca, N.Y.: Cornell University Press, 1963), p. 110.

However, increasing military pressure from the KMT took its toll. In late 1933, Chiang Kai-shek launched the fifth in a series of campaigns against the Jiangxi Soviet, and by the latter part of 1934 this campaign had forced the Communists to abandon their stronghold and set out on the Long March to Shaanxi.

Although the soviet period culminated in military defeat, it brought major changes to the Communist Revolution. It resolved a bitter intraparty struggle between urban and rural orientations in favor of the latter. After the establishment of the Soviet Republic in 1931, central party organs began to move from Shanghai to Jiangxi, tacitly acknowledging that the CCP's center was in the countryside. This shift was formalized in early 1935 when Mao Zedong, the foremost proponent of the rural revolutionary strategy, became party leader. Second, the period marked the origins and development of the Chinese Red Army, which was henceforth to be the bulwark of the CCP in its struggle for survival and power. Indeed, the movement became nearly inseparable from its military arm, with territorial influence being chiefly a function of Red Army strength and effectiveness. Virtually all CCP members acquired military experience, while the Red Army itself was thoroughly penetrated by party organization and controls.[67] Finally, these years witnessed the crystallization of Mao's military strategy, in which major emphasis was placed on guerrilla-type units operating from a territorial base area with extensive popular support,[68] and the beginnings of CCP governmental experience. In the Jiangxi Soviet, the Communists had their first opportunities to establish governmental organs and to experiment with various economic and social policies, particularly land policy. These efforts met with mixed results, but the experience gained had considerable influence on later patterns of CCP rule.[69]

[67] On the origins and early years of the Red Army, see Samuel B. Griffith, II, *The Chinese People's Liberation Army* (New York: McGraw-Hill, 1967), pp. 1–46.

[68] A convenient collection of Mao's military writings is *Selected Military Writings of Mao Tse-tung* (Peking: Foreign Languages Press, 1963). The major works in question date mainly from 1936–1938, when Mao had time to reflect and write on his Jiangxi experiences.

[69] See Ilpyong J. Kim, "Mass Mobilization Policies and Techniques Developed in the Period of the Chinese Soviet Republic," in A. Doak Barnett, ed., *Chinese Communist Politics in Action* (Seattle: University of Washington Press, 1969),

The Second United Front, 1935–1945. While the Chinese Communists were on the Long March to Shaanxi, which their first units reached in October 1935 in greatly weakened condition, a second United Front with the KMT was taking shape as a response to growing Japanese pressures on China. Although the CCP had urged resistance to Japan for many years, it was only after 1935 that this slogan acquired concrete political significance. The Comintern's 1935 call for an international united front against fascism, the increasing threat of renewed Japanese advances, and the CCP's removal to an area closer to the North China trouble spots, all made the KMT-CCP cooperation a possibility. The path to a new alliance was not easy, given profound suspicion and hostility on both sides, but after the Xian [Sian] Incident of December 1936 the groundwork had been laid. With the beginning of full-scale war between China and Japan after July 7, 1937, the second United Front became a reality.[70]

This alliance was significantly different from the first, however, being essentially an armed truce in the interests of anti-Japanese unity. The KMT gave up its campaigns to crush the Communists, while the CCP abolished the Soviet Republic and agreed to regard its areas and armies as formally subordinate to the national government. In fact, there was little cooperation between the two parties; there was a loosely observed understanding that the two parties would not go to war and that Communist-controlled territories and forces would retain de facto independence. The CCP used the security thus gained to expand its influence at the expense of both Nationalist and Japanese authorities. In January 1937, Mao's forces occupied the town of Yanan in northern Shaanxi, which was to become the center of a new stable base area known as the Shaanxi [or Shaan-Gan-Ning] Border Region. Throughout the Anti-Japanese War, Yanan was not only the capital of Shaan-Gan-Ning, but also the de facto capital of a growing number of other border regions and anti-Japanese bases that accepted Communist leadership. By 1945, according

---

pp. 78–98; and James R. Townsend, *Political Participation in Communist China* (Berkeley: University of California Press, 1967), pp. 43–51.

[70] Van Slyke, *Enemies and Friends*, pp. 48–93.

to Communist sources, there were nineteen such areas, most of them in North China but some in the lower Yangtze region and South China as well; the CCP had grown to over 1.2 million members, had armies totaling 910,000 men, and governed areas with a population of 95.5 million.[71] Since CCP strength at the end of the Long March was only a fraction of its Jiangxi peak, the Yanan period was one of truly impressive Communist growth and expansion.

The second United Front was a decisive period in the evolution of Chinese Communism. The remarkable increase in CCP strength that occurred between 1937 and 1945 transformed the terms of Chinese politics. Communist forces entered the postwar period still inferior to the Nationalists in numbers and armaments but, for the first time, as genuine competitors for national political power. Supporting this growth of raw power was a consolidation of party leadership, in both personnel and techniques, that reflected the maturation of the CCP as an organization. Mao Zedong's rise to leadership in 1935 had not eliminated all his competitors, but in Yanan he discredited or drove out of the party any who might contest his dominance. Through the *zheng-feng* (*cheng-feng*, rectification) campaign of 1942–1944[72] and the decisions of the party's Seventh National Congress in April–June 1945,[73] Mao established his "thought" as the CCP's guide for the application of Marxism-Leninism to China. With the relatively stable political conditions that prevailed in Shaan-Gan-Ning (although not necessarily in other Communist bases), this consolidation of Mao's political and doctrinal authority was translated directly into practice; Maoist methods for educating and disciplining party members, controlling bureaucracy, leading and working with the masses, organizing the economy, and

[71] Townsend, *Political Participation*, p. 52.

[72] For documentation of this campaign, see *Mao's China: Party Reform Documents, 1942–44*.

[73] The revised Party Constitution adopted at the Seventh Congress included a specific reference to Mao's thought as the guiding principle of party work. See Brandt, Schwartz, and Fairbank, *A Documentary History*, pp. 419, 422. Shortly before the Congress opened, the Central Committee also adopted a "Resolution on Certain Questions in the History of Our Party," which affirmed the rectitude of Mao's political career and scored his various opponents for their errors and deviations. The text is in *Selected Works*, vol. 3, pp. 177–225.

many other tasks were applied systematically and formalized as integral parts of the CCP's political style.[74]

Another development of the 1935–1945 years was the nationalization of the CCP's appeal. During the soviet period, the CCP had retained a basic class orientation, demonstrated in the Central Committee's attempts to build a proletarian party and in the Soviet Republic's land policy, which was at times harsh and confiscatory toward the wealthier rural classes. After the emergence of the United Front, the CCP moved toward more moderate economic policies that would permit multiclass support. The focus of the movement became national struggle rather than class struggle, a shift reflected in doctrinal statements about the character of the Chinese revolution and in the ardently nationalistic propaganda of the period. The real significance of the second United Front was not, then, meaningful cooperation with the KMT, which was never realized, but rather its impact on the Communist Revolution. The United Front was a statement of Communist revolutionary strategy, a strategy that saw the road to power as built on the broadest possible national base rather than on narrow or rigid class lines. It was a strategy of "uniting with all who can be united," and to give meaning to it, the CCP adopted not only nationalistic propaganda but also an operational style that attracted positive support from a broad multiclass base. Superficially, the United Front appeared to suggest cooperation between two parties, each representing a different class base; in fact, the CCP used it to establish itself as the leader of a truly national movement.[75]

The Civil War, 1946–1949. For a brief period after the Japanese surrender in August 1945, the two major contenders for power negotiated, with American mediation, for a peaceful solution to their conflict. The American role was compromised from the first, however, by its past and continuing support for the

[74] For analysis of major CCP policies in Shaan-Gan-Ning, emphasizing their centrality in the post-1949 Communist system, see Mark Selden, *The Yenan Way in Revolutionary China* (Cambridge, Mass.: Harvard University Press, 1971).

[75] Van Slyke, *Enemies and Friends*, pp. 99-116. See also Chalmers A. Johnson, *Peasant Nationalism and Communist Power: The Emergence of Revolutionary China, 1937–1945* (Stanford, Cal.: Stanford University Press, 1962).

Nationalist government; while the profound suspicion and hostility between the KMT and CCP made workable agreements unlikely. By 1946, a civil war had begun, raising to an unprecedented military scale the struggle that these two parties had waged for twenty-five years. The Nationalist armies were superior on paper and scored some initial successes, but the Communists soon made evident their superiority in the field. The tide had turned by 1948, and within a year the Nationalist forces were defeated. The KMT retreated to the island of Taiwan, and the CCP established its new government on the mainland.

For the CCP, the civil war was yet another military struggle for survival, a campaign fought on a larger scale than ever before but still a continuation of the reliance on armed force that had marked party history since the late 1920s. It was a continuation, too, of the effort to build and lead a national movement. Of course, the shift from a Japanese foe to a Chinese foe sharpened class distinctions between opposing political forces. The CCP appealed to poor and landless peasants with a radical land program that made most rural elites targets of the revolution. Many Chinese whose anti-Japanese credentials had been acceptable to the Communists during the war were now reclassified as "enemies" if they opposed the party's revolutionary socioeconomic goals. Nonetheless, despite the actual and impending rise of class conflict, the CCP continued to define its movement as a national one with a multiclass base. The leadership was "proletarian"—that is, the CCP—but the Communists insisted the movement still rested on a United Front that all Chinese, except for a relatively small number of reactionaries and traitors, could join.

The pattern of party history, sketched so crudely in these pages, will be a frequent source of reference in later chapters. Additional details will illuminate specific aspects of post-1949 politics. It is important, however, to emphasize a few salient features of CCP historical experience that shaped the Maoist approach to PRC development. Although they appear less influential since Mao's death, they remain an important part of the CCP's political tradition.

Mobilization and Struggle. The CCP came to power with the conviction that mobilization and struggle are the essence of politics. Until the very end of the revolutionary period, it was a threatened minority movement beset by hostile military forces and a social environment frequently unsympathetic to its cause. Military-type virtues—enthusiasm, heroism, sacrifice, and collective effort—acquired great value. Passivity smacked of opposition and was all the more troublesome because it was a common response in the traditional political culture of the Chinese peasant.[76] When victory finally came, it was a product of successful political mobilization growing out of a wartime struggle for national survival. To the CCP elite, therefore, politics was not simply a matter of peaceful political competition or administration, but it was an effort to mobilize and activate human resources in a crisis situation.

The Mass Line. Closely related to these themes is the party's "mass line," a fundamental CCP principle that has its origins in the circumstances faced on the road to power.[77] In one dimension, it is a method of leadership that stems from the party's reliance on popular assistance in its revolutionary base areas. It is a recognition of the fact that the movement could not be sustained by party members alone but depended also on the intelligence, food supplies, new recruits, and even performance of administrative duties that the nonparty masses could provide. Leadership remained a party prerogative, but leadership could not be effective or achieve permanent results without mass support.

In a second dimension, the mass line has a control function with respect to bureaucrats and intellectuals. The Chinese Communists have been highly sensitive to the bureaucratic-intellectual tradition in which they have operated. Their hostility toward the traditional official as representative of a feudalistic and oppressive culture was joined by suspicion of the modern bureaucrat, who was likely to be ideologically sympathetic toward the KMT or foreign powers. The mass line responded to these concerns by insisting that officials have contact with the masses,

[76] See Richard H. Solomon, "On Activism and Activists: Maoist Conceptions of Motivation and Political Role Linking State and Society," *China Quarterly*, no. 39 (July–September 1969), esp. pp. 76–79.

[77] The best description of the empirical conditions fostering the mass line is in Selden, *The Yenan Way*. For more general discussion, see Lewis, *Leadership in Communist China*, pp. 70–100; and Townsend, *Political Participation*, pp. 46–64, 72–74.

by entrusting many administrative duties to popular groups and by urging citizens to scrutinize the behavior of bureaucrats and intellectuals.

Finally, the mass line is an expression of populism, of identification with and commitment to the welfare of the people. The Chinese Communists spent most of their years before coming into power in intimate association with the peasantry, experiencing firsthand the conditions of Chinese life that generated so much of the revolutionary impulse in that society. The party unavoidably grew away from this experience after 1949, but mass line exhortations to "eat, live, work, and consult with the masses" were ongoing reminders not to lose touch with the popular needs said to legitimize the revolution.

This last dimension of the mass line is directly relevant to Mao Zedong's "rural orientation" referred to earlier. In the soviet period, Mao was the main spokesman for a rural-based revolution, one that could survive and grow in the countryside with the capture of cities postponed until they were surrounded by the rural bases. Mao recognized early that revolution in an overwhelmingly agrarian society required a revolution in the countryside. The villages were not simply a staging area for proletarian revolution; they were the stronghold of the old society and a primary arena in which revolutionary change must occur.[78] In other words, the mass line necessarily carried with it a strong orientation toward the peasants, simply because the Chinese Communists could not talk about their popular base or obligations without talking about the peasantry.

Self-Reliance. The idea of self-reliance is a third element of CCP political style that draws strength from historical experience. The conditions encouraging it were the relative geographic, economic, and political isolation of Communist base areas from 1927 on. These areas were generally shut off from significant contacts with the outside, and even with each other, by military and economic blockades; moreover, they were relatively backward in themselves, being poorly served by surface and wire commu-

[78]Mao's classic statement on these themes is his 1927 "Report on an Investigation of the Peasant Movement in Hunan," *Selected Works*, vol. 1, pp. 23–59.

nications. Each base area was largely on its own, depending for survival on its own military and economic self-sufficiency.

The principal of self-reliance has both national and international implications. On the national scale, it has fostered in Chinese Communism a preference for local units that are relatively self-sufficient and that hold considerable responsibility for the maximum development of their own resources with a minimum of external assistance. It is a preference for a system with decentralized features, although decentralization is in some ways a misleading word, since the party places even greater emphasis on maintaining the primacy of central authority. What self-reliance really suggests is a system in which local units are clearly subject to central control and discipline but, in practice, meet their obligations on their own without requiring much central interference or assistance.

Mao was equally firm about the importance of self-reliance in international affairs. He saw CCP victory in China as due to its own efforts and resources; foreign assistance, as during the first United Front, was actually counterproductive. Chinese views on this question clearly draw on Mao's interpretation of national as well as party experience. They remain sensitive to the way in which a foreign presence may lead to foreign interference and control. They are sensitive, too, to their country's limited capacity for providing material assistance to other countries. Although they welcome international support and will offer it themselves to other countries and movements with which they sympathize, the still insist that each must rely essentially on its own resources to accomplish its goals.

Ideological Education. The most difficult doctrinal problem the Chinese Communists have faced as Marxist-Leninists has been how to create a socialist revolution and build a socialist society in an agrarian country so close to its feudal past. How could this cause succeed in the absence of a proletarian base? The question emerged in full force after 1927, when the CCP was forced to seek survival in a distinctly nonproletarian setting. Mao responded by building a Red Army, composed of peasants, former bandits, Nationalist soldiers, and other motley elements whose ideological commitment was to be instilled by education. Subsequently, the party applied the same principle to its new peasant and intellectual recruits, to its base-area populations, and ultimately to the Chinese people as a whole.

The Maoists never assumed that the educational road to ideological purity would be easy, and they warned repeatedly (the Cultural Revolution being the best example) that powerful nonproletarian influences can corrupt even those who seem to have been converted. Hence they devised techniques of education, indoctrination, and rectification to overcome these obstacles and threats. The techniques referred to—mass propaganda media, political study, guided small-group discussions, constant criticism and self-criticism—appeared in the soviet period, matured in Yanan, and were institutionalized after 1949.

But education is a slow process, and what is instilled by one kind of education can presumably be undone by another. How could education alone be a workable tool for revolution? For Mao Zedong, at least, there was another necessary ingredient: human will. It can be the decisive factor in any given situation and should be guided by ideological understanding; but it is the initial human will to act that is crucial and permits the educational process to work through the testing and application of ideas in practice. The entire history of the CCP, with its struggle and ultimate victory under extremely adverse conditions, reinforced the strength of this conviction.

CONCLUSION

This chapter has emphasized the influence of China's past, the way in which the political tradition, the revolutionary setting, Soviet Communism, and the CCP's own history helped shaped the post-1949 system. Perhaps the clearest legacy from the past is the continuing tension between authoritarianism and populism—between tendencies to concentrate power in a small elite with a statist, bureaucratic approach to government and inclinations to distribute throughout society the material, psychic, and political rewards of the revolution. Authoritarianism comes directly from the imperial tradition, reinforced by the crisis of revolution that demanded even stronger and more concentrated authority to cope with domestic crisis and foreign penetration. Soviet Communism and decades of civil war hardened CCP attitudes toward political opponents and nourished the CCP's insistence on party dictatorship.

Populism, too, has its roots in the old order, which set peasants apart from the Confucian elite, isolated them from government, and supported a long tradition of popular rebellion. Inherited resentment of oppression by the elite joined with the new ideology of class conflict and working class leadership and with the rural-based revolutionary strategy to produce a movement strongly oriented toward mass mobilization and participation. Both authoritarianism and the reaction against it are part of the PRC's inheritance.

The origins of the PRC reveal its link with the past; but linkage is not identity. The Chinese political system of the 1980s is very different from that of the 1960s, just as Cultural Revolution Maoism was different from the Yanan version. Although current elites claim Maoism as a guide and continue to talk about struggle, the mass line, self-reliance, and the importance of political education, their interpretation of these themes is different from Mao's. The contrast between Communist and imperial systems is even stronger. The imperial state was relatively passive, acting largely to maintain the status quo and to restore balance in the wake of human or natural disruptions. It kept affairs of state to itself and hoped that its subjects and tributaries would behave properly without requiring imperial intervention. The new state aggressively pursues social change, regulating an immense sphere of human activity. It assumes social conflict is unavoidable, intervenes to control and channel that conflict, and expects citizens to lend active support to its efforts. It recognizes the international forces that affect its interests and tries to shape them to its own advantage. Whatever the links with political tradition, the revolution brought fundamental changes to Chinese politics, and the postrevolutionary era continues the process by restructuring its inheritance.

CHAPTER III

The Political Framework: Institutions and the Evolution of Policy

THE STUDY OF STABLE POLITICAL SYSTEMS, whether democratic or authoritarian, often begins with analysis of the institutional framework within which politics takes place. Political structure is a logical place to start because it channels the flow of political transactions and usually offers a more durable image of the system's character than do the political personalities or issues that dominate particular periods. Institutions are not immutable, of course, nor do they determine political outcomes, but in most cases it is helpful to understand institutional structures and relationships before attempting to analyze political processes.

In revolutionary regimes, institutions are less important. Revolutionary elites are usually committed to the destruction of some institutions, suspicious of others, and reluctant to devote their energies to building new ones. There is still a structure of political activities, of course, but it often consists of informal personal relationships, polemics over strategies and policy programs, shifting power relations within the revolutionary movement that are largely concealed from outsiders, and the like. The effective structure is not likely to be found in formal political institutions, which typically come and go with bewildering speed or, if they endure, simply fail to exercise the powers attributed to them.

The elusive role of institutions in a revolutionary system is a problem for the student of Chinese politics. During the years surrounding the revolutionary victory of 1949 and during the long Maoist push of 1958–1976, Chinese political institutions were generally in flux and often in disarray, providing few guidelines for understanding the political scene. Yet, briefly in the mid-1950s and especially since 1976, PRC institutions have been more important as guides to the actual distribution and management of political power. Moreover, a few institutions have been relatively stable for most of PRC history and all of them have been part of the vocabulary of Chinese political debates, so the student still needs to know the names and relative importance or durability of the principal institutions. Accordingly, we begin analysis of the political framework with a brief discussion of some relatively constant organizational principles, followed by a look at the CCP, the state structure of the PRC, and the mass organizations.

Identifying institutions is still only a first step toward understanding the framework of Chinese politics. This is so because that framework derives primarily from two other sources: first, the policy sets, models, or "lines" that have dominated key periods of post-1949 history, and second, the ideology of the ruling party. The pattern of post-1949 policy changes provides the single most important component of the political framework because it establishes the general characteristics of each period— the policies, campaigns, and goals as well as institutional relationships—that have in fact been the focus of most Chinese political debate and action. Without an appreciation of this kind of periodization, one cannot understand *why* the significance of formal institutions fluctuates and *how* the framework has evolved over time. Hence, after its opening survey of institutions, the chapter extensively discusses the evolution of post-1949 policy, treating institutional development as only one of several key indicators of changes in the political framework. Ideology, the other major source of systemic guidelines, is analyzed in Chapter 4 in an effort to reconcile enduring features of the Communist framework with patterns of change within it.

A. POLITICAL INSTITUTIONS

CONSTANTS OF CHINESE POLITICAL ORGANIZATION

Although Chinese politics appears to change completely in each phase of its development, some organizational features are present to a greater or lesser degree in all phases. They concern levels of hierarchy, the principle of democratic centralism, and ambiguity of power and procedure. These constants of Chinese political organization are important for understanding the salience of institutional arrangements for actual political behavior.

Levels of Hierarchy. Almost all institutions and policies involve four broad levels of organization: center, intermediate, local, and basic. The center has always been in Beijing. The most important intermediate level has usually been the province (including "autonomous regions" and the three largest cities), but there are often other intermediate levels as well. Generally, counties and cities have been the most important local level of hierarchy, and the basic level includes a variety of units within counties and cities. The interrelationships of these levels are frequently the target of discussion and reforms; however, the situation of a multilevel organizational structure appears inescapable, and the features of each level are fairly constant.

The center is the policy-making level. From its vantage point, all other organizational levels are "local."[1] The scope of its powers is not restricted by rights or responsibilities reserved to intermediate or local levels. It is quite common for the center to intervene in provincial and even local and basic level affairs, and any significant action by a lower level is reported to the center. Center personnel are quite aware of their political importance, but they are also vulnerable to policy shifts and struggles within the higher leadership. Therefore, the political atmosphere in Beijing is more exciting, tense, and volatile than in the rest of China—quite comparable to "Potomac fever" in Washington, D.C.

The primary task of intermediate levels is to manage lower levels of government in the implementation of center policy. The size of China makes intermediate management a necessary task. The average province has a population of over 30 million, compared to the average American state's population of less than 5 million. Because they are indispensable, intermediate

---

[1] Official documents referring to "local" (*difang*) organizations usually mean all levels except the center. For instance, "The Organic Law for All Levels of Local People's Congresses and All Levels of Local People's Governments of the PRC" discusses state organization from the township through the province.

levels have their own weight and momentum vis-a-vis the center, even though they lack key policy-making rights. Inevitably, they control a vast reach of personnel and administrative decisions that are beyond the routine oversight of the center. In addition to the provinces, the intermediate level has included multiprovincial regions that were especially important in 1949–1954 and prefectural districts between the provincial and county levels. Since 1983, the importance of major cities as an intermediate level of government has increased rapidly. One-fourth of China's counties are now under the administration of a city government.[2]

The execution of policy occurs at the local level. Comprehensive local-level administration is coordinated by the county in rural areas and by towns or city districts in urban areas. This is the lowest level at which the organizational apparatuses of the party and state are complete. At over 300,000, the average population of county-level units is still quite large. Local government is responsible for more activities than the comparable level in capitalist countries because the public ownership of enterprises puts them under government control, and the smaller ones are often directly under local government control. Still, many of the problems handled at this level include zoning, lighting, and roads, which would be familiar to counterparts elsewhere. Like the province, the county has been a durable level of administration despite fluctuations in its powers.

In contrast to the levels of administration discussed above, which were inherited from earlier Chinese governments, fundamental innovations in political structure have been made at the basic level. The proliferation of grassroots organizations puts every Chinese in touch with government policies and enables large-scale mobilization of popular energies. The success of the revolution was made possible by effective basic-level organization in the countryside, and yet the most notable organizational failures have also occurred there. One example of organizational failure is the commune, a combined political-economic unit that was introduced in 1958 and replaced by the township (*xiang*) in 1983.

The basic-level organizations below the county are the townships—averaging between 15,000 and 20,000 people—and

[2]*China Daily*, February 28, 1984, p. 1.

below them are the villages (formerly "brigades") and teams. The comparable urban levels of basic administration are the street and lane, or the work unit. As its name suggests, the "work unit" is the place where one works, but it is also a political, social, and residential entity. A large work unit will have its own schools, party committee, and election district for the people's congress as well as housing and canteens, and it may also own farms and organize sideline enterprises for unemployed children or spouses of workers. Since there is very little labor mobility between work units, they provide a stable and close "urban village" environment. The lowest levels of party, state, and mass organizations coalesce at the work unit and provide political structure and direction in this informal and familiar setting.

Relationships between levels of the hierarchy are a constant source of concern to the leadership. If center control is too strong, then the bureaucracy becomes topheavy, policy becomes too uniform, and local initiative is discouraged. On the other hand, if the center is too lax, then abuses of power occur at the lower levels, and effective planning becomes difficult. According to Mao Zedong, relations between the center and lower levels were one of the "ten major relationships" of Chinese politics.[3] The fact that lower levels are completely vulnerable to upper-level intervention encourages undesirable bureaucratic behavior. Cadres tend to be cautious about assuming responsibility for decisions, but they enjoy the power they have over underlings and outsiders. Each official is the anvil of his superiors and the hammer of his subordinates.

Democratic Centralism. Democratic centralism is the major operational principle of Chinese organizations. Its premise is that there should be full democracy before decisions are made and complete centralism in implementation. Although borrowed from Bolshevik party organization, the years of Chinese revolutionary experience have given the term a special meaning. On the one hand, democratic centralism commits decision makers to a constant process of consultation and investigation. Any decision maker or leading body is surrounded by ever-widening

[3] Mao Zedong, "On the Ten Major Relationships," *Selected Works*, vol. 5, pp. 284–307.

circles of persons and institutions who can expect some form of access. As a result, leaders often complain of confronting "a mountain of documents and a sea of meetings." On the other hand, there is really no appeal against a decision once it is made. There are no rights of opposition, and there are no immunities against intervention from authority. Inevitably, centralism is more powerful than democracy.

Among organizations, democratic centralism implies the hegemony of the party. The function of mass organizations and even of the state and the people's congress system is on the consultative side of the process. To oppose party leadership on an issue would be quite risky, and to organize opposition could be condemned as factionalism. However, the party is obligated to consult and to exercise its leadership through persuasion. Centralism is the power of the party; democracy is its recommended style.

Ambiguity of Power and Procedure. Power is difficult to define in any political system, but in China it is particularly ambiguous. One reason is that the guerrilla style of leadership combined military, political, and economic functions. This experience reinforced and gave a special twist to the traditional Chinese esteem for the omnicompetent scholar. Since the party's leadership style has been practical and generalist, it avoids organizational patterns that fragment problems into specialist and professional bailiwicks. Not only do the party and the center generally feel free to intervene wherever they see fit, but powerful persons do not feel bound to currently assigned roles. The relationships of important persons often displace the lines of command shown on organizational charts. Often, it seems that the importance of the organizational role is measured by the importance of the person filling it. The guerrilla style also encouraged mass mobilization campaigns that often by-pass or disrupt organizational formalities.

Another contributing factor is the antilegislative bias of Marxism-Leninism. Since Marx criticized the capitalist equality of citizens under the law as a sham that masks class rule, Communist states have adopted a very different constitutional structure. In China and other Communist states, the class leadership of the proletariat is openly expressed in the leadership of the

Figure 3.1. CCP Structure: Center, Province, and City: 1982 Party Constitution

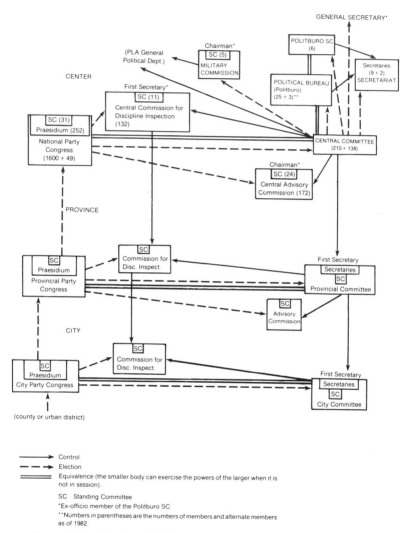

Control

Election

Equivalence (the smaller body can exercise the powers of the larger when it is not in session).

SC   Standing Committee

*Ex-officio member of the Politburo SC

**Numbers in parentheses are the numbers of members and alternate members as of 1982.

Sources: "Constitution of the Communist Party of China," adopted September 6, 1982, *BR* vol. 25, no. 38 (September 20, 1982):8–21; *Zhongguo gongchandang di shi'er ci quanguo daibiao dahui wenjian huibian* (Collection of documents from the Twelfth National Congress of the CCP). (Beijing: Renmin Chubanshe, 1982).

Communist Party, while the equality of citizens and democratic control of the state are expressed in the people's congress system. It would appear from the constitution that the people's congress system would provide a powerful democratic control over the state and also exercise important legislative powers, but in fact the party's monopoly on policy making, as well as its controlling influence within the people's congress, vitiate the importance of the elective part of government.

These constants of Chinese political organization are an intimidating introduction to Chinese political institutions. The ambiguity of power reduces the salience of the organizational charts and constitutions that will be discussed in this chapter. The principle of democratic centralism gives a special and rather restricted meaning to the more consultative areas of Chinese political organization and amplifies lines of authority as they run from the center or from the party. The many levels of Chinese hierarchy ensure that any organizational arrangement will have a complicated structure, and policies adopted at the center may be slowed or modified in the process of transmission.

THE CHINESE COMMUNIST PARTY

Center, Province, and City. The formal organization of the Chinese Communist Party (CCP) is set forth in the party constitution. The most recent party constitution was adopted by the Twelfth Party Congress in 1982. Although the party is now declared to be subordinate to the state constitution and laws, its tasks of providing political, organizational, and ideological leadership assure its position as the dominant political organization. According to the constitution, the party "must see to it that the legislative, judicial and administrative organs of the state and the economic, cultural and people's organizations work actively and with initiative, independently, responsibly, and in harmony."[4]

The party exercises its leadership functions through the party members active in other organizations. The positioning of some

[4]"Constitution of the Communist Party of China," *BR*, vol. 25, no. 38 (September 20, 1982): 10. Beginning in 1979, *Peking Review* changed its name to *Beijing Review*, hereafter cited as *BR*; *Peking Review* (pre-1979) is cited as *PR*.

form of party organization alongside state organs strengthens CCP leadership of the political system by encouraging institutional supervision and the assignment of many party cadres to overlapping roles in both hierarchies. Whatever formal powers a state organ holds, it is the party organ at the corresponding level that is the politically authoritative voice. Major organizations at the central and provincial levels have "leading party members' groups" (*dang zu*) that are directly under the control of the provincial or central party committee and are responsible for the implementation of party directives. At lower levels, the party structure within each organization is responsible for that organization's compliance with party wishes.

The organizational principle of democratic centralism takes a particularly centralized form within the party. Lower organs are expected to "request instructions and make reports" (*qing shi baogao*), transferring as much discretion as possible to their superiors. The representative organs meet so infrequently that their powers are necessarily assumed by small groups of leaders. Nevertheless, the "democratic" side of democratic centralism does not disappear. Collegial decision making is emphasized. A leader should not squelch differing viewpoints and should submit to the majority. Party members at all levels are expected to comply with the same norms of behavior, and all have certain rights of expression, criticism, and self-defense.

The party constitution defines the representative congresses as the "leading bodies" at their respective levels. However, as in the state system, the committees elected by these congresses—or the standing committees and secretaries elected by the full committees—exercise congressional powers while the congress is not in session. Moreover, higher party committees have the power to review leadership elected by lower congresses and can assign leadership to lower levels without their approval. The constitution states that the National Party Congress shall be convened every five years and that it may be convened early or postponed. Historically, party congresses have been irregular. Each of the last five has produced a new constitution and elected a significantly altered Central Committee (CC).

Although national party congresses have marked changes in party leadership, the delegates have little control over the proceedings. The agenda and nominations for offices are controlled by the standing committee of the congress praesidium. The praesidium standing committee, which had thirty-two members at the Twelfth Party Congress, is elected by the praesidium, which in turn is nominally elected by the congress delegates on the day before the congress opens. During the congress, delegates spend much of their time in small groups discussing leadership reports and candidate lists for the CC, the Commission for Discipline Inspection, and the Advisory Committee. Although election procedure now provides for more candidates than positions, there is no open election competition.

The CC acts for the Congress and is the most important representative body in the PRC. It is identified by the number of the congress that elected it, with its full meetings known as "plenums." Thus the first full meeting of the CC elected by the Twelfth Congress was the First Plenum of the Twelfth CC. Plenums are to be held at least once a year. Besides the plenums, there are many partial, informal, and enlarged meetings of CC members. Sometimes, CC plenums merely confirm decisions hammered out at preceding informal meetings. The historic "Communique of the Third Plenum of the Eleventh CC" of December 1978, which confirmed the party's commitment to economic modernization, was actually the result of a month-long working meeting that preceded the brief plenum.

The active political leadership of the PRC is provided by the Secretariat, the Politburo, its Standing Committee, and the General Secretary of the party. All of these are elected by the CC, and the General Secretary is the presiding officer of the CC, the Politburo, and its Standing Committee. The title of the General Secretary replaced that of Party Chairman when Hu Yaobang succeeded Hua Guofeng in 1981.

There is an informal division of labor within the Politburo and, less clearly, in its Standing Committee. With only six members, the Standing Committee cannot carry specialization too far, but one position is reserved for the chairman of the Military Commission, another for the First Secretary of the Central Commission for Discipline Inspection, and another for the chairman of the Central Advisory Commission. Two of these reserved positions are now concurrently held by Deng Xiaoping. In the Politburo, the portfolios (*kou*) of individual members are more evident, although they are still informal.

Politburo members speak out frequently and with an authoritative tone in areas of their responsibility.

While the Politburo and its Standing Committee are the highest decision makers, the administrative and detail work of the party center is handled by the Secretariat. The Secretariat was disbanded during the Cultural Revolution because of bureaucratism, but it reemerged as a very influential organization in 1980 and regained constitutional status in 1982. Four of its nine secretaries are Politburo members, and the rest are CC members. It is elected by the CC but works under the direction of the Politburo and its Standing Committee. The Secretariat's work is carried out by a large number of departments. Through this bureaucracy, the Politburo controls the execution of day-to-day party work from the central level down to the basic party groups that are established in every unit of Chinese society.

The Military Commission is elected by the CC and controls the military through the army's General Political Department. Its function of political control over the military might appear to overlap with the state's Central Military Commission, but in fact the membership of the two organizations coincides.

The military is a unique and powerful organization in Chinese politics. The success of the revolution was based on the victories of the People's Liberation Army, and many top leaders have had some military experience. Mao Zedong was a founder of the army and the originator of its strategy of guerrilla warfare. Because Lin Biao had politicized the army along Maoist lines before the Cultural Revolution, the army was spared that campaign's disorganizing effects and stepped in to restore order in 1967. The army's organizational challenge to the shaken hegemony of the party reached its apex in Lin Biao's foiled attempt to assassinate Mao in 1971. The army retains a strong but diminished role in central politics. It tends to be a less progressive influence within the leadership, perhaps because it benefitted from some Cultural Revolution policies that reformers now criticize. The army emphasizes ideological discipline and has less to gain from experimental forms of economic modernization.

The Central Commission for Discipline Inspection has a very broad charge to investigate the implementation of party policy and to handle disciplinary matters regarding party organizations and members. Its members are elected by the National Party

Congress, and it is responsible to the CC. Lower-level commissions are responsible both to their respective party committees and to the higher commission. Although the party has had similar organs since the 1950s, they have been especially prominent since their reestablishment in 1979 and the promulgation of the "Regulations Concerning Inner-Party Life."[5] The center's desires to restrict "feudal" abuses of power by local leaders and to prevent the erosion of the party by the pressures of modernization have contributed to a heightened interest in discipline.

The Central Advisory Commission is a new organ created by the 1982 party constitution to help ease the transition in leadership personnel from the older generation of Long March survivors to younger successors. Its members must have been party members for at least forty years. It has a consultative rather than a decision making function. Its members can attend plenary sessions of the CC as nonvoting participants, and its vice-chairmen may attend plenary meetings of the Politburo. Its chairman is an ex-officio member of the Politburo Standing Committee. Deng Xiaoping became the first chairman of the Advisory Commission in order to lend his prestige to the organization and encourage the retirement of older party leaders. The commissions are viewed as temporary organs for the benefit of the current older generation.

The structure of the party at the provincial level is a copy of the center on a smaller scale. The provincial level is comprised of all administrative units directly under the center, including the major cities of Beijing, Shanghai, and Tianjin, five autonomous regions, and twenty-one mainland provinces. Taiwan is listed as a province but, of course, is not under PRC administration. The provincial party congresses also meet once every five years, and their primary functions are to elect the provincial party committee, discipline inspection commission, advisory commission, and delegates to the National Party Congress. The provincial committee and its standing committee correspond to the CC and the Politburo. The committee meets once a year, as do all other CCP committees down to the general branch level. The provincial first secretary has the most powerful political position in the

[5] Graham Young, "Control and Style: Discipline Inspection Commissions Since the Eleventh Congress," *China Quarterly*, vol. 97 (March 1984): 24–53. See also, "Guiding Principles for Inner-Party Political Life," *BR*, vol. 23, no. 14 (April 7, 1980): 11–20.

province. Party leadership in provincial ministries, writers' associations, trade unions, and the like is exercised through leading party members' groups (*dang zu*). The province directly appoints leadership at the prefectural level (the intermediate administrative level between the counties and the province), but it is also in firm control of the nominally elected leadership at lower levels. Party organization at the city level, which includes autonomous prefectures, follows the pattern of the provincial level, with reduced staffing and complexity. City party congresses meet once every five years.

Party Organization: Local and Basic. County-level organization includes the districts (also translated "wards") of large cities, smaller cities that are not divided into districts, and autonomous counties and banners. It is a major level of administration, especially in rural areas. The county party congress meets once every three years and elects its committee, standing committee, and secretary. The party had a policy of periodically transferring county party secretaries and government heads in the 1950s and revived the practice in 1984.

The basic levels of party organization correspond to the basic organizations of Chinese society, described in the party constitution as "factories, commercial enterprises, schools, institutions, streets, people's communes, cooperatives, rural markets, military companies, etc." If an organization has at least three party members, it can establish a basic party organization. Generally, the party organization of a unit is then responsible for the implementation of party directives within the unit. However, if the unit has a *dang zu*, then its party organization is under the policy leadership of the *dang zu* as well as the higher levels of party authority.

The number of party members in the unit determines its level of organization. If there are more than one hundred members, a basic party committee may be established. This highest level of basic organization is similar in structure to the county and also has three-year terms of office, but its representative congress meets once a year. Party members belonging to a basic party committee are further organized into general branches and branches corresponding to subdivisions (shifts, workshops, academic departments, brigades, etc.) of their unit.

Figure 3.2. CCP Organization: Local and Basic

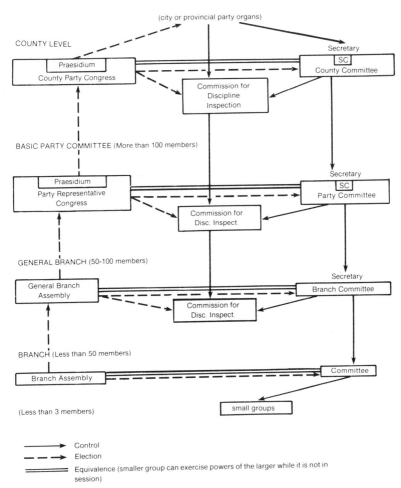

(city or provincial party organs)

COUNTY LEVEL

Secretary

Praesidium
County Party Congress

SC
County Committee

Commission for
Discipline
Inspection

BASIC PARTY COMMITTEE (More than 100 members)

Secretary

Praesidium
Party Representative
Congress

SC
Party Committee

Commission for
Disc. Inspect.

GENERAL BRANCH (50-100 members)

Secretary

General Branch
Assembly

Branch Committee

Commission for
Disc. Inspect.

BRANCH (Less than 50 members)

Branch Assembly

Committee

(Less than 3 members)

small groups

Control
Election
Equivalence (smaller group can exercise powers of the larger while it is not in session)
SC Standing Committee

Sources: Dang di zuzhi gongzuo wenda (Questions and answers on party organizational work), edited by the organizational research office of the Central Organization Department of the CCP (Beijing: Renmin Chubanshe, 1983); *Dang di zuzhi gongzuo wenda* (Questions and answers on party organizational work), Lan Wenrong and Yuan Shengli (Xi'an: Shaanxi Renmin Chubanshe, 1981).

95

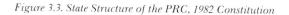
Figure 3.3. State Structure of the PRC, 1982 Constitution

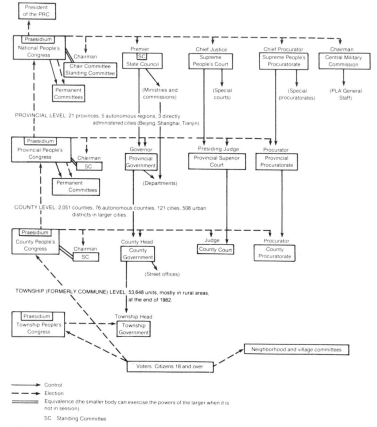

Source: "Constitution of the People's Republic of China," BR, vol. 25, no. 52 (December 27, 1982).

A general branch will be established if there are more than fifty but less than one hundred party members in a unit. The entire membership of a general branch meets twice a year. The general branch committee, which also meets twice a year, is elected for a two-year term. There is no standing committee, so the secretary is not as tied to collegial decision making at this level.

The party branch is the lowest level of party organization. A unit with more than three but less than fifty members may be organized into a branch, and all other levels of party organization have branches as their lowest unit. Every party member should be a member of a branch. Especially for noncadres, party life is organized at the branch level, and decisions concerning admission and expulsion of members are made here. The branch membership meets four times a year and elects a branch committee of three to seven members for a two-year term. One organization manual lists eight posts within the branch committee: secretary, assistant secretary, organization, propaganda, discipline inspection, security, youth, and women. Branch members may be further organized into small groups of three to five members for discussion and study purposes, but these have no decision making powers and therefore do not constitute a level of party organization.

PRC STATE STRUCTURE

China has a unified state organization that includes four major hierarchies: the people's congress system, the government, the courts, and the procuratorate. Although the army could be included as a part of the state according to the definition used in China, it is usually treated separately. The people's congresses are representative assemblies meeting once a year. According to the state constitution, they are the highest organs of state power, and their ability to oversee governmental affairs was strengthened in 1979 by the creation of standing committees at the provincial, city, and county levels. The government, from the state council to local administrators, is the executive and administrative bureaucracy of the state. Typically, its highest officials are elected by the people's congress at each level. Officials of the two legal hierarchies, the judiciary and the procuracy, are also elected by the people's congress. Although the army sends delegates to people's congresses, it is largely independent of the civilian governmental system except at the highest level.

The state structure of the PRC has some similarities to Western governments, but it would be a mistake to assume that it is simply a copy of familiar institutions. Communist constitutional theory is fundamentally different from that of capitalism, and as a result even apparently similar institutions function differently. The most important difference is the explicit class basis of the PRC; it is a people's democratic dictatorship. *People* is a political concept. It means friendly classes—those allied with the working class—as opposed to enemy classes. The government of China is supposed to be a democracy among the people, but a dictatorship toward internal enemies. Class enemies presumably have rights as citizens, but these are ambiguous given the constitutional hostility of the state.

The class basis of the PRC did not change when Hua Guofeng announced the abolition of enemy classes as such in 1979. According to the official viewpoint, hostile elements are being produced continually by internal and foreign influences, and the possibility exists for problems with class enemies in the future. The utility of the class enemy category is that it gives the government a free hand in defining and dealing with political criminality—in effect, they become nonpeople to the People's Republic of China. However, it precludes a truly universal citizen-based state or legal system.

The constitutional history of the PRC reflects the major turns of Chinese politics. The first Communist governments in China were organized in the Jiangxi base areas in 1928–1934. From the beginning, the Russian model of people's soviets and party leadership were predominant, but the situation of guerrilla war required the Chinese Communists to be more concerned than the Russians were with the quality of mass participation. However, this concern was more reflected in the party's political style than in institutional innovations.[6] The PRC's initial state structure, from 1949 to 1954, was a temporary administrative system

---

[6]For an extended discussion of the evolution of political participation in China down to the Cultural Revolution, see James R. Townsend, *Political Participation in Communist China* (Berkeley: University of California Press, 1967).

that relied heavily on regional military units to oversee reconstruction and early reforms; the Chinese People's Political Consultative Conference (CPPCC), a holdover from the pre-1949 United Front, served as the nominal national representative authority under the Common Program, a provisional constitution drafted by the CPPCC in September 1949. The first state constitution was adopted in 1954, establishing a centralized government on a modified Russian pattern. From 1954 until the Anti-Rightist campaign of 1957, serious efforts were made by a part of the CCP leadership to develop a working legal system and to standardize administrative procedures. Soon, however, the Great Leap Forward (1957–1960) brought important changes. Decentralization and CCP assertiveness weakened central state organs, while the introduction of people's communes in 1958 created new patterns of local administration. The Cultural Revolution (1966–1969) further unsettled the 1954 system. Although the 1954 constitution was not formally abolished, many of its provisions for institutions, procedures, and rights were disregarded. State structure remained in limbo, with no legal guidelines in operation, until a second constitution was adopted in 1975. The 1975 constitution incorporated many Cultural Revolution principles and significantly altered the previous structure. After the death of Mao Zedong and the fall of the Gang of Four in 1976, another constitution, which was closer to the 1954 model, was adopted in March 1978.

Toward the end of 1978, with the decisive victory of Deng Xiaoping's "practice faction" within the top leadership of the CCP, new reforms began to be contemplated that would move significantly beyond the efforts of the 1950s. The second session of the Fifth National People's Congress in 1979 adopted for the first time direct elections for the county-level people's congresses, an election system with more candidates than positions, and standing committees for intermediate and local people's congresses. The trend of "democratic and legal institutionalization" (*minzhu zhiduhua faluhua*) continued with measures to increase the autonomy of government officials vis-a-vis the party and to make the people's congresses more effective. The reforms culminated in the 1982 state constitution, the product of two years of drafting, revision, and public comment. The following discussion is based on the 1982 constitution and its accompanying legislation.[7]

A major business of the National People's Congress (NPC) is to discuss and approve work reports and the state plan, to discuss and approve legislative drafts, and, during the first session of its term, to elect the major officials of government. It is a large body with approximately 3,000 delegates who meet once a year for a five-year term. Delegates to the NPC are elected by provincial-level people's congresses. Provincial delegations meet before each session to discuss agenda items. The NPC has six permanent committees: minorities, law, finance, foreign affairs, overseas Chinese, and one that covers education, science, culture, and health. Legislative drafts and motions of inquiry or censure are submitted to the appropriate committee. A praesidium with a standing committee presides over sessions of the NPC and controls the agenda, the routing of legislation, and nominations for offices. The main function of the NPC is to symbolize the regime's legitimacy and popular base, rather than to chart the political course of the country. The latter is the function of the CCP. Nevertheless, the post-Mao reforms in the state structure have strengthened the consultative role of the NPC. Research by Dorothy Solinger has shown that significant policy debates are discernible at NPC meetings.[8]

The NPC's extensive formal powers of legislation and oversight are exercised by its Standing Committee, a much smaller body (155 members in 1983) meeting once every two months. It serves essentially as a clearing house for the ratification and issuance of state decisions. A certain degree of autonomy is provided for the Standing Committee by the stipulation that government officials

[7]Recent reforms in China's political structure are discussed more fully in David S. G. Goodman, "State Reforms in the PRC since 1976: A Historical Perspective," in N. Harding, ed., *The State in Socialist Society* (London: Macmillan, 1983), pp. 277–98; Lowell Dittmer, "The Formal Structure of Central Chinese Political Institutions," in Sidney Greenblatt, Richard Wilson, and Amy Wilson, eds., *Organizational Behavior in Chinese Society* (New York: Praeger, 1981); and Brantly Womack, "Modernization and Democratic Reform in China," *Journal of Asian Studies*, vol. 43, no. 3 (May 1984): 417–40. Interesting information on the actual behavior of China's top leadership organs is provided by A. Doak Barnett, "A Peek at China's Foreign Policy Process," *New York Times*, August 13, 1984.

[8]Dorothy Solinger, "The Fifth NPC and the Process of Policy-Making," *Asian Survey*, no. 12 (December 1982): 1238–75.

are ineligible for membership. The Standing Committee has in turn an even smaller group, the chair committee, that controls its agenda. The chair committee is led by the chairman of the Standing Committee, currently Peng Zhen, and includes the vice-chairmen and the secretary, a total of twenty-two members. The Standing Committee also has specialized subcommittees that are active in coordinating legislation between different governmental organs and in communicating with provincial governments and standing committees. Interlevel contact is encouraged by allowing the leadership of provincial standing committees to attend meetings of the NPC Standing Committee. NPC delegates are encouraged to attend the sessions of the provincial people's congress that elected them.

The 1982 constitution reinstituted the office of chairman of the PRC government, and Li Xiannian was elected for a five-year term in 1983. This office has the function of ceremonial head of state. Mao held the office from 1954 to 1959, succeeded by the ill-fated Liu Shaoqi (1959–1966). The office had been omitted in the 1975 and 1978 constitutions.

The State Council is the chief administrative organ of government. The State Council usually meets once a month and has a standing committee meeting twice a week, which consists of the premier, vice-premiers, secretary, and state counselors. It issues decisions, orders, and administrative regulations and can submit legislative proposals to the NPC. It is headed by the premier—Zhou Enlai from 1954 until his death in 1976, Hua Guofeng from 1976 to 1980, and now Zhao Ziyang, who was reelected to a five-year term in 1983. It also includes several vice-premiers and the ministers who head the ministries and commissions of the central government. The State Council consists almost entirely of high-ranking party members. As the central administrative clearing house for governmental actions at all levels, it is the functional center of state power, if not the center of political decision making. The priority of economic modernization since 1978 has increased the influence of the State Council.

The Central Military Commission is a new organ charged with the direction of China's armed forces. The chairman of the Commission nominates the membership of the committee for approval by the NPC. On the vital question of control of the military, there is no semblance of separation of party and state.

The chairman (Deng Xiaoping) and vice-chairmen of the CCP military committee are the chairman and vice-chairmen of the state organ. As Peng Zhen said in introducing the 1982 constitution, "The leadership by the CCP over the armed forces will not change with the establishment of the state Central Military Commission."[9]

The legal system of the PRC is based on the Russian model, with a system of general courts and procurators corresponding to major administrative levels, as well as numerous special courts. The Supreme Court and the Supreme People's Procuratorate are responsible to the NPC and its Standing Committee, and the provincial and local courts and procurators are responsible to their respective people's congresses. Procurators are supervisory, investigative, and prosecutory officials who are involved in the investigation of individual cases and also in the supervision of the legality of government work and the proper operation of the court system. There have been important reforms in Chinese law, which will be discussed in Chapter 7, but the structure of the legal institutions is the same as it was in the 1950s.

Recent reforms have made provincial state organization even more similar to the central structure. Until 1980, the provincial people's congress did not have a standing committee, so it could not exercise the supervisory role of the NPC. Also, the provincial people's congress first received the power to pass local legislation in 1980. Since the adoption of these two basic reforms, the provincial congress has enhanced its organization and activities each year on the model of NPC functions. It has permanent committees, which become involved in governmental policy in their areas, and its standing committee meets once every two months to supervise activities of the provincial government. Meanwhile, the devolution of considerable economic decision making power to provincial and lower levels has increased the importance of provincial government, although it has not changed its constitutionally vulnerable status in a unitary and centralized system.

[9]Peng Zhen, "Report on the Draft Constitution," *BR*, vol. 25, no. 50 (December 13, 1982): 18.

The provincial-level, city-level, and county-level people's congresses each elect the heads of their respective governmental organs and discuss and approve their annual reports and the budget. They and their standing committees have the power to remove officials and to demand explanations for official actions. Perhaps more importantly for the individual delegate, any motion made and seconded by three other delegates obligates the appropriate government authorities to make an official response. Hundreds of these motions are made at each people's congress session, many dealing with very concrete items of constituent interest. Delegates are encouraged to be in close contact with their constituents.

One of the most interesting political reforms since the death of Mao was the adoption in 1979 of an election system with more candidates than positions and with direct elections to the county level. Previously, the Chinese had appeared even more disdainful of elections than the Soviet Union. The Soviet Union has direct but noncompetitive elections to every level of its system of soviets, but China's elections above the basic level were both noncompetitive and indirect—and often irregular as well. The 1979 election law presented basic changes. It provided for a more open nomination process, a secret ballot with a choice of candidates, and the possibility of primary elections. The new election procedure not only applies to the election of county people's congress delegates but also to the election of delegates to higher-level people's congresses and to the election of government officials. The more candidates than positions approach has also been adopted by the CCP for elections within the party and is also used in many work units for the election of factory directors and other leaders. It is easy to overestimate the practical effect of the procedural change. The more important the position to be filled, the less likely it is to be left to chance. Nevertheless, it is an important procedural reform. In combination with direct election at the county level, the establishment of a county standing committee, and the major economic reforms at the local level, the management of public affairs at the county level could change significantly in some localities.

At the basic level, state organization tends to lose its distinction from party, economic, and mass organizations. In large work units, state and party activities follow the structure of the unit, and state functions and personnel can be hard to distinguish from party and union business. In rural areas, the people's commune combined governmental, economic, and party functions from 1958 to 1983. The recent establishment of township (*xiang*) government to replace the commune is difficult to evaluate given the other momentous changes in rural policy. At the most basic level in rural areas, that is the production team, leadership has been elected since the early 1960s, subject to the approval of the brigade party leadership.[10] Similarly, the progressive trend in urban areas is toward the election of work unit leadership.

The presence of autonomous regions, autonomous counties, banners, and so on among China's administrative units is a reflection of a policy toward national minorities that promises self-administration in places where a minority is the dominant ethnic group.[11] Although the Chinese population as a whole is overwhelmingly of the Han nationality, the other ethnic groups tend to be concentrated in border areas where they constitute the majority of the local population. Following the example of the Soviet Union, where the nationalities problem is much more extensive, certain provincial-level, prefectural-level, and county-level units are designated at autonomous units. They are charged with protecting the political, economic, and cultural peculiarities of their ethnic groups, and special efforts are made to guarantee ethnic participation in leadership. Even in areas where minorities do not constitute a large fraction of the population, they are guaranteed at least proportional representation in the people's congresses.

MASS ORGANIZATIONS

Chinese political structure also includes many mass organizations that mobilize ordinary citizens and supplement and support the party and state institutions. In general, mass organizations are national in scale and have a hierarchy of units extending

---

[10] John Burns, "The Election of Production Team Cadres in China, 1958–1974," *China Quarterly*, no. 74 (June 1978): pp. 273–97.

[11] For an analysis of minority regions and policy, see June Teufel Dreyer, *China's Forty Millions* (Cambridge, Mass.: Harvard University Press, 1976).

downward from the central level to a mass membership defined by a common social or economic characteristic (e.g., youth, women, workers, or other occupational groups). These organizations play a key role in implementing the party's mass line of "coming from the masses and going to the masses." They provide a sounding board for popular opinions, channel representatives into state and party structures, and mobilize support for CCP policies from different segments of the population. In some cases, they perform administrative and service functions for the groups they represent.

The most important mass organization before the Cultural Revolution was the Communist Youth League (CYL). During the 1950s and early 1960s, the CYL was responsible for leadership over all youth activities and other youth organizations, was a major source for new recruits for the CCP, and generally assisted in the basic-level implementation of all party policies. Another organization that played a unique role in the early period was the Chinese People's Political Consultative Conference (CPPCC). It included members of the CCP as well as members of eight political parties that sided with the CCP late in the civil war. After serving as the provisional national legislature from 1949 to 1954, the CPPCC remained active as a symbol of multi-party cooperation in PRC programs. Other important mass organizations in the period before the Cultural Revolution included the Young Pioneers, for children aged nine to fifteen years old (seven to fifteen years old since 1965); the All-China Women's Federation; the All-China Federation of Trade Unions; and a variety of associations for specialized occupational and professional groups.

All of these mass organizations were suspended during the Cultural Revolution. Indeed, the term *mass organization* took on an entirely different meaning with the appearance of the Red Guards in 1966. Instead of orderly hierarchies of persons assisting the party and state, the revolutionary mass organizations of the Cultural Revolution appeared spontaneously, criticized party and state officials, and eventually engaged in armed warfare among themselves. These groups were formed at the work-unit level and joined in alliances against opposing groups. In early 1967, there was an attempt to base provincial-level government on these groups, but it was quickly abandoned. Instead, "revolutionary three-in-one combinations" were endorsed, which included mass representatives, party and government officials, and army representatives. Gradually, the influence of the mass representatives declined, and after the Lin Biao affair in 1971 the role of the army lessened as well.

The pre-Cultural Revolution mass organizations began to revive after 1969. By the early 1970s, the CYL, the All-China Women's Federation, the All-China Federation of Trade Unions, and Young Pioneers were reorganizing at the local level, as were some of the professional associations. Rebuilding was slow, however, suggesting that these organizational forms remained controversial. Following the death of Mao and the fall of the Gang of Four in 1976, reactivation accelerated, and national congresses of the CYL, the All-China Women's Federation, and the All-China Federation of Trade Unions, as well as a national science conference were held in 1978. At the same time, the disruptive mass activities of the Cultural Revolution were officially criticized.

Since 1978, the postrevolutionary institutionalization of Chinese society has been exemplified by a strengthening and proliferation of mass organizations. One of the most interesting cases has been the rebirth of the CPPCC. Its constituent parties have recruited new members and are engaged in a variety of educational and cultural activities. The national, provincial, and city congresses of the CPPCC are held at the same time as the respective people's congresses and are given comparable attention. Evidently the new purpose of the CPPCC is to encourage a united front of patriotic intellectuals to contribute to China's modernization. The other major mass organizations have also expanded, and the number of professional societies holding meetings and publishing journals is larger than it has ever been. The basis of membership in mass organizations has shifted away from class membership and toward functional and professional criteria. For example, the Young Pioneers recently announced it would raise its recruitment target from 80 percent to 100 percent of the appropriate age group.[12] This indicates a shift from restricting membership only to those children with good class background

[12]*China Daily*, October 14, 1984, p. 3.

to opening the organization to all, a change that might be an important socialization experience for Chinese children of the 1980s.

This brief review has identified principal PRC political institutions and some of the major changes in them since 1949. We turn now to a different kind of survey, one of post-1949 policy periods, that puts institutional analysis in a different light.[13] Although most of the institutions just described appear from time to time in this survey, what is striking is the way in which they have been shaped or even discarded to meet the demands of political campaigns. Institutions do not channel politics but rather serve as its targets or even enemies, whereas programs concerned with the direction, timing, and pace of change—as reflected in campaigns or developmental models—establish differing political guidelines for each policy period. Although the post-1976 institutionalization suggests that campaign dominance of institutions may be a thing of the past, or at least greatly reduced, that dominance has been a fundamental characteristic of the PRC for most of its history.

B. THE EVOLUTION OF POST-1949 POLICY

RECONSTRUCTION, 1949–1952

The CCP came to power in 1949 with good reason for confidence. The Red Army had inflicted a decisive military defeat on the Nationalist forces, producing for the first time in decades a Chinese government that did not face the threat of large-scale armed opposition within its mainland territory. The party was disciplined and experienced by its long years of struggle, including considerable practice in administration of large areas of rural China. Its political authority was solid for a new revolu-

---

[13]The survey focuses on national policies as seen from the center. For analysis of how policies are implemented and sometimes modified in localities, see Ezra Vogel, *Canton Under Communism: Programs and Politics in a Provincial Capital, 1948–1968* (Cambridge, Mass.: Harvard University Press, 1969); William L. Parish and Martin King Whyte, *Village and Family in Contemporary China* (Chicago: University of Chicago Press, 1978); and Martin King Whyte and William L. Parish, *Urban Life in Contemporary China* (Chicago: University of Chicago Press, 1984).

tionary regime, partly due to positive support generated by its
nationalist and reformist programs—particularly among youth
and intellectuals and within the areas in which it had operated—and partly due to its demonstrated military and political
effectiveness, which brought widespread acceptance, if not support, from a population very weary of strife and uncertainty.
These conditions stimulated high hopes for the rapid emergence
of a China in which the citizen might find increased opportunity
as well as national respect. For a variety of reasons, however, the
new system was to take shape more slowly and with much more
turmoil than these factors would suggest.

The Sino-Japanese War, the civil war, Russian confiscation
of industrial equipment in Manchuria, and the collapse of KMT
governmental authority had left a shattered and inflation-ridden
economy. For the first few years, therefore, the Communists
concentrated on restoring plants, production, and transportation
facilities and on bringing inflation and governmental revenues
under control. By the end of 1952, economic reconstruction was
basically completed, with production levels restored in the main
to peak prewar levels.[14] While it was in progress, however, the
CCP had little choice but to postpone its plans for the socialization
of the economy.

A second major problem was that the CCP was simply not
prepared in 1949 to establish direct control throughout the
political system. Although its national leadership was visible
and unquestioned, it did not possess the resources to staff all
posts necessary for carrying out its objectives. Extensive experience
in rural administration, much of it under wartime conditions,
was inadequate training for the varied and complicated tasks
faced in reconstruction of the entire country; many party members
were illiterate and unaccustomed to urban life, let alone its
administration. Yet, even if the quality of party membership had
been better suited to its new responsibilities, its numbers were
insufficient. KMT resistance had collapsed so quickly from late
1948 on that Communist forces had acquired large areas that
were politically unassimilated. Despite rapid recruitment, the
CCP could not consolidate its political control immediately. To

[14]See the discussion in W. W. Rostow, *The Prospects for Communist China*
(New York: Wiley and the Technology Press, 1954), pp. 237–54.

deal with this situation, it adopted a dual strategy of institutional temporizing and popular mobilization.[15]

In the case of government institutions, the new leaders accepted temporary solutions, permitting many existing arrangements and officials to stand, albeit without any guarantee of permanence. Thus the central government functioned under the nominal authority of the CPPCC, with many nonparty members within the United Front assigned to high positions. Six large administrative regions were established for the country, each coinciding with a military region so that the pattern of military conquest flowed naturally into a decentralized system of regional governments based on a combination of civil and military authority. At lower levels, many former officials remained in office, with local party organs playing a relatively discreet role. In short, the CCP simply postponed the creation of a permanent governmental structure until its political control was consolidated. It used the interim period to build its organizational strength, while trying to weed out unreliable officials and party members. Much of this basic political work was accomplished in the 1949–1952 period, although the new state structure was not established until 1954.

Political Mobilization. While economic reconstruction and political consolidation delayed the establishment of a socialist system, encouraging many nonparty intellectuals, businessmen, overseas Chinese, and former officials to commit themselves to the People's Republic, there was no delay in efforts to mobilize the population. During the earlier course of the revolution under both Communist and non-Communist leadership, many groups in Chinese society had experienced political mobilization, a term that denotes the process by which resources—in this case, human resources—are made available for use by political authorities. Yet, this mobilization had been partial and sporadic in terms of Chinese society as a whole and was based on a level of socioeconomic development that made it difficult to sustain. The population in 1949 was overwhelmingly rural, illiterate,

[15]For details, see A. Doak Barnett, *Communist China: The Early Years, 1949–55* (New York: Praeger, 1964); and Kenneth G. Lieberthal, *Revolution and Tradition in Tientsin, 1949–1952* (Stanford, Cal.: Stanford University Press, 1980).

and poorly served by modern transportation and communications. Traditional avoidance of external concerns and demands remained strong in the villages. In areas under their control, the Communists had proven their ability to combat these difficulties by promoting their programs through intensive face-to-face contact, but prior to 1949 only a minority of the population was so affected. Identification with the nationalist mobilization against Japan had given the CCP substantial legitimacy beyond its own areas, which assisted greatly the establishment of its authority, but there was no guarantee that popular energies could be similarly employed in socialist construction. Accordingly, the new leaders decided that a thoroughgoing mobilization to support political consolidation and preliminary social reforms must precede institutionalization of the new system.

The primary vehicle for this task was a series of mass movements, each aimed at the twin goals of attacking a particular political or social issue and mobilizing popular resources under CCP leadership. The land reform movement, begun earlier in "liberated" areas but carried out throughout China in 1950–1952, established peasants' associations to redistribute the land and to smash the power and status of the landlord class. A campaign for "implementation of the marriage law" began in 1950, aiming at reform of the traditional marriage system and the prevailing inequality of women in all spheres of social life. "Resist America–Aid Korea," a movement in progress throughout the Korean War of 1950–1953, worked to support the Chinese war effort and arouse anti-American sentiments. In 1951, the CCP carried out a "suppression of counterrevolutionaries" campaign to eradicate remnants of armed resistance and other enemies of the regime. A "three anti" movement (against "corruption, waste, and bureaucracy" in government offices) in the winter of 1951–1952 reviewed and disciplined officials, both party and nonparty, who failed to meet CCP standards. A subsequent "five anti" movement (against businessmen allegedly engaged in "bribery, tax evasion, theft of state property, cheating on government contracts, and stealing state economic secrets") drastically reduced the economic resources and political status of the urban middle class. In the "thought reform of intellectuals" campaign, all higher intellectuals underwent challenge, criticism, and self-examination in which their basic beliefs were tested for loyalty to the new order.

These new campaigns followed in rapid succession, involving almost every citizen in some way. None of the specific issues was permanently resolved (each campaign was to be renewed or modified in later ones), and the impact on the people was mixed. For some, the movements brought upward mobility and a new sense of involvement in political action; for others, they brought personal losses, uncertainty, and fear, for there were excesses and an element of calculated and spontaneous terror, particularly in the movements for land reform and suppression of counterrevolutionaries. These early mass movements nonetheless contributed heavily to Communist political consolidation through the expansion of mass organizations, the establishment of propaganda networks, the recruitment of new activists and party members, the elimination of opponents, and the initiation of new social relationships. Later events cast doubt on the thoroughness of the mobilization achieved; but in this area, too, the CCP achieved something of fundamental importance by surpassing previous levels of mobilization and redirecting it from predominantly nationalist goals to those of radical social and economic change. From the CCP's viewpoint, the way was prepared for socialist construction.

THE FIRST FIVE-YEAR PLAN, 1953–1957

The First Five-Year Plan (FFYP), officially in effect from 1953 through 1957, was not made public until 1955 and was to undergo a profound reappraisal before its conclusion. Despite this evidence of irresoluteness, which is vital to an appreciation of later events, it is important to emphasize that the FFYP years constitute a distinctive phase in the history of the People's Republic. Generally, the mid-1950s was a period of rapid economic development along the lines of the Soviet model, accompanied by a trend toward moderation and institutionalization in political life relative to the reconstruction era.

The FFYP's concentration on industrial development, especially heavy industry, was its most pronounced characteristic.[16] To achieve the control of economic resources necessary for

---

[16] For an official description of the Plan, and its first published exposition, see Li Fuchun (Li Fu-ch'un), "Report on the First Five-Year Plan" (July 5–6, 1955), in Harvard University, Center for International Affairs and East Asian

massive industrial investment, the leaders moved quickly to establish centralized and planned direction of the entire economy. Private industrial and commercial operations were eliminated, except for the smallest entrepreneurs, by transforming them into cooperatives or joint state-private enterprises in which state control was paramount and by setting up state enterprises in key sectors. Rationing and quotas for state purchase and supply of major agricultural products controlled consumption and guaranteed extraction of resources from the agricultural sector to support state investment. The CCP also had plans for agricultural collectivization, which moved slowly from 1952 to 1955. From late 1955 on, however, following an important statement by Mao in July of that year,[17] the pace of collectivization accelerated. By the end of 1956, virtually all agricultural households were in collectives, and the socialization of the economy was essentially complete (see Table III.1). The economic results of FFYP efforts, which were assisted by Soviet aid in the most critical construction projects, were impressive. Estimates of average annual growth in the national product for 1952–1957 range from a low of 5.6 percent to an official Communist report high of 9 percent; even the lower estimates place China high in international rankings of economic growth for this period.[18] The weak point in the Plan was agriculture, where production increases were probably only slightly ahead of population growth.[19] Since agriculture was a major drag on average growth rates, industrial gains were obviously much greater than suggested by the preceding figures.

A number of significant political and social trends accompanied rapid industrialization. The state apparatus established in

Research Center, *Communist China, 1955–1959: Policy Documents with Analysis* (Cambridge, Mass.: Harvard University Press, 1965), pp. 42–91. This documentary collection is cited hereafter as *Communist China, 1955–1959*.

[17]Mao Zedong, "The Question of Agricultural Cooperation" (July 31, 1955), in *Communist China, 1955–1959*, pp. 94–105.

[18]For citation and discussion of various estimates of growth, see Ta-chung Liu, "Economic Development of the Chinese Mainland, 1949–1965," in Ping-ti Ho and Tang Tsou, eds., *China in Crisis*, vol. 1 (Chicago: University of Chicago Press, 1968), esp. pp. 617, 625–27.

[19]Choh-Ming Li, *Economic Development of Communist China: An Appraisal of the First Five Years of Industrialization* (Berkeley: University of California Press, 1959), pp. 71–74.

1954 assumed direction of the economy and developed as a highly centralized and bureaucratized structure; the central economic and planning ministries became particularly powerful organs in the new system. The party and Youth League were recruiting heavily to meet demands for more officials and cadres. Urban population and the industrial labor force grew rapidly, as did the number of students (particularly those training in scientific and technical fields) in educational institutions. Expansion and improvements were also notable in transportation, communications, publications, and public health and sanitation. The FFYP was, in brief, a period of real modernization.[20]

With increasing emphasis on economic growth and material progress, some of the political tensions of the early years began to recede. Mass campaigns become more oriented toward increasing production. Revived drives against counterrevolutionaries and so-called bourgeois intellectuals in 1955 were reminders of the CCP's determination to suppress political opposition. However, by 1956 a climate of relative liberalization was apparent in a more open communications policy that permitted some questioning of party behavior and orthodoxies. In foreign policy, following the Korean Armistice of 1953, the People's Republic adopted a "peaceful coexistence" stance that led to expanded diplomatic contacts and negotiations with non-Communist countries.

"Liberalization" and the Debate of 1956–1957. "Liberalization" culminated in the "hundred flowers" campaign of May–June 1957, a brief outburst of criticism, largely by intellectuals, that led to a political reaction and ultimately to a rejection of much that was implicit in the FFYP approach to China's development.[21] Far more was at issue in both the cultivation and later weeding of these "flowers" than the limited question of tolerating

[20]For figures on the trends referred to here, see Nai-Ruenn Chen, *Chinese Economic Statistics* (Chicago: Aldine, 1967); and *Ten Great Years: Statistics of the Economic and Cultural Achievements of the People's Republic of China* (Peking: Foreign Languages Press, 1960).

[21]For documentation and analysis of the hundred flowers period, see Roderick MacFarquhar, *The Hundred Flowers Campaign and the Chinese Intellectuals* (New York: Praeger, 1960) and MacFarquhar, *The Origins of the Cultural Revolution, I: Contradictions Among the People, 1956–1957* (New York: Columbia University Press, 1974).

TABLE III.1 *Development of Collectivized Agriculture*

	Household	Small village or village section (20–40 households)	Large village or village cluster (100–300 households)	Rural marketing area
1949–1952	Land reform ends large holdings & tenancy, destroys old rural elite.			
1952–1955		Mutual aid teams of 4–10 households lead into lower agricultural producers' cooperatives, which become BAU.[a]		
1955–1957	Households retain small private plots.	Early co-ops become production teams within higher co-ops.	Higher agricultural producers' cooperatives emerge, become BAU, full collectivization begins.	
1958–1959	Private plots absorbed by communes.	Become production teams within communes.	Become production brigades within commune.	People's communes formed & become BAU; early total of 25,000 large-scale communes, many exceeding marketing area in extent.

Experimentation with highly collectivized communities; large-scale rural labor mobilization for water conservation and other construction projects.

1960–1978	Private plots returned to household with limited free markets for household production.	Production team becomes BAU.	Production brigade runs primary schools, small rural industries; a few serve as BAU.	Communes reduced in size & increased in number (about 50,000 after 1970); roughly coterminous with marketing area.

"Agriculture as the Foundation" policy prevails: Increased attention to rural areas with push for agricultural modernization (mechanization, use of chemical fertilizers, growth of small-scale rural industry) and, after the Cultural Revolution, improved social services; rural institutions basically stable despite Cultural Revolution pressures to abolish private plots and raise BAU to a higher level.

1979–1985	Private plots & free marketing expanded; household becomes de facto BAU.	Production team contracts most production to smaller groups, households, or even individuals.	Production brigades & communes manage a few large-scale rural economic activities, but *xiang* replaces commune as the basic-level governmental unit.

"Responsibility System" appears: To increase agricultural production and raise peasant standards of living, production teams transfer use of land, draft animals, and tools to groups or households, which are then responsible for most decisions on production and earn profits when they exceed quotas contracted with the team. Collective ownership principle (of land and other major means of production) remains, but reforms greatly expand the scope and profit incentives of household farming, in effect ending the commune system.

---

[a]BAU = basic accounting unit. This is the unit responsible for making work assignments, organizing agricultural production, and collecting and distributing the agricultural product. It handles its own accounting and is responsible for its own profits and losses; hence, it is an important indicator of the level of collectivization.

intellectual dissent. What was involved was a serious debate about how China was and should be developing. The debate was carried on mainly in 1956–1957; however, some of its issues had been signaled earlier, and most were to remain as increasingly bitter points of conflict from 1959 through the Cultural Revolution. The debate centered on CCP dissatisfaction with, or uneasiness about, the emerging results of the FFYP; hence it is easiest to discuss within that context. Rather than trying to specify individual or factional positions within the leadership, generalized conservative and radical responses to the FFYP will be noted to suggest the boundaries of the debate.[22]

A salient issue was the proper balancing of agricultural and industrial development and how to attain it. CCP elites were united in insisting that industrialization must proceed; yet they also acknowledged that the development of agriculture and light industry was relatively weak and must be strengthened to ensure adequate resources for investment in heavy industry. The growth of urbanized populations and consumer demands heightened their fears of shortages in agricultural and consumer products. Accordingly, they approved modest increases over FFYP targets for state investment in agriculture and light industry, but the conservatives were unwilling to go much beyond that. They were pessimistic about the results of rural collectivization in both production and peasant response; they preferred to go slowly, to avoid upsetting the agricultural scene, and to let industrialization lead the peasants gradually into a more collec-

---

[22] Intraparty conflict is treated at greater length in Chapter 6 of this book. The "conservative" and "radical" labels are admittedly vague but seem preferable to alternatives (Liuists and Maoists, pragmatists and idealists, revisionists and revolutionaries) that imply a degree of personal or ideological cleavage not clearly evident at the time. The 1956–1957 debate was not one in which rigid, unchanging positions were taken; differences were real, but compromises, shifts of circumstance, and a strong desire to maintain unity blurred their lines. Most of the key documents relevant to the discussion in the text are available in *Communist China, 1955–1959* and *Eighth National Congress of the Communist Party of China*, vols. 1–2 (Peking: Foreign Languages Press, 1956). One important document not included is Mao Zedong, "On the Ten Great Relationships" (April 1956), translated in Jerome Ch'en, ed., *Mao* (Englewood Cliffs, N.J.: Prentice-Hall, 1969), pp. 65–85; also in *Selected Works*, vol. 5, pp. 284–307. For detailed analysis of policy shifts in this period, see Parris H. Chang, *Power and Policy in China* (University Park: Pennsylvania State Press, 1975); and Franz Schurmann, *Ideology and Organization in Communist China*, 2nd ed. enl. (Berkeley: University of California Press, 1968).

tivized economy. Radical opinion favored a more forward policy, pushing ahead with collectivization and relying on the forces generated by it to bring about rapid social and economic change in the countryside. The struggle between these positions, beginning with Mao's promotion of accelerated collectivization in late 1955, led to several fluctuations in agricultural policy during 1955–1957.

A second acknowledged defect of the FFYP was its encouragement of excessive centralization and bureaucratization, leading to general agreement that the central ministries should transfer some powers to lower units and that criticism of bureaucratic behavior was in order. The radicals wanted simplification and staff reductions in the bureaucracy—in 1956 Mao proposed a two-thirds cut in party and governmental organs[23]—and wanted expanding committee or popular supervision over leading cadres. This position had considerable support, since state ministerial power was a growing challenge to party authority and a symbol of Soviet influence. In one of its earliest retreats from Soviet-style arrangements, the CCP had already rejected the "one-man management" system in enterprises in favor of greater control by party committees; by the Eighth Congress in September 1956, the idea of strengthening leadership by party committees in all lines of work was established policy.[24] However, conservatives had little enthusiasm for any general dilution of the authority structure, nor were they ready to renounce the value of bureaucratic and technical specialization. It remained to be seen how far the radicals could go in pushing the mass line (not simply strengthened party committees) as a counterweight to bureaucratism.

Finally, the FFYP period raised fundamental questions about the CCP's relations with other groups in Chinese society— questions underscored by the sobering impact of Khrushchev's denunciation of Stalin in early 1956 and subsequent upheavals in Poland and Hungary. Here, too, there was at least a partial consensus within the CCP elite that political consolidation and the establishment of a socialist economic system had basically unified China, so that the danger of counterrevolution was no

[23] Mao, "On the Ten Great Relationships," in Jerome Ch'en, *Mao*, p. 77.
[24] Schurmann, *Ideology and Organization*, pp. 263–87.

longer great and so that the party could be less authoritarian in its relations with nonparty elements. These were the convictions that encouraged the liberalization of 1956–1957; but the leaders were by no means of one mind concerning their implications. A more conservative viewpoint saw economic and political consolidation as marking the end of the revolutionary period; henceforth, the CCP could exercise leadership through its new institutions rather than through mass movements, now deemed necessary in their time but prone to error, excess, and inefficiency. In place of continued political mobilization and struggle, this viewpoint suggested codification of laws, stricter observance of institutional procedures, and the granting of some material concessions to the people, particularly to intellectuals and technicians whose skills were necessary but still underutilized. Essentially, the conservatives leaned toward placating or co-opting nonparty groups without emphasizing or expanding their political role. Mao's famous speech, "On the Correct Handling of Contradictions Among the People," was the best expression of a more radical position.[25] Its central thesis was that "nonantagonistic" contradictions exist even in socialist society and must be debated openly to achieve resolution. While affirming basic party leadership and rectitude, Mao assigned nonparty groups a crucial, dialectical role in the political process—a role that not only would transform the groups but also would prod the socialist system to strengthen itself. It was this push from Mao, against the reservations of some of his colleagues, that enabled liberalization to become briefly the "hundred flowers."

The CCP soon found the criticism by intellectuals too severe and the dangers of its spreading too great to permit the "hundred flowers" experiment to continue. Critics were silenced and in some cases punished, while the party moved to resolve its debate by establishing a new approach. The result was the Great Leap Forward, which began to take shape in late 1957 and was to dominate Chinese politics for the next three years. The Leap also marked a shift away from the Soviet model that had guided

---

[25] Text in *Communist China, 1955–1959*, pp. 273–94. The original speech, given at an enlarged meeting of the Supreme State Conference on February 27, 1957, was never made public. The official version ultimately released in June 1957, after the hundred flowers outburst had been cut off, contained admitted alterations.

policy making in 1949–1957 and toward the Maoist model that would prevail for much of the next twenty years. Significantly, when the CCP arrived at its second major watershed around 1978, moving from Maoist to socialist modernization models, it resurrected many of the 1956–1957 conservative arguments described previously.

THE GREAT LEAP FORWARD, 1957–1960

The Great Leap Forward was not a concrete plan with consistent guidelines or objectives, but rather a set of policies held together by a political mood or frame of mind. (The beginning of the Leap coincided roughly with the Second Five-Year Plan for 1958–1962, but that Plan soon fell by the wayside.) This mood was expressed in highly rhetorical terms full of overpowering claims and exhortations. The rhetoric implied that all of China was moving together, whereas in fact there were numerous variations or deviations of time and place. It implied unified and permanent commitment, but Leap policies were not fully formed until the fall of 1958 and were undergoing partial revision almost immediately, indicating that commitment to the movement was not as firm as claimed. In other words, there was a good deal of uncertainty about the Leap's objectives, performance, and even duration; yet its impact on Chinese politics was immense.

Great Leap Themes. Four interlocking themes that permeated the rhetoric of the Great Leap Forward convey a general impression of the movement's quality.[26] One was a fervent optimism that proclaimed China's ability to accomplish monumental tasks in a short period of time and insisted that earlier problems had been identified and corrected. Another was the glorification of the mass line principle that human effort and will are the

[26] The best expression of the Great Leap approach, displaying all of the themes mentioned here, is Liu Shaoqi, "Report on the Work of the Central Committee of the Communist Party of China to the Second Session of the Eighth National Congress" (May 5, 1958), text, under a different title, in *Communist China, 1955–1959*, pp. 416–38. The fullest scholarly account of the Leap is Roderick MacFarquhar, *The Origins of the Cultural Revolution, Vol. 2: The Great Leap Forward, 1958–1960* (New York: Columbia University Press, 1983).

decisive factors and hence that popular mobilization is an effective method for resolving problems in all spheres of action. This elevation of the mass line placed a great emphasis on the quantity of manpower mobilized, extolled the virtues of sacrifice and manual labor, and devalued the specialized skills and professional knowledge of the intellectual elite. One specific result was the practice of *xiafang* (hsia fang) ("downward transfer"), in which office workers and intellectuals were sent down to lower levels to engage in more menial lines of work.

A third theme was "politics takes command," which asserts that correct political consciousness is the best and indeed the only proper base for social action. This principle demanded the widest possible propagation of official ideology in an effort to ensure that mass mobilization be motivated and guided by political considerations. It also had great implications for the CCP, which as the sole judge of political rectitude was the only organization capable of defining which politics would be in command. The result was a sharp increase in the power of party committees as they moved to implement central policies.

Finally, the Great Leap rested on the belief that simultaneous advances in all economic, political, and cultural spheres were possible and on the refusal to admit that there were insurmountable limitations or mutually exclusive possibilities in development. The idea of an all-around advance was expressed in what was perhaps the most representative slogan of the period: "Build socialism by exerting our utmost efforts and pressing ahead consistently to achieve greater, faster, better, and more economical results." As the slogan and Liu Shaoqi's discussion of it suggest,[27] the Great Leap philosophy insisted that speed could be combined with efficiency, quantity could be combined with quality, and agricultural and local development could be combined with industrial and national development. The key to such development was to be a loosening of institutional restraints—to be implemented through decentralization and mass movements— that would encourage each social unit to develop its own capacities to the fullest extent.

Emergence and Origins. The apparent unanimity with which these themes were articulated from late 1957 on obscures the

[27] Ibid., pp. 424–32.

Leap's gradual and controversial emergence. Many of its features actually appeared in late 1955 and early 1956, following Mao's July 1955 speech on agricultural collectivization. In his report to the second session of the Eighth Party Congress in May 1958, Liu referred to this earlier "leap" of 1955–1956 as setting the proper pattern for China's socialist development.[28] Mao's conservative opposition persisted, however, halting the 1955–1956 "leap" and bringing on the 1956–1957 debate. Even after the "antirightist" campaign in the summer of 1957 had silenced the "hundred flowers" critics, conservative economic policies were still in evidence. The critical decisions that initiated the Great Leap Forward came only at the Central Committee's Third Plenum in September–October 1957.[29] Two actions of this plenum are of particular interest. One was a decision to expand the antirightist struggle—until that point largely concerned with the "hundred flowers" experience—into a thorough, nationwide rectification campaign that would provide socialist education for the masses of workers and peasants and eradicate "rightist" and various erroneous tendencies within the party and other elite groups.[30] The other action of the plenum was approval of a program of decentralization in which control over many enterprises and financial resources would be transferred from the central ministries to provincial authorities. These decisions provided the basis for a general intensification of ideological indoctrination, for purging or eclipsing conservative party officials, and for raising the authority of party committees (particularly at the provincial level) at the expense of central state organs.

During the winter of 1957–1958, a massive labor mobilization was undertaken in the countryside for work on irrigation and flood control projects. The expanded scale of rural organization provided incentive for merging some existing cooperatives into large units. With the spring planting of 1958, the mobilization extended to agricultural production itself, stressing a variety of labor-intensive techniques. The nonagricultural population was also pressed into productive service by organizing units for labor in the countryside, in street factories, or in various sideline and

[28] Ibid., pp. 424–27.

[29] See the discussion in Schurmann, *Ideology and Organization*, pp. 195–210.

[30] See Deng Xiaoping (Teng Hsiao-p'ing), "Report on the Rectification Campaign" (September 23, 1957), in *Communist China, 1955–1959*, pp. 341–63.

spare-time enterprises. This massive outpouring of human effort, which was essentially an effort to raise production dramatically without major reallocation of capital resources, stimulated optimistic economic forecasts that steadily raised output targets. The first experimental rural people's communes appeared in the summer of 1958, carrying further the merging of rural organization into larger units that had begun in the winter; in August the Central Committee formally approved them and called for their nationwide establishment.[31] Within a few weeks, communes had become the primary production and administrative units for the rural population, essentially completing the framework of the Great Leap Forward.

How can one explain the CCP's adopting of the Great Leap approach when it was contrary to many more conservative tendencies in the party and was to lead to such damaging results? The decisive factor was probably the authority and persuasive powers of Mao Zedong, who initiated Leap policies and campaigned vigorously for their realization. The question remains, however, as to why Mao's arguments carried the day. For one thing, the Leap had a powerful, inherent attraction for CCP elites. It affirmed their desire for rapid socioeconomic change, for "catching up" with the advanced countries; it reasserted familiar revolutionary themes, such as heroic struggle, mass mobilization, self-reliance, and the like; and it drew on the consensus that had developed in 1956–1957 about the need for decentralization, stronger party leadership, and more rapid agricultural development. It had sturdy roots, therefore, in both historical experience and recent policy positions.

Moreover, much of Mao's fire was directed at conservatives who praised the efficacy of socialist institutions and the expertise of intellectuals and technicians; whereas, the results of the "hundred flowers" seemed to show that bourgeois ideology still thrived among educated elites and that socialist institutions had not yet made China a secure socialist society. In such circumstances, it seemed necessary to keep the revolution going and seemed a mistake to institutionalize it too soon. Thus, even

---

[31] "Resolution of the Central Committee of the Chinese Communist Party on the Establishment of People's Communes in Rural Areas." (August 29, 1958), in *Communist China, 1955–1959*, pp. 454–56.

though Mao had promoted the liberalization of 1956–1957, its outcome supported his call for a new revolutionary push based on ideological militancy and popular mobilization.

Finally, the Leap's damaging effects came not so much from its logical rationale—labor mobilization and ideological incentives made sense for a country rich in manpower and weak in capital and technology—but from the fanaticism with which it was pursued. There were a number of factors in 1957–1958 that combined to make CCP elites unduly optimistic about how far they could leap in a short time.[32] Domestically, the economy was on the upswing after a disappointing lag in 1956–1957; the antirightist and rectification campaigns seemed to have consolidated the party's leadership; and the 1958 harvest was to be excellent, the early signs of which prompted the progressive raising of economic targets that took place that year. In the troubled field of Communist bloc relations, where "dark clouds" were acknowledged in 1956, the defeat of counterrevolution in Poland and Hungary, the consolidation of Khrushchev's power in the Soviet Union, and the management of a compromise statement at the Moscow Conference of Communist Parties in November 1957 all contributed to a belief that the solidarity and strength of the camp was growing. Perhaps most significant of all was the Chinese belief that the cold war balance of power had shifted to its side, expressed in Mao's statement that "the east wind prevails over the west wind." The Soviet Union's growing technological prowess—revealed most dramatically in the October 1957 *Sputnik* launching—and a moderate recession in the West were other primary elements in this favorable estimate of the international situation. It is easy in retrospect to note how fragile these trends were, but they nonetheless led CCP leaders to act with confidence bordering on recklessness.

Communes and Economic Crisis. Some of the consequences of the Great Leap approach—its constant meetings and indoctrination to stimulate maximum efforts—are implicit in what

[32] All the following points are expressed in Liu Shaoqi, "Report to the Second Session," pp. 416–38; and Zhou Enlai, "The Present International Situation and China's Foreign Policy" (February 10, 1958), in *Communist China, 1955–1959*, pp. 401–10.

has been said; however, there are others that demand special attention. The people's communes, for example, had a profound impact on rural society because they concentrated economic and political powers in a basic-level unit significantly larger than any that preceded it (see Table III.1). Before communization, the basic rural administrative unit was the *xiang*, of which there were about 220,000 in 1952–1955; however, a policy of amalgamation after 1955 increased their size so that by the summer of 1958 there were only some 80,000 *xiang*. The basic agricultural production unit was originally the peasant household, numbering over 100 million in the early 1950s, but collectivization gave the Agricultural Producers' Cooperative (APC) primary responsibility for managing and distributing the agricultural product. There were about 750,000 APCs in 1958, most of them based on natural villages. After communization, both administrative and production responsibilities were combined in the management committees of some 25,000 communes. This concentration of power in a larger and unfamiliar political-economic unit caused great disruption and uncertainty, due to boundary changes, shifts of personnel, and conflict with established production and marketing relationships.[33]

The impact of the communes went far beyond the disruption of institutional patterns, however. As seen by the leadership, they were to be large, self-sufficient communities that would lead their members rapidly toward modernization and a communistic way of life. They were to establish their own factories, schools, nurseries, mess halls, and militia units to provide for maximal development and deployment of manpower under collective management. Most "private plots," the small lots of land retained for individual household use in the APCs, were absorbed into collective production, and there were experiments with a "free supply" system of payment according to need rather than according to work. These changes were far too abrupt for easy management and acceptance.

[33] For a detailed analysis, see Roy Hofheinz, "Rural Administration in Communist China," *China Quarterly*, no. 11 (July–September 1962): 140–59; G. William Skinner, "Marketing and Social Structure in Rural China," part 3, *The Journal of Asian Studies*, vol. 24, no. 3 (May 1965): 363–99; and Kenneth R. Walker, *Planning in Chinese Agriculture: Socialization and the Private Sector, 1956–1962* (Chicago: Aldine, 1965), esp. pp. 3–19.

Economically, the Leap had some positive accomplishments; however, it ended in a severe crisis in 1959–1961.[34] Bad weather had an adverse effect on the 1959 harvest, but the all-around deterioration that followed reflected basic faults in the approach itself. Agricultural decline continued in 1960, leading to shortages of investment funds and raw materials that forced a slowdown in industry. Food shortages lowered both physical and psychological work capacity, reinforcing downward production trends. Personnel transfers at the basic level brought inexperienced men to new posts and disrupted the cohesion of work groups. Disregard of specialists led to errors in attempted technological innovations. Ideological indoctrination produced diminishing returns as it cut into the scant leisure time of an overworked labor force. Planning and accurate statistical reporting languished, and overly ambitious or enthusiastic cadres pushed the commune policy to radical extremes. The deepening rift with the Soviet Union and the departure of Soviet technicians in 1960 added to the bleakness of the picture.

The severity of the 1959–1961 economic crisis had major political consequences. The overworked and hungry population became resentful and began to turn against the party cadres who were so totally identified with implementation of the Leap policy. Apathy, disobedience, and even instances of insurrection spread in rural areas. The position of basic-level cadres was particularly acute, for they were caught between popular discontent and directives from higher levels. Their response ranged from illicit concessions to the people to authoritarianism and brutality, or simply to an abdication of official responsibility and integrity. In short, the crisis involved political authority as well as the economy.[35] Inevitably, it produced great tension within the political elite, which faced the task of changing a policy to which it had, at least publicly, committed itself so heavily. The change took place in a period of retrenchment, but it also raised many new and old controversies about the wisdom of the Great Leap Forward.

[34] For a summary of economic problems in this period, see Alexander Eckstein, "On the Economic Crisis in Communist China," *Foreign Affairs*, vol. 42, no. 4 (July 1964): 655–68.

[35] Evidence of these difficulties is found in *Gongzuo Tong xun (Kung-tso Tung hsün)*, ("Bulletin of Activities"), a secret journal of the PLA General

RETRENCHMENT AND RECOVERY, 1961–1965

The years from 1961 to 1965 form a less distinct period than those discussed previously. What cohesion they have stems largely from an economic retrenchment policy that emerged in 1961 and continued in force through 1965. Many of its basic features remained even through the Cultural Revolution. On the political side, however, there was a significant break in this period, coming at the Tenth Plenum of the Central Committee in September 1962. Before that date, a climate of political retrenchment, moderation, and uncertainty prevailed; following it, a complex struggle between mobilization and institutionalization took place, leading to the open conflict of the Cultural Revolution.

The preceding discussion has indicated the conditions that made some kind of retreat from the Great Leap virtually inescapable. Indeed, the first signs of retreat came as early as December 1958 at the Central Committee's Sixth Plenum,[36] when it was noted that full communism was still a long way off, that the "free supply" system should be limited, that commune members must be guaranteed adequate hours for rest, and that tighter planning and organization was necessary. It was this meeting that announced Mao's decision to retire from the chairmanship of the government—a move which was not forced upon him but which certainly was recognized by senior elites as reducing his political responsibilities. Leap policies came under direct attack at the Eighth Plenum in July–August 1959, with Defense Minister and Politburo member Peng Dehuai (P'eng Teh-huai) serving as spokesman for the critics. The Plenum dismissed Peng from his position in the Defense Military (but not from the Politburo), launched an intensive campaign against "right opportunism" and "conservatism," and reasserted the rectitude of the communes and the Great Leap Forward. This was done, however, only by a

Political Department of which twenty-nine numbers for the January–August 1961 period are available. They are translated in J. Chester Cheng, ed., *The Politics of the Chinese Red Army* (Stanford, Cal.: Hoover Institution, 1966). For a brief analysis of their contents that is particularly relevant to points discussed here, see John Wilson Lewis, "China's Secret Military Papers: 'Continuities' and 'Revelations'," *China Quarterly*, no. 18 (April–June 1964): 68–78.

[36]For documentation, see *Communist China, 1955–1959*, pp. 483–503.

great investment of Mao's personal prestige, indicating that support for the Leap was wavering.[37] During 1959 and 1960, the communes were quietly modified to lessen their disruptive impact.

Retrenchment Policies. Economic retrenchment became official at the Ninth Plenum in January 1961, which conceded that Leap policies had created errors and opposition.[38] A new slogan of "taking agriculture as the foundation of the national economy" acknowledged the need for new measures to support agricultural development. Private plots were restored to households, rural markets were expanded, and rural mechanization was promoted to stimulate agricultural production and distribution. The Plenum also emphasized economic planning, consumer goods, and quality and diversity in industrial products. Experts and central ministries regained some powers lost to party committees.

Perhaps the greatest changes came in the structure of communes, which had settled into a system of "three-level management" by 1958–1959 (see Table III.1). Each commune was divided into production brigades, generally the same as the previous village-based advanced APCs, and each brigade was divided into production teams of twenty to forty households each. Initially, the commune was the "basic accounting unit" (BAU) that managed agricultural production and distribution; however, during 1959 the brigade became the BAU. By 1962, after retrenchment, the production team was the BAU, returning primary agricultural responsibility to about the same level of collective organization as existed in 1955. Communes and brigades remained important organizations that managed larger-scale economic and governmental tasks, but the original communes, which had been large rural units often covering several rural marketing areas, were divided into a larger number of smaller ones closer in size to marketing areas.

---

[37] The official published documents of the Eighth Plenum are in *Communist China, 1955–1959*, pp. 533–40. Much additional documentation on the Peng affair became available during the Cultural Revolution and has been translated in *The Case of P'eng Teh-huai* (Hong Kong: Union Research Institute, 1968), esp. pp. 1–47.

[38] See *China Quarterly*, no. 6 (April–June 1961): 183–90.

The Leap's disruption of both economic and statistical systems ushered in two decades of uncertainty and controversy in estimates of Chinese economic performance. Nonetheless, it seems recovery was underway by 1962, with most 1957 output levels regained or surpassed by 1965 (see Appendix B). As in earlier years, gains in industry were stronger than in agriculture, which remained the critical economic problem area.[39] The retention of the major retrenchment policies through the 1970s indicates at least minimal satisfaction of the elite with their results.

Retrenchment initially penetrated politics as well as economics. During most of 1961–1962, there was a noticeable slackening of ideological indoctrination and mass movements coupled with an inward-looking party rectification campaign. The primacy of politics receded as agricultural, industrial, and educational units were encouraged to devote more time to their nonpolitical functions. For nonparty intellectuals, there was a revived "blooming and contending" that encouraged resumption of academic research and debate, although not the outspoken political criticism of 1957. Party officials were not so restrained, however, and some of them began to publicize views that were critical of the Leap, Peng Dehuai's dismissal, Mao's policy leadership, and even Mao's abilities and personality.[40] Much of this criticism came in subtle form through the medium of drama and literary essays, but Maoists later charged that in 1962 Peng actively sought reinstatement and vindication with the support of Liu Shaoqi by circulating a lengthy defense of his position among party leaders.[41]

New Political Offensive. The Tenth Plenum in September 1962 marked the end of political retrenchment and the beginning of a new political offensive. Although its official communiqué

[39] For a sampling of estimates for 1957–1965 and the difficulties and controversy that surround them, see Ta-chung Liu, "Economic Development" in *China in Crisis*, pp. 631–50, and the "comments," ibid., pp. 650–90.

[40] Merle Goldman, "The Unique 'Blooming and Contending' of 1961–62," *China Quarterly*, no. 37 (January–March 1969): 54–83.

[41] "From the Defeat of Peng Teh-huai to the Bankruptcy of China's Khrushchev," *Hongqi* editorial, no. 13 (August 17, 1967), in *PR*, no. 34 (August 18, 1967), pp. 18–20, 35.

referred only briefly to the existence of "opportunist" and "revisionist" elements within the CCP,[42] subsequent developments made clear that the Plenum had launched a new effort to counter the anti-Maoist tendency of 1961–1962. The next three years brought a number of campaigns aimed at stimulating class struggle and ideological education in the name of Maoist orthodoxy. Two of the most important of these were a socialist education movement and the drive for "cultivation of revolutionary successors." The former was actually a series of campaigns that sought to remedy persistent defects in lower-level cadre work by intraparty rectification combined with mass criticism and education; it insisted on continuing class struggle to defeat bourgeois and revisionist influences both within and outside the CCP.[43] The latter addressed itself to young people who were in line for political leadership but who lacked the actual revolutionary experience of their seniors; they were to immerse themselves in physical labor, ideological study, and class struggle to acquire the experience and attitudes necessary to "carry the revolution through to the end."[44]

These movements, combined with the polemics of the now open Sino-Soviet conflict and a number of related campaigns, fostered an intense political rhetoric reminiscent of the Great Leap Forward. In fact, political tension seemed in some ways higher than in 1957–1960, since struggle was said to be against class enemies and anti-Maoist ideology, whereas the Leap had fought mainly against nature and institutional limitations on productive capacities. Yet, somehow the 1962–1965 rhetoric was not translated fully into practice. The socialist education movement dragged on indecisively, and the peasant associations that were to be revived to help implement it never acquired much promi-

[42] Text in *PR*, no. 39 (September 28, 1962), pp. 5–8.

[43] For analysis and documentation, see Richard Baum and Frederick C. Teiwes, *Ssu-Ch'ing: The Socialist Education Movement of 1962–1966* (Berkeley: University of California, Center for Chinese Studies, 1968). A valuable collection of primary data on cadre problems in this period in a Fujian county is C. S. Chen, ed., *Rural People's Communes in Lien-Chiang*, trans. Charles Price Ridley (Stanford, Cal.: Hoover Institution, 1969).

[44] See *Training Successors for the Revolution Is the Party's Strategic Task* (Peking: Foreign Languages Press, 1965); and Hu Yao-pang, *Revolutionize Our Youth!* (Peking: Foreign Languages Press, 1964).

nence. Experts and youth participated in campaigns to revolutionize themselves, but in a regularized way that permitted continuation of their professional work or study. Revolution, in short, was becoming an institution of the regime, a routinized procedure for education and training that would support rather than alter the system. In that tendency lay some of the basic controversies that brought on the Cultural Revolution. Before discussing that topic, however, we should examine briefly one structure in which the Maoist revival did have a dramatic impact—the People's Liberation Army (PLA).

As noted earlier, military organization was very prominent during the reconstruction period. Following the end of the Korean War and the establishment of the new state system, the PLA's political power declined. Its budget and size were reduced, and it began to assume a more standardized professional role. However, Lin Biao's replacement of Peng as defense minister in 1959 initiated a process of politicization that was to make the PLA Mao's ultimate power base in the Cultural Revolution.[45] Mao's determination to maintain a politicized army is understandable given the CCP's historically intimate identification with its military arm, and his reliance on military models for political action was demonstrated in the Great Leap's heavy use of military metaphors.[46] Still, the forcefulness of the PLA's rise was surprising particularly in view of the resistance Mao's ideas were meeting elsewhere. Under Lin's direction, the PLA's General Political Department and party organization within the army were greatly strengthened, while the study of Mao Zedong thought was promoted vigorously. By 1963–1964, as these efforts bore fruit, the PLA and individual soldier-heroes became the foremost Maoist models for emulation by the rest of society. The army's political department system began to spread to party and government structures, with new political departments appearing under the Central Committee and most of the economic ministries. Army cadres were prominent in the staffing and organizing

[45] See Chalmers Johnson, "Lin Piao's Army and its Role in Chinese Society," *Current Scene*, vol. 4, nos. 13–14 (July 1 and 15, 1966); and Ralph L. Powell, "The Increasing Power of Lin Piao and the Party-Soldiers 1959–1966," *China Quarterly*, no. 34 (April–June 1968): 38–65.

[46] See T. A. Hsia, *Metaphor, Myth, Ritual and the People's Commune* (Berkeley: University of California, Center for Chinese Studies, 1961).

of these new organs. On the eve of the Cultural Revolution, the PLA was publicly identified as the most successful organizational practitioner of Maoism, and it had acquired, through the preferential placement of demobilized soldiers as well as the new political departments, a network of political influence throughout the system.

THE CULTURAL REVOLUTION DECADE, 1966–1976

The Great Proletarian Cultural Revolution was one of the most significant events in modern Chinese history. It was also one of the most confusing because it had a dual character and has been interpreted quite differently by Chinese leaders themselves. Although the Cultural Revolution refers to a specific political struggle campaign that lasted from 1966–1969, it also refers to the decade of 1966–1976, when policies and factions produced by the campaign continued to agitate Chinese politics. In this latter sense, the Cultural Revolution refers to a broader period, process, or set of policies. When Maoist forces were ascendant during 1966–1976, Chinese statements lavishly praised the Cultural Revolution's accomplishments and goals. After 1976, especially after 1978, Chinese leaders began to condemn it as an unmitigated disaster. We analyze these complex issues more carefully in other chapters, presenting here an introductory description of the Cultural Revolution's dual character and its two major stages, the first from 1966–1969 and the second from 1969–1976.[47]

---

[47] Translated Chinese documents provide excellent coverage of the Cultural Revolution: see *CCP Documents of the Great Proletarian Cultural Revolution, 1966–1967* (Hong Kong: Union Research Institute, 1968), cited hereafter as *CCP Documents*; Mark Selden, ed., *The People's Republic of China: A Documentary History of Revolutionary Change* (New York: Monthly Review, 1979); and *Classified Chinese Communist Documents: A Selection* (Taipei: Institute of International Relations, 1978). Two fascinating firsthand accounts are Liang Heng and Judith Shapiro, *Son of the Revolution* (New York: Random House, 1983); and David Milton and Nancy Dall Milton, *The Wind Will Not Subside: Years in Revolutionary China* (New York: Pantheon Books, 1976). Valuable scholarly monographs focusing on or emphasizing the period include Byung-joon Ahn, *Chinese Politics and the Cultural Revolution* (Seattle: University of Washington Press, 1976); Lowell Dittmer, *Liu Shao-ch'i and the Chinese Cultural Revolution* (Berkeley: University of California Press, 1974); Hong Yung Lee, *The Politics of the Chinese Cultural Revolution* (Berkeley: University of California Press, 1978); Lucian Pye, *The Dynamics of Chinese Politics*

Dual Character of the Cultural Revolution. The Cultural Revolution often refers to a national political movement organized and directed by a group of political elites under the leadership of Mao to rectify the CCP in accordance with Maoist policies. As a rectification campaign, the Cultural Revolution sought to test the quality of all officials, particularly those at high levels, reforming or purging those who were not following Mao's prescriptions for Chinese society. The Maoists regularly described the Cultural Revolution as an organized political campaign with centrally defined leadership, guidelines, and stages, although they did not define it exclusively in these terms and did not in fact maintain central control throughout its course. The Cultural Revolution was, therefore, comparable to other political movements in the history of the CCP and was directly related to some of them, particularly the rectification of 1957–1958, the drive against Peng Dehuai's so-called right opportunism in 1959, and the socialist education movement. It stands apart from other campaigns, however, because of its duration and impact (although land reform was a competitor on this score) and because the central leadership was so deeply divided by it.

In a second sense, the Cultural Revolution refers to the whole period of 1966–1976, when Maoists tried to transform the thought and behavior—that is, the culture—of the Chinese people. As a process of attempted cultural transformation, the Cultural Revolution period involved all Chinese (not just active participants in the campaign), raised issues long debated by Chinese leaders and intellectuals (not just Maoists or even Communists), and had its roots deep in modern Chinese history (not just in CCP squabbles of the 1960s). In fact, the phrase *cultural revolution* was an old Communist term, used partly because of its links to non-Communist cultural reform efforts such as May Fourth and the "new culture" movements of the early twentieth century.

(Cambridge, Mass.: Oelgeschlager, Gunn and Hain, 1981); Stanley Rosen, *Red Guard Factionalism and the Cultural Revolution in Guangzhou (Canton)* (Boulder, Colo.: Westview Press, 1982); and Frederick C. Teiwes, *Leadership, Legitimacy, and Conflict in China* (Armonk, N.Y.: M. E. Sharpe, 1984). A history of the PRC giving primary attention to Maoism and the Cultural Revolution is Maurice Meisner, *Mao's China: A History of the People's Republic* (New York: Free Press, 1977).

The Cultural Revolution as a movement was inseparable from the broader period or process because so much of its debate centered on cultural issues. The movement began with attacks on writers and party officials responsible for cultural expression. It addressed directly the content of art and literature, insisting it celebrate the nationalistic and proletarian values of socialist society, rejecting the values of traditional China and of foreign or domestic class enemies. It emphasized from the first a thorough reform of the educational system to make it more accessible to workers, peasants, and soldiers and to place it wholly in the service of Maoist goals. Generally, it upheld ideals of populism, political activism, and self-sacrifice for collective interests, while inveighing against aspects of Chinese lifestyle that seemed opposed to these Maoist virtues: the "four olds" (old ideas, culture, customs, and habits); "selfish" desires for material gains; personal ties that diluted political obligations; bureaucratic or elitist behavior; and the special honor or status accorded purely intellectual pursuits. Such cultural concerns were obviously political, but that is precisely the point. For the Maoists, a revolutionary campaign was necessary to establish leaders who would promote cultural transformation; yet only cultural transformation would ensure that "correct" leadership would prevail and endure. The two Cultural Revolutions were inseparable in Maoist ideology and therefore became inseparable for all those affected by or interested in the campaign.

Stages of the 1966–1969 Campaign: Mobilization, Red Guards, Power Seizures, and Consolidation. The Cultural Revolution became an official, open campaign in mid-1966, but its first phase of mobilization lasted from the fall of 1965 through July 1966. In this period, the central leadership engaged in a largely hidden struggle over how to respond to Mao's call (at a September 1965 meeting of the Central Committee) for a major assault on revisionist influences. Open criticism was directed at a small number of intellectuals and party propagandists who had published anti-Maoist pieces in 1961–1962, but the top antagonists were not initially identified. Much of this inner struggle centered around the work of a Central Committee Cultural Revolution Group set up to direct the campaign. The conflict exploded in May–June 1966 when the Central Committee repudiated its first

Cultural Revolution Group (subsequently establishing a more radical one), purged several high-ranking leaders, and reconstituted the Peking Municipal Party Committee.[48] The most prominent victim was Peng Zhen (P'eng Chen)—mayor of Peking, first secretary of the Peking Party Committee, and a member of the Politburo and the first Cultural Revolution Group—who was identified as the main culprit in the Cultural Revolution Group and the patron of revisionist intellectuals in Peking. During June and July, the Cultural Revolution broadened into an open mass movement to uncover all bourgeois authorities, particularly in educational and propagandist institutions. However, many party leaders continued to restrain its most radical tendencies.

A second stage of public attack, dominated by Red Guard activities, lasted from August through November. It was initiated at the Eleventh Plenum (August 1–12, 1966), which adopted a crucial "Sixteen Point Decision" on the Cultural Revolution marking the ascendancy of Maoist forces at the party center.[49] This decision aimed the movement at "persons in authority who are taking the capitalist road"—gradually revealed to be Liu Shaoqi, Deng Xiaoping, and a host of other senior elites—and named the mass movement, especially "large numbers of revolutionary young people"—the Red Guards—as the main force for implementing it. With this official sanction, facilitated by an earlier closure of the schools, Red Guard organizations mushroomed, bringing millions of young people into the streets to demonstrate support for Chairman Mao, to denounce and ter-

---

[48] See, in particular, the "May Sixteenth Circular" of the Central Committee, text in *CCP Documents,* pp. 20–28.

[49] Text in *CCP Documents,* pp. 42–54. Use of the word *Maoist* throughout this discussion seems necessary for simple reference to the promoters of the Cultural Revolution as distinguished from those who resisted or tried to defuse it in some way. It does not imply they all held precisely the same views or supported the movement for the same reasons. In fact, there was great controversy about who was really a Maoist and who was not, and many participants were doubtlessly surprised by the labels ultimately attached to them. Nor is it certain that the Maoists, even in this qualified sense, had a genuine majority on the Central Committee at the Eleventh Plenum, due to the presence of nonmembers and the possibility of intimidation at that meeting. From August 1966 on, Maoists controlled communications issued in the name of the Central Committee, but the course of the Cultural Revolution suggests that they did not have a formal majority on the Committee until after the purges of 1966.

rorize those said to be his opponents, and to destroy various symbols of bourgeois or reactionary culture. However, while their actions revealed near fanatical devotion to Mao, they could not drive his opponents from office. Red Guards began to differ on who was truly Maoist or revisionist, splitting into competitive and even hostile organizations—a development naturally encouraged by party officials who were under attack. By late 1966 the Maoist leaders were preparing a new offensive in which a literal "seizure of power" by "revolutionary rebels" would take place in all party, state, and economic organizations.

The seizure of power stage, which lasted from December 1966 through September 1968, markedly escalated the Cultural Revolution by extending it into the countryside, economic enterprises, and government and party offices. The new revolutionary rebel groups were drawn largely from the working population and hence were significantly broader mass organizations than were the student-based Red Guards. The very idea of a power seizure from below was a direct assault on local power authority and organization. Understandably, the first efforts to seize power produced immediate confusion and violence, as local "rebels" struggled with officials and each other for control of offices and communications centers. Localized civil disorders, occasionally becoming armed conflict between rival mass organizations, continued for roughly the next two years, although their intensity fluctuated constantly depending on time and place. The Maoists in Peking must have accepted this upheaval as necessary and to some extent desirable, but they acted quickly to place limits on it. Most important, they issued instructions in January 1967 that the PLA was to intervene with any force necessary on the side of the "leftists" and that it was to assume control of key communications, transportation, and other facilities.[50] In effect, China came under a kind of martial law in which the PLA became the de facto administrative authority and arbiter of local disputes; local CCP organization simply ceased to function, and even central party organs went into partial eclipse. Moreover, the tactic of power seizure by mass organizations soon was modified by an endorsement of "revolutionary committees" based on a

---

[50] See the directives in *CCP Documents*, pp. 186, 195–97, 200–01, 208, 211–13.

"three-way alliance" as the appropriate organs for replacing the old state and party committees.[51] The "three-way alliance" meant that revolutionary committees were to be composed of "leaders of revolutionary mass organizations, PLA representatives, and revolutionary leading cadres." In practice, this permitted many former cadres to remain in office, significantly reduced the influence of mass organizations on the committees, and gave the PLA a decisive voice in negotiating the establishment and membership of the committees.

The twenty-one months required to set up revolutionary committees in all provincial-level units were full of conflict and policy shifts; however, when the last was formed in September 1968, it was clear that a trend toward restoration of order and authority was under way. Army commanders and former cadres held most leading positions on the new committees; mass organizations were being broken up and repressed; and students were under orders to go back to school or to work in the countryside. Party organization was still a shambles, however, and the provincial revolutionary committees had barely begun to straighten out the reorganization of power in their subordinate units. Accordingly, a fourth and final stage of consolidation ensued in which the leadership claimed overall victory in the Cultural Revolution but acknowledged that substantial tasks of party building and general economic and political stabilization remained.[52] Although the Twelfth Plenum in October 1968 had claimed that "ample conditions had been prepared" for a Ninth Party Congress, that Congress—marking the conclusion of the Cultural Revolution as a rectification campaign—did not meet until April 1969.

Maoist Reform and Factional Conflict, 1969–1976. The Ninth Party Congress formally committed the CCP to reform the Chinese system in accordance with Mao's prescriptions. For a variety of reasons, however, the effort fell short of the ideals articulated early in the Cultural Revolution. For one thing, the

---

[51]"On the Revolutionary 'Three-in-One' Combination," *Hongqi* editorial, no. 5 (March 30, 1967), in *PR*, no. 12 (March 17, 1967): 14–16.

[52]See "Communiqué of the Enlarged 12th Plenary Session," *PR*, supplement to no. 44 (November 1, 1968).

post-1969 leadership was not united in its interpretation of the Cultural Revolution's legacy and soon succumbed to renewed factional conflict. Second, the institutional uncertainty and disarray produced by the campaign complicated efforts to advance new policies. Finally, the PRC now faced new issues—most importantly, Mao's approaching death and how to deal with the Soviet threat—that would transform the stakes and substance of Chinese politics. As a result, the practice of Maoism in 1969–1976 was different from the rhetoric of 1965–1967. Nonetheless, reforms after the Cultural Revolution had a great impact on Chinese society and came to represent—both in China and abroad—at least a modified application of the Maoist model. We will note some of the most important reforms and then review the problems that altered or obstructed their progress.[53]

One striking feature of the immediate post-1969 period was an effort to maintain the spirit of the Cultural Revolution by infusing public life with its symbolism. Mao's personal authority continued to serve as the legitimator of policy, and Maoist themes—self-reliance, mass line, continuing the revolution, the primacy of politics—permeated all areas of Chinese life. Official statements held that the Cultural Revolution was still in progress, that Chinese society was still engaged in a fierce struggle between the Maoist and revisionist lines that would require militant action, as well as more cultural revolutions, against those who would compromise the goals of the revolution. This radical rhetoric discouraged specification of national policies and plans, encouraging instead an experimental approach that permitted much local diversity and aimed more at reform of thought and behavior than at attainment of quantifiable targets.

More concretely, the idea of continuing the revolution was translated into measures designed to foster a more egalitarian society by shifting resources and status to less privileged sectors

---

[53]For detailed analysis of this period, see Jürgen Domes, *China After the Cultural Revolution* (Berkeley: University of California Press, 1977). A substantial collection of key documents for 1973–1978, illustrating conflicting programs within the CCP leadership before 1976 and the post-1976 polemics against the Gang, is Raymond Lotta, ed., *And Mao Makes Five: Mao Tsetung's Last Great Battle* (Chicago: Banner Press, 1978). The editor's introduction argues that the Gang of Four were the real Maoists and that their purge represented a right-wing coup against the true Chinese Left.

of Chinese society—that is, from elites to masses and from city to countryside. Bureaucratic organizations were simplified, their personnel reduced. All cadres spent several months in May Seven Cadre Schools, where they engaged in a mixture of manual labor and ideological study. Technical and professional specialists were urged to integrate with the masses and renounce their bourgeois dreams of individual recognition and advancement. There were reports of salary reductions at the upper end of the pay scales, coupled with the pressure on all citizens to renounce privileged life styles. Revolutionary committees, which had become the administrative organs of government, were extended into other units, thereby providing some mass representation in the management of factories, enterprises, schools, and other institutions.

Maoist reforms had their greatest impact in the areas of education, culture, and public health. As schools reopened after the closures of the late 1960s, several changes became evident (see Chapter 5 for fuller discussion). Primary school attendance swelled, becoming nearly universal as resources were concentrated on this effort; middle school (secondary level) enrollment also grew rapidly, but university enrollment remained far below the pre-1966 years. Courses of study were shortened; grades, examinations, and theoretical study were downplayed; political education, applied and practical studies, and experience in manual labor held priority. Virtually all middle school students received rural work assignments on graduation. Cultural policy promoted simple revolutionary themes in a populist style, limiting cultural expression to a few officially approved forms, while criticizing anything resembling feudal or bourgeois influences; foreign influences were also objects of suspicion. In public health, as in education, there was a major effort to serve rural areas. Large numbers of doctors and medical teams moved to the countryside. The general thrust of reforms was to provide minimal health care for the population as a whole, rather than specialized care for the few who had access to advanced medical centers in the cities. Medical training emphasized training of generalists and armies of paramedics (the so-called barefoot doctors) who could extend simple treatment or referral services into the villages.

Despite the Cultural Revolution's attacks on Liu Shaoqi's revisionist economic policies, the broad outlines of the economic policies of the early 1960s remained in place. "Agriculture as the foundation," the three-level commune system with the production team as the basic accounting unit, and household retention of private plots persisted, although there was some discussion of reviving more collectivist measures. The Cultural Revolution spirit did, however, encourage an "antieconomist" stance that was critical of emphasis on material incentives or production goals. Local initiative, development of rural, small-scale industry, and worker participation in management received greater attention than in the past.

These reforms had heavy rhetorical support and considerable impact, but they soon ran into difficulties. Sino-Soviet border clashes in 1969 and the beginning of American retreat from Vietnam led to the limited Sino-American rapprochement signaled in the Shanghai Communiqué of February 1972. The PRC began to reorient its foreign relations toward greater contact with capitalist countries to build a united front against the USSR; the Soviet threat also raised serious questions about China's economic and technical development that put Cultural Revolution assumptions about the primacy of politics in a different light (see Chapters 4 and 7 for further discussion). Moreover, Mao's failing health and declining role in governmental affairs compelled other leaders to face the political and strategic implications of the post-Mao era, even though they were reluctant to depart from the leader's prescriptions while he was alive.

Institutional uncertainties also obstructed the reforms. State and party organs were slow to recover from the shattering events of 1966–1969. Many experienced cadres were purged or temporarily relieved of their original work assignments. The 1954 state constitution was discredited, but a new one was not adopted until January 1975. The CCP was taking in many new members, even though the fate of old cadres was not yet clear. The role of mass organizations and the PLA was in flux, the former beginning to revive and the latter retreating from its political prominence of the late 1960s. The resolution of these institutional issues was in itself a matter of dispute, but as long as they remained unresolved, they weakened administrative effectiveness.

Most importantly, these problems combined with the residue of Cultural Revolution factionalism to produce serious splits within the leadership (see Chapter 6 for further discussion of elite conflicts). The initial post-1969 leadership was a coalition of three groups: the most ardent Maoists or radicals who drew strength from their close association with the Chairman and their manipulation of his directives—Jiang Qing (Chiang Ch'ing), Mao's wife, was the key figure in this group; the military elite who, although not united, benefitted from Defense Minister Lin Biao's designation as second-in-command and Mao's chosen successor; the veteran administrators, led by Zhou Enlai, who represented what was left of the moderate position in Chinese politics.

This coalition proved unstable. A major rupture occurred in 1971 with the purge of Lin Biao for allegedly plotting a coup against Mao.[54] Lin's downfall—apparently due mainly to his ambitious drive for power but also involving more obscure differences with Mao, particularly on policies toward the Soviet Union and the United States—was accompanied by the purge of several other high-ranking military leaders and was followed by a reduction of PLA influence, leaving the radicals and moderates in uneasy balance. The former tried to protect the more radical version of Cultural Revolution reforms, whereas the latter tried to moderate their effects and concentrate more on economic development. There was backsliding on some of the reforms as Zhou Enlai sponsored the restoration of many old cadres who had been purged in the Cultural Revolution. The most prominent example was the return of Deng Xiaoping, who had been linked to Liu Shaoqi as a leading capitalist-roader in the Cultural Revolution but who had, by 1975, moved into virtual leadership of the government as Zhou's health failed. The 1972–1976 period, then, was marked by increasing tension within the leadership, with discordant interpretations of key campaigns (particularly the "criticize Lin Biao and Confucius" movement),[55] by increasing labor disputes and social unrest, and by a pronounced economic slowdown in 1974–1976. When Zhou Enlai died in January 1976, the radicals—apparently with Mao's support—

[54] For documentation and analysis, see Michael Y. M. Kau, ed., *The Lin Piao Affair: Power Politics and Military Coup* (White Plains, N.Y.: International Arts and Sciences Press, 1975).

[55] Merle Goldman, "China's Anti-Confucian Campaign, 1973–74," *China Quarterly*, no. 63 (September 1975): 435–62.

engineered Deng's second purge, the premiership going to a relative newcomer, Hua Guofeng. However, Deng's removal exacerbated the conflict, providing further unrest manifested in an unruly demonstration in Tiananmen Square in Peking in April 1976. Mao's death on September 9, 1976, removed the last barrier to an open confrontation.

SOCIALIST MODERNIZATION AND THE POST-MAO PERIOD, 1976–1985

Socialist modernization has been the dominant theme in Chinese politics since the death of Mao, with emphasis on material incentives, efficiency, social stability, and expanded ties with the world economy to realize China's modernization and economic development. The effort to define and implement this general goal moved through three phases between 1976 and 1985. In the first, Hua Guofeng tried to consolidate his leadership with a modernization push that continued many Maoist symbols and policies. This effort failed to stem the rising influence of Deng Xiaoping, who replaced Hua as de facto leader in 1978, launching a second phase of far-reaching reform and reassessment of Maoism. In a third phase emerging about 1981, the CCP adopted a more cautious "readjustment" strategy that struck a balance between reformist and conservative forces. We describe each phase briefly, concluding with a preliminary assessment of China's transition from a revolutionary to postrevolutionary era.[56]

Hua Guofeng and the Transition from Maoism, 1976–1978. In early October 1976, Hua Guofeng arrested the Gang of Four—the epithet chosen for the four leading radicals (Jiang Qing, Yao Wenyuan, Zhang Chunqiao (Chang Ch'un-ch'iao), and Wang Hongwen)—and unleashed a vitriolic campaign against them for distorting Mao's directives, sabotaging the government and

[56]For detailed analysis of post-Mao politics, see Jürgen Domes, *The Government and Politics of the PRC* (Boulder, Colo.: Westview Press, 1985); Peter R. Moody, Jr., *Chinese Politics After Mao* (New York: Praeger, 1983); and Victor Nee and David Mozingo, eds., *State and Society in Contemporary China* (Ithaca, N.Y.: Cornell University Press, 1983). Foreign policy since 1976 is assessed in Harry Harding, ed., *China's Foreign Relations in the 1980s* (New Haven, Conn.: Yale University Press, 1984); and Michael Yahuda, *Towards the End of Isolationism: China's Foreign Policy After Mao* (New York: St. Martin's Press, 1983).

economy with their factional activity, and generally following a rightist line under the guise of radicalism. Hua became Chairman of the CCP and of the CC's Military Affairs Commission, while continuing to hold the premiership. For the next several months, the new leadership concentrated on consolidating its position and charging the Gang with responsibility for nearly all of China's problems over the preceding decade. This was done in the name of Mao, who was said to have picked Hua as successor and to have recognized the Gang's disruptive and deviant character well before his death. Hua and his colleagues clearly wanted to retain Maoist legitimacy and avoid explicit departures from the Maoist legacy. At the same time, criticism of the Gang inevitably suggested criticism of the Cultural Revolution and pointed toward changes in Cultural Revolution policies.

These changes began to take form after the Eleventh National Congress of the CCP in August 1977, which produced a new party constitution and confirmed Hua's leading position. Equally important was the reinstatement of Deng Xiaoping (as CCP vice-chairman and later vice-premier of the government), who quickly became a spokesperson for new policies. In March 1978, the Fifth NPC, with its adoption of a new state constitution, gave further impetus to the emergence of a new line. These two meetings, plus a number of national conferences on particular policy areas, elaborated Hua's "four modernizations" theme: to attain the modernization of agriculture, industry, national defense, and science and technology by the year 2000, placing the Chinese economy in the front ranks of the world and approaching or even overtaking some of the most developed capitalist countries. A Ten-Year Plan for 1976–1985 advanced equally ambitious short-run goals for accomplishing this monumental task.[57] Hua argued that Zhou Enlai had called for a modernization drive several years earlier only to see the Gang sabotage it; removal of the Gang brought a new period of socialist unity and order that would propel China toward modernization. He also called for new policies to strengthen education, workplace discipline and social order, foreign trade, and economic planning and management; however, it was difficult for a leader so dependent on

[57] See Hua's "Report" to the First Session of the Fifth NPC, text in *PR*, no. 10 (March 10, 1978): 7–40.

Mao's legacy to advocate fundamental change in the Maoist system. Hua's Ten-Year Plan bore a strong similarity to the Great Leap Forward—an all-out development push that set high targets across the board without acknowledging the unwelcome trade-offs that might accompany it.

Hua's moderate Maoism came under increasing fire in 1978 from Deng Xiaoping and his supporters. By the latter part of the year, this so-called practice faction (named because of their pragmatic slogans, such as "seek truth from facts" and "practice is the sole criterion of truth") was pushing for full repudiation of the Cultural Revolution and more comprehensive reforms. In policy addresses, academic journals, and a new burst of popular debate around posters at "Democracy Wall" in Peking and other places, they pressed their case against Hua. Many issues came together in demands for a "reversal of verdict" on the Tiananmen Incident of 1976, because that protest against radical policies had been labelled "counterrevolutionary" to justify police action against the critics, the second purge of Deng, and the confirmation of Hua as premier. Official announcements in November that the affair was "completely revolutionary" indicated that the victims of the 1976 event—Deng and other opponents of the Cultural Revolution—had won the day and that the primary beneficiary of the Incident, Hua Guofeng, was no longer in charge.

"Shift of Focus to Socialist Modernization": The Third Plenum and Deng's Reforms, 1978–1980. The Third Plenum (of the Eleventh CC) in December 1978 proclaimed a "shift of focus to socialist modernization" that marked a decisive departure from Hua's transitional leadership and indeed from China's revolutionary era.[58] The "shift" replaced Hua's grandiose development goals and claims to Maoist legitimacy with a readiness to do whatever was necessary, within the bounds of socialism, for China's modernization. It brought changes in party leadership as Deng's forces assumed command; in interpretation of party history and doctrine, with a critical view of Mao, Maoism, and the whole Cultural Revolution episode; and in many domestic

[58] See Text of the Plenum's Communiqué in *PR*, no. 52 (December 29, 1978): 6–16.

and foreign policies, including basic organizational principles of the existing system, to make them more effective servants of modernization. Some of these changes were underway before December 1978 (although none was completed at that time), but the Third Plenum symbolized the break with Maoism and set the CCP on the course of reform.

Leadership changes at the Third Plenum brought demotion of Hua's highest-ranking supporters and promotion of many of Deng's group. Struggle among these and other factions continued, but the die was cast. The crucial remaining members of Hua's group were purged in early 1980, with Hua yielding the premiership to Zhao Ziyang in September 1980 and his party leadership post to Hu Yaobang in June 1981. Zhao and Hu were protégés of Deng, who was the dominant political figure in China throughout the 1978–1985 period, even though he held formal leadership of neither state nor party. Deng faced continual opposition and was not uniformly successful in his initiatives, but the Third Plenum had shifted the balance of power at the top toward those eager to leave the Cultural Revolution behind and establish a new long-term development strategy.

Reinterpretation of party history and doctrine was a central issue in debates leading to the Third Plenum. Deng's victory at that meeting signaled a shift in emphasis on three major doctrinal points: material goals and incentives, especially the primacy of national economic development and the appropriateness of material rewards to motivate producers, replaced Cultural Revolution emphasis on ideological goals and incentives; images of social harmony, of a society united by its socialist system and hence no longer in need of mass struggle campaigns, replaced Maoist insistence that sharp class struggle persisted in China and required a "continuing revolution"; institutional procedures of socialist law and democracy replaced the personal word and authority of the leader in legitimating policy and doctrine. This obvious reformulation of Maoism left open the question of how to assess Mao's individual role in party history. The answer to such a delicate question could only be worked out gradually; however, the Third Plenum's mandate required that it be faced.

Open criticism of Mao and the Cultural Revolution appeared first in public posters, without formal approval by party elites, during the "democratic movement" of 1978–1979. Then, in

September 1979, Ye Jianying—a top military and political figure placed between Hua and Deng on the CCP political spectrum—delivered a major address acknowledging that many post-1957 Mao policies were wrong, calling the entire Cultural Revolution an "appalling catastrophe," and announcing that the CCP intended to hold a meeting to sum up its assessment of these difficult issues.[59] Thereafter, official criticism of the Maoist period became common, although the promised resolution on party history did not appear until June 1981.[60] Both the delay and substance of the document attested to the issue's controversiality. The CCP retained Mao Zedong Thought as a guiding principle, insisting that Mao's contributions to the Chinese revolution far outweighed his failings. At the same time, he was reduced to the level of an ordinary mortal who made gross mistakes during the Cultural Revolution, with these mistakes and the Cultural Revolution's flaws spelled out in detail. Although less than a full-scale "de-Maoification," the resolution drew a sharp doctrinal distinction between so-called correct pre-1957 and post-1978 lines and the errors of the Maoist period.

Reform policies unfolded rapidly after the Third Plenum, touching almost every area of Chinese life. Efforts to restore and raise academic standards were undertaken, with a sharp increase in university enrollments based on admission by competitive examination. Party leaders emphasized the importance of science and technology, and of intellectual contributions in general, to the success of modernization. A limited academic and cultural liberalization permitted experimentation with previously taboo subjects or forms of expression. Liberalization had political dimensions as well, leading to some open political dissent in 1979 along with the officially approved reconsideration of Maoism. The strengthening of socialist law and democracy became a common theme, with promulgation of a new criminal code, expansion of legal and judicial organs, and new laws in local government and elections that gave greater scope to popular political participation. CCP leaders insisted that cadres must also observe the new standards of legalism, discipline, and efficiency as "no one is above the law."

[59] Text in *BR*, no. 40 (October 5, 1979): 7–32.
[60] Text in *BR*, vol. 24, no. 27 (July 6, 1981): 10–39.

Economic reforms included increased benefits for consumers and experiments with market socialism. The Third Plenum raised state prices for agricultural products while lowering prices paid for key farming inputs, thereby giving rural areas their first substantial increase in disposable income in decades. There were also wage increases for salaried workers, bonuses for the most productive workers, and a new concern for raising the quantity and quality of consumer goods.

"Market socialism" is an imprecise term for diverse efforts to raise economic production and efficiency. Decentralization of some decisions to lower levels, greater reliance on experts and technology, improved management systems, and insistence that enterprises account for their profits or losses did not necessarily challenge the structure of China's command economy. On the other hand, the expansion of private plots and free markets in the countryside, and experiments allowing some rural and urban production units to gear their product and prices to the market and dispose of their profits as they wished (so long as state quotas were met) *were* reforms that departed significantly from the established system. For example, the launching of the responsibility system in agriculture, which returned most farming decisions to the household and allowed it to buy and sell on the market after meeting a contractual obligation to the state (see Table III.1), effectively dismantled the system of agricultural collectivization that had emerged in the mid-1950s.

In external affairs, the Third Plenum brought a decisive commitment to an "open door foreign policy" that would accelerate modernization through expansion of China's international contacts. Some aspects of this opening simply continued the growth of PRC trade with capitalist countries and the general widening of diplomatic contacts associated with the strategic shift of the early 1970s, symbolized by the Sino-American Shanghai Communiqué of 1972. But Deng's foreign policy was more ambitious than the limited anti-Soviet united front pursued through most of the 1970s. Full normalization of relations between the United States and the People's Republic of China in December 1978, followed by China's invasion of Vietnam in February 1979—immediately after Deng's return from a historic visit to the United States—fueled speculation that China and the United States were moving toward an actual alliance against the Soviet Union. Sharp increases in foreign trade accompanied new policies approving borrowing on the international market and some direct foreign investment in China. To pay the bill for greater commodity and capital imports, the PRC began crash programs to develop exports and attract tourists. Initiation of large-scale cultural and academic exchanges—primarily with capitalist countries—was another part of the "open door" package that seemed to have reversed Maoist self-reliance. However, in both domestic and foreign policy, the initial thrust of reform gave way to a "readjustment" phase that modified some reform policies while strengthening others.

Readjustment and the Sixth Five-Year Plan, 1981–1985. "Readjustment" of the Chinese economy was one of the slogans of the late 1970s, so its emergence as a central theme in 1980–1981 was neither surprising nor a repudiation of reform. Rather, it indicated the desire of CCP leaders to carefully examine their reforms, readjusting those that seemed most problematic. This second look had a conservative bias, yet its effect was only to modify, not stop or even deflect, the reform program. The primary rationale for readjustment was continuing evidence of inefficiency and low productivity in the Chinese economy, coupled with growing deficits in the state budget due to increased imports, investments, and subsidies. Concern about China's economic capacity to sustain rapid development while satisfying long-suppressed consumer demands merged with fears of the political and cultural consequences of "liberalization" and the "open door." Internationally, the continuing irritant of American relations with and military support for Taiwan showed that normalization of diplomatic relations had not cleared the way for a U.S.-PRC alliance. Issues such as these enabled Deng's opponents to challenge his reform package, which resulted in three main areas of readjustment.

Economic readjustment was the centerpiece of the Sixth Five-Year Plan for 1981–1985. This Plan aimed at steady but modest growth for the period, and indeed for the subsequent 1986–1990 period as well, with high growth rates scheduled to resume only in the 1990s.[61] Its core was restraint in new state investments, increased efficiency in existing enterprises, and reliance on careful planning and technological inputs for production increases. The goal was to concentrate on raising productivity as a foundation for more rapid future growth.

A second area of readjustment was foreign policy, with a cooling of Sino-American relations and some signs of thaw—principally increased trade and diplomatic contacts—in Sino-Soviet relations. The PRC returned to relatively evenhanded criticism of both superpowers, asserting its closeness to Third World countries and its self-reliant, independent stance in world affairs. In fact, China's differences with the USSR over Afghanistan, the northern border, and Soviet support for Vietnam, coupled with its increasingly important economic and cultural ties with capitalist countries, kept it oriented much more toward the West (including key Asian members of the world market) than toward either the East or the South. Nonetheless, the shift reaffirmed China's determination to play an independent international role and ended speculation about early emergence of anything like a Sino-American alliance.

Finally, readjustment curtailed some of the liberalizing tendencies of the late 1970s. Open dissent was silenced; intellectuals were reminded of the political limits to cultural expression and academic debate; and Chinese citizens were cautioned about the danger of ideological pollution in contacts with foreigners. As noted earlier, the party resolution on Mao's historical role stopped far short of repudiation. Mao Zedong Thought held its place with Marxism-Leninism, socialism, party leadership, and proletarian dictatorship as guiding principles of the system that could not be compromised. In short, the CCP reasserted its dominant place in Chinese society and the correctness of its ideology. How to enforce its role and principles—whether by campaigns, purges, ideological education, police controls, or the like—remained controversial among party elites, but there was no doubt that they were determined to counter any serious political or ideological opposition that might develop from reform policies.

[61] See Zhao Ziyang, "Report on the Sixth Five-Year Plan," *BR*, vol. 25, no. 51 (December 20, 1982): 10–35.

Within the confines of readjustment as described, many reform policies continued to thrive. In fact, economic readjustment itself extended some reforms precisely because it emphasized fiscal sobriety, economic efficiency, and technological development. This approach put a premium on motivating enterprises to reform themselves and on attracting more foreign trade, capital, and technology. For example, the responsibility system in agriculture spread to almost all rural households, many of them branching out into freewheeling contracting and subcontracting for specialized production and services. Legal ownership of land remained with the collective; however, household contracts for land were extended to fifteen years to encourage peasant investment in land improvements. Success of the rural responsibility system in increasing production encouraged extension of the contract system to urban enterprises and entrepreneurs as well. A major CC decision in October 1984 loosened price controls and strengthened enterprise autonomy in the urban/ industrial sector.[62] In effect, market socialism forged ahead in response to some readjustment considerations, even though it seemed to confirm the ideological fears of the readjusters.

Another striking example of broadening reform was in policy toward foreign investment. Initially, the CCP limited such investment mainly to development loans or credit, participation in joint ventures in which China retained a controlling interest, and special undertakings in four small special economic zones along the Guangdong-Fujian coast. However, readjustment put borrowing and expensive purchases of foreign goods (especially complete plants) in disfavor, while expanding opportunities for direct foreign investments that entailed little cost for the Chinese. A variety of options, including full foreign ownership and operation, were offered; fourteen major cities and ports along the whole eastern seaboard were designated for intense economic development through encouragement of foreign trade and investment; and the concessionary terms offered to foreign investors were liberalized. There was no rollback in tourism or cultural

---

[62]Text of the decision in *BR*, vol. 27, no. 44 (October 29, 1984). The reforms are further clarified by Zhao Ziyang, "The Current Economic Situation and the Reform of the Economic Structure," *BR*, vol. 28, no. 16 (April 22, 1985): i–xv.

and academic exchange, despite explicit warnings about the ideological and even criminal dangers associated with these foreign contacts. In general, therefore, readjustment represented an effort to rationalize and refine the reform program (and to guard against dangers associated with it) but not to change its basic mission of accelerating the socialist modernization of China. Dramatic evidence of the reform movement's continuing vitality came at a September 1985 CC plenum, where Deng secured the retirement of over 100 senior officials, including 10 Politburo members and 64 CC members, and brought in many younger cadres with professional experience more suited to the modernization program.[63]

It is too early to discuss the success or failure of the modernization effort or to predict its future course. Although the basic program remained in place through the mid-1980s, with mixed but generally satisfactory economic results (see Appendix B), there are formidable obstacles ahead. These obstacles include questions about economic management and distribution and the nature of political leadership, that is, about the basic character of the socialist system. During the first sustained reform period (1978–1985), experiments with market socialism gained ground at the expense of the command economy, and consumer interests seemed at times to challenge the primacy of state interests. But central planners and the state still hold decisive power, so reforms in these crucial economic areas remain controversial and vulnerable to reversal.

Also controversial are political reforms that tried to increase the popular or representative role in politics, to regularize intraparty procedures, and to institutionalize separation of state and party functions. All had some effect but, like the economic reforms, they pushed against the entrenched interests and habits of party bureaucrats long accustomed to a near monopoly of power. Reform in socialist China requires a bureaucratic establishment to share a significant portion of its power with other claimants. Initial reforms brought some diffusion of power to lower-level units, to nonparty units, and to technical and professional elites whose qualifications differed markedly from old-line

[63] *The New York Times*, September 17, 1985, pp. 1, 6.

bureaucrats, but the issue is far from settled. Subsequent chapters will analyze in more detail the political dimensions of this problem.

Despite uncertainty about prospects for China's modernization and even the form that Chinese socialism may assume, there is no doubt about the significance of the PRC's transition to a postrevolutionary era. The CCP has recognized this shift in its doctrine and disassociated itself from many prescriptions of revolutionary Maoism. It has established new policies that support economic transformation, with particular emphasis on technology and material incentives. It has moved from a relatively self-reliant international posture to a degree of interdependence not unlike that of many other developing countries. Changes such as these have altered fundamentally the context of Chinese politics.

CHAPTER IV

The Communist System: Ideology and Change

COMMUNIST SYSTEMS RAISE major conceptual problems in the study of comparative politics. We touched on this in Chapter 1, particularly in reference to the inadequacies of the totalitarian model, and now we must explore it more carefully in generalizing about the Chinese system. What makes conceptualization difficult, as one student of comparative Communism has pointed out, is that Communist systems tend to be identified in general typologies as stable and institutionalized; whereas studies of specific Communist countries reveal acute problems in coping with change and institutionalization.[1] Indeed, tensions between stability and change seem to be inherent in such systems, which seek to stabilize and concentrate power in the political system in order to transform the social system. In practice, the political system cannot attempt to alter society without serious repercussions. As demonstrated in the preceding chapter, China is a prime example of the way in which efforts to transform society threaten the stability of the regime promoting that transformation.

Ideology appears to provide more coherence to the study of Communist systems than do institutions or policies. Richard

[1] Chalmers Johnson, "Comparing Communist Nations," in Chalmers Johnson, ed., *Change in Communist Systems* (Stanford, Cal.: Stanford University Press, 1970), pp. 1–3 passim.

152

Lowenthal argues that it is ideology that differentiates Communist systems from other revolutionary nationalist movements that also seek "politically forced development." The primary characteristics of Communist systems, according to Lowenthal, stem from a drive for rapid development—the "politically forced development" that links them to other revolutionary nationalist movements in developing countries—plus a commitment to attain a classless society on a world scale.[2]

The more concrete aspects of this ideological commitment are the following: the economic strategy of development is socialism, requiring collectivization and centralized planning of the economy; the political vehicle of development is the dictatorship of the proletariat, requiring a virtual monopolization of state power by the ruling Communist party; the ultimate objective of development is a classless communist society, requiring the creation of a new socialist man through continued class struggle and repeated efforts to establish a uniform collectivist consciousness; the world context of development is seen as a strategic situation of unremitting struggle between capitalist and socialist systems. In 1979, the ideological heterodoxy of the dissidents writing on Democracy Wall in Peking caused Deng Xiaoping to formulate these basic beliefs into a set of four principles that must be upheld: the socialist road, the leadership of the CCP, the dictatorship of the proletariat, and Marxism-Leninism Mao Zedong Thought. To question openly one of these principles is tantamount to a political crime.

We must emphasize, however, that these commitments establish only the most basic structure and goals of the system. Although sufficient to distinguish the Communist system from other types for purposes of general classification, they leave room for diametrically opposed interpretations and applications. The commitment to modernization and socialization of the economy does not resolve questions about the rate and timing of economic advance, the balance among sectors, and the permissible extent of deviations from socialist principle. The exercise of proletarian dictatorship does not specify a single model of party composition, procedures, and style; the attempt to create a classless

[2]Richard Lowenthal, "Development vs. Utopia in Communist Policy," in Johnson, ed., ibid., p. 33.

society based on the new socialist man does not reveal how this effort will relate to division of labor and differentiation demanded by rapid economic modernization; global opposition to capitalism and imperialism leaves open the degree to which considerations of national interest, security, and resources will govern foreign relations. Moreover, institutional and policy formulations inevitably reflect the social, political, economic, cultural, and geographic conditions of the society in question and the changes that occur in these conditions over time. In short, the basic ideological credo establishes long-range goals and a rough framework for achieving them but does not provide solutions for the crucial policy choices that the leaders of Communist countries face. At the same time, it requires that all decisions be justified in terms of its basic tenets in order to retain the legitimacy and identity of the system.

As the discussion of pre-1949 politics in Chapter 2 makes clear, the roots of Chinese Communist ideology are complex. The initial interest in Marxism was part of a general attraction to progressive Western ideas, strengthened by the anti-imperialism of Chinese intellectuals, the impressive victory of the October Revolution, and Bolshevik efforts to proselytise and to organize an international communist movement. However, the CCP could not remain a mere copy of the Communist Party of the Soviet Union (CPSU). Forced to the countryside in 1927, the CCP's struggle to survive led to the development of a specifically Chinese revolutionary strategy, political style, and leadership cohort. The primary author and leader of China's adaptation of Marxism was Mao Zedong,[3] and his very influential but problematic ideological legacy is known as "Mao Zedong Thought."

---

[3]The classic works on Mao Zedong are Edgar Snow, *Red Star Over China* (New York: Random House, 1937); Benjamin Schwartz, *Chinese Communism and the Rise of Mao* (Cambridge, Mass.: Harvard University Press, 1951); Stuart Schram, *The Political Thought of Mao Zedong*, rev. ed. (New York: Praeger, 1969); Stuart Schram, *Mao Tse-tung* (New York: Simon and Schuster, 1966); and Jerome Ch'en, *Mao and the Chinese Revolution* (New York: Oxford University Press, 1965). More recent works include John Starr, *Continuing the Revolution* (Princeton, N.J.: Princeton University Press, 1979); Ross Terrill, *Mao: A Biography* (New York: Oxford University Press, 1980); Helmut Martin, *Cult and Canon* (Armonk, N.Y.: M.E. Sharpe, 1982). A useful review of literature on Mao is Stuart Schram, "Mao Studies: Retrospect and Prospect," *China Quarterly*, no. 97 (March 1984): 95–125.

Mao is not credited with originating a new world view, but with creatively and successfully applying Marxism to Chinese conditions. The practical ideology identified with Mao has been the operating value system of the CCP since the 1940s. Although Mao's leftism and authoritarianism from 1957 until his death weakened his personal credibility, Mao Zedong Thought remains one of the basic pillars of Chinese orthodoxy. Beyond the official acceptance of Mao Zedong Thought, the influence of Mao's four decades of leadership have become part of the self-image of Chinese Communism.

In this Chapter, we will first consider the emergence of Mao Zedong Thought and some of its structural features. Since ideology is viewed as a guide to understanding reality in order to change it, we then consider patterns of change in the PRC.

IDEOLOGY AND MAO ZEDONG THOUGHT

Development of Mao Zedong Thought. Mao Zedong was primarily a leader engaged in revolutionary politics, not a theoretician. As a result, his thinking and writings were tied to practical political problems. Very few of his essays deal with exclusively theoretical questions. Because Mao's views and values are enmeshed in practical concerns, the question of what general doctrines constitute Mao Zedong Thought is one of interpretation. The Gang of Four, Hua Guofeng, and Deng Xiaoping all hold very different views of Mao Zedong Thought, and all are based on Mao's writings. Moreover, it is clear that Mao's thought continued to develop throughout his career. Although the Cultural Revolution gave the impression that Mao was an isolated, idealistic, and idiosyncratic thinker, he had a very different reputation earlier in his career. It is necessary to retrace Mao's political career in order to understand Mao's thought and the interpretations to which it has been subject.

Early twentieth-century China, the environment of Mao's youth, was in great turmoil. Feuding warlords trekked through his home province of Hunan; China's traditional culture appeared outmoded; and new ideas from the West were being introduced with dizzying rapidity. Young scholars still felt the mission to rule, but there was no longer a legitimate, bureaucratic path to power. The most idealistic and revolutionary Western doctrines had great appeal. Mao was an active local leader of the

May Fourth Movement of 1919, the anti-imperialist popular movement described in Chapter 2. At that time, Mao preferred Kropotkin's anarchism to Marxism because he thought that the latter's class struggle would taint the future society with the violence of the old. In his major pre-Marxist work, "The Great Union of the Popular Masses,"[4] Mao makes the suggestion that people with common problems form groups, and that alliances of such groups demand a new society. Such a "Great Union" would prevail over the small handful of actual exploiters without violence and usher in a new world era of enlightened, nonoppressive society.

The waning of the May Fourth Movement did not make Mao any less revolutionary, but it did convince him that mass enthusiasm by itself was insufficient.An organization of dedicated revolutionaries was necessary in order to create favorable conditions and to lead the masses to victory. The success of the Russian revolution made Marxism-Leninism especially attractive to frustrated May Fourth radicals such as Mao. He attended the founding congress of the CCP in Shanghai in 1921 and organized its Hunan branch. Mao was expelled from Hunan at the time that the first KMT-CCP United Front was forming, and he became involved as a CCP representative in various KMT activities. In 1925, Mao's interest in the revolutionary potential of the peasantry was rekindled by a visit to Hunan, and he became an impassioned advocate for active peasant participation in the anti-imperialist, antiwarlord revolution. The peasant activities against landlords that Mao encouraged hastened the split between the KMT and the CCP in 1927. The KMT and its warlord allies were very much stronger militarily than the CCP, and soon the remaining members of the CCP were escaping to distant rural areas. With a few hundred followers and bandits for allies, Mao settled in the Jinggang Mountains (Chingkangshan) on the Hunan-Jiangxi border and struggled to survive.

The combination of the necessity of surviving in rural areas surrounded by more powerful enemies and Mao's rev-

[4]Translated and introduced by Stuart Schram in *China Quarterly*, no. 49 (January 1972): 76–105. See also Robert Scalapino, "The Evolution of a Young Revolutionary—Mao Zedong in 1919–1921," *Journal of Asian Studies*, vol. 42, no. 1 (November 1982): 29–61.

olutionary-populist predisposition led Mao to develop a rural strategy for the Chinese revolution. The rural strategy involved much more than to "surround the cities from the countryside." Mao was venturing in untried directions, and Marxism-Leninism and the Bolshevik experience were of little help to him. Considerable trial and error were involved in its evolution, and ultimately the rural strategy was a complex and interdependent synthesis of military, political, and economic elements. Techniques of guerrilla warfare were an important element. Flexible maneuvers in friendly territory, surprise, and utilization of informal military assets helped Mao's isolated base area cope with its deficiency in material resources. Later, these techniques were useful against the invading Japanese. However, guerrilla warfare was only the military element of Mao's rural strategy, and it could not have succeeded without political and economic elements.

The political prerequisite of the rural strategy was to attract and sustain broad peasant support for CCP policies. Confiscating the land of landlords and rich peasants and distributing it to poor peasants was an important first step, but it was not sufficient for effective political mobilization. The CCP had to develop its claims to allegiance by pursuing tasks that benefitted the peasants and by becoming intimate enough with each village to recruit new activists and to isolate its enemies. The cardinal sin of a bad cadre was "estrangement from the masses." A cadre that was not in touch with the masses would be more likely to pursue unpopular or unsuccessful policies and, in any case, would be ineffective in transforming peasant appreciation for CCP policies into recruitment and mobilization. Therefore, Mao strongly criticized bureaucratic and dogmatic habits and insisted that cadres investigate the concrete conditions of their locality and be flexible in their policies. The strategy of staying close to the masses in order to mobilize them through effective leadership was later formulated as the "mass line."

Mao had more difficulty in arriving at a viable economic policy for his rural base areas. These were naturally poor areas; many of the old base areas were still receiving special economic assistance in 1984. The task of taking over a subsistence agrarian economy from its indigenous elite, recruiting an army from its best labor power, and then supporting both the population and the army would have been challenging for anyone. In addition, the base areas sustained the damage of blockades and invasions. Besides the general resource problems of the base areas, politically necessary policies, such as land redistribution, further reduced productivity. Land reform satisfied the land hunger of the peasants, but many did not have sufficient labor power or tools to work their share. Agricultural production in the Jiangxi Soviet usually dropped for the first few years after land reform, adding to the deprivations caused by war and forcing the CCP to rely on wealth seized from landlords for the major part of its budget. Although Mao began to stress cooperation and self-sufficiency in 1933, it was not until the 1940s that the encouragement of mutual-aid teams, mobilization of the army for production, and more moderate land reform policies began to resolve the economic bottleneck of rural revolution.

The development of Mao's personal political power during the 1930s was as slow and painful as the development of his policies. Although Mao was in charge of his first base area in 1927–1929, he was subject to continual meddling by emissaries from the Central Committee. When he moved to his larger base area in southern Jiangxi, he seemed to be in greater control initially, but within a year the Central Committee decided to move from its underground headquarters in Shanghai to his base area. After 1931, Mao lost political and then military control of the base area, although he remained in charge of government administration. The Central Committee was controlled by the "28 Bolsheviks," a group of Moscow-trained Stalinists, and their policies were virtually the opposite of those Mao was developing. Policies became dogmatic and Russian-derived; an extreme policy of class struggle was implemented; and military policy became more formal. Ultimately, the base area in Jiangxi was destroyed by Chiang Kai-shek, and in 1934 the CCP began the Long March, a legendarily long and difficult escape from Jiangxi to China's northwest.

Mao began his leadership role in the CCP on the Long March. He was in a good position to criticize the 28 Bolsheviks because of his own military and political successes before they assumed command of his base area, and he became chairman of the military commission at the Zunyi Conference in January 1935. Mao's role had expanded to general political leadership by 1936; however, he continued to face challenges from the Moscow faction until the early 1940s.[5] The responsibilities of general leadership that Mao faced after 1936 required that he formulate his techniques for rural revolution into guidelines for CCP activities. Moreover, the war with Japan that began in 1937 required a rethinking and reorientation of policy toward a patriotic united front. From 1936 to 1949, Mao wrote a number of works concerning military strategy, united front work, and the rectification of CCP political style; these became the official formulation of Mao Zedong Thought. From 1942 on, CCP members were required to study Mao's writings and master his approach to politics.

The consolidation of Mao's leadership in the 1940s depended on the continued success and development of his rural revolutionary strategy. Guerrilla warfare provided an effective form of resistance in areas under Japanese occupation, and by the end of the war, the CCP's base areas had a total population of 100 million. The political technique of the mass line encouraged the replacement of traditional village leadership by activists committed to the CCP. By 1945, CCP membership had grown to 1.2 million. Economic policy was successful enough to permit the CCP to survive KMT blockades and the burdens of war mobilization. When the postwar struggle between the CCP and the KMT for the control of China began, the solidity of CCP leadership and policies led to a sweeping victory by 1949, years earlier than Mao had anticipated.

The founding of the People's Republic of China (PRC) elevated Mao to head of state as well as Chairman of the CCP. In both the Leninist-Stalinist tradition and the Chinese imperial tradition, Mao now occupied the position of infallible leader. As the guardian of orthodoxy, Mao was now in a position to command rather than to persuade in ideological matters. Consequently, his public writings became much less frequent and were replaced by private, authoritative comments. An official four-volume edition of Mao's *Selected Works* was issued. Although the process of establishing Mao as China's Stalin had begun in the early 1940s, the success of the revolution and his

[5]See Gregor Benton, "The Second Wang Ming Line (1935–1938)," *China Quarterly*, no. 61 (March 1975): 61–94; and Raymond Wylie, *The Emergence of Maoism* (Stanford, Cal.: Stanford University Press, 1980).

position as an impeccable leading figure of state raised Mao far beyond his colleagues.

The task of ruling China induced Mao to write two important works in the 1950s. The first, "On the Ten Major Relationships" (1956),[6] argues against the assumption that in order to do one thing well other tasks must be neglected. Mao makes the dialectical argument that tasks are interdependent. For instance, one should not neglect agriculture and light industry in order to concentrate on heavy industry, because the development of heavy industry depends on the development of agriculture and light industry. Similarly, the relationships of center and localities, coastal and inland areas, the Hans and minority peoples, and other apparent dichotomies should be viewed as interdependent. Mao is not arguing for a static balance of resources, but he is against seeing options as trade-offs. Apparently, Mao would prefer a general effort that would attempt to tackle all related aspects of a problem at once.

Another important work of the 1950s was "On the Correct Handling of Contradictions Among the People" (1957). Influenced by the criticism of Stalin and unrest in Poland and Hungary, Mao admitted that incorrect leadership could lead to strife even after exploiting classes had been eliminated. Although "contradictions among the people" were essentially nonantagonistic, they could become antagonistic if they were mishandled. At the time this was used as an argument for tolerance, but the implication that political leadership could determine the character of socialist society paved the way for the Cultural Revolution's criticism of the party.

In the Great Leap Forward of 1958, Mao implemented the "general effort" approach to modernization that he recommended in his "On the Ten Major Relationships." Investment and industry were decentralized; bold new social reforms were introduced; and production was expected to mushroom on all fronts. China was expected to "grasp revolution and promote production" at the same time, because in Mao's view they could not be done separately. However, the Leap turned into a full-scale disaster despite some initial successes, and Mao had to permit the effort to restore production to take precedence. Meanwhile,

---

[6]Mao's major writings for 1949 to 1957 are in *Selected Works*, vol. 5.

Mao's forcing of Leap policies on the party and his subsequent attempt to control criticism of its failure created a fatal rift between Mao and the institutionalized party leadership under Liu Shaoqi. In 1962, Mao himself criticized his leadership in the Leap and proclaimed the need for democratic centralism within the party.[7] However, Mao had already begun to play an imperial revolutionary role. Concerned about the emergence of a bureaucratic class of party cadres and frustrated by its passive resistance to his radical initiatives, Mao opened the Cultural Revolution by calling on the masses to "bombard the headquarters." Although Mao did not anticipate that the criticism would be as widespread and violent as it became, he was sufficiently alienated from the party organization and concerned about the future of the revolution to permit the chaos and to identify with its radical direction.

Mao was not as dogmatic or as antiestablishment as the leftist ideologues whom he patronized (now known as the Gang of Four). The restoration of social order and the rebuilding of the party would have been impossible without Mao's active endorsement. Zhou Enlai and later the reinstated Deng Xiaoping remained symbols within the top leadership of Mao's lingering commitment to production as well as revolution. Mao's reluctance to choose between economic needs and revolutionary ideals led to policy oscillations in 1967–1976, as he shifted from one to the other. His inability to admit that there could be a conflict between the two aims gave the high ground of propaganda to the leftists, because their assumption that production would follow from revolution could not be contested openly. Thus Mao ended his political career, which had been based on the pragmatic evolution of a successful rural revolutionary strategy, publicly identified with a dogmatic leftism that threatened the material foundation of his regime.

Within a month of Mao's death on September 9, 1976, the leftists were easily swept aside by a broad coalition of more moderate leaders. The first concern of the new leadership was to establish the legitimacy of its rule. Hua Guofeng was presented

---

[7]Mao elaborated his views on democratic centralism in a very interesting speech with the title, "Talk at an Enlarged Working Conference Convened by the Central Committee of the CCP," *PR*, no. 27 (July 7, 1978): 6–22.

as Mao's faithful and hand-picked successor, and the Gang of Four was exposed as corrupt and hypocritical manipulators. Hua took the lead in homage in Mao. He had a mausoleum built in Tiananmen in record time, he edited the fifth volume of Mao's *Selected Works*, and he began to shape his personal image after Mao's. Nevertheless, the content of Mao Zedong Thought had already begun a major shift. The works highlighted by Hua were from the 1950s and underscored Mao's interest in production. Hua retained Mao's dictum about taking class struggle as the "key link," but he also declared the end of the Cultural Revolution and the need for "great order across the land." China had entered a new era of modernization, and it was unclear how much relevance was retained by Mao's directives.

Transition from Hua Guofeng's efforts to reorient Maoism to Deng Xiaoping's rejection of the Cultural Revolution and criticism of Mao occurred in 1978. Using Mao's saying "Seek truth from facts," Deng's supporters said that policy should be based on current realities rather than on Mao's directives. Deng argued that Mao himself had opposed blind dogmatism in politics; and, in a new era, China should follow Mao's example rather than his words. After a factional struggle fought around the slogan of "Practice is the only criterion for determining truth," Deng consolidated his control over the party at the third Plenum of the eleventh CC in December 1978.

The new official interpretation of Mao Zedong Thought was provided by the "Resolution on Certain Questions in the History of Our Party Since the Founding of the PRC."[8] This complicated document passed by the Sixth Plenum of the Eleventh CC criticized the excesses of the 1957 anti-rightist campaign and the Great Leap forward, while condemning totally the Cultural Revolution. Mao is said to have "initiated and led" the Cultural Revolution, although he is given some credit for preventing a total degeneration of the party and state. On the other hand, Mao's leading role in the success of the revolution is recognized, as is his contribution during the 1950s to socialist construction. Mao is viewed as the principal author of Mao Zedong Thought, but not as its proprietor. According to the document, the

[8]*BR*, vol. 24, no. 27 (July 6, 1981): 10–39.

"erroneous 'left' theses, upon which Mao Zedong based himself in initiating the 'cultural revolution,' were obviously inconsistent with the system of Mao Zedong Thought, which is the integration of the universal principles of Marxism-Leninism with the concrete practice of the Chinese revolution."[9] Thus Mao Zedong thought has become separated from Mao Zedong not only by death but by official interpretation.

STRUCTURAL FEATURES OF MAO ZEDONG THOUGHT

Despite the development and changes in Mao's thinking, there are certain elements that may be called structural features of Mao Zedong Thought. The first two, revolutionary populism and practicality, are the most fundamental. The remaining three features are dialectics, the importance of process, and unity through struggle.

Revolutionary Populism. Even before he became a Marxist, the premise of Mao's politics was that the organized masses would ultimately prevail. In suggesting a "Great Union of the Popular Masses" in 1919, Mao expected China and the world to be transformed from below by a broad organization of society's lower classes. Mao thought that mass participation was the only way to bring about a real revolution in society and politics and that organized mass support would be invincible. Elite regimes were not only illegitimate, they were weakened by their small popular base.

Marxism-Leninism shaped Mao's view of revolutionary populism in two respects. First, as Jerome Ch'en has shown,[10] class struggle became the framework of Mao's view of society. From the early 1920s, Mao's social investigations were formulated in terms of economic classes related by exploitation. Second, a certain type of elitism was justified, namely the revolutionary leadership of the party, that is, the "vanguard of the proletariat." But broad mass participation remained the touchstone of Mao's

[9]Ibid., p. 30.

[10]Jerome Ch'en, "The Development and Logic of Mao Tse-tung's Thought," in Chalmers Johnson, ed., *Ideology and Politics in Contemporary China* (Seattle: University of Washington Press, 1973), pp. 78–116.

politics.[11] Mao always tried to achieve a maximum alliance of forces against an isolated handful of enemies.

The Cultural Revolution demonstrated that Mao was more committed to revolutionary populism than he was to Marxist-Leninist orthodoxy. When he felt that the CCP itself was becoming an elite isolated from the masses, Mao exposed the party to mass criticism. To be sure, Mao couched his attacks in terms of "party persons in power going the capitalist road," but the Marxist economic definition of classes is stretched beyond recognition by such a usage. The same example of the Cultural Revolution shows that populism did not imply a democracy in which the wishes of the masses determined government policy. The content of populism was assumed to be revolution against exploitation, and popular support was gauged by success in mobilization, not by ballots.

Practicality. Despite the revolutionary romanticism of his later years, one of the strongest characteristics of Mao's writings was his concern for effectiveness. Mao's practicality had a definite empirical dimension. Mao insisted on personal, concrete investigation and once raised the slogan of "no investigation, no right to speak." He often criticized higher authorities for relying solely on reading reports in their offices or for substituting dogma for reality, and his own lengthy investigations of rural conditions were models of fact-finding. Clearly, Mao's empiricism had dwindled by the time of the Great Leap Forward, but he still adjusted his leftist interventions in the light of unwelcome facts about their effects.

The most important dimension of Mao's practicality, and one which distinguishes him from Marx and Lenin, is his attention to the problems of political leadership. From Mao's point of view, leaders at all levels were involved in a constant effort to combine their experience, investigation among the masses, ideology, and commands from superiors into decision making that would best fit their opportunities. The complex and shifting nature of the world meant that some mistakes were inevitable,

[11] Maurice Meisner has shown that Mao's populism diverged from Leninism in the direction of the Russian populists. See Meisner, *Marxism, Maoism and Utopianism* (Madison: University of Wisconsin Press, 1982).

but they could be minimized by experience and prompt correction of misunderstandings. Leaders who were too dogmatic or who allowed themselves to become separated from the masses by bureaucratic habits were courting disaster. Correct leadership for Mao was situationally appropriate leadership. By contrast, leadership quality is only an incidental concern for Marx, and Lenin tended to focus on the ideological correctness of leadership.

Even Mao's most theoretical contributions were inspired by the practical concerns of leadership. Mao's essay "On Practice"[12] analyses the problematic relationship between theory and practice that makes necessary constant alertness and flexibility. The main thesis of his essay "On Contradiction" is that "the particularity of contradiction is universal," which means that each problem must be analysed on its own terms and on the basis of concrete investigation. In his theoretical works, Mao never questions his Marxist-Leninist framework but instead concentrates on the theoretical dimensions of the problems of political leadership.

Dialectics. A third structural feature of Mao's thought is dialectics. Mao's dialectics has roots in both Marxist and traditional Chinese philosophy. In contrast to ordinary logic, which stresses the identity of things and therefore their autonomy, dialectics stresses the essential interrelationship of things and therefore the possibility of one thing transforming into another thing or even into its opposite. Dialectics sees a changing world driven by internal contradictions, rather than a static world of separate objects. Dialectics is especially important to Marxism, because the contradiction of class struggle is expected to be transformed by revolution into a new socialist society.

For Mao, dialectics was primarily a very flexible method of political analysis that allowed him to concentrate his attention on one problem while affirming the interrelationship of that problem with other problems. In his essay "On Contradiction," Mao claims that situations have a principal contradiction and a principal aspect of the contradiction. This justifies the concentration of effort on only one aspect of a complex situation, with

---

[12]"On Practice" and "On Contradiction" are both included in *Selected Works*, vol. 1.

the expectation that the focus will shift as the situation develops. Such an approach encourages a dynamic imbalance in policy.

Another set of dialectical categories important to Mao's thought is that of antagonistic and nonantagonistic contradictions. Antagonistic contradictions are those "between the enemy and ourselves," in which the victory of one side means the defeat of the other. Class struggle is the chief example of an antagonistic contradiction. A nonantagonistic contradiction is a conflict between individuals or groups with basically harmonious interests. Because of the underlying common interests, nonantagonistic contradictions can be handled by education or persuasion. Within socialist society, most contradictions are "among the people," and therefore nonantagonistic. However, such contradictions can develop into antagonistic ones if they are mishandled by the leadership.

Importance of Process. Perhaps because of his dialectical outlook, Mao more highly valued political processes and movements than he did institutions and professionalism. Revolution, the ultimate process, was not viewed by Mao as a stepping stone to a perfect, unchanging society, but rather as a transition to a different kind of process. As he put it in "On Practice": "The epoch of world communism will be reached when all mankind voluntarily and consciously changes itself and the world."[13] Later, Mao formulated his idea as "uninterrupted revolution," and during the Cultural Revolution he called for more cultural revolutions in the future. Underlying Mao's preference for process was a conviction that only massive collective efforts could raise society to a new level. Problems that, taken individually, were tedious or difficult to solve were removed with little effort when part of a general campaign. For example, political education of the peasants was not easy, given their limited horizons and suspicion of outsiders; however, if there was class struggle in the village, then convincing analogies to warlords and imperialism could be drawn.

The mass campaign is a political process that was developed in the base areas and is still influential in PRC politics. In 1933, Mao developed a comprehensive campaign technique in which

[13]"On Practice," ibid., vol. 1, p. 308.

cadres were carefully prepared and an enthusiastic mass campaign was launched that integrated political, economic, and military tasks.[14] Such campaigns worked very well in the base areas because their goals of survival and fighting Japan were easily understood, and because they made use of mass enthusiasm in place of scarce material and professional resources. The technique of mass campaigns was more problematic after 1949 because they disrupted normal operations and often led to excesses, factionalism, and feigned enthusiasm.

The corollaries of Mao's faith in political process were a low opinion of routine political institutions and a suspicion of professionals. Mao thought that neither the internal disciplinary procedures of the party nor elected institutions such as the people's congresses could ensure a closeness between leaders and masses. Government by a Communist party was, in the last analysis, still government by officials, and in time they would take on bureaucratic airs and interests. Many analysts view the Cultural Revolution as an attempt to negate the routinizing of Chinese politics.

Professionalism is somewhat analogous to organizational routine because it assumes that problems are best handled by experts. Although Mao was not crudely anti-intellectual, he was deeply suspicious of the effectiveness and motivation of professionalism. By claiming that expert knowledge is necessary in order to handle certain problems properly, professionalism poses subtle limits to both mass activism and to party power. The challenge to party power was answered by the demand that cadres be "both red and expert." Mao also encouraged the opening up of professional spheres to mass activity. Probably the most successful case was the "barefoot doctor" program, which created a vast corps of peasant medical workers who brought basic medical care to the villages. During the Cultural Revolution, Mao's populist responses to the implicit stratification and privileges of professionalism devastated China's intellectual and technical institutions. Experts were transferred to low-level jobs;

[14]The origins of Mao's campaign strategy are described in Brantly Womack, *Foundations of Mao Zedong's Political Thought, 1917–1935* (Honolulu: University of Hawaii Press, 1982), pp. 144–187. Their application in Yenan is described in Mark Selden, *The Yenan Way in Revolutionary China* (Cambridge, Mass.: Harvard University Press, 1971).

higher education was closed down; entrance examinations were abolished; and intellectuals were considered (in a vituperative radical slogan) the "stinking ninth category" of bad-class elements. The reversal of such policies was a major source of the popularity of the post-Mao regime.

Unity through Struggle. Coordination and targeting of effort is a major strategic question for a political party. Mao's basic response to this problem was to assume that the CCP led a broad coalition of basically compatible classes unified by a collective interest and arrayed against a small number of clear and irreconcilable enemies.

> Who are our enemies? Who are our friends? This is a question of first importance for the revolution.... To ensure that we will definitely achieve success in our revolution and will not lead the masses astray, we must pay attention to uniting with our real friends in order to attack our real enemies.[15]

Throughout the history of the Chinese Communist movement runs this attempt to identify the "people" (all those with whom the CCP can unite) and the "enemies" (all those who are targets of the people's struggle) in such a way as to maximize the coalition without compromising revolutionary objectives.

Three variant formulations of the coalition have been offered since Mao came to power in 1935. During the Yanan period, the formulation was relatively easy and nationalistic. The "people" were essentially all patriotic Chinese; the "enemies" the Japanese and their Chinese collaborators. Class issues were not forgotten but were made secondary to the national issue, permitting a highly inclusive united front. During the Civil War of 1946–1949 and the early years of the PRC, Mao returned to a class-based definition that excluded some Chinese who might earlier have belonged to the anti-Japanese "people."

> Who are the people? At the present stage in China, they are the working class, the peasantry, the urban petty bourgeoisie and the national bourgeoisie.... They enforce their dictatorship over

[15] Mao Zedong, "Analysis of the Classes in Chinese Society," in *Selected Works*, vol. 1, p. 13.

the running dogs of imperialism—the landlord class and bureaucrat-bourgeoisie, as well as the representatives of those classes, the Kuomintang reactionaries and their accomplices.[16]

This definition reduced the scope of "the people" and authorized sharp internal conflict within Chinese society, but it still portrayed a high degree of national unity. The Korean War, the program of national reconstruction, and the relative smallness and distinctness of the enemy classes permitted retention of much of the patriotic flavor of the wartime period. Moreover, the enemies were presumably doomed as class components, although not necessarily as individuals, within mainland society—the landlords and bureaucrat-bourgeoisie by land reform and socialism, the KMT forces by suppression of counterrevolutionaries. In effect, the definition forecast rapid progress toward total national unity simply by elimination of the enemy. By 1956–1957, the CCP was proclaiming unprecedented national unity, the effective defeat of the enemy classes, and the secure establishment of socialism.[17]

However, it was precisely at this juncture that Mao offered a third definition of the people, shifting the operative distinction from class status to ideological commitment. The shift is explained most forthrightly in Mao's 1957 speech, "On the Correct Handling of Contradictions Among the People." Mao opened by asserting that "Never has our country been as united as it is today"—recording his recognition, too, of progress toward eradication of class enemies. His real message in this regard was to observe that "the people" change in composition from one historical period to another. Noting the meaning of the term in the two earlier periods, as described above, he then said,

> At this stage of building socialism, all classes, strata, and social groups which approve, support, and work for the cause of socialist construction belong to the category of the people, while those

[16]"On the People's Democratic Dictatorship," in ibid., vol. 4, pp. 417–18.

[17]One of the major pieces of leftist evidence about Liu Shaoqi's revisionism was his articulation of these points in his "Political Report" to the eighth Party Congress in September 1956. Text in *The Eighth National Congress of the Communist Party of China. Volume 1: Documents* (Peking: Foreign Languages Press, 1956), pp. 13–112.

social forces and groups which resist the socialist revolution and are hostile to and try to wreck socialist construction, are enemies of the people.[18]

For the following twenty years class struggle was redefined in terms of ideological commitment as evidenced by attitudes and behavior. During the 1960s, relatively minor differences in ideology were often magnified into struggles between the proletariat and the bourgeoisie. Of course, one's assigned class background was also important. Attacks on old enemy classes and tension between children of "good" and "bad" family background were prominent features of the Red Guard movement in the early Cultural Revolution.[19] Generally, the Maoist period brought heightened insistence on ideological education and a tendency to interpret all political conflict as ideological conflict, with the enemy class designation attributed to those said to deviate from Mao.

From one perspective, the ideological distinction between people and enemies has symbolized a high degree of national integration because it has excluded relatively few Chinese from the ranks. "The people" invariably are said to be over 90 percent of the population, whereas the enemies are usually said to be a handful. Obviously, however, there is a forced and insecure quality to the constantly professed unity of the people, for it relies heavily on the threat of expulsion from community ranks of anyone in opposition. Those branded as enemies lose their right to participate in the political community to express and defend their position. In other words, they are not allowed to damage the unity of the people either conceptually or politically. Although few are actually assigned enemy status, virtually everyone is vulnerable to exclusion. The purges of Liu Shaoqi, Lin Biao, the Gang, and other top leaders are dramatic evidence of the uncertainties produced by this ideological definition of political community.

If political conflict within the system is tentatively legitimized but made hazardous by the possibility of being defined as antag-

---

[18] Mao, *Selected Works*, vol. 5, p. 385.

[19] For an overview of the political effects of class background, see Anita Chan, "Images of China's Social Structure: The Changing Perspectives of Canton Students," *World Politics*, vol. 34, no. 3 (April 1982): 295–323.

onistic, what form does its expression take? Issue-oriented conflict is typically carried out among the elite in a cryptic style in which the positions and personalities in opposition are not made explicit. Yet, the infrequent occasions in which the debate is open and broader segments of the population join in are extremely significant. The most prominent examples of relatively open-ended public debate and criticism are the "hundred flowers" period of 1957, the early Cultural Revolution, and the "democracy wall" period of 1978–1979. It is instructive to note that periods of relatively intense popular political activity have coincided with serious intraparty debate over basic developmental choices. Despite the generally controlled character of popular politics in the PRC, crisis periods seem to create opportunities for mass participation.[20]

CYCLICAL CHANGE

Reflecting on the course of Mao Zedong's politics and the structural principles of his thought, it is clear that change, whether intentional or unintentional, has been a dominant feature of Chinese political life. The doctrine of uninterrupted revolution symbolized the leftists' absolute preference for mass activity over institutionalization. Even the post-Mao regime, which is far more committed to institutionalization than Mao ever was, is not opposed to change. It hopes to stabilize the disorderly ebb and flow of mass politics that characterized the Cultural Revolution in order to accelerate economic and social change. In other words, the current regime prefers a secular change, one that proceeds ABCDEF..., to a cyclical surge of ABABAB.... However, the two cannot be separated entirely, and the cyclical pattern of change is still very important in PRC politics.

Cyclical change may be defined as regular movement from one condition to another, each phase representing the recurrence of some previous condition. The movement may be frequent and even extreme, but the larger pattern has a static quality

[20]For a discussion of crisis periods, in which great pressures for change and adaptation in a political system produce heightened levels of system activity and significant developmental choices, see Gabriel Almond, "Political Development: Analytical and Normative Perspectives," *Comparative Political Studies* vol. 1, no. 4 (January 1969): 454–57.

owing to its repetition of previous phases. In its simplest form, this type of change may be oscillation between two poles, or it may involve progression through a more complicated cycle of several stages. Description of cycles in social history necessarily simplifies and distorts reality; there is always some evolutionary change in human affairs so that no cycle is exactly like its predecessors.

Mobilization-Consolidation. Recurring mass campaigns have been a distinctive feature of CCP politics since 1933 and have been a major pattern in the government of the PRC since its inception.[21] Despite their bewildering diversity in scope, duration, goals, and intensity, these campaigns progress through mobilization and consolidation phases. The mobilization phase defines, tests, and attacks campaign goals, while the consolidation phase assesses, corrects, and consolidates the results. Campaigns tend to give Chinese political life a pulsating quality of advance and retreat, of political intensification and relaxation. The tone of politics in a particular locality or policy sector depends heavily on whether or not a campaign affecting that unit or sector is in progress and, if so, what phase it is in. The mobilization phase tends to drain energy and attention away from regular tasks, so rural campaigns (other than production campaigns) usually are not begun during seasons of peak agricultural production. When the 1984 party rectification campaign was in full swing in Beijing, leading cadres in central ministries were divided into two groups, one to manage the campaign within the ministry and one to handle regular duties. The enthusiasm of the mobilization phase encourages excesses, but victims usually must wait until the consolidation phase—or a future campaign that counters the thrust of the first one—to press their grievances.

It is tempting to extend campaign characteristics to larger cycles in the Chinese political process. The most elaborate and provocative effort has described a six-phase cycle in rural policy,

[21] See Gordon Bennett, *Yundong: Mass Campaigns in Chinese Communist Leadership* (Berkeley: University of California, Center for Chinese Studies, 1976); and Charles Cell, *Revolution at Work: Mobilization Campaigns in China* (New York: Academic Press, 1977).

with eight cycles initiated between 1949 and 1965.[22] It is also possible to distinguish some generalized mobilization and consolidation periods in national politics—the former dominated by major national campaigns, the latter sorting out and modifying the results. Mobilization periods occurred, for example, in 1949–1952 (land reform and other early campaigns), in 1955–1956 (accelerated collectivization), 1957–1958 (the Great Leap and communes), and in 1965–1967 (the early Cultural Revolution). Each was followed by a consolidating relaxation and/or modification of campaign goals and policies. One can see "radical" initiative in the mobilizations and "moderate" guidance in the consolidations.

The student of Chinese politics must be sensitive to the campaign syndrome and its relationship to the tone of national politics but must not push this type of generalization too far. Campaigns have been too numerous and diverse to yield a single, consistent pattern in the system as a whole. The larger national cycles seem most valid for the 1950s and possibly the early 1960s, when relative consensus within the CCP permitted policy oscillation. It is much harder to sort out mobilization and consolidation phases from the early 1960s and later, since radical and moderate positions hardened into more open and constant conflict. Rather than alteration, there was confused competition in which rival factions turned campaigns on each other. These conflicts also exposed details, or alleged details, of earlier campaigns, thereby revealing some of the inadequacies of simplified cyclical models for Chinese politics. Instead of a policy cycle, these struggles often displayed a factional cycle of out-groups replacing in-groups. It is even more difficult to characterize the

[22] William Skinner and Edwin Winckler, "Compliance Succession in Rural Communist China: A Cyclical Theory," in Amitai Etzioni, ed., *Complex Organizations: A Sociological Reader*, 2nd ed., (New York: Holt, Rinehart and Winston, 1969), pp. 410–38. The approach was criticized by Andrew Nathan, "Policy Oscillation in the PRC: A Critique," *China Quarterly*, no. 68 (December 1976): 720–33. It was rebutted by Edwin Winckler, "Policy Oscillations in the PRC: A Reply," ibid., pp. 734–50. Further, more quantitative discussion is provided by Charles Cell, "The Utility of Mass Mobilization Campaigns in China: A Partial Test of the Skinner-Winckler Compliance Model," in Sidney Greenblatt, Richard Wilson, and Amy Wilson eds., *Organizational Behavior in Chinese Society* (New York: Praeger, 1981). pp. 25–46.

post-Mao period in terms of campaign cycles. Since Mao's death there has been a paradox of institutionalizing campaigns in which reforms meant to regularize life in China are pushed in a mobilizational style. There have also been long-term policy developments that promise to have no immediate ebbtide of retrenchment. Despite these cautions concerning the applicability of the campaign model, it is worthwhile to examine two areas in which campaign mobilizations have had significant impact.

Institutional Instability. The political structure of the PRC has experienced periods of both institutionalization and institutional instability, with the most intense national campaigns serving as the primary source of instability. The distinction here is not simply institutional growth versus institutional destruction; obviously, some parts of the political structure have been more durable than others, so that the changes referred to have never been total reverses. Rather, it is one between development of institutions along prescribed or established lines in certain periods and open-ended experimentation with institutional forms in others. In periods of institutionalization, the elements and interrelationships of the structure have been fixed so that its development has followed predictable patterns; in periods of institutional fluidity, existing forms have been challenged or new ones introduced so that the outcome has been in doubt. Stability has been characterized by centralization and greater security for both the party and specialist elites, while instability is usually accompanied by decentralization and an expansion of active nonelite political participation.

Between 1949 and 1953, China experienced a period of institutional fluidity, since many institutional arrangements were temporary and a great deal of experimentation was occurring. By the end of 1953, the basic outlines of socialist political and economic structure had been established, bringing a period of institutionalization, generally coinciding with the First Five-Year Plan and formalized by the 1954 constitution. There were continued institutional changes during these years, particularly the acceleration of collectivization in 1955, but they were essentially changes in the pace or timing of existing plans. The Eighth Party Congress in 1956 still tended toward institutionalization. The Great Leap Forward was a period of pronounced institutional fluidity characterized by general rejection of the Soviet model and experimentation with new forms and relationships. Institutionalization resumed in 1960, building on a combination of pre-Leap patterns of organization and some of the policies initiated in the Leap—for example, the commune framework, at least verbal commitment to class struggle and revolutionary transformation, and repoliticization of the PLA. This period continued until 1966, when the Cultural Revolution shattered the prevailing pattern of institutional development and opened the system to major structural innovations. After the Ninth Party Congress, prescriptive guidelines for renewed institutionalization on Maoist terms were established, however, in this case the intensifying elite controversy over Cultural Revolution reforms and succession paralyzed the process. After 1976, the post-Mao leadership explicitly encouraged an institutionalization that bore many similarities, in both tone and structural content, to the mid-1950s institutionalization that accompanied the FFYP and the 1954 state constitution. Some current areas of reform were introduced by the re-publication of policy speeches from the 1950s.

Variations in Popular Political Life. Grass roots political life in China is deeply affected by whether or not campaigns are based on class struggle, that is, the antagonistic contradiction between the state and groups of individuals considered "enemies of the people." Frequently occurring in mobilization phases, "antagonistic" struggle produces great political tension owing to the severe consequences—public denunciation and sanctions— that attend identification as an "enemy." Examples include mobilizations against landlords and counterrevolutionaries in 1950–1951, against rightists in the summer of 1957, against capitalist-roaders in 1965–1967, and against the Gang and their supporters in 1976–1977. Early class struggles led to the ostracism of the victims. However, they became so extensive during the Cultural Revolution that factionalism resulted as people banded together to protect themselves and to attack others.

"Nonantagonistic" struggle is more likely to occur between campaigns or in consolidation phases, when coexistence among different classes in socialist society is being emphasized. Errors and deviations are criticized, but the object is education and reform rather than punishment or expulsion from the ranks of the people. Nonantagonistic struggle attempts to "cure the illness to save the patient" in order to resolve "contradictions among the people," in Mao's terminology. Rectification campaigns within the CCP are primarily nonantagonistic struggles. Other examples include investigation of land reform results in 1951, the early "hundred flowers" criticism in 1957 (before the CCP initiated class struggle against the critics), and the criticism during 1961–1962 of cadre behavior during the Great Leap. In both the Cultural Revolution and the campaign against the Gang, class struggle eventually focused on a few key enemies, promising reintegration for others who reformed. Alternation between these different forms of struggle is neither neat nor predictable, but it is an important campaign-related feature of Chinese politics.

Mobilization and consolidation have also produced variations in the degree of party control over popular political action. The mass line leads the CCP to mix its concern for organizational control with calls for mass spontaneity and initiative. As a result, mobilization phases have sometimes produced cases in which local initiative has carried the movement beyond its central guidelines; whereas consolidation phases have been vulnerable to popular reactions exceeding the leadership's view of appropriate correction of mistakes.

The reconstruction years and the Cultural Revolution stand out as periods in which the looseness of controls relative to the intensity of the campaign permitted considerable spontaneous mass activity. In some cases, the actions in question—primarily by peasants' associations in land reform and by Red Guard factions in the Cultural Revolution—had official approval but not direct leadership. In other cases, they usually attacked the center's targets but did so with excessive violence or zeal. In the most extreme cases, they rejected central authority and became a vehicle for localized interests hostile to central objectives. The early part of the Great Leap was another period of considerable latitude in local implementation of directives. Here, initiative led not so much to excessive or unauthorized political struggle as to overly ambitious efforts by local cadres to realize the Leap's more radical features. The peasants and basic-level leaders generally did not encourage this spontaneity (although some apparently pushed for the free supply system), but they were inevitably caught up in it through the mass meetings and discussions that the movement required.

While spontaneity in mobilization phases has tended toward unwanted violence and radicalism, its rare occurrences in consolidation phases have been in reaction or even rebellion against party authority. For example, most of the criticism by intellectuals during the hundred flowers campaign was within the guidelines of the CCP's call for rectification, but some of it did attack the party's leadership as such. More important, student critics engaged in physical assaults on cadres and efforts to organize interuniversity exchanges of experiences and ideas. Peasant and worker unrest during the same period was relatively high, with many reports of peasant withdrawals from cooperatives.[23]

Once again, the point is not to argue that there is a clear correlation between campaign phases and popular political spontaneity; both variables are too complex for that. For example, there was a good deal of spontaneous dissident activity throughout 1974–1979, including factory disruptions, dissident wall posters, the Tiananmen Incident of April 5, 1976, and underground publications, that was not linked clearly to particular phases of a campaign cycle. What is significant here is that popular political action has repeatedly exceeded officially prescribed limits at both ends of the political spectrum, suggesting that such swings are not aberrations but a regular part of the political process. Its limitations notwithstanding, cyclical analysis makes an important contribution in reminding us that there is no single version of "normal" politics in China.

SECULAR CHANGE

Purely cyclical interpretations of Chinese politics founder on the reality of secular change. That is, even if there is a tendency to follow an oscillating pattern of mobilization and consolidation, long-term evolutionary change alters the issues and context so that earlier cycles cannot be repeated. Even if the form of cyclical change remained unaffected, the content and outcome of each cycle would be different, and we have seen that the campaign

[23] Roderick MacFarquhar, *The Hundred Flowers Campaign and the Chinese Intellectuals* (New York: Praeger, 1960), pp. 130–73, 231–47.

form itself has been affected by larger developments. This section identifies four particularly important areas of secular change— change in economic resources, socioeconomic change, changes in political culture and participation, and change in political leadership. The discussion will be quite general, drawing on the historical survey of Chapter 3 and anticipating some points to be developed more fully in later chapters.

Change in Economic Resources. The horizons of political decisionmaking are set by available resources.[24] As resources change over time, the starting point, goals, and priorities of political decisions change. China's achievements in economic development since 1949 have transformed the resource context of Chinese politics in some areas and have affected it less in others. Data describing the changes are presented in Appendices A, B, and C. As a result of the inevitably uneven development, the issues of politics have shifted.

Paradoxically, some of China's most impressive accomplishments have been in slowing certain kinds of secular change, namely those of population growth and redistribution. Although China's population has almost doubled from 542 million in 1949 to 1.015 billion in 1982, the birth rate since 1971 has been very low compared to other developing countries. Nevertheless, population control is still a major area of policy emphasis, and current regulations are the most stringent in PRC history. China's population has remained overwhelmingly rural despite industrialization and the attractions of urban life. In 1982, the population was still 79 percent rural, only a 10 percent decline since 1949. Also, there has been little interprovincial shift in population. The rural economy has had to bear the brunt of population increases, and rural industry has made a considerable contribution to industrialization. By contrast, some developing countries

[24]The statistics used in this section are derived from the following sources: *China: Socialist Economic Development,* 3 vol., World Bank (Washington: World Bank, 1983); Zhu Qingfang, "Major Economic and Social Achievements" *BR,* vol. , no. 40 (October 1, 1984): 16–28; *Zhongguo tongji nianjian 1983* (1983 Statistical Yearbook of China), Beijing: Zhongguo Tongji Chubanshe, 1983; Wu Dingguang, "Wo guo nongye laodong renkou yu gengdi di guanxi" (The relationship between the agricultural labor population and arable land) *Shehui kexue yanjiu (Social Science Research),* no. 5 (1984).

have more urbanization than industrialization, resulting in large urban slums. The population has become better educated: in comparison to 1952, enrollments in 1982 were six times higher at the college level, fifteen times higher at the high school level, and three times higher at the primary school level. Current investment in higher education is dictated by its slow growth relative to middle schools in the preceding decades. The population is now bound together by much higher levels of communication and commerce, although the road system remains one of the least developed in the world.

In general, the productivity of the Chinese economy has risen much faster than population growth. By 1983, the total output value was twenty times that of 1949, and industrial assets had grown seventeen times. In 1983, Chinese industry could produce the output value of 1949 in eight days. Compared to other developing countries, the output of China's industrial sector is large, the service sector is small, and agriculture is average. Energy production has tripled since 1965, and coal, oil, and hydroelectric reserves promise further development. Chinese industries make intensive albeit inefficient use of energy, while household energy consumption is still quite low. Increase in agricultural productivity has been less dramatic than that of industry, registering a threefold growth since 1952, an average of 2.7 percent per year. However, the conditions for agricultural growth were much less favorable. The amount of cultivated land actually declined due to new nonagricultural construction, and with population increase the amount of sown land for each agricultural worker has dwindled one-third. To put the agricultural situation in world perspective, in 1978 each agricultural worker in China had an average of three-quarters of an acre of arable land, compared to 1.5 acres in Japan, 4.8 acres in the Soviet Union, 39.4 acres in the United States, and 38.5 acres in Canada. Even though the productivity per acre is high—1,612 kilograms per acre compared to 1,417 in the United States and 759 in the Soviet Union—the productivity of each agricultural worker is limited by the land at his or her disposal. From 1960 to 1978 productivity per agricultural worker grew only 23 percent in China, compared to 215 percent in the United States, 247 percent in the Soviet Union, and 143 percent in Canada. Despite these disadvantages, Chinese agriculture has moved forward by means of reorganization, irrigation, and fertilizer. Progress since 1977 has been exceptionally good, comparable to or better than that of agriculture in developed countries. The sector most often neglected in Communist countries is that of services, and China has been no exception. Socialization in the middle and late 1950s led to a withering of urban small-scale enterprises, and leftist pressure against rural sideline industries and fairs had the same effect in the countryside. In the past few years, the economy has again diversified to include more individual laborers and marketing enterprises.

Despite the continuing poverty in China, the economic advances sketched above have led to significant tangible benefits for the population. Per capita income (adjusted for inflation) increased almost seven times from 1949 to 1983, although it remains only one-tenth that of advanced countries. According to the World Bank, "China's most remarkable achievement during the past three decades has been to make low-income groups far better off in terms of basic needs than their counterparts in most other poor countries."[25] Life expectancy has increased at twice the rate of other developing countries, rising from 36 years in 1950 to 69 years in 1980. This increase reflects Chinese accomplishments in the distribution of basic health care and nutrition. Meanwhile, inflation has been quite modest. The total retail price index was up only 57 percent between 1950 and 1983. In keeping with China's socialist orientation, many goods, services, and opportunities that would be allocated by price in capitalist countries are subsidized, rationed, or allocated by work unit.

China's long-term growth has been modulated by the Cultural Revolution, and especially by the Great Leap. In both cases, many economic indicators showed a year or two of sharp downturn followed by recovery. The period of 1958–1978 was generally one of somewhat slower growth. During this period, the total output value of society grew by 7 percent per year, compared to 8 percent per year in the 1978–1983 period. In general, the post-Mao era has been quite successful in economic growth, although at the cost of greater inflation and budget deficits. Previous economic success poses somewhat different economic tasks for the post-Mao regime. It must rectify the gross inefficiencies in earlier economic

[25] World Bank, *Socialist Economic Development*, 1:11.

construction, readjust the pace of development in order to overcome bottlenecks caused by uneven progress, and evolve a policy and managment mechanism appropriate to a more complex economy and society. Whether or not these challenges are met, Chinese politics in the 1980s faces an agenda different from that of earlier periods.

Socioeconomic Change. Socioeconomic change in post-1949 China has altered significantly the social basis of Chinese politics, creating new sources of influence and conflict within the system. This does not mean that Communist efforts at economic development have been uniformly successful or that Chinese social structure has undergone a total transformation since 1949. Nonetheless, Chinese society has experienced fundamental changes that have altered the relative weights of various political actors and issues. These changes are a result of rapid modernization and socialization of the system, either accelerated or initiated following the Communist victory in 1949.

One of the most pronounced changes has been the elimination or political neutralization of some social strata and the expansion of others. The landlords, merchants, and industrialists who held dominant political influence before 1949 have disappeared, while the ranks of industrial workers, state employees, and intellectuals (including middle school graduates as well as more highly trained technical and professional personnel) have increased sharply. Although the urban population remains only 20 percent of China's total, it has increased almost fourfold, from 58 million in 1949 to 212 million in 1982. Significant changes have also affected the countryside, for collectivization transformed the peasant from tenant or owner-cultivator to an agricultural laborer whose labor and rewards were largely determined by the local collective. Since 1979, another fundamental transformation has been occurring in which peasants contract on an individual or family basis with the collective for tasks and resources. Although current policies do not simply return peasants to their precollective situation, they do mark a major and long-term reversal of the trend toward larger rural units of production.

A fundamental alteration in the relationship between Chinese government and society occurred between 1949 and the late 1950s, centering on an unprecedented expansion of governmental

resources, personnel, operations, claims, and power. This alteration did not take place at one stroke in 1949–1950 with the shift
from KMT to CCP political leadership; rather, it occurred as a
consequence of that shift and the program of industrialization
and socialism promoted by the new national leadership. It was
only after the completion of the First Five-Year Plan that the
new relationship of government to society was really established.
The old indicators of economic and social status—wealth, land
ownership, education, age, sex, and kinship ties—had declined
rapidly as sources of political power, although they certainly
continued to have political relevance, particularly at the basic
level. Indeed, the scope of governmental programs and demands
was such that the citizen's economic and social status had become
largely a function of governmental policy or of an explicitly
political definition of favored and disfavored classes. Political
power in the new relationship fell exclusively to manifestly
political roles, that is, to authoritative positions in the party,
state, or army hierarchies, recruitment to which was controlled
by CCP policies. As of 1957, it appeared that the physical
location of governmental power, and of those most likely to gain
access to it, increasingly was located in the cities in the complex
of government offices, state economic enterprises, and educational
facilities that seemed to be the vanguard of China's socialist
future.

The leftist phase that began in the late 1950s modified initial
developments in two important respects. First, it limited urban
growth, while promoting rural economic and social development. The limitation of urban growth was not a leftist policy
but a necessary response to a resource bottleneck. By 1960, urban
areas were overcrowded, and the Great Leap had created acute
supply problems. The restriction of urban residency has been
very effective. Ninety percent of the proportional growth of
China's urban population occurred in the first eleven years, and
only 10 percent occurred in 1961–1983. Recruitment of peasants
to work in urban industries continued, but most were recruited
as contract workers, hired and paid through their rural work
units, with no claim to urban residency or to the benefits of
regular state employment. Generally, the policies of residency
control adopted after the Great Leap created a rural population
with no geographic mobility and only such economic mobility

as they could create for themselves. Since large-scale urbanization was out of the question, the egalitarian leadership of the 1960s and 1970s concentrated on encouraging rural industry, the mechanization of agriculture, and increasing crop yields through a variety of labor-intensive improvements. There was also a major shift of health, educational, and communications resources to rural areas. During this period, the socioeconomic revolution penetrated deeply into the countryside, distributing its gains much more broadly throughout Chinese society.[26] However, rural living standards remain substantially lower than urban ones, as detailed in Appendix C.

The complex effects of the accentuation and broadening of class struggle constitute a second major area of change during the 1957–1977 era. Class struggle in the 1950s had been led by the party against fairly well-defined economic classes. The enemy classes were either engaged in exploitation made possible through the ownership of the means of production, or they were avowed enemies of Communism. The Anti-Rightist campaign of 1957 began a process of ideological redefinition of class enemies in which deviations perceived by the accuser became sufficient grounds for class struggle. The anxiety, violence, suffering, and arbitrariness of class struggle during the leftist phase caused widespread factionalization in society and latent alienation from the regime. The intelligentsia was especially hard hit, but even peasant villages felt its effects. The official commitment to egalitarianism led to compressed wage differentials and emphasis on political and class criteria for educational and occupational opportunities; while, at the same time, the weakening of central control led to growth of many local domains of individual or factional power, that is "kingdoms," where almost feudal conditions of arbitrariness and corruption could exist. The unquestioned political hegemony of the party organization and the functional justification of power and privilege were in a shambles.

In other respects, however, the main trends established in the 1950s continued. Industrialization continued to progress faster

---

[26]For vivid accounts of developments in specific rural areas, see William Hinton, *Shenfan* (New York: Vintage, 1983); and Richard Madsen, Jonathan Unger, and Anita Chan, *Chen Village* (Berkeley: University of California Press, 1984).

than agricultural growth, with the Chinese economy interacting more with the world economy and moving into areas requiring more sophisticated technology. New industrial centers emerged, hastening national economic integration. Increased manufacturing potential and modest gains in per capita income brought growing consumer demands. As foreshadowed by the 1950s, the government's scope of responsibility expanded, its tasks becoming more complex and controversial. The revolution's leveling tendencies—pushed forward by Maoist egalitarianism—reduced the sharpest social cleavages of the past; however, abundant conflicts over development and distribution of the social product remained.

Just as the Chinese society of the 1960s was different from that of 1949, the society of the 1980s is different from that of the 1960s. The contrary pressures of the leftist attempt to prevent the institutionalization of a new urban-bureaucratic elite pitted against the social and organizational needs of a growing political economy has yielded decisively in favor of the latter. Modernization has been the party's primary goal since 1979, and it is acknowledged that modernization requires political stability and an unequal division of labor, power, and reward. There has been a general diversification of Chinese society, due in part to the ideological relaxation after Mao and in part to the continued success and growing credibility of post-Mao modernization. Rural areas have been, to a large extent, decollectivized, thereby increasing the gap between rural rich and poor but decreasing the rural-urban income gap. With the reestablishment of the traditional prestige of intellectuals, there is great pressure on the educational system to expand and improve and upon students to do well and serve themselves and the people. However, even if a smooth economic future is assumed, material wealth, diversification, and increasing self-confidence of various sectors of society will press new political demands. It may be anticipated that some of these pressures will be for a corresponding diversification of the political process.

Political Culture and Participation. The CCP's socialization and mobilization efforts have changed the mix of Chinese political culture, raising the general level of political awareness and increasing the proportion of politically involved citizens. The substance and degree of this change is controversial, since much of the evidence that relates to it is indirect or ambiguous. The proposition rests, however, on some solid foundations. One is that the CCP has undertaken a political education movement of great magnitude, backed by an organizational and communications network surpassing anything known in China's past. Another is that the CCP has mobilized the population for direct participation in political campaigns and basic-level affairs. Heavy party controls raise questions about the meaning of this participation, but it surely contributes to popular politicization. Finally, formal education has spread, increasing political skills, literacy, and knowledge.

Equally significant is the expansion and diffusion throughout Chinese society of those who constitute China's political elite and subelite, that is, people who have received a relatively intense kind of political education and, as either cause or effect, have assumed distinctive political roles. We should recall here an important aspect of China's political heritage: although traditional Chinese political culture was dominated by feelings of powerlessness and isolation with respect to political authority, there was always in Chinese society a small elite of scholar-officials marked by a highly developed sense of political obligation and participation. What the Chinese Communists have done is to reinforce this sense of elite political responsibility (although altering the determinants of elitehood), while greatly expanding the numbers of those who qualify for it. The size of the CCP—the simplest indicator of political elitehood in contemporary China—gives one, relatively conservative, measure of this expansion. The 40 million party members in 1982 may be contrasted with the 1–2 million gentry who were the actual and potential political elite of late Qing China.

The significance in this comparison is not simply the difference in absolute numbers, but the fact that the pool of potential political leadership in contemporary China is so readily expandable. Since political elite or subelite status depends initially on the acquisition of a political education or experience that is now almost automatic for young people, the pool of potential political recruits is truly enormous. This is in sharp contrast to the pool in imperial China, which was normally limited to those who could afford to pursue exacting and lifelong scholarly study.

Although for many of the old guard the necessary credentials came through a lifetime of revolutionary activity, since 1949 they have been attainable in rather ordinary ways. For example, any Chinese who has served in the PLA or received a middle school education—unless he or she has some specific political liability—is really part of the subelite. After three decades of Communist rule, this pool is so numerous and so widely diffused throughout Chinese society that the leadership can no longer assume that only a small, easily identified stratum is politically relevant. Between officialdom and what still may be a politically unsophisticated mass of citizens, there is now a broad intermediate stratum, relatively youthful, a political influence of some importance.

The expansion of political education, activity, and potential elite membership among the Chinese population does not necessarily produce a uniform political culture. There is ample evidence—particularly in the Cultural Revolution and the turmoil of 1974–1978—that mobilization of the Chinese citizenry has led to sharp conflicts at the popular level. In some cases, these mirror elite differences; in others, they reveal more distinctly local or popular issues. What the expansion signifies is, first, that the body of citizens mobilized for politics since 1949 now dwarfs the old guard of revolutionaries. Second, it signifies the intermediate political stratum is very diverse in its social background and interests. The result is to inject into the system new influences that necessarily after the perceptions of key issues in Chinese politics.

Political Leadership. The structure of political leadership has also evolved since 1949, going through three major stages that correspond to major stages in party policy. The first stage lasted roughly from 1949 to 1957 and was characterized by a general growth and strengthening of public organs—party, state, army, and mass organizations. These organs had all existed in the base areas, but after 1949 they had to be developed into comprehensive, national institutions. Initially, the new regime's organizational power rested heavily on the PLA and a variety of rather loosely constructed local groups (e.g., the peasants' associations). From the early 1950s, tasks of national, regional, and local government increasingly were brought under the umbrella of the new state structure. As active military tasks receded and the PLA underwent modernization, its political administrative role was assumed by the state. Meanwhile, the mass organizations continued to grow in membership and organizational sophistication, although they remained primarily grass roots organs limited to designated areas of activity. The CCP and the Communist Youth League recruited at a rapid rate and consolidated the party's leading position throughout the public institutional structure. By 1955, the CCP had already doubled its 1949 membership. Recruitment had a much broader geographic base and stressed the admission of urban members who could help with the party's new tasks of socialist construction. As state power over economy and society was consolidated, the basis was laid for an effective political hegemony of the party at all levels and in all areas. Pressures for a degree of institutional autonomy and pluralism were generated by the strengthened state and mass organs, and these were expressed in the 1954 state constitution and in various proposals made during the hundred flowers campaign. But the anti-rightist campaign and the advancement of the "politics takes command" slogan in 1957 signaled the weakening of central state organs vis-a-vis the party; the CCP's unquestionable dominance of the system was clear.

The second stage, from 1957 to 1977, contains a more complex set of developments. The whole period is characterized by a rift between Mao and most of the other top party leaders over the basic direction of Chinese politics. The rift was first apparent in the hundred flowers campaign and widened considerably with the failure of many of Mao's initiatives in the Great Leap Forward. By the early 1960s, Mao and the party organization were pursuing distinctly different policy directions—the party toward the consolidation of a party-state on the Leninist-Stalinist model, and Mao, with an unclear agenda of his own, unsuccessfully intervening on behalf of ideological education, collective incentives, and mass political participation.

Before the Cultural Revolution, these differences did not seem to presage major change in the political system. Although the State Council played a significant policy role, the influence of the people's congresses, united front organs, and mass organizations continued to decline. The only exception from the general picture of party consolidation and institutional routinization was the army. Since 1959, Lin Biao had turned the PLA's attention away from military professionalization and toward ideological renewal, using Mao Zedong Thought as his guide. When the Cultural Revolution escalated to general media and mass criticism of CCP personnel, the PLA became a model of successful ideological transformation. It was thus spared the destructive effects of mass criticism and was in position to take over political administrative leadership from the shattered and discredited party organization in 1967. But Lin Biao's attempt to consolidate his power against the reemerging party organization failed in 1970–1971, leaving the party left and party right as the major factions. Both sides contended for power by admitting adherents into the party and advancing (in the case of the right, rehabilitating) them to power. By 1977, nearly half of the party's membership had been admitted since the Cultural Revolution, most in the early 1970s. There was no secret of complete CCP control of political life. The people's congresses were not functioning; government at the provincial level and below was in the charge of revolutionary committees directly controlled by the corresponding party secretary; and in the absence of undisputed standards for appointments, admission to school, change of residence, and so on, power in society gravitated toward party leadership. But the party was not the ideologically and organizationally unified body that it had been. It was deeply factionalized, and many cadres had become used to a life of great power and little discipline in an organizational structure that preached mass involvement but did not contain effective checks from outside or below.

The death of Mao Zedong in late 1976 not only marked the end of the second phase of political leadership in the PRC, it marked the end of a revolutionary era that had culminated in a destructive impasse between ideology and practice—an impasse that had been sustained by Mao's personal prestige and his suspicion of institutionalization. Within a month of his death, the Gang of Four was removed from power and a post-Mao leadership emerged that proclaimed a "new era" in PRC history. The initial coalition included all those who were critical of the Gang, but by 1979 the power of remaining leftists and left-moderates had been broken at the center. Since then, there have been significant policy disputes at the center, but they have occurred within Deng Xiaoping's ruling coalition.

One of the most significant problems of political leadership in the 1980s has been that of discipline within the CCP. The continuing influence of leftism is one aspect of the problem. Although the new direction of central leadership was confirmed by late 1978, foot-dragging and unenlightened attitudes have been common at lower levels. Cadres who were promoted because of their leftism during the Cultural Revolution are reluctant to support policies that appear revisionist and are, in any case, poorly suited for leadership in modernization. The "Oppose Spiritual Pollution" campaign of 1983 was essentially a leftist campaign, and it was opposed and finally halted by leaders committed to modernization.[27] At the other extreme, a number of cadres are disillusioned with the CCP's political hegemony and encourage more radically pluralizing reforms than the regime is willing to support. Quite aside from these ideological extremes of left and right, the new economic policies of the post-Mao era have opened lucrative opportunities for graft and corruption. Disciplinary problems have led to a number of campaigns since 1978, culminating in the major party rectification campaign of 1983–1986.

Current political leadership is similar to that of the 1950s in a number of respects. It has adopted popular policies and institutionalizing reforms that promise some autonomy for nonparty organizations, revamped united front policies, invited intellectuals to join the CCP, reformed the legal system, and strengthened the people's congress system. There are, however, several important differences between these reforms and their counterparts from the 1950s. First, current reforms are not a naïve imitation of the Soviet Union or a simple extension of base area policies, rather they are a determined effort to create stable societal institutions. The reforms of the 1950s are now criticized for being too weak to prevent the "feudal-fascist dictatorship" of the Cultural Revolution. Indeed, by enduring four or five years, the post-Mao reforms have already exceeded the lifespan of their predecessors. Second, the regime is more completely committed to economic modernization as the primary political task than was the leader-

[27] The tensions between leftist orthodoxy and modernizing progressivism are well described in Stuart Schram, "'Economics in Command?': Ideology and Policy Since the Third Plenum, 1978–84," *China Quarterly*, no. 99 (September 1984): 417–61.

ship of the 1950s. It acknowledges that modernization requires a division of labor and unequal rewards, and its social and political reforms reflect this view of modernization. Third, leftist egalitarianism has been largely discredited as a political alternative by the experience of the Cultural Revolution and the Gang of Four. The writings of Mao Zedong will remain fertile ideological ground for leftist thoughts, but political leftism in the future would have to disassociate itself from the Gang, unless it appears as a primitive rural rejection of modernization or the current regime stumbles on its own mistakes. These differences, as well as the long-term changes in China's material conditions and socioeconomic circumstances, imply that political institutionalization in the 1980s cannot simply repeat political institutionalization in the 1950s.

How do patterns of cyclical change relate to this periodization, which rests on and emphasizes secular change in PRC history? The cyclical perspective reminds us that the periods are not sharply delineated, that their characteristics are not exclusively the property of a single period. Separation between periods is blurred by the fact that each is largely a response to its predecessor and hence continues some of the earlier debates and features. Indeed, one could borrow from cyclical analysis to portray the periods (adding one earlier period) as dialectical alternations of mobilization and consolidation: there is a first revolutionary mobilization that begins with the KMT-CCP civil war in 1946 and ends with completion of land reform in 1952; the FFYP is a consolidation period; the Maoist period is a prolonged second mobilization, synthesizing elements of the first two periods; the modernization period brings renewed consolidation, now synthesizing the second and third periods.

Cyclical analysis also calls our attention to contrary impulses within each period. The transitional period contained forerunners of the Maoist period in the peasants' associations, in the "little leap" of 1955–1956, and in a broad debate, beginning as early as 1954, on the wisdom of following the Soviet model. The Maoist period contained at least two more conservative interludes in the retrenchment of the early 1960s and, more erratically, in mixed retreats from the Cultural Revolution peak. The slogan of the "four modernizations" dates from the 1960s, and much of Hua's modernization program of 1977 was borrowed from plans made by Deng Xiaoping in 1975. The modernization period began with a struggle against the Gang of Four, and campaigns requiring ideological orthodoxy have recurred regularly. There has been a right and a left, with individuals scattered between the poles, on nearly all important issues in post-1949 politics. The policy stance of right and left changes as the issues change. At the same time, representatives of right and left will continue to define their positions with reference to the precedents of the Chinese past, keeping alive a sense of recurring conflicts and of known alternatives to the dominant policies of the moment.

CLASSIFYING THE CHINESE SYSTEM

The identification of three different periods in the post-1949 evolution of the Chinese Communist system recognizes important changes but stops short of arguing that it has changed from one type of system to another. The relationships between the periods, their elements of change and continuity, will emerge more clearly in the remaining chapters that probe Chinese political processes in more detail. However, the approach suggested here conflicts with other perspectives and does not resolve the classification issue. For example, the Almond and Powell classification of China (see Chapter 1) as a "penetrative-radical-authoritarian" system pursuing an "authoritarian-technocratic-mobilizational" strategy must be qualified to account for variations among the three periods. The classification is most appropriate for the Soviet period. It loses considerable force in the Maoist period when the system became more "radical," when its "authoritarian" character perhaps became truly "totalitarian" during the peak Cultural Revolution years, and when populism seriously eroded the "technocratic" elements of the strategy. The labels fit better in the modernization period—especially the technocratic strategy, which has finally come into its own—yet the system and strategy seem less "penetrative, radical, authoritarian, and mobilizational" than in the two earlier periods. The classification remains a suggestive characterization of Third World Communist systems, with China belonging to that group and exhibiting some degree of all the characteristics noted. Yet we must emphasize that the PRC has displayed some of these characteristics sequentially and in different mixes rather than as a single package.

A second problem concerns the looseness of boundaries implied by viewing all post-1949 changes as "within the Communist system." Is this an abdication of judgment, a definition so broad that everything is included and all distinctions are lost? Our approach is to accept broad boundaries, so that only the most extreme Red Guards and the bourgeois intellectuals are clearly outside the system. The former veered close to anarchism in their assault on party centralism, while the latter had hopes for a legitimate political opposition. Neither position fits within the normal horizons of a Communist system. The left and right are included, however, as the marginal extremities of the Chinese Communist political spectrum, as positions that have been occupied by important party elites and that often blend into the central mainstream, so that it is difficult to exclude them without excluding a healthy proportion of post-1949 political activity.

A closely related problem is how to deal with the substance of the charges that some Chinese leaders have violated the requirements of a Communist system. Of the many instances of such charges in post-1949 politics, four are of particular importance and interest: (1) the Maoist charge that Liu Shaoqi and others had forsaken socialism and were embarked in the early 1960s on a road leading to capitalist restoration; (2) the Soviet argument that the Cultural Revolution represented an antiparty movement smacking of idealism, petty bourgeois nationalism, and Trotskyism; (3) the assault by the post-Mao leadership on the Gang of Four for an ultraleft, subjective distortion of historical materialism, leading to the sabotage of the socialist economy and party discipline; and (4) the counterattack in defense of the Gang that charges the Deng leadership with betraying Maoism, class struggle, and Third World revolution, while following revisionist policies and forging an alliance with the capitalist world.[28] The positions represented in these polemics are too complicated to analyse here, but the fact that each claims adherence to Marxism-Leninism indicates the difficulty of deciding when a nominally socialist system has lost its claim to purity.

The important points to glean from this exercise in relativism are these. First, none of the major groupings in Chinese politics has abandoned its formal commitment to the four principles of a socialist economy, party leadership, the dictatorship of the proletariat, or Marxism-Leninism Mao Zedong Thought. Despite

[28] For a sampling of analyses and documentation on each of these positions, see the following: 1. Charges against Liu are thoroughly analysed in Lowell

the mutual hostility of contending factions, they have shared some common ideological ground that differentiates them from non-Communist systems. Second, there has been a relatively broad mainstream of Chinese politics—from center-left to center-right—that has carried most policies and actors along with it. However, the mainstream itself has shifted from time to time, leaving former mainstream participants stranded in ideological heresy. As it veered left in the early Cultural Revolution, Liu Shaoqi and Deng Xiaoping were stranded; as it veered right after 1976, Deng was freed and the Gang was left stranded. More frequently, the party leadership has attempted to narrow the acceptable mainstream through ideological rectification, using the methods of study campaigns, criticism, and self-criticism (that is, encouraging individuals to criticize themselves). Third, the ideological differences between factions are exaggerated by the winner in order to consolidate its own position and discredit the opposition. Within Marxism, there is no tradition of legitimate opposition, and therefore conflict that cannot be suppressed or mediated finally expresses itself as a contradiction between the triumphant vanguard of the Chinese people and a manipulating class enemy that led China to the brink of disaster. Needless to say, the painting of this picture involves invidious interpretations of the ideology, policies, and historical record of the opposition. In fact, there are numerous continuities in personnel, policies, and even ideology between vastly different periods.

A final question of particular interest to Western observers of China is the extent to which the PRC remains committed to

---

Dittmer, *Liu Shao-ch'i and the Chinese Cultural Revolution* (Berkeley: University of California Press, 1974); 2. For Soviet critiques of Mao and the Cultural Revolution, see Wang Ming, *Cultural Revolution or Counter-Revolutionary Coup?* (Moscow: Novosti Press, 1969); B. Zanegin et al., *Developments in China* (Moscow: Progress Publishers, 1968); and the articles translated in *Chinese Law and Government*, vol. 1, no. 3 (Fall 1968): 3–62; 3. For charges against the Gang of Four, see Hua Guofeng, "Political Report to the Eleventh CCP Congress," *PR*, no. 35 (August 26, 1977): 23–57; 4. For criticisms of the current regime as revisionist, see Charles Bettelheim, "The Great Leap Backward," *Monthly Review*, vol. 30, no. 3 (July–August 1978): 37–130, and Raymond Lotta, ed., *And Mao Makes Five* (Chicago: Banner Press, 1978). For a less ideological critique of current rural policies, see William Hinton, "Transformation in the Countryside," *US-China Review*, vol. 8, nos. 3, 4, 5 (1984).

opposition to capitalism. This is the litmus test of a Communist system for many people, and China's position seems to have fluctuated wildly since 1949. In the 1950s, China shared Stalin's view of a strengthened socialist camp pitted against a weakened capitalist one and felt a special bond with national liberation movements. As John Foster Dulles's refusal to shake Zhou Enlai's hand at the 1954 Geneva Conference graphically illustrates, the militant anti-Communism of the West contributed to the bipolar gulf. Internally, there was a peaceful transformation of the holdings of Chinese capitalists into state enterprises paying salaries and interest to former proprietors, although many were harassed in the Five-Anti and Anti-Rightist campaigns. China's ideological purism of the 1960s increased verbal opposition to capitalism and suspected all Communist states except Albania of revisionist tendencies. Meanwhile, U.S. involvement in Vietnam gave continuing evidence of the virulence of international capitalism. Internally, former capitalists suffered extremely during the Cultural Revolution, and they were joined by numerous capitalist-roaders. Attempts by individuals to provide a service or product for payment were denounced as capitalist. On the other hand, it must be remembered that Mao played a personal role in the dramatic breakthrough in U.S.-China relations formulated in the "Shanghai Communiqué" of 1972. It was also in this period that China entered the UN and began its rapid expansion of international diplomatic ties.

In the post-Mao period, the former capitalist-roaders are back in power, joint ventures of capitalist firms in China are encouraged, the tilt toward the Soviet Union of the 1950s is tentatively replaced by a tilt—at a smaller angle—toward the West, and many internal policies encourage market and entrepreneurial activities. Although not without precedents in China and in other Communist countries, these developments so exceed their precedents in momentum and degree that some see China as giving up on socialism and copying capitalism. However, these policies are better understood as innovative attempts within the Chinese socialist tradition to cope with the problem of modernization. Criticisms of international and internal capitalism continue, although they are greatly muted compared to the Cultural Revolution. The campaign against "spiritual pollution" of

1983 was an attempt to curb the ideological influence of increased foreign exposure and social experimentation. The older image of a rabid China out to push the world into a war from which it would emerge victorious through sheer numbers has never been correct, and, likewise, it seems unlikely that China is now embarked on a smooth convergence with capitalism.

CHAPTER V

Political Socialization and Communications

THE MISSION OF THE CHINESE LEADERS to create a new socialist society gives them an intense concern for the processes of political socialization and communications. They cannot accept socialization as a given process that simply maintains existing attitudes and orientations, but they insist that the process itself must change in order to facilitate transformation of popular social consciousness. By the same token, they see the establishment of new patterns in the structure and content of socialization and communications as essential to the attainment of the desired political culture. In the absence of adequate data on popular attitudes, assertions about contemporary Chinese political culture are highly speculative. We can become better informed, however, by studying the relationship between revolutionary values and the inherited political culture, CCP efforts to structure agents of socialization, the Cultural Revolution's impact on socialization, and the post-1976 modification of Cultural Revolution reforms.

REVOLUTIONARY VALUES AND THE INHERITED POLITICAL CULTURE

A useful way of introducing post-1949 socialization and communications processes is to draw a broad contrast between the values promulgated by the regime and China's traditional political culture. Neither of these categories is precise or even demonstrably real. Traditional political culture is a loose category that conceals major differences and discontinuities in patterns of political attitudes existing in China before 1949. Revolutionary values are essentially ideal prescriptions that have guided CCP socialization efforts for most of PRC history; they have not been unchallenged even as an ideal, however, and actual practice has fallen short of such standards. Moreover, the content and urgency of revolutionary values have varied greatly, from dogmatic exaggeration during the Cultural Revolution to significant modification during the post-Mao period. Nevertheless, it is possible to isolate some common values to which the CCP has always been committed. The contrast identifies key themes that have exerted great influence on CCP socialization debates and policies and that establish a framework for evaluating the direction of change in Chinese political culture.[1]

[1]The following discussion attempts to synthesize a complex subject, on which a substantial scholarly literature has emerged. The work most directly relevant to the question addressed here is Richard H. Solomon, *Mao's Revolution and the Chinese Political Culture* (Berkeley: University of California Press, 1971). Reviews challenging Solomon's assertions about traditional and/or Maoist culture include Pi-chao Chen, "In Search of Chinese National Character Via Child-Training," *World Politics*, vol. 25, no. 4 (July 1973): 608–35; and those by Thomas Metzger and F. W. Mote in *Journal of Asian Studies*, vol. 32, no. 1 (November 1972): 101–20. See also Lucian Pye, *The Spirit of Chinese Politics: A Psychocultural Study of the Crisis in Political Development* (Cambridge, Mass.: MIT Press, 1968); Thomas Metzger, *Escape From Predicament* (New York: Columbia University Press, 1977). Continuities between Confucian and Chinese Marxist assumptions about human nature and the proper functions of government are emphasized in Donald J. Munro, *The Concept of Man in Contemporary China* (Ann Arbor: University of Michigan Press, 1977). The initial impact of the Communist Revolution on Chinese social institutions is analyzed in a two-volume study by C. K. Yang, *Chinese Communist Society: The Family and the Village* (Cambridge, Mass: MIT Press, 1968); a short essay on this topic is Francis L. K. Hsu, "Chinese Kinship and Chinese Behavior," in Ping-ti Ho and Tang Tsou, eds., *China in Crisis*, vol. 1 (Chicago: University of Chicago Press, 1968), pp. 579–608. An important recent work on Chinese society, emphasizing the tenacity of some traditional social patterns, is William L. Parish and Martin King Whyte, *Village and Family Life in Contemporary China* (Chicago: University of Chicago Press, 1978). Other useful studies of Chinese political socialization processes include William Kessen, ed., *Childhood in China* (New Haven, Conn.: Yale University Press, 1975); David M. Raddock, *Political Behavior of Adolescents in China* (Tucson: University of Arizona Press, 1977); Susan Shirk, *Competitive Comrades* (Berkeley: University of California Press, 1982); Amy Auerbacher Wilson et al., eds., *Deviance and Social Control in Chinese Society* (New York: Praeger, 1977); and Martin King Whyte, *Small Groups and Political Rituals in China* (Berkeley: University of California Press, 1974). See also Richard W. Wilson, *Learning To Be Chinese: The Political Socialization of Children in Taiwan* (Cambridge, Mass.: MIT Press, 1970), and material cited elsewhere in this chapter.

Collectivism. Communism calls for a redefinition of the social units to which primary loyalties are due and from which authority flows. In traditional China, the dominant social institution was typically a kinship unit: individuals geared their actions to its maintenance and prosperity and accepted the authority of its leaders over a wide range of their social behavior. The family or lineage, however, was only the most obvious beneficiary of a particularism that favored exclusive and personal relationships over inclusive and public ones. In other words, individuals saw their loyalties and responsibilities largely in terms of their own particular experience, creating a web of obligations that would protect and benefit the insiders (those who shared a particular experience or relationship) at the expense of outsiders. Although kinship claims were normally most formidable in this network, it supported as well the claims of native village or locality, common school or work associations, and so forth, against the claims of external social groupings. Particularism restricted individualism as well as larger community interests, but it tended to place selfish interests—in the sense of those identified with one's limited personal associations—above those of the public realm. Local organizations could not easily ignore or flout the dictates of political authority, since imperial power was ultimately supreme in both theory and practice; however, they were the operative authority in most cases, and their hold over individuals was strong enough to offer real competition to the demands of the political system.

In the Communist ethic, collectivism replaces particularism as the determinant of both loyalty and authority. Political authority, at whatever level, is superior to the claims of constitutent elements within the community: loyalties belong to the collective regardless of personal associations and ties. As Maoist slogans like "serve the people" and "fight self" suggested, this principle requires dedication to the public cause and a conscious suppression of inclinations to place selfish concerns above those of the collective. The shift here is partly one of degree, since in traditional China, too, the individual was expected to subordinate his interests to those of a larger group. The difference is that under socialism the collective is a wider and more inclusive one. For example, the locality, which in imperial times was a relatively large and inclusive group as seen from individual perspective, is in the revolutionary view one of the lowest collectives in an ever-widening sphere of political community that blends into the national political system and even an international political movement. The shift is also qualitative, however, in its insistence that political authority is supreme in all areas of life and that the individual's obligation extends to all members of his community, not just to those with whom he has a personalized or particular relationship.

Collectivism was particularly stressed during the Cultural Revolution, while particularistic needs and desires have received greater recognition in the post-Mao period. The Cultural Revolution's slogan of "all public and no private" implied that the only legitimate motivation was the public good. Profit-making activities and material incentives such as bonuses were viewed as bourgeois influences. Government policies in the 1980s have reversed such judgments, claiming that the principle of socialism is "to each according to his labor." Material incentives are used to spur production, and individuals are encouraged to pursue profitable enterprises. However, collectivist values have not been abandoned. They are part of the "socialist spiritual civilization" that the regime promotes. Models of selfless behavior are often cited and praised, including the army hero Lei Feng, who was much touted during the Cultural Revolution. February has been proclaimed "socialist morality month," and at that time work units vie with one another to provide courteous and sometimes free service to customers. Collectivism tends to be interpreted as generosity and good manners rather than as a sharp class struggle, but it is still an important part of China's official ethics.

Struggle and Activism. The traditional orientation emphasized the maintenance of harmony in social relations. People were to be orderly and peaceful, avoiding or suppressing displays of antagonism. Reality fell short of this ideal, of course, as the system had its share of rebellions and individual hostilities; the insistence on suppression of conflict may, in fact, have encouraged violent and disorderly action when the restraining norms were broken. The tendency to restrain conflict was nonetheless powerful and was made relatively effective by insistence on submission to authority and an acceptance of "face-saving" or compromise solutions to disputes. The political realm was recognized as particularly susceptible to conflict and, the values of its scholar-elites notwithstanding, quite capable of harsh and arbitrary action—hence the common image of the tiger of government. Both prudence and social norms therefore dictated great caution in dealing with conflict, which easily led the common man with his relative political ignorance and powerlessness to political passivity or avoidance of political issues.

By contrast, we have seen in the previous chapter that struggle is a key revolutionary value. Society is permeated with class struggle both as a consequence of exploitation and a condition of social progress. Citizens are expected to participate actively and voluntarily in this struggle, sharpening its features and challenging openly those whose positions or actions stand in the way of the socialist path. Commitment to political activism and struggle must replace old inclinations toward passivity and harmony.[2] Since the Cultural Revolution, official emphasis has shifted away from antagonistic struggle and toward activism for modernization. The slogan "dare to rebel" has been replaced by "stability and unity." However, metaphors suggesting military struggle against an enemy still abound in the Chinese media, and struggle techniques such as criticism and self-criticism are still approved and utilized. Class struggle continues in the milder but still important form of the struggle against bourgeois influence.

Self-Reliance. Traditional authoritarianism and the strictures against challenging its harmonious ordering of society led to a heavy dependence on those holding positions of authority. Paternalistic protection from superiors was the primary guarantee of security and gain. Pursuit of goals without elite approval risked failure as well as possible displeasure from those whose blessings counted most. Diverse practices of religion and superstition, through which most Chinese sought protection and signs of good or bad fortune from suprahuman forces, supplemented dependency on human authority. If all protection failed,

---

[2]See Richard H. Solomon, "On Activism and Activists: Maoist Conceptions of Motivation and Political Role Linking State to Society," *China Quarterly*, no. 39 (July–September 1969): 76–114; and Arthur F. Wright, "Struggle vs. Harmony: Symbols of Competing Values in Modern China," *World Politics*, vol. 6, no. 1 (October 1953): 31–44.

a sense of fatalism could cushion the blow—although again we should note that rebellion was a periodic response to adversity and oppression. Self-reliance is the socialist virtue preached against this dependency orientation. It insists that human efforts can overcome all obstacles, and it urges the people to employ their own initiative and capacities to accomplish the tasks that face them. Dependence on religion, superstition, and higher authorities is discouraged, as is resignation to one's fate. The proper outlook, in the new culture, is that individuals need not and should not expect paternalistic protection and assistance from any source, including the government.

In some respects, the principle of self-reliance has been strengthened in the 1980s. There have been numerous campaigns against the "iron rice bowl" of total job security, and individuals who have succeeded through their own efforts are encouraged and their successes are publicized. On the other hand, the principle of self-reliance is no longer interpreted as self-sufficiency. During the Cultural Revolution, units and regions were encouraged to supply all of their own needs, and the leadership was very cautious about dependence on foreign trade. China did not have a significant foreign debt. Currently, an emphasis on commodity production and cooperation has replaced self-sufficiency. Agricultural and industrial units are encouraged to produce for maximum profit (within plan guidelines), rather than to cover all of their own needs. China now expects international trade and credit to play a key role in modernization. In this area, self-reliance remains a caution against excessive dependence on the import of technology.

Egalitarianism and Populism. Hierarchical relationships were viewed as natural and necessary in the ordering of traditional Chinese society. The principles governing social hierarchy were complex, involving mixed considerations of age, generation, kinship, sex, wealth, scholarly attainment, and official status. Nonetheless, individuals knew who their superiors and subordinates were in various settings, so that a demarcation of authority and status was clear in most social relationships. Persons in higher roles in the hierarchy expected deference from those in lower ones and were characterized not simply by authority but by privilege and symbolic superiority relative to those beneath them. The Chinese Communist view of social stratification is much more egalitarian, especially in the Maoist version of revolutionary values. Although recognizing the existence of classes, the inevitability of some division of labor in society, and above all the necessity of maintaining political authority, this view is hostile toward the elaboration and reinforcement of hierarchy. It seeks to minimize material and psychological inequalities generally and to eradicate what it regards as irrational subordination, such as that of younger generations and women. In the inescapable political and administrative hierarchy, it is hostile toward privileges, symbols, and economic differences that set elites apart as a special group and give them an aura of superiority extending beyond their specific political roles. Despite current policies, permitting the accumulation of wealth and larger wage differentials, egalitarianism remains a value in Chinese politics. Justifications of rural decollectivization emphasize its benefits to poorer peasants and hotly deny that it has led to polarization.[3] Policies that allow some to get rich first are defended by saying that the social value of production exceeds the individual reward, and, therefore, society as a whole is better off. Regardless of the merit of such arguments, egalitarianism remains a potent political value in China.

The revolutionary orientation is similar to the traditional one in assigning elites a role as model for the most valued life style, but the style itself differs greatly in the two cases. The ideal life style in traditional society was that of the scholar-official elite, whereas in the Maoist ethic it is that of the common man. The former placed the burden of attainment on the people, allowing elites to perpetuate their way of life; the latter places a distinct burden of change on elites who are expected to model a style of life traditionally considered beneath them. In more specific terms, traditional culture valued intellectual attainment and pursuits, bureaucratic or managerial roles, mental labor, and the contemplative life; the Maoist ethic values practical work, participation in the "front line" of production, manual labor, and the active, physical life. Although not overtly materialistic, the former encouraged material gain to support pursuit of elite

[3]See, for instance, Wang Dacheng, "Take the Road to Common Prosperity," *BR*, vol. 26, no. 39 (September 26, 1983): 4.

status and some conspicuous consumption to demonstrate its attainment; the latter encourages self-denial, savings, and frugality, making a virtue of what was and remains an economic necessity for most of the people.[4] The recent formulation of revolutionary values has modified these Maoist themes, becoming more tolerant of mental labor, rewards for the skilled, and desires to enjoy higher living standards. Nonetheless, it remains significantly more populist than the traditional view.

This outline greatly simplifies the contrast between revolutionary values and traditional political culture and says little about actual political orientations in contemporary China. Neither model has been so pure and static in its application, and neither represents adequately the complex mix of attitudes that now prevails in Chinese political culture. Yet, despite its limitations, the outline does suggest why political socialization has such a prominent place in Chinese politics. At issue here is not simply the transferral of allegiance to a new regime but the creation of a new political community in which all individuals will transform their images of public life and their roles within it. The values affirmed indicate the general direction of desired change and the magnitude of the task. They also help explain why the CCP has tried to expand the scope of socialization—to include adults as well as children, elites as well as masses—and to establish political control over all socializing agents.

Realization of a socialist political community may be remote and possibly utopian, but there are some conditions that favor the struggle to attain it. With its relatively homogeneous cultural tradition and common written language, China does not face severe ethnic or cultural cleavages. The national minorities constitute only about 7 percent of the population and live largely in frontier and mountainous areas. They figure prominently in questions of national security and integration but have little effect on general policies relating to political socialization.[5]

---

[4]For stimulating discussion of Maoist populism, see Maurice Meisner, "Leninism and Maoism: Some Populist Perspectives in Marxism-Leninism in China," *China Quarterly*, no. 45 (January–March 1971): 2–36.

[5]For a general survey of ethnic and cultural patterns in China, see Hu Chang-tu et al., *China: Its People, Its Society, Its Culture* (New Haven, Conn.: Human Relations Area File Press, 1960), esp. pp. 64–139; and Leo J. Moser, *The Chinese Mosaic* (Boulder, Colo.: Westview, 1984).

Cultural variations among the Han Chinese are probably a greater problem. For example, the adoption of standard Chinese (Mandarin) as the official language in dialectic-speaking areas, particularly the provinces of southeastern China, created tensions between local and outside cadres and special complications in education and communications. Variations in lineage organization, with their impact on land ownership patterns, have led to different timing and results in land reform and collectivization.[6] On balance, however, the Chinese sense of cultural unity and identity overshadows these local variations and tends to support the acceptance of a new political culture that places such emphasis on national uniformity. The Chinese government traditionally has played a direct role in setting the moral and cultural tone of society. The principles advanced now are new, but the nationwide articulation of an official doctrine by representatives of the political system is not.

Moreover, changes already under way in Chinese society have blurred the confrontation between traditional and Maoist political cultures. The demise of state Confucianism, the imperial bureaucracy, and the examination system early in this century removed the political system's institutionalized support of the old culture. Political upheaval, economic change, the growth of modern schools, and the emergence or importation of new ideas encouraged social ferment and mobility. A "family revolution" began to disrupt the old society's dominant socializing agent.[7] To a great extent, the political orientations encouraged by the unfolding revolution were supportive or anticipatory of those demanded by the CCP. The mobilization of mass support for transcendental causes such as national unity and independence, the practice of KMT one-party rule with its intolerance of political opposition, and a growing conviction that China needed a new dispensation of political authority were preparing the way for reception of the Communist political style. As one scholar has suggested, the Chinese people in 1949 were in a sense ready for

[6]Guangdong (Kwangtung) province is an excellent example on both points; see Ezra F. Vogel, *Canton Under Communism: Programs and Politics in a Provincial Capital, 1949–1968* (Cambridge, Mass.: Harvard University Press, 1969), esp. chaps. 2, 3, and 5.

[7]Marion J. Levy, Jr., *The Family Revolution in Modern China* (Cambridge, Mass.: Harvard University Press, 1949).

the CCP's demand for political commitment, if only to resolve the terrible divisions and uncertainties of preceding decades.[8] The old orientations had not disappeared, of course, but the institutions that had maintained them were in flux, and there was at least some receptivity to the official political culture of the new government.

Finally, we should take note of the manifest political resources of the CCP. Backed by substantial experience in mass political mobilization, widespread acceptance of its legitimacy, a dedicated cadre of party members and supporters, and demonstrated military superiority, the Communist government was able to establish a network of political organization unparalleled in Chinese history. With these resources vigorously brought into play, the prospects for inducing significant changes in Chinese political culture were at least credible, although not guaranteed.

It is important to recall, however, the difficulty of implanting a new socialization process in China. Powerful influences external to the Communist system were present in 1949 and inevitably were to continue in force for some time to come. The CCP clearly benefits, in its desire to remold political attitudes, from the relative youth of the population. Over 55 percent of the population was under twenty-five in 1953, and by 1983 over 75 percent of the population had reached school age after 1949.[9] In other words, the age structure of the population creates good opportunities for influencing the socialization experience. Yet in 1949, this was a future-oriented advantage that did little to resolve the immediate problem, which was that virtually the entire adult population had received primary socialization and education in a non-Communist setting. There was nothing the CCP could do to alter the fact that the parents, teachers, and workers of the first decade would reflect a pre-Communist socialization process, necessarily transmitted to some degree to the next generation. Moreover, even the most rigid control of the

[8]Lucian W. Pye, "Mass Participation in China: Its Limitations and the Continuity of Culture," in John M. H. Lindbeck, ed., *China: Management of a Revolutionary Society* (Seattle: University of Washington Press, 1971), pp. 15–19.

[9]Calculated from *Zhongguo 1982 nian renkou pucha 10% xiuyang ziliao* (10% Sampling Tabulation in the 1982 Population Census of the People's Republic of China), Beijing: Statistical Press, 1983, pp. 264–73.

social environment could not exclude some extrasystemic influences. For example, KMT and American propaganda directed at the mainland, the passage of Chinese back and forth from the mainland (especially through Hong Kong), and the presence of foreign travelers and residents in China ensured some external inputs of information. Most significant during the 1950s were Chinese contacts with other Communist countries, especially the Soviet Union. Hundreds of Russian teachers and thousands of Russian experts served in China in this period, while some tens of thousands of Chinese had studied in the Soviet Union by the early 1960s.[10] As the CCP admits, the influence of feudalistic, capitalist, and revisionist ideas remains long after the establishment of the socialist system.

Deficiencies in the tools of socialization were another formidable problem, given the 1949 level of economic and technical development. Schools, teachers, and books were in short supply for an effort aiming at universal education. CCP political biases aggravated these shortages through destruction of library resources judged politically faulty and through suspicion of existing mass communications media. The rate of illiteracy—exactly unknown but estimated as high as 85 to 90 percent of the population in the early years[11]—was an obvious liability, as were the differences in spoken languages in different parts of the country. Socialization occurs regardless of such deficiencies, of course, but it was not easy for the CCP to transfer the burden of political socialization to those public institutions where its control was most secure.

Underlying all of these problems is the fact that the structure of human relationships does not necessarily govern their content. The resources of the CCP came to bear most forcefully and effectively on social structure, changing the institutions of Chinese society and their relationship to each other. There is no need to review here the specific changes in question, the most relevant of which will be discussed in subsequent sections. Generally, the CCP has changed the structure of political socialization by reducing the role of kinship organization and by expanding greatly the scope of public, politically dominated mechanisms of socialization. However, this cannot guarantee that the content

[10]R. F. Price, *Education in Communist China* (New York: Praeger, 1970), pp. 101–04.
[11]Ibid., p. 202.

of attitudes associated with declining institutions will disappear or that the content of those associated with new relationships will follow the expected pattern. The CCP itself is a case in point. A new institution in Chinese society, carefully structured to embody the political orientations desired by its leaders, the party nonetheless failed to live up to Mao's expectations. If the vanguard of the revolution could not rid itself of the influences of the past, how effective has been the reform of less politicized institutions? The Cultural Revolution is, of course, the crucial episode for an analysis of this question. We will return it to after discussion of the agents of socialization including the family, the educational system, the communications network, and political and social experience.

AGENTS OF SOCIALIZATION

The Family. The Chinese family has been and continues to be a stronger social unit than the Western family. Bonds and obligations among family members are stronger and more explicit, divorce is rare, and the family is the basic unit of the rural economy. Relationships, whether of kinship or of friendship, play an extremely important role in daily life. Chinese Communist policy is based on the family unit but has also remolded it by changing its context and by challenging its power. In doing so, the CCP is continuing sixty years of family reform begun by Western-oriented urban progressives; however, it is also confronting the particularistic resistance of the family with collective values and claims to total allegiance.

The traditional Chinese family was the controlling institution of daily life, a position confirmed by the high regard of Confucianism for familial responsibilities and ritual. Marriage was primarily a family event, so the questions of the alliance of families and financial advantages often dominated arrangements. Family structure was strongly patriarchal; the head of the family was the unquestioned ruler, and wives were very vulnerable subordinates because they became a part of the husband's family and were isolated from the support of their own parental families. Corporal punishment of wives and children was common. The purchase of wives for the purpose of begetting children was upheld by the Chinese Supreme Court in 1919, and the generally progressive Chinese Civil Code of 1931 did not prohibit polygamy.[12] Even today, many older Chinese women can be seen hobbling about because their feet had been bound when they were children. Local society in traditional China was organized in terms of particularistic relationships, of which kinship relations were the most important. Especially in Southeast China, lineage organization often provided the structure of power below the county level. The large extended families of landlords, officials, and merchants provided disciplined, loyal personnel for maintaining the family's prosperity and defending its power. Family size was smaller at the lower end of the economic ladder, and its solidarity was buffeted by famine, migration, infanticide, and the selling of children.

Even before large-scale Western influence, the abuses of the traditional family system prompted reform measures from the Taiping rebels. By the turn of the century, Western missionaries and Chinese progressives were arguing against footbinding and for free choice in marriage.[13] Ba Jin's famous 1920s novel, *Family*, depicted the dilemmas of a large Chinese family in transition, and Western works such as Ibsen's *Nora*, which dealt with similar themes, were popular. The founding members of the CCP were enthusiastic supporters of family and reform for women. Some of Mao's earliest articles were against the suppression of women. Family reform, including equal property rights for women, free consent in marriage, and accessible divorce have always been a part of CCP policy. The formation of women's associations, first in the base areas and later in the PRC, played an important role in the reform of familial structure and behavior. The effect of the party's commitment to equality for women can be seen in the enrollment of 84 percent of primary-school-age girls, as compared to an average of 56 percent in developing countries. Nevertheless, reality falls far short of ideals of sexual equality, and at all levels China remains a male-dominated society.[14]

---

[12]Maurice Freedman, "The Family in China, Past and Present," in G. William Skinner, ed., *The Study of Chinese Society: Essays by Maurice Freedman* (Stanford, Cal.: Stanford University Press, 1979), pp. 240–54.

[13]An interesting account of Mrs. Archibald Little's campaign against footbinding can be found in Nigel Cameron, *Barbarians and Mandarins* (Chicago: University of Chicago Press, 1970), pp. 361–70.

[14]World Bank, *China: Socialist Economic Development* (Washington, D.C.: World Bank, 1983) vol. 1, p. 96.

Unlike some extreme Bolshevik reforms in the early years of the Soviet Union, the family revolution supported by the CCP was not a revolution against the family. Some features of the old system were marked for destruction: the organizational power of the lineage; traditional marriage practices that symbolically and in practice helped perpetuate the subordination of women and youth to family elders; and those values articulated in both state Confucianism and popular religion that made kinship obligations paramount within the sphere of social relationships. However, aside from destruction of lineage organizations that extended their influence over several families and even whole villages, Communist policy with respect to basic kinship structure has not been particularly radical. The unit of distribution in land reform was the family, and it remained the basic unit providing for the welfare of the young and the old, especially in the countryside. Although divorce is allowed, it is greatly discouraged, and the major tactics in dealing with problems such as wife beating and philandering are persuasion and arbitration. Except for some short-lived experiments with common mess halls and dormitories during the Great Leap Forward, normal domestic functions are left to the family. Many families are strengthened by better living conditions and increased life expectancies, resulting in larger and multigeneration families. Restricted geographical mobility and housing shortages help prevent some of the disintegrating effects normally associated with modernization. Although the destruction of traditional characteristics deserves emphasis, so does the effort to establish what may legitimately be called a modern family system.[15]

With reference to political socialization, the basic intent of Communist policy has been to transfer major responsibility to the public realm and to secure compliance within the family to norms established by political authority. Since the public institutions of socialization will be discussed later, we focus here on efforts to shape and define the family's role in the new society. Broadly speaking, there have been several fairly distinct stages in the post-1949 development of CCP attitudes toward the family.

The first stage, from 1949 to the Great Leap Forward, was one of attempted neutralization of the family's traditional power by

[15]Maurice Freedman, "The Family Under Chinese Communism" *Political Quarterly*, vol. 35, no. 3 (July–September 1964): 342–50.

explicit attacks on familial authority. The most important step was adoption of the "marriage law" in 1950, followed over the next few years by a campaign to propagate and enforce its provisions. Basic provisions of the law included the following: the establishment of marriage as a civil act entered into only upon "complete willingness" of both parties and registered by government authority; the prohibition of "polygamy, concubinage, child betrothal, interference with the remarriage of widows, and the exaction of money or gifts in connection with marriage"; the establishment of full legal equality of both sexes in home and social matters; the granting of divorce on both parties' consent, or on one party's demand if backed by legal approval.[16] Over 500,000 divorces were filed for each of the first five years after the new law. The marriage law also offered legal protection for children against abuse by their parents, a principle given teeth by the marked rise of young activists to positions of political responsibility. The assault on subordination of youth to elders was publicized dramatically in denunciations by youth of alleged political crimes of their elders, including close relatives. The confiscation and redistribution of lineage lands and holdings, coupled with the establishment of new organs of local government, eroded the power of extended kinship organizations.[17] These efforts were by no means completely successful or even uniformly implemented. The marriage law campaign encountered such resistance that implementation was somewhat relaxed after 1953. On the other hand, the direction of CCP law, policy, and propaganda was unmistakable. The influence of the old kinship system might continue informally but only in a context of legal restrictions and political intimidation.

The first wave of family reform receded during the institutionalization of the middle 1950s, but the Great Leap brought a second wave that challenged briefly the structure of the nuclear family itself. Although a radical restructuring of the family was not a primary goal of the Leap, the mobilization of 1958 was a serious challenge to the single-family home. Expansion of the labor force took many women out of the home, while some work

---

[16]See Yang, *The Family and the Village*, esp. "The Chinese Family in the Communist Revolution," chaps. 2–4; the marriage law appears as an appendix on pp. 221–26.
[17]Ibid.

projects required splitting of families, residential change, or overnights away from the family. Communal mess halls were to provide meals, permitting confiscation of many home utensils, and communal nurseries and old-age homes were to care for the very young and very old. Yet the commune experiment did not continue along these lines. The most radical features of communal living were never established uniformly and were moderated during the winter of 1958–1959. The Great Leap's political threat to the family was replaced by the physical threat of poor harvests over the following three years. Hard times are reflected in a dramatic reduction of births; the number of surviving children from the worst year, 1961, was only 42 percent of the number from 1964, a recovery year.[18]

With the post-Leap retrenchment came a new official view of the family's role in socialist society. Earlier an object of suspicion to be neutralized or even sacrificed in the course of revolution, the family was now regarded as a possible ally of the state in socialist construction. One of the best indicators of the new attitude was a relatively sympathetic portrayal in literature of kinship relationships and traditional authority figures such as fathers and "old peasants."[19] From the official viewpoint, expressed in retrenchment policies and editorial comment as well as in literature, the relaxation of earlier pressures on the family was not an abdication to traditional values as such. Rather, it was an acknowledgment that social change is a long-term process that can be promoted by models of correct behavior within the reformed institutions of the old society. The family and the village could become positive agents of socialization, reinforcing state policy by their encouragement of production skills, hard work, community service, and respect for authority.

However, the CCP's attempt to co-opt the family's socializing influence ran a serious risk. How could it be sure that a warmer attitude toward traditional social institutions, even if partially reformed, would not encourage demonstration of old values as well as new? In fact, evidence in the early 1960s revealed the

[18]Calculated from 1982 census data reported in *BR*, vol. 27, no. 3 (January 16, 1984): 22.

[19]For documentation and analysis, see Ai-li S. Chin, *Modern Chinese Fiction and Family Relations: Analysis of Kinship, Marriage and the Family in Contemporary Taiwan and Communist Chinese Stories* (Cambridge, Mass.: Center for International Studies, MIT, 1966).

continued existence of kinship influence in local politics, arranged marriages and sale of brides, corruption and personal aggrandizement and other feudalistic practices.[20] This tendency was not condoned by the leadership, nor could it be attributed solely to social policy since it thrived on the revisionist economic reforms of the period. Nonetheless, a certain tolerance of traditional kinship practices was implicit in the effort to capitalize in the family's stabilizing influence.

Attitudes toward the family mirrored the basic dilemma of the 1960s—how to reconcile maintenance of authority and stability with continued revolution—and were, therefore, necessarily involved in the socialist education campaigns and the Cultural Revolution. As might be expected, the early stages of the Cultural Revolution brought sharp attacks on relationships suggestive of traditional prerogatives. Once more, the independence of youth was encouraged, sometimes taking the form of denunciation of parents and elders. The family was not a target of special hostility, but neither was it immune from revolutionary struggle; it was to "revolutionize" itself, fearlessly rooting out any evil tendencies that might persist or arise within it.[21] Besides families that were disrupted by the fates of individual members, many were disrupted by ideological conflict and by a desire to be disassociated from relatives who were vulnerable to criticism.[22] Despite the increase in intrafamily tensions during the Cultural Revolution, the basic family pattern followed the trends of the early 1960s.[23]

The organized power of the lineages was gone, the status of youth and women had risen significantly, and the state or collective had established its formal authority over kinship units. Yet the nuclear or stem family remained the primary residential and child-rearing unit, continued to serve as an important eco-

[20]John Wilson Lewis, "The Leadership Doctrine of the Chinese Communist Party: The Lesson of the People's Commune," *Asian Survey*, vol. 3, no. 10 (October 1963): 457–64; and C. S. Chen, ed., *Rural People's Communes in Lien-chiang*, trans. Charles Price Ridley (Stanford, Cal.: Hoover Institution, 1969), esp. pp. 44–49.

[21]Tsao Hsin-hua, "Using Materialist Dialectics to Revolutionize the Family," *PR*, no. 47 (November 20, 1970): 10–12.

[22]A poignant case of the effects of class struggle on a family is presented in Liang Heng and Judith Shapiro, *Son of the Revolution* (New York: Vintage, 1983).

[23]The authoritative study is Parish and Whyte, *Village and Family Life*.

nomic unit by pooling its members' incomes and expenditures, provided some education and health care expenses, and cared for most of the aged in Chinese society. Despite progress in the direction indicated by the marriage law reforms, many traditional marriage practices—payment of bride prices, patrilocal residence for newlyweds, and some (less than formerly) parental involvement in mate selection—remained common, tolerated if not approved by cadres. Urban families were closer to the official model than those in rural areas, where one might expect a gradual weakening of traditional customs, but it seemed that the family revolution had reached a plateau in which the attainment of many initial reforms had essentially satisfied state demands.

The 1980s have again introduced a stage of major change for Chinese families. Many burdens on family life that had been growing in the 1960s and 1970s have been lightened. The new marriage law that went into effect in September 1980 facilitated divorce by allowing it on the grounds of alienation of affection, which has induced a surge in divorce applications. The legal change helped spark a spirited discussion of the proper grounds for marriage and divorce.[24] Perhaps more importantly, the ideological pressures on family relationships have eased, and prosperity is softening economic problems and the housing shortage. The housing shortage had forced young couples to remain in the parental household and had led to the premature registration of marriage in urban areas so as to qualify earlier for the housing waiting list. Since 1980, a number of cities have opened up "marriage introduction institutes," which provide a new form of socialist matchmaking to young people. In general, the current tolerance and provision for more private and materialistic concerns have moved issues associated with the family and daily life higher on the public agenda.

The changes occasioned by the household responsibility system in agriculture may well be more important for rural family life

---

[24]For contemporary trends in marriage and family matters, see David Chu, trans. and ed., *Sociology and Society in Contemporary China, 1979–1983*, a special issue of *Chinese Sociology and Anthropology*, vol. 16, no. 1–2 (Fall–Winter 1983–84); also contributions by Marilyn Young, Margery Wolf, Gail Hershatter, and Emily Honig to a symposium on "Courtship, Love and Marriage in Contemporary China," *Pacific Affairs*, vol. 57, no. 2 (Summer 1984): 209–69.

than changes in marriage regulations. The household responsibility system, introduced in 1979 and confirmed as a long-term policy in 1984, permits families to contract resources from their production team, deliver an agreed product to the team, and keep the surplus. In effect, although the family does not become the owner of team resources, it does resume its role as a production unit as well as a unit of consumption. From the time that cooperatives were formed in the 1950s until 1979, the unit of production was larger than the family. The family was respected as a social unit and a unit of consumption, but production decisions, task assignments and remuneration were collectively determined, and family income was closely linked to the income of the team as a whole. Now there is no limit set on family income, and a number of peasant families have become quite wealthy. The control of resources and the prospect of family success or failure binds its members together much more closely than before and strengthens its authority structure. This in turn weakens local party control and the capacity of the party to mobilize energies for its projects. The resurgence of superstition in rural areas is a symptom of ideological and/or organizational weakness. The new policies also introduce a potentially volatile polarization between wealthy and poor families. Even if everyone benefits from modernization policies, more successful peasants may expand their wealth exponentially because of opportunity for reinvestment of profits, and they are encouraged to become involved in local leadership. One would expect that a growing gap between rich and poor, powerful and weak, would create egalitarian pressures at the local level. Of course, it can be expected that the CCP will react to emerging problems with new policies, but the current leadership would want to retain the basic thrust of current policies while ameliorating negative consequences, rather than to change policy direction.

One policy that puts the regime at odds with the private desires of Chinese families is population policy. There have been several phases in Chinese population policy.[25] In 1949–1953, the government looked favorably on population growth and so restricted abortion and prohibited sterilization. From 1953 until

[25] For a short official account of China's population policy, see Qin Xinzhong, "Evolution of China's Population Policy," *BR*, vol. 27, no. 3 (January 16, 1984): 17–19.

the 1970s, there was a recognition of a population problem, but control measures were ineffective. In the meantime, increasing life expectancies and prosperity coupled with decreasing infant mortality were causing a population explosion that peaked in 1963–1972. In rural areas, births were encouraged not only by traditional views that a large family was a source of wealth and security in old age, but also by distributive policies in the communes. By the early 1970s, Mao Zedong, who initially was critical of population control, supported a nationwide drive for late marriages and stronger birth control. These policies began a significant decline in the rate of population growth. In the 1980s, however, the regime is faced with a very difficult situation. The baby boom generation of the 1960s comes to marriageable age in this decade, and their desire to have children is augmented by prosperity and stability, rapidly improving housing, and strengthening of the family as a unit of production. However, because the child-bearing cohort is so large, even one child per family would result in a population increase of 200 million by the year 2000, and two children per family would produce an increase of 400 million. Consequently, the regime has adopted a strict policy of one child per family except in specified unusual circumstances. This policy has had the unintended effect of encouraging female infanticide because only male children continue the family line. The government has responded with a vigorous campaign for the rights of women and children. The contradiction between the private good of the family and the public necessity of population control may remain the greatest source of tension between the government and the family in the 1980s.

The family's emergence as a cooperating rather than target institution in Communist society is due in part to its residual strength, its capacity to meet human needs that cannot be satisfied elsewhere. Elites have also discovered that extreme disruption of family life, as in the first push toward marriage reform or in the mobilization of 1958, is counterproductive. In other words, there is an economic rationale to the implicit toleration of some traditional practices, a toleration that seems to enhance social stability and economic production, just as retaining family responsibility for certain welfare costs reduces public expenses in these areas. Finally, reforms in other areas (education, collectivization of the economy, and creation of new political organizations) both shape and limit the family's socializing role. As time goes by, parents influenced by other socializing agents are more likely to reflect the official ethic, while institutional changes reduce the family's role relative to public organizations. All of these considerations help to explain why the CCP has compromised some of its revolutionary values, such as the drive for full equality of women in marital practices and roles, in exchange for stabilization of the family's place in the new society.

The Educational System. The system of public education that has emerged in China since 1949 is one of the state's most extensive and effective agents for altering Chinese political attitudes. Success in establishing and expanding the system has been impressive. Primary schools now admit 93 percent of their cohort, a figure that is close to that of industrialized countries, thirty percentage points better than the average for the developing world, and remarkable considering that in 1949 admission was at 25 percent. Junior middle schools admit 50 percent of their cohort, up from 5 percent in 1949. One-third of junior middle school graduates go to senior or specialized middle schools, and one-tenth of senior middle school graduates go to college.[26] With a total enrollment approaching 250 million, the Chinese educational system services about 40 percent of all students in the developing world.[27] There are also massive television educational programs, adult programs, and teacher retraining programs.

The educational system has been both the beneficiary and the victim of the regime's interest in political socialization. For twenty years, from 1957 to 1977, the primary purpose of education was one of propagating revolutionary values, such as the dignity of manual labor and the importance of the collective. The egalitarianism of the Maoist period made it the time of greatest expansion of educational opportunity, but at the same time its anti-intellectual bias caused a severe slip in quality. Since 1978, education has been reoriented toward the service of economic

[26]Calculated from 1982 census data and the *Almanac of China's Economy 1983*, pp. iv–153. Also World Bank, *Socialist Economic Development*, vol. 3, pp. 134, 147.
[27]World Bank, ibid., vol. 3 p. 146.

modernization, and ideological work has assumed a less important although still prominent role. The change in educational priorities has led to a shift of emphasis from the quantitative extension of education to its professional quality. Primary school enrollment has dropped in response to decreasing numbers of school-age children, but the constriction of secondary school enrollment shown on Table V.1 is the result of consolidation and the closing of substandard schools. Education continues its socializing mission, however, it does so in accordance with the new priorities of the post-Mao regime.

This is not to say that a system that once produced devoted Maoists is now educating young modernizers. Education can never be a wholly successful instrument for establishing attitudes favored by future elites. The influence of other socializing forces, conflict among elites over the functions and content of education, and limitations on the capacity of schools to accomplish what is demanded of them ensure that students will never conform to any single attitudinal pattern. Still, the educational system carries a heavy long-term responsibility for change. Unlike the family, which affects everyone at an impressionable age but is difficult to penetrate, the schools are subject to a high degree of state control. In contrast to the communications network and generalized political experience, which have their greatest impact on adults in rather uneven and unpredictable ways, the schools provide a mechanism for sustained and structured contact with most school-age citizens.

The Chinese educational system rivals that of the United States in complexity and local variation; and, moreover, its policies have changed dramatically over the years, so generalizations about the system must be very general indeed.[28] It includes five major branches: preschool programs, primary schools, middle schools (including junior and senior levels, plus a variety of vocational and technical schools), institutions of higher education, and various television, part-time, and spare-time schools that overlap in level with the more standardized full-time schools.

[28]See Marianne Bastid, "A la Recherche d'une Strategie de l'Education: Ecole et Developpement Economique depuis 1949," *Tiers Monde*, vol. 22, no. 86 (April–June 1981): 317–38; also the discussion in Leo A. Orleans, "Communist China's Education: Policies, Problems and Prospects," in *An Economic Profile of Mainland China*, vol. 2, pp. 505–12.

TABLE V.1 *Enrollments and Graduates by Level of School (in Thousands)*

	Primary schools		Middle schools		Universities	
Year	Enrollment	Graduates	Enrollment	Graduates	Enrollment	Graduates
Peak year prior to						
1949	23,683	4,633	1,879	399	155	25
1949	24,391	2,387	1,268	352	117	21
1952	51,100	5,942	3,126	289	191	32
1958	86,400	16,225	9,990	1,504	660	72
1960	N/A	N/A	N/A	N/A	955	135
1965	116,000	N/A	14,318	N/A	674	170

The Cultural Revolution: All schools closed for at least two years, with primary schools the first to reopen, universities the last. The closures produced a noticeable lag in graduates from middle schools and universities.

	Primary schools		Middle schools		Universities	
1967	N/A	N/A	N/A	690	N/A	10
1970	N/A	N/A	N/A	1,266	N/A	40
1975	130,000	N/A	34,000	N/A	400	N/A
1977	150,000	N/A	59,079	N/A	584	N/A
1979	146,629	20,900	60,248	N/A	1,020	162
1980	146,269	N/A	56,778	16,298	1,143	146

1981	143,328	N/A	50,145	17,100	1,280	139
1982	139,720	20,689	47,548	15,978	1,154	457
1983	135,780	N/A	46,873	N/A	1,207	335
(1989 projection)	98,000	N/A	72,452	N/A	N/A	N/A

Sources: Figures for the years down to 1958 are from John Phillip Emerson, "Employment in Mainland China," United States Congress, Joint Economic Committee, *An Economic Profile of Mainland China* (Washington: Government Printing Office, 1967), pp. 424–25. The 1960 university enrollment is from Emerson, "Manpower Training and Utilization of Specialized Cadres, 1949–68," in John Lewis, ed., *The City in Communist China* (Stanford, Cal.: Stanford University Press, 1971), p. 200. Enrollments for 1965 are from *Peking Review*, no. 5 (February 3, 1978), p. 17. Enrollments for 1975 are from *The Unites States and China, A Report to the Senate Foreign Relations Committee and the House International Relations Commitee, United States Congress* (Washington: Government Printing Office, 1975), p. 21. Graduates for 1960, 1965, 1967, and 1970 are from Leo Orleans, "China's Science and Technology," in United States Congress, Joint Economic Committee, *People's Republic of China: An Economic Assessment* (Washington: Government Printing Office, 1972), pp. 218–219. Enrollments for 1977 are from Suzanne Pepper, "An Interview on Changes in Chinese Education After the 'Gang of Four,'" *China Quarterly*, no. 72 (December 1977): 815–16. Most of the 1979 to 1982 data are from Marianne Bastid, "Chinese Educational Policies in the 1980s and Economic Development," *China Quarterly*, no. 98 (June 1984): 189–219. The 1983 figures are from the State Statistical Bureau, "Communiqué on the Fulfillment of China's 1983 National Economic Plan," (April 29, 1984), published in *BR*, vol. 27, no. 20 (May 14, 1984): x. The 1989 projections are World Bank projections from *China: Socialist Economic Development*, vol. 3, pp. 220–26.

Although the system is a centralized one, governed throughout by regulations and/or control from central ministries that establish national standards for administration and content, it has much variety within it. Quality of institutions at the primary level varies from urban key schools, where students enjoy the best available teaching and material resources, to rural schools that have no glass in the windows, that have local peasants as teachers, and that are equipped only with textbooks, tables, and benches. Particularly at preschool, primary, and part-time and spare-time levels, there are some nongovernmental schools established by local units or volunteers; although subject to governmental approval and regulation, and possibly recipients of subsidies, such schools inject an element of citizen participation into educational operations. Lengths of term and courses of study are not uniform for all schools of the same level, and there have been frequent revisions of central educational policies since 1949.

In terms of political socialization, progress toward universal education has been the system's most consistent objective. To shift the burden of socialization toward the public realm and to establish widespread mass literacy to facilitate continued political education and upgrading of skills, the schools must approach universality of enrollment for school-age population groups. Universal education for the entire population is, of course, a difficult goal. In 1956, with an illiteracy rate of 70 percent among young people, a twelve-year program for the elimination of illiteracy was adopted. In 1983, with illiteracy remaining at 34 percent of the adult population, the campaign against illiteracy was renewed, and a target date of 1990 was set for the achievement of universal primary education. Of course, a 46 percent reduction in illiteracy is a monumental accomplishment, especially considering the difficulty of achieving literacy in the Chinese language.[29] In practice, a high and increasing proportion of enrollment

---

[29] See World Bank, *Socialist Economic Development*, vol. 3, pp. 123–230 for data. Minimal literacy in Chinese requires the memorization of at least 1,000 characters. Since the characters are complicated and not phonetic, this feat is more similar to memorizing 1,000 telephone numbers than it is to being able to recognize 1,000 alphabetic words. Reasonable literacy requires knowledge of 3,000 characters, which takes 40 percent of class time for five years of primary school.

of school-age children also represents significant progress. Although primary school enrollment is decreasing as the age cohort is decreasing (due to birth control), the percentage of the cohort entering primary school is gradually increasing. However, given the intense concern of Chinese elites for universal attitudinal change, what might be considered "significant progress" by some does not guarantee the satisfaction of the elite—hence the frequency and centrality in Chinese politics of controversy over the educational system.

The primary schools carry the major burden of efforts to achieve universal education and the basic literacy associated with it. Before the Cultural Revolution, the standard primary course was a six-year program, which began at about the age of seven and customarily was divided into four-year junior and two-year senior primary schools. The current structure is a five-year unified program followed by junior middle school. Enrollment increased sharply during the 1950s, reaching 86.4 million in 1958 (see Table V.1)—a figure representing 67 percent of the primary school age group (seven to twelve years) at the time. In effect, the percentage receiving *full* primary education was certainly lower than this. Some overage students would be included due to late starts, and enrollment as such was no guarantee of completing the six-year program. In many rural areas, completion of only the junior primary course was apparently the norm. Moreover, 1960 probably marked the high point of attendance in the regular schools prior to the Cultural Revolution (at least as a percentage of school-age population), as enrollments slowed or fell in the early 1960s, while population continued to grow.[30]

Middle schools expanded even more rapidly during the 1950s but remained accessible to a very small number of people. Their basic function was to provide advanced academic, vocational, and political training to select students who formed the pool from which China's new elite would be recruited. This task rested mainly on the regular middle schools, which trained the

[30]Ibid.; and Price, *Education in Communist China*, p. 128. The continued growth of primary and middle enrollments down to 1965, shown in Table V.1, probably indicates inclusion of various part-time school enrollments in the totals for that year.

vast majority of new teachers, technicians, and low-level government cadres. Middle school enrollment is difficult to estimate, owing to the variety of schools operating at this level; but regular middle schools probably reached a peak enrollment of about 10 million in 1958–60. Thus, only about 10 percent of primary graduates continued on to regular middle school, and most who did so completed only the three-year junior middle school course; about one out of six junior middle school graduates went on to senior middle school.[31]

The most rapid expansion in the early and mid-1950s occurred in higher education. Admission increased from a miniscule .3 percent of the age cohort in 1949 to 1.6 percent in 1958, a fivefold increase within a decade. The number of universities and colleges expanded from 205 to 791. The late 1950s were a golden age for going to college. By 1957, there were more university openings than there were senior middle school graduates.[32] In 1960, higher education achieved a peak enrollment of almost 1 million, a figure not surpassed until 1979. Adjusted for population, the 1960 figure may not be attained until the late 1980s.

In general, the regular school system greatly expanded educational opportunities during the late 1950s; however, the expansion was imbalanced in favor of advanced education in urban areas. Planners were intimidated by the sheer magnitude of the task of providing universal education to rural areas, and the tasks of modernization demanded the rapid expansion of specialized training. The rationale for educational policy was a mixture of traditional Chinese respect for education, the progressive belief throughout the twentieth century that modern education was the key to solving China's problems, and the influence of the Soviet model. By the mid-1950s, educational progress was clearly out of balance, and the system lacked a clear revolutionary focus. The system was seen as giving relatively advanced and prolonged education to the few (encouraging in them hopes for a purely official career), while limiting the educational benefits to rural areas and the working population.

Two major lines of reform appeared in response. One was proposed reform of the regular system itself, with calls for reduction in years of study, less emphasis on specialized academic

---

[31] Orleans, "Communist China's Education," pp. 505–12.
[32] Bastid, "A la Recherche," pp. 317–38.

programs, and the injection of some working or production experience into the regular school schedule. The other was a strenuous effort during the Great Leap Forward to expand worker and peasant access to education and to reduce illiteracy. Besides redirecting the attention of the educational establishment in this direction, two important new policies were introduced. The first was the policy of "management by the people with the assistance of the government." This was an arrangement whereby localities would establish their own schools, building the buildings themselves and providing food for the teachers. This lessened the dependence of educational expansion on central planning and financing. As a result, enrollment increases reported for 1958 were astonishing: 34 percent in primary schools and 42 percent in middle schools in one year.[33] The second policy was to expand spare-time and part-time (half-work, half-study) schools. Such schools had existed in various forms since the early 1950s, but their intensified promotion as an alternative to the regular full-time schools was a distinctive feature of the Great Leap Forward. Spare-time schools are essentially courses in adult education frequently organized by local production units to provide basic training in literacy, occupational skills, and politics for the working population. Part-time or half-work, half-study programs are diverse, operating at many levels under different forms of management and offering different combinations of study and work experience. Aimed mainly at young people, they attempt to offer an educational program nominally approximating that of the regular schools but without separating the student from his or her production responsibilities. The best example is the agricultural middle schools, which flourished in the late 1950s as a response to the regular schools' failure to provide adequate education for rural youth.[34] In 1958 alone, enrollment in part-time primary schools went up 333 percent, middle schools 85 percent, and higher education 100 percent.

[33] The 1958 enrollment statistics and much of the discussion of changes in educational policy are based on ibid.

[34] For details on spare-time and part-time education in the late 1950s and early 1960s, see Robert D. Barendson, *Half-Work Half-Study Schools in Communist China* (Washington, D.C.: U.S. Department of Health, Education and Welfare, Office of Education, 1964); and Paul Harper, *Spare-Time Education for Workers in Communist China* (Washington, D.C.: U.S. Department of Health, Education and Welfare, Office of Education, 1964).

As the 1958 enrollment statistics indicate, educational reform was caught up in the illusion of instant progress that characterized the Great Leap. The collapse of the Great Leap, the economic crisis and retrenchment policies that followed, and the general inertia or resistance of many within the school system required massive retrenchment and reorientation in education. In theory, the regular schools committed themselves to a more proletarian line, giving prominence to politics and the working class in their policies and requiring their staff and students to participate in productive labor. In practice, these measures were routinized to minimize their impact. Test performance was the major criterion for admission and achievement: in practice, this meant that middle class children succeeded disproportionately.[35] The spare-time and part-time schools survived, continuing to serve at least some of their intended functions by bringing political and practical education to millions excluded from the regular schools; however, they remained subordinate to the latter in academic quality and social prestige. Tensions between Maoist egalitarianism and incipient stratification led to a frontal assault on the educational establishment in the Cultural Revolution.

In part, the Cultural Revolution brought a return of the educational policies of the Great Leap in a more extreme form. Proletarian values were paramount. All educational institutions were supposed to operate on a half-work, half-study basis; students were required to spend two years in manual labor before going to college; and teachers were sent to "May Seventh cadre schools" to reestablish their links with the masses. Entrance exams and even academic performance were replaced as primary criteria for advancement by evaluations of personal revolutionary qualities. The primary, secondary, and tertiary curricula were reduced to five, four, and two to three years respectively, with 10 percent of class time occupied by political study.[36] While university enrollment was reduced drastically, primary enrollment increased and secondary enrollment quadrupled. The educational trend of the 1950s was completely reversed, and the opposite imbalances were created.

[35]Statistics on the class background of students at the Shanghai Foreign Languages Institute in 1966 are given in Neale Hunter, *Shanghai Journal* (Boston: Beacon, 1969), p. 60.

[36]Bastid, "A la Recherche," pp. 326–7.

Another, more destructive, aspect of the Cultural Revolution was the effect of its emphasis on class struggle in the educational system. By the end of 1966, the entire school system was closed. The primary schools reopened in the spring of 1968, the middle schools in the fall of 1968, and the universities in 1970.[37] But the loss of up to four years of education was not the most serious harm done. Intellectuals were reviled as the "stinking ninth category" of bad class elements; campuses and schoolyards became battlegrounds for mortal factional wars; and priceless historical objects were destroyed in the name of proletarian culture. The Cultural Revolution denied normal educational advancement to an entire generation of Chinese youth. The deprivation is especially cruel because the post-Mao leadership places great emphasis on educational qualifications.

Educational policies since 1978 appear to be a return to those of the 1950s, but they are also a response to the accomplishments and imbalances of the intervening twenty years. Higher education is again emphasized, as in the 1950s; however, the great expansion of primary and secondary education in the Maoist period has made the emphasis more reasonable and urgent. The earlier expansion also calls for qualitative retrenchment, especially necessary because of the chaos and anti-intellectual values of the Cultural Revolution. Findings that 53 percent of elementary school teachers and 70 percent of junior middle school teachers were unqualified led to massive inservice retraining programs. In 1983, one-fifth of all teachers were involved in some form of further study.[38] Qualitative retrenchment also led to a closing of many middle schools and a consequent reduction of middle school enrollment, as shown in Table V.1. The most controversial reform has been the reestablishment of key schools, that is, elementary and middle schools with priority treatment in educational resources and competitive enrollment policies. Key schools were originally established in the 1950s but were criticized during the Cultural Revolution for elitism and disbanded.

Not all change has been constrictive, however. Expansion continues in educational budgets, graduate schools, universities,

[37] Ibid., p. 326.
[38] Marianne Bastid, "Chinese Educational Policies in the 1980s and Economic Development," *China Quarterly*, no. 98 (June 1984): 189–220.

television education, and kindergartens. The Central Radio and Television University, established in 1979, had 410,000 students by the end of 1982, 35 percent of the regular university enrollment. In both expansion and retrenchment, the educational system is responding to the needs of a more sophisticated economy.

The role of the educational system in CCP-directed political socialization remains important, but it has been confused by the reversal of Cultural Revolution values, the deemphasis of ideology, and the reemphasis of the training mission of education. Successful students have reason to be positively inclined toward modernization, since their education will qualify them for a leading role. But the ideological flip-flops of the 1970s have produced a cynicism concerning ideological propaganda among college-age adults. Among younger students, the influence of current priorities is visible. In a primary school survey in Shanghai, the four most preferred occupational assignments were: scientist/engineer, PLA soldier, worker, and "obey assignment by the homeland." Among graduating senior middle school students in Shanghai, the top choices were: engineer, doctor, technician, journalist.[39] However, at both levels, agriculture was by far the least desirable occupation; and, in the grade school, politics was by far the least popular subject.

Although students do not simply accept the values preached to them, the schools have had a great influence on political socialization in post-1949 China. By any comparative standard, they have been highly politicized in terms of large blocks of time devoted to explicit political education, the injection of political information and desired political attitudes into basic subjects of instruction (most prominently, into the materials used in the standard readers), an effort to permeate the classroom with official views of public and private morality, and the establishment of party supervision and control over the system as a whole. As a result, certain political themes have been a heavy and inescapable part of the school experience. None of them is surprising, given the nature of the system, but the most salient of them should be noted. One is patriotism, the attempt to transmit basic information about China, its accomplishments and resources, and to instill feelings of love, loyalty, and respect for it. Another

[39]These surveys are translated in David Chu, *Sociology and Society*.

is support for the Communist political system, encouraged through transmission of knowledge about the history and achievements of the CCP and its leaders, particularly Mao Zedong, and the portrayal of the party as the benevolent and righteous leader of the country. Coupled with this is explicit criticism of negative political models, such as the old feudal system, the KMT, imperialism, and the Gang of Four. Finally, political education has emphasized strongly the qualities of the model citizen: hard work, sacrifice, and discipline for the sake of society and the collectivity.[40] With most of the population now exposed to some regular education under Communism, and with the variety of irregular educational programs that have supplemented the regular schools, we can assume the emergence in China of widespread subject orientations—founded on a basic identification with the national political system—coupled with growing enclaves of citizens holding more specialized knowledge about politics and more participant orientations toward their own role in it.

The assertion rests on the simplistic proposition that the political content of Chinese education is sufficiently forceful to have some long-term effect on a population that is increasingly composed of citizens who have partaken of it. There are, of course, many other influences that resist and even oppose the pressures of the educational system—for example, the enduring dictates of the traditional political culture and the possibility of contradictory socializing experiences elsewhere in comtemporary society. Nor is the educational system itself without its internal conflicts over political socialization—conflicts that compromise its capacity to transmit unequivocally the elements of a revolutionary political culture. One of the sharpest conflicts in the Maoist period was between obedience to political authority and encouragement of individual activism; the former's subject orientation toward unfailing acceptance of party leadership cannot always be reconciled with the latter's more participant

---

[40]For a detailed analysis of political socialization in Chinese schools, see Charles Price Ridley, Paul H. B. Godwin, and Dennis J. Doolin, *The Making of a Model Citizen in Communist China* (Stanford, Cal.: Hoover Institution Press, 1971), pp. 3–208; sample selections from primary-school readers are included on pp. 239–404. See also Price, *Education in Communist China*, passim.

orientation toward individual political initiative and action. The major tension of post-Mao socialization is between the collectivist structure and values of society and the material incentives upon which modernization policies are based. There is conflict on the fundamental question of how prominently political socialization should figure in the general educational process. At the root of this is the "red-expert" problem: the question of how to balance competing demands for political education in the service of attitudinal change and for technical education in the service of economic transformation, as well as how best to manage national development given limited educational resources.[41] As the subsequent discussion will argue, these are conflicts that continue to plague the political socialization process. Yet their very existence and the seriousness with which elites debate them suggest that the new educational system is making its mark on the Chinese political culture.

The Communications Network. Political communications in China, as in other societies, include an immense variety and volume of messages. Although China may be considered a relatively closed system in which communications patterns and media are usually restricted by government controls, its tendency to politicize so many areas of human action ensures a heavy flow of communications about politics. Our interest here is primarily in media policy, inasmuch as media policy both reflects the regime's attitudes toward information availability and shapes the content of publicly available information.[42] Other major sectors of political communications, such as the expression of

[41]See Donald J. Munro, "Egalitarian Ideal and Educational Fact in Communist China," in John M. H. Lindbeck, ed., *China: Management of a Revolutionary Society* (Seattle: University of Washington Press, 1971), pp. 256–301; Suzanne Pepper, "Educational and Political Development in Communist China," *Studies in Comparative Communism*, vol. 3, nos. 3–4 (July–October 1970): 198–223; and Bastid, "Chinese Educational Policies."

[42]For a comprehensive overview of Chinese media, see Harold Jacobson, *Systems of Internal Communication in the People's Republic of China* (United States Information Agency Research Report R-22-83, December 1983). The richest source of data on Chinese media is *Zhongguo Xinwen Nianjian* (Almanac of Chinese News), which began publication in 1982. See also John Howkins, *The Media in China* (London: Nord Media Ltd., 1980); Godwin Chu, ed., *Popular Media in China: Shaping New Cultural Patterns* (Honolulu: University Press of Hawaii, 1978); Alan Liu, *Communication and National Integration in*

political interests and the demands and exchanges relating to the making and implementation of decisions, will be examined in subsequent chapters.

The public communications network in China is almost exclusively an official (state or party) operation, subject in its content and management to the control of central political authorities. The organization of this official monopoly on public communications is complex. State agencies administer most major media—such as the New China [Xinhua] News Agency, radio and television stations, the film industry, and most publishing enterprises—but the CCP and its supporting mass organizations also publish important newspapers and periodicals. General newspapers are directly under the party committees at the respective level. For example, the *People's Daily* is an organ of the Central Committee, the *Shaanxi Daily* is an organ of the Shaanxi provincial party committee, and the *Xi'an Evening News* is an organ of the Xi'an municipal party committee. Regardless of the administrative source or level of operation, however, all media are subject to the general controls and policies established by the CCP Central Committee's Propaganda Department. Through its sections for specific communications areas and its authority over propaganda departments within lower-level party organizations, it seeks to ensure that all media follow central party policy in the dissemination of information and ideas through the printed and spoken word.

Party supervision of all public communications cannot guarantee in practice that the media always speak with one voice. The division of operational control among state, party, and mass organization units at various administrative levels has produced some deviation from the central line. Moreover, the central line as such has been ambiguous or disputed at times, resulting in intended or unintended conflicts between messages put forth by different sources. The Propaganda Department itself was torn apart in the first year of the Cultural Revolution,

China (Berkeley: University of California Press, 1971); Frederick T. C. Yu, *Mass Persuasion in Communist China* (New York: Praeger, 1964); and Jorg-Meinhard Rudolph, "China's Media: Fitting News to Print," *Problems of Communism* vol. 33, no. 4 (July–August 1984): 58–67.

highlighting a particular vulnerability of the media to changes in political line. The departures from total control do not alter two generalizations that follow from the attempt to achieve it. The first is that virtually all information disseminated through the network is that which central leadership or subordinates acting on their perceptions of central intent have approved for public release. The public is told what the leadership wants it to know; competing or contradictory messages have no organized vehicle for response. Thus almost every news item in the Chinese press has a quasi-official quality; it is there because it relates positively to current policy. Politically neutral news, such as accidents and minor disasters, are ignored, and published news that conflicts with current policy is usually a sign of dissension or of impending policy change. The other generalization is that a clear sense of hierarchical authority permeates the system and is in fact essential to its effective operation. Communications from more authoritative sources will overrule those from subordinate ones; contradictions and confusion require direction from above for resolution. In the absence of consistent messages from the highest authorities, lower communications agents and the body politic as a whole tend toward inaction or conflict.

A second characteristic of political communications in China is the governing influence of ideology and its special vocabulary. As Schurmann points out, the "closing" effect of official control over communications is not simply secrecy or censorship—much significant information is transmitted publicly—but rather the requirement that communications be cast in the language of the official ideology.[43] The ideologically specific meaning of concepts and terms becomes a separate language system for public discourse; it provides a unifying bond and mechanism for those who "speak" it, while at the same time screening out those who do not or those concepts that have no place in it. As with all languages, employment of it involves not simply the use of certain words but internalization of the manner of thinking that makes those words intelligible. As a result, much of what passes through the communications system is aimed in the first instance at elites or subelites who have the capacity to understand

---

[43] Franz Schurmann, *Ideology and Organization in Communist China*, 2nd ed., enl. (Berkeley: University of California Press, 1968), pp. 58–68.

it and the responsibility to disseminate it with appropriate explanation and reference to local circumstances to the general population.

Finally, the style of public communications is distinctly pedagogical. Questions are posed, arguments listed, and conclusions drawn; reason and persuasion attempt to guide the recipient to a specific position; slogans and catchword devices (such as the use of numbered sets of points, commonly identified by numbers only once the points are known) that lend themselves to memorization and repetition abound; good and bad "models" illustrate how policies should be implemented—which experiences should be emulated and which shunned. As the Great Leap slogan put it, "the whole nation is a classroom," and the communications system plays a vital part in the education or reeducation of the nation's population. Although the media is much less ideological and pedagogical in the post-Mao period, these features are still strikingly present when contrasted to Western media. In a major policy statement issued in 1985, Hu Yaobang strongly reaffirmed the media's role as "the mouthpiece of the party" and rejected suggestions that media operate as autonomous, profit-making enterprises.[44]

Political communications in China vary in their intended audience and the kind of medium employed. In terms of the intended audience, we may distinguish among foreign-oriented media, "internal" (*neibu*) or secret media, specialized media, and mass media. The category of mass media may be further divided into print, radio, and television. The major foreign-oriented media consist of shortwave broadcasts in six languages, Xinhua news releases, various magazines (especially *Beijing Review*), and the English language daily newspaper *China Daily*. The last has a significant domestic readership as well; two-thirds of its readers are Chinese. It began publishing in May 1981, and in its first two years had 64,000 subscribers.[45]

Ironically, only China's many internal media have the primary function of providing information to their audiences. Because the audience of internal media is restricted, the information in

[44]*Renmin Ribao (People's Daily)*, April 15, 1985.

[45]Jacobson, *Systems of Internal Communicaton*, pp. 278–79; *Almanac of Chinese News 1983*, p. 528.

the media does not have to be as closely controlled. The internal media system is very extensive and has many uses, but details of its operation are of course unavailable to outside observers. Many inhouse journals are classified *internal*; for instance, the Shaanxi Provincial Journalism Research Institute publishes an internal quarterly, *Journalism Research*, which is primarily for professional journalists.[46] Likewise, textbooks that have not yet been cleared for publication may circulate on an internal basis, and many party levels have their own restricted publications. Some internal publications include less inhibited discussions and disputes concerning current policy. The basic principle for determining circulation of internal publications is "need to know"—work units have access to internal material appropriate to their function.

The most interesting internal publications from the point of view of political socialization are those that make available more news of the outside world. Two are especially noteworthy: *Reference News (Cankao Xiaoxi)* and *Reference Materials (Cankao Ziliao)*. The latter is by far the most restricted. It is published twice a day in 80–90 page issues, the equivalent of 300–400 typed pages per day, and consists mostly of translated items from the foreign press.[47] It is similar to the United States Central Intelligence Agency's Foreign Broadcast Information Service *Daily Report*, except that the *Daily Report* is unclassifed while the *Reference Materials* is highly restricted. By contrast, *Reference News*, a daily, four-page compilation of foreign wire service reports, is probably the world's most popular "secret" media. Sometimes, the articles translated in *Reference News* are distorted, but by and large it is a faithful rendering of material from world news services; it does include material critical of China. Its circulation of 8.5 million is considerably larger than that of *People's Daily* (5.2 million), and comparable to the combined circulation of the ten largest U.S. newspapers. Through *Reference News*, the educated Chinese citizen has available a considerable variety of high-quality international news.

Specialty publications are by far the fastest-growing category of Chinese media. Their circulation grew by 320 percent in 1982

[46]*Almanac of Chinese News 1982*, p. 401.
[47]See Rudolph, "China's Media," pp. 61–62.

alone, although a good deal of that growth was due to inclusion of Chinese equivalents of *TV Guide* which, as in the United States, have the largest periodical circulations. Besides the consumer and sports magazines, the specialty and professional publications play an increasingly important role in providing relevant information to various sectors of society. In time these specialty and professional periodicals will probably strengthen the collective identity and self-consciousness of different sectors in Chinese society.

Mass media consist of publicly available general news sources. These come in a great variety and have a definite pecking order. Although television and radio have larger audiences, the print media, as the news of record, have the most prestige. Within the print media, the hierarchy is set by the status of the party committee to which the newspaper is attached. *People's Daily (Renmin Ribao, Jen-min Jih-pao)* is the authoritative national newspaper, the equivalent of the Soviet Union's *Pravda*. However, *People's Daily* is generally considered a dull newspaper, and its important articles are reprinted in all other newspapers. Provincial-level newspapers have a combined readership approximately twice that of *People's Daily*, and the readership of lower-level newspapers is twice that of the provincial press.[48] The fastest growing segment of the mass print media is the municipal evening newspapers. These usually feature more lively and investigative reporting than the more stodgy provincial and national press, and of course they present more local news and entertainment information.

Bordering on the specialty media are national newspapers such as *Worker's Daily, Liberation Army Daily, China Peasant News*, and the *China Youth News (Zhongguo Qingnian Bao)*, the organ of the Communist Youth League. The most important semispecialty periodical is *Red Flag (Hongqi)*, which is the theoretical journal of the Central Committee (CC) and provides ideological guidance to the CCP. Although generally available, only those with a considerable interest in CC theoretical and political concerns would read it regularly. More readable information about national politics and personalities is provided by

---

[48]Calculated from 1982 data supplied in *Almanac of Chinese News 1983*, pp. 527–48.

the new journals *Semi-Monthly Talk (Banyue Tan)* and *Observation Post (Liaowang)*.

Radio is probably the most widely used media in China, although television is rapidly increasing its audience share. The radio news system extends from central broadcasting through the province down to a wired radio network that reaches almost the entire rural population. Each level carries the national news and then adds its own news, entertainment, and educational programs. Very precise standard Chinese is used in most radio programming, but many provinces also broadcast in minority languages and local dialects. Audience interest in programming varies widely. In a Beijing survey, 76 percent of urban listeners were interested in the news, while only 39 percent of rural listeners were. By contrast, 62 percent of rural listeners liked serialized novels, but only 37 percent of urban listeners did.[49]

Television is rapidly assuming importance as an information medium comparable to its role in the West. In Beijing, 86 percent of urban workers' families and 33 percent of peasant families had televisions in 1982.[50] Of course, Beijing could be expected to be far ahead of the rest of China in television ownership, but the broadcast network is improving (with the help of a Chinese communications satellite launched in 1984), and private ownership of televisions is growing very rapidly. Although news is the most popular item in urban areas, peasants are even less interested in television news than they are in radio news and are correspondingly more interested in movies and drama. The latter are also well received by urban audiences, and when a very popular dramatic series is shown, such as a martial arts thriller broadcast in the spring of 1984, it seems that all of China is tuned in.

Media in China have undergone tremendous changes since the founding of the PRC. As Table V.2 indicates, the dominant trend has been one of growth; however, the Cultural Revolution severely affected some aspects of media development. It had some effects on the volume of print media, but its most severe effect was the restriction of variety and content. At least one-third

[49]*Almanac of Chinese News 1983*, p. 261.
[50]Ibid.

TABLE V.2 *Media Growth in China*

Year	Book Titles	New Book Titles	Magazines	Newspapers	Radio Stations	TV Stations
1950	12,153	7,049	295	382	49 (1949)	
1955	21,071	13,187	370	285	61 (1957)	
1960	30,797	19,670	442	396	94 (1962)	14
1965	20,143	12,352	790	343	87	12
1968	3,694	2,677	22	49	—	—
1970	4,889	3,870	21	42	80	31
1975	13,716	10,633	476	180	88	32
1980	21,621	17,660	2,191	188	106	38
1981	25,601	19,854	2,801	242	114	42
1982	31,784	23,445	3,100	277	118	47

Source: Zhongguo Tongji Nianjian 1983 (Statistical Yearbook of China), edited by the State Statistical Bureau (Beijing: Chinese Statistical Press, 1983), pp. 529–34.

of the books printed between 1966 and 1968 were copies of five compilations of Mao's works, including the "Little Red Book" of Mao quotations of 2 billion copies.[51] In essence, the Cultural Revolution reduced centrally controlled media to its propaganda function, and control of the media remained a major strength of the leftists until Mao's death in 1976. Since 1978, the informational component of media has expanded well beyond its pre–Cultural Revolution heights, although the control of the party, the boundaries set by ideological orthodoxy, and the pedagogical tone of most news/propaganda stories are still present.

Of course, the question concerning the credibility of media is not answered by data concerning its availability. Do Chinese citizens fit the 1950s image of brainwashing, so well described by the following observer?

> The head of a good Chinese citizen today functions like a sort of radio receiving set. Somewhere in Peiping [Beijing] buzzes the great transmitting station which broadcasts the right thought and

[51]Calculated from *Statistical Yearbook of China* and Jacobson, *Systems of Internal Communication.*

the words to be repeated. Millions of heads faithfully pick them up, and millions of mouths repeat them like loudspeakers.[52]

Or are the Chinese sophisticated and somewhat jaded consumers of propaganda, much like American consumers of advertising? Answering this question requires survey data of the Chinese media audience, and hitherto there have been no studies that would confirm or deny conjectures. However, in 1982 the Journalism Institute of the Chinese Academy of Sciences carried out a large-scale sample survey of the Beijing media audience, including questions concerning the credibility of news. These results, which are translated in Table V.3, show a highly critical but not totally alienated audience. Although the differences between the categories of respondents are interesting, in general the majority finds the news "basically believable"; however, only a minority asserts that it is totally credible. The reasons given for distrusting the news relate to the distortion and stereotyping that is endemic in propaganda. Evidently, the regime pays a high price in audience trust for the subordination of media to policy. On the other hand, access to foreign news through *Reference News* or directly through Voice of America, BBC, and Radio Moscow as well as rumor and their own experience apparently convince citizens that they are not simply being presented a dream world by the official media.

Mass media other than news media include films and live dramatic performances. The Chinese film industry is active, although it is still developing and is peculiarly vulnerable to political shifts. Enough films and facilities have been produced since 1949 to make viewing common in the cities. Rural viewing has been expanded greatly by traveling projection teams and efforts to set up permanent projection facilities in communes. In contrast to newspaper reading, which may be a chore even for the literate, film viewing is easy and entertaining. It has tremendous potential for government communication with the masses, even though most peasants still see only a few films a year. Dramatic performances (plays, opera, ballet, and variety shows) are frequent and popular in the cities, with traveling troupes offering less frequent rural performances.

---

[52] Robert Guilain, *600 Million Chinese* (New York: Criterion Books, 1957). Quoted in Jacobson, *Systems of Internal Communication*.

Although it is impossible to say exactly what impact the political communications network has on Chinese political attitudes, a few comments about variations in the intensity of the communications experience may shed some light on this question. First, it is safe to assume that reception of political propaganda is nearly universal and fairly frequent for all Chinese citizens. That is, virtually all are exposed regularly to the messages of at least some of the formal media—primarily press, radio, and films—all of which have a high political content. The cumulative effects of this reception probably have raised the general level of knowledge about political personalities and affairs, created a greater sense of identification with the national political system, and encouraged among citizens greater receptivity to the demands and values of political elites. However, the degree of attitudinal change as contrasted to a greater awareness of and knowledge about politics may be minimal, simply because ordinary propaganda does not require a response. No matter how frequent and extensive its coverage, media propaganda permits the recipient to remain passive. If passivity is a cover for resistance, then repeated exposure to the message may even have negative effects.

The preceding discussion has identified some of the audiences and media that are involved in the Chinese communications network but has said nothing about one of its most important and distinctive forms—face-to-face contact in meetings or small-group encounters. Although such meetings are much less frequent and intense than they were during the Cultural Revolution, they are still an important part of life at least for state workers and cadres. In any case, all party cadres are expected to stay in frequent, informal contact with the masses of their unit and explain and justify party policy. Several factors may account for the Chinese emphasis on direct, personal contact in political communications. One factor is surely the problem of illiteracy, which, as noted, affects the use of formal media as well by elevating radio and film use relative to that of the printed media. Another factor is the example of the Soviet Union, where every factory has its agitprop teams to deliver the party's message personally to fellow workers.

The CCP's historical experience of mass mobilization, under circumstances in which face-to-face contact was sometimes the only possible means of communication, also influences its contemporary style. Apart from these societally specific influences,

TABLE V.3 *The Credibility of Chinese Media among the Beijing Audience*

Question: What is your view of the news reports carried in newspapers?

Answer	Sex		Household		Occupation		
	Male	Female	Urban	Rural	Worker	Peasant	State Cadre
Believable	25.6	22.5	22.7	33.8	16.8	35.5	26.5
Basically believable	57.8	50.0	57.9	35.2	57.3	35.5	66.2
Not greatly believable	3.2	3.4	3.4	2.8	4.7	3.2	1.5
Unbelievable	.5	.5	.3	1.4	.3	.8	0
Can't say for sure	12.8	23.5	15.6	26.8	20.9	25.0	5.9

Answer	Student	Business employee	Teacher	Scientist/ Technician	Retired	Unemployed
Believable	25.7	22.9	25.0	22.5	50.0	12.5
Basically believable	48.6	55.4	66.1	66.2	35.4	50.0
Not greatly believable	3.7	2.4	1.8	4.2	2.1	0
Unbelievable	1.8	1.2	0	0	2.1	0
Can't say for sure	20.2	18.1	7.1	7.0	10.4	37.5

Reasons given for incomplete credibility

Percent of Respondents	Reason
44.3	"The content of some news reports does not correspond to reality."
43.7	"In some reports everything is all good or all bad."
29.2	"Sometimes only good news is reported."
27.0	"Some reports are unreal."
17.0	"All of the above."
9.3	"Can't say."

Areas in which the news is not completely credible

Percent of Respondents	Area
30.1	"Reflecting the voice and demands of the masses."
28.4	"Successes in production and raising living standards."
25.9	"Can't say."
19.9	"Improvements in party style; the party serving the people."
17.1	"Socialism is good, capitalism is bad."
16.2	"Praise of models and encouragement of new morality and directions."
16.1	"Criticism of bad tendencies and attacks on economic criminals."
14.4	"Various aspects together."
12.9	"Propoganda for Marxism-Leninism, Mao Zedong Thought and policies."

Responses are from a representative sample of the Beijing population to a survey conducted in the summer of 1982. This set of questions had 1,837 respondents.

Source: Zhongquo Xinwen Nianjian 1983 (Yearbook of Chinese News 1983), Beijing: Chinese Social Sciences Press, 1983, pp. 278–80.

there is the fact that face-to-face contact is a highly effective means of communication in any society.[53] These factors have combined to produce in China a communications system that favors direct, personalized communications.

The resource that makes this possible is an army of political cadres and activists sufficient in number to penetrate every working and/or residential collectivity in China. In the early years of the PRC, when party and mass organization ranks were thin and the formal communications network was yet to be established, the CCP trained "propagandists" and "reporters" with specific responsibility for carrying government messages to the people. As administrative and political posts were filled, and as the regime gained experience in coordinating mass movements with the growing communicatons network, these specialists became unnecessary. Responsibility for direct contact with the masses came to rest on members of the local subelite: basic-level cadres, designated or natural leaders of work or residential groups, party or Youth League members not holding higher cadre posts, persons with middle school or higher education, demobilized soldiers, and others whose personal motivation had led into activism without special background or experience. Higher-level cadres supervise their work and, when necessary, supplement it with personal visits. These low-level cadres and activists are expected to grasp political issues revealed in the formal media and call them to popular attention, explaining and persuading as necessary to secure mass support. They may do this through regular discussion and study groups that examine current news and issues, through special meetings called for problems of particular urgency, or simply through the give-and-take of daily conversation. Of course, there is no guarantee that the full potential of this form of communication is realized, due to variations in ability and motivation of the intermediaries; however, the possibility of establishing personal contact with and response from individual citizens is one of the great strengths of the network.

The most intensive political communications in China occur in what the CCP calls "rectification," "struggle," and "thought

[53]Gabriel A. Almond and G. Bingham Powell, Jr., *Comparative Politics: System, Process, and Policy*, 2nd ed. (Boston: Little, Brown, 1978), pp. 142–43.

reform." Here, particular individuals or groups are criticized in a highly structured setting that allows no escape from confrontation with norms prescribed by the elite. Rectification campaigns, such as the 1984–1985 party rectification campaign, aim at various levels or sectors of the elite, especially CCP members. Normally, they identify certain categories of shortcomings and subject officials to close scrutiny to determine which among them might manifest the deficiencies under attack. Although a few negative models might be named at the outset, the political disposition of most members of the target group depends on their response during the course of the campaign. Rectification (that is, acknowledgment of errors and renewed commitment to the orthodox party line) and not purge is the result for most. Yet some will be found seriously deficient, the consequence being demotion or purge and more hostile struggle. Struggle and thought reform are the extreme forms of political education brought to bear on individuals whose political guilt is already established, whether through a rectification campaign or through information developed in other ways. The structural and psychological dynamics of struggle and thought reform are too complex for analysis here,[54] but there is little question about their capacity to produce extreme disorientation in the subject, while not necessarily creating a permanent attitudinal change in the desired direction. It must be remembered that relatively few Chinese have been on the receiving end of these techniques—at least since the early postliberation years, when whole social groups such as landlords or intellectuals were designated for struggle and reform. Rectification is basically a form of communication and control among the elite. Struggle and thought reform are political and psychological assaults on even more limited numbers, primarily deviant elites and those identified as enemies of the regime.

To summarize, China has acquired the superstructure of a modern communications system and continues to develop its infrastructure. Coverage is most complete for the cities and for the more literate and better-educated citizens. Political communications rely heavily on face-to-face contacts that supplement

[54]For a pioneering exploration of this topic, see Robert Jay Lifton, *Thought Reform and the Psychology of Totalism* (New York: Norton, 1961).

the formal media, particularly by encouraging individual response. The overall impact of communications is greatest for elites, who experience its most intensive forms more frequently and at a higher level of interaction and who are more likely to encounter the full range of media output. In terms of socialization, the system is most effective in expanding knowledge about politics and heightening sensitivity to political issues, although its reception is by no means uncritical. Its role in inducing attitudinal change is more questionable, but in face-to-face contact, it has a mechanism that can penetrate to the level of individual attitudes and that probably has encouraged more participant orientations toward politics.

Political and Social Experience. Socialization is not a process that ends with childhood or formal education. It continues throughout life, as the pattern of daily life and perceptions of major events reinforce, challenge, and alter the orientations formed in earlier years. The leaders of post-1949 China have tried to capitalize on this fact, using their power to structure public organization and activity in ways that provide an environment supportive of the political culture they hope to establish. Mao Zedong, in particular, insisted on the necessity of "combining theory with practice," of providing or even forcing opportunities for the testing and practice of abstract political concepts.[55] From the Maoist perspective, it is not enough to study political ideas and principles; they must be applied in social action before they truly become part of one's social being. The CCP's attempt to create political and social experiences that will assist internalization of the desired political culture is most evident in political campaigns and organizations at the basic level and in the compulsory dilution of elite status and privilege. We also want to consider briefly the impact of more generalized, unstructured political experiences on the Chinese population.

One of the CCP's most ambitious goals has been to involve every Chinese citizen in regular, organized political activity at

[55] The theme permeates Mao's writings and political style; for a formalized statement, see "On Practice," *Selected Works* vol. 1, pp. 295–309. See also Brantly Womack, "Theory and Practice in the Thought of Mao Tse-tung," in James Hsiung, ed., *The Logic of Maoism* (New York: Praeger, 1974), pp. 1–35.

the basic level, largely through mass movements, representation in basic-level government, membership in mass organizations, and participation in the management of primary production and residential units.[56] All of these are multifunctional political phenomena. They are structures for the implementation of central policy, for political recruitment and control, and to some extent for local interest articulation and decision making. Their function of socialization is important and at times paramount. The point is simply this: in pre-Communist China, most citizens had no role in political life and were divorced in any positive sense from the processes of formal government; the Communist goal, on the other hand, is to ensure that every citizen begins to experience some political roles by participating in rallies, meetings, discussions, and elections that relate to public affairs. In most cases, real initiative and control in these activities rests with higher authorities, and no doubt some participants simply are performing assignments for which they have little understanding or enthusiasm. Yet these are not overriding limitations with reference to socialization. Even if the setting is structured and the conduct of the activity ritualistic, the participant is learning something about the governmental process, the possibilities of political association, and his or her relationship to politics. The act of participation may foster positive awareness of political identity even if its real efficacy is low.

These phenomena are not uniformly effective, however, in providing meaningful political experiences. The system of elections and basic-level congresses flourished briefly in 1954–1957 and had an important symbolic role in affirming the popular base of government, but it was disrupted by the Great Leap and the Cultural Revolution. Local branches of the nationally organized mass organizations, such as the unions and Women's Federation, have offered opportunities for mass involvement in specialized projects (for instance, labor insurance and welfare, child care, mediation of local disputes), although they have been

[56] See the outline of major campaigns and basic-level organization in Chapter III, this book. A fuller discussion is found in James R. Townsend, *Political Participation in Communist China* (Berkeley: University of California Press, 1967), chaps. 5–7. See Liu, *Communication and National Integration*, chap. 5, for an analysis of mass movements with particular reference to their role in political communications.

very much a part of the national bureaucratic hierarchy and accordingly were pushed aside during the Cultural Revolution. Afterward, these forms of institutionalized mass participation not only reappeared but were strengthened in their operations. The strengthening of the electoral system and responsibilities of the people's congress system, which was described in Chapter 3, is not an isolated phenomenon.

Mass campaigns can be viewed as an alternative to institutionalized mass participation, although it should be remembered that the two are mutually exclusive only in their extreme forms. The socializing impact of the mass campaigns is ambiguous. As the focal point of political life and the vehicle for the most intense political activity, they have done more than any other mechanism to involve the population in the full range of political situations the system offers. They have probably increased the salience of politics for all, generated (at least on occasion) enthusiasm for collective action for many, and led substantial numbers into genuine political activism. Their negative effects also have been great, however, due to their frequently excessive demands and politically threatening nature. Most Chinese have seen their own lives disrupted by one or more of these campaigns or know of people who have suffered heavily from them.[57] The most constructive settings for political socialization have probably been the production and residential groups that have encouraged considerable popular participation in the management of their affairs (such as work assignments, public improvement projects, remuneration systems, etc.). While higher-level authority and policy penetrates these groups freely, they have provided the

[57] This disruptive potential is illustrated by the increased flow of emigrants from the mainland to Hong Kong that has occurred in the later stages of nearly all major campaigns. The occurrence of some negative socialization experiences does not mean, of course, that campaigns are counterproductive as a whole; for a careful evaluation of campaign accomplishments and shortcomings, see Charles P. Cell, *Revolution at Work: Mobilization Campaigns in China* (New York: Academic Press, 1977), pp. 117–69. For direct analysis of campaign socialization processes, see Sidney Greenblatt, "Campaigns and the Manufacture of Deviance in Chinese Society," and Gordon Bennett, "China's Mass Campaigns and Social Control," in Wilson, et al., eds., *Deviance and Social Control*, pp. 82–139. For a fascinating case study of one student's movement from early enthusiasm to later disillusionment in the Cultural Revolution, see Gordon A. Bennett and Ronald Montaperto, *Red Guard: The Political Biography of Dai Hsiao-ai* (Garden City, N.Y.: Doubleday, 1971).

most stable setting for open discussion and action on community problems.

Elites and subelites have participated more heavily than the masses in the activities described thus far and, in addition, have been the target of several measures designed to force a reduction in their status and privilege. Some of these have been explicitly egalitarian, such as the abolition of rank insignia and titles in the PLA by Lin Biao and reduction of wage differentials during the Cultural Revolution. By far the most ambitious, however, was the practice of *xiafang* (assignment to lower levels) and related efforts to give cadres, students, and intellectuals experience in manual labor.[58] Voluntary and compulsory programs of this sort thrived during the Great Leap Forward and the Cultural Revolution, and some voluntary efforts, much reduced, have continued in the post-Mao era. Like the mechanisms for mass participation, *xiafang* was a multifunctional policy aimed at reducing bureaucratic staff and transferring underutilized urban resources to the countryside as well as establishing more populist orientations. The socialization function was still important, however, for both the privileged strata directly affected and the masses who observed the results. For those already employed in various bureaucracies, *xiafang* meant temporary or permanent assignment to a lower level or a system of participation in manual labor at regular intervals. For students, it meant an initial work assignment in rural or frontier areas (increasingly over the 1960s a permanent assignment) or some formula for interrupting academic study with work experience. Whatever the specifics, the practice sought to give those holding or aspiring to official positions a taste of what manual labor is like, to

[58] Theoretical and developmental underpinnings of *xiafang*, and its multi-functional character, are analyzed in Pi-chao Chen, "Overurbanization, Rustication of Urban-educated Youths, and Politics of Rural Transformation," *Comparative Politics*, vol. 4, no. 3 (April 1972): 361–86; and Rensselaer W. Lee, III, "The *Hsia Fang* System: Marxism and Modernisation," *China Quarterly*, no. 28 (October–December 1966): 40–62. A comprehensive study of the transfer of urban youth to the countryside is Thomas P. Bernstein, *Up to the Mountains and Down to the Villages: The Transfer of Youth from Urban to Rural China* (New Haven, Conn.: Yale University Press, 1977). *Xiafang's* impact on bureaucracy is assessed in Khien Theeravitaya, "The *Hsia-Fang* System: Bureaucracy and Nation-Building in Communist China, 1957–1969," (Ph.D. diss., University of Washington, 1971).

overcome any notions in their minds that educational or political credentials exempt them from discomfort and hard work, and to persuade the masses that elites in the New China will not be permitted to isolate themselves from the sometimes harsh realities of the common man's life situation.

Xiafang has encountered resistance not only from elites who have no sympathy for its objectives or believe it a waste of their talents but also from peasants or basic-level cadres who may see it as disruptive and ineffectual or who may feel that those sent down still get the best work available. Breaking down barriers of status cannot be painless in a society where scholars and officials traditionally held such privileged positions and where political authorities today command such power. Any measure designed to counteract the separation of elites and masses would produce resentment and disorientation. For many, the social learning experience was probably counterbalanced by the resentment of being forced into internal exile. Moreover, the policy meant the continuous disruption of the work, research, and academic careers of the people involved. Given the shortage of technically qualified personnel, it did not make sense in terms of modernization to have a sizeable percentage doing menial jobs. Therefore, to the great satisfaction of many, *xiafang* policies were gradually reduced and then discontinued in 1977. However, some youths sent to the countryside during the 1960s and 1970s continue to demand return to their cities of origin. Despite their politically embarrassing protests, the government thus far has refused to honor their demands.

Political attitudes may also reflect life experiences not structured, sanctioned, or anticipated by the government as socializing devices. The most dramatic example is the economic crises of 1959–1961, due in part to natural disasters, which shook popular confidence in the CCP and encouraged a retreat into traditional political orientations. More generally, the alternating pattern of mass movements and the apparently interminable search for new "enemies" and "renegades" may lead to a certain political weariness even among those basically sympathetic with the overall direction of government policies. Perhaps the constant striving for a political ideal that is never reached will ultimately create a counterculture of public accommodation and private cynicism. However, we should not assume that the general pattern of post-1949 events has had a negative impact on the bulk of the population. Despite economic fluctuations and the evident unpredictability of politics, the standard of living and China's international standing have improved. Although certain groups may be disillusioned with politics, there is no real challenge to the CCP's legitimacy. Even many dissidents see themselves as loyal reformers of the current system rather than as antagonistic radicals. Most Chinese have accepted the present government—we cannot answer with confidence the crucial question of how different motivations and degrees of commitment distribute themselves among the population—and consequently, they have unavoidably participated in the establishment of a collectivized society, the sacrifice of some personal interests in favor of national goals as defined by elites, the effort to elicit political activism at the grass roots, the practice of a populistic social ethic, and all the personal and group struggles generated by these changes.

SOCIALIZATION AND THE CULTURAL REVOLUTION

Agents and processes of political socialization became a prime issue and a target for reform in the Great Proletarian Cultural Revolution. Why were the Maoists so dissatisfied with a system that seemed to penetrate society thoroughly and to show plainly the influence of Mao's hopes for a new Chinese political culture? What were the results of the assault on the established system? What does the Cultural Revolution and its aftermath suggest about long-term patterns of change in Chinese political culture?

The first point to emphasize is that the attack on the socialization process was by no means a total one. Although campaign rhetoric sometimes suggested an across-the-board failure by the "authorities following the capitalist road" to promote socialist values, the Maoists, in practice, showed little desire to alter policies and institutions in certain key areas. For example, as noted earlier, the Cultural Revolution brought little concrete change in policy toward the family, indicating that the advance of socialism had so circumscribed the social influence of this institution that it was no longer a center of controversy. The disruption of the communications system, which was one of the campaign's most startling features, seems in retrospect to have been a symptom rather than a motivating factor of the conflict;

that is, it was due to a struggle to control the communications network rather than to change it. The Maoists recognized early that they could not succeed without control of the public media, which were largely dominated by their opponents in the state and party bureaucracies. The effort to reverse this situation brought purges of party propaganda departments, suspension of key organs such as *People's Daily* and *Red Flag*, physical seizures by the PLA and Red Guards of printing and broadcasting facilities, the emergence of a variety of unofficial and unauthorized Red Guard publications, and general decline and confusion in the output of authoritative information. However, once the capitalist-roaders were purged and some social order restored, the new leadership began to reconstruct an even more centralized, authoritative communications system, as Table V.2 indicates.

Dissatisfaction with the established pattern of political social-ization centered, then, on the educational system and the general quality of public life. The details of the educational critiques and policies of the Cultural Revolution have been discussed earlier, but in simplest terms, the Maoist argued that the revi-sionists were structuring mass participation and organization to serve their own bureaucratic requirements and interests rather than to maximize popular political activity and bring cadres and citizens closer together. Liu Shaoqi served as the scapegoat for the principal example of this tendency. Much of the criticism against him was hyperbolic in tone and divorced from the context of his actions and statements, but there is little doubt that he represented a political style that emphasized the preroga-tives of authority and the need for discipline and obedience from the rank of file.[59] Charges that Liu wanted people to serve as "docile tools" and "stainless screws" and that he supported the ideas of "joining the party to become an official" convey the spirit of Maoist fears that his administration encouraged a "sub-ject" rather than "participant" political culture for the masses and an elitist orientation within the entrenched bureaucracy. In the socialist education campaigns and the early stages of the Cultural Revolution, the Liuists apparently tried to limit mass criticism, to direct it away from the real centers of power, and to mobilize the established mass organizations for their own defense

---

[59]See Lowell Dittmer, *Liu Shao-ch'i and the Chinese Cultural Revolution* (Berkeley: University of California Press, 1974), esp. pp. 214–93.

rather than for opening up the mass movement. The lessons likely to be gained from political action under these circumstances were of course in conflict with the expressed values of the official propaganda media. From the Maoist perspective, an effort to stimulate mass activity and crack the apparent invulnerability of elites and large-scale organization was necessary to make social practice supportive of the desired values.

The upheavals of 1966–1967 shattered the institutional context of political socialization. Schools closed in the summer of 1966, not to reopen for formal instruction for two or three years. In the interim, educational facilities became staging areas for political debate, organization, and struggle, and in some cases command posts for student combat. Cadres at every level came under mass criticism, frequently leading to public humiliation and dismissal. The old mass organizations fell into disarray or inactivity, while new associations of Red guards and other so-called "rebel" groups sprang into action sometimes forming citywide federations and commanding real power and constituencies at the local level. As the communications system ceased to provide authoritative direction, these groups began to develop their own information, platforms, and publications in the midst of a barrage of competing political messages. This exercise in spontaneous mass action was not, however, to continue for long. Alarmed by the threat of anarchy and civil war, heightened by factionalism within its own ranks, the Maoist coalition began to suppress disorder.

For ordinary citizens, the Cultural Revolution also brought significant changes in socializing experiences. One change was increased popular participation in primary units, especially through the revolutionary committees set up in factories, schools, offices, hospitals, neighborhoods, and so forth. Mass representatives on these committees provided a vehicle for acting on Maoist themes, such as popular supervision and criticism of cadres, that the Cultural Revolution had advanced. The decentralizing tendencies of the campaign also made participation in primary units more significant by giving them a greater role in managing social services and making decisions in production and worker remuneration.

A second shift affecting the general population was a new cultural policy associated with Jiang Qing. The range of cultural expression was curtailed, with a sharp drop in the variety of books and periodicals published relative to the pre-1966 period. Magazine titles dropped from 790 in 1965 to 22 in 1968, while the number of newspapers dropped from 343 to 49 in the same period (see Table V.2). Public performances were limited mainly to a few revolutionary dramas, presented over and over on stage and in film. Worker-peasant art and creativity was praised, individual virtuosity downplayed, and most traditional and foreign cultural influences viewed with suspicion. Populism, nationalism, and Maoist revolutionary themes pervaded not only culture narrowly defined but also much of the general tone of Chinese public life.

Finally, the Cultural Revolution left a certain combativeness or struggle orientation that had not been so marked before the great campaign. Chapter 6 will address this trend more carefully; however it is important to note that in 1969–1976 there were many signs of popular conflicts or tensions, indicating that factionalism developed during the Cultural Revolution remained and that many were still willing to air disagreements publicly. While some of this discontent was directed against the Cultural Revolution policies, its spirit was in line with the campaign slogan "it is right to rebel."

POST-1976 SOCIALIZATION

The events that followed Mao's death altered the pattern just described. Although new socialization processes are still evolving, with uncertain long-term effects, the major post-1976 changes can be summarized. Let us begin with education, which is the most significant area of change in socialization and where, by the fall of 1978, a new policy had taken shape.

At the heart of the new educational policy was a centralizing, regularizing trend aimed at raising academic standards. Time devoted to academic subjects increased, with a corresponding decline in the earlier stress on political study, labor experience, and practical applications. Classroom discipline, respect for teachers, and academic grading and examination systems were promoted. Educational authorities reinstituted the policy that had existed before the Cultural Revolution of designating certain schools as key schools, with higher academic standards and an admissions policy that would channel the academically stronger students into them. Tracking within schools emerged, with official endorsement, dividing students into faster and slower classes according to academic performance.

The new policy had its greatest impact on universities, which began to recruit rapidly on the basis of new college entrance examinations given for the first time in December 1977 (producing nearly 300,000 new college students in 1978). Relaxation of the requirement for precollege work experience permitted many middle school graduates, apparently 20–30 percent of the new admissions, to enter college directly. By the 1980s, almost the entire entering cohort were fresh senior middle school graduates. Graduate study resumed, with much publicity given to research scholars and the necessity for advanced theoretical research. The new leaders invoked Mao's name in blessing these changes, saying that he had never opposed examinations or academic study as such; the educational policy of the Cultural Revolution was generally linked to the Gang and denounced as sabotaging China's modernization.

Official commentary acknowledged that these changes would favor children from cadre and intellectual families and from urban areas due to their advantages on the examinations determining entrance to key schools, faster classes, and higher-level schools. They acknowledged, too, that elimination of the three great differences—between town and country, worker and peasant, and mental and manual labor—would be delayed as a result.[60] In this compromise on the broadest of Maoist socialization ideals was a fundamental shift of perspective. The defense of the shift argued that the differences cannot be eliminated quickly in any case, that they will disappear only as a result of material changes stemming from modernization, and that the new educational policy will contribute to their ultimate disappearance by hastening modernization; further, since modernization requires advanced science and technology and high performance in all intellectual sectors, those who work in these areas are really "laboring" people, too, working for socialist progress just as workers and peasants were. In other words, the egalitarian, classless society of the future can only be a product of material change, not of ideological rhetoric divorced from objec-

[60]See, for example, *PR*, no. 30 (July 28, 1978): 18–19, 22.

tive reality, so that the promotion of material change and modernization has first priority in the attainment of communism.

This invocation of the primacy of material factors, with its repudiation of ideological sloganeering and of emphasis on subjective factors, was related to other changes in socialization practices. One of the most obvious changes was in the broader cultural and intellectual sphere; it experienced a marked opening to less politicized expression, a revival of many long-dormant academic and cultural publications, and some interesting debates on subjects virtually taboo during most of the previous decade. The slogan of "let a hundred flowers bloom" took on new meaning in this atmosphere, which nourished a more open interest in foreign and traditional culture. Although in 1978 the regime moved to reaffirm ideological control by requiring allegiance to the "four fundamental principles," and in 1983 attacked many progressive ideas in the "oppose spiritual pollution" campaign, there are no signs of a return to the ideological terrorism of the Cultural Revolution. The "oppose spiritual pollution" campaign showed the power of forces scandalized by the rapid social and intellectual changes since 1977, but it also showed their weakness. The campaign was much milder in its methods than earlier, comparable campaigns. Moreover, it ran into considerable resistance at every level and was abandoned prematurely.

Greatly expanded study and research exchanges with foreign countries, although justified mainly in terms of the priority of scientific and technological development, has profound long-term implications for the socialization experiences of Chinese intellectuals. In 1984, it was reported that over 33,000 Chinese had gone overseas to study since 1978, approximately 26,000 funded by the government and 7,000 privately funded. By 1984, 14,000 had already returned to China. This six-year total already doubles the number of Chinese students abroad from 1961–1977.[61] Moreover, only 10 percent of the older cohort had pursued advanced studies, compared to 78 percent of the current group. The returned foreign students may be expected to favor even

---

[61] Xinhua press release, in FBIS, November 28, 1984, p. K23. It should be noted that Soviet sources give higher figures for Chinese students in the 1950s. See Price, *Education in Communist China*, pp. 101–04.

more rapid modernization, and, just as importantly, the prospect of going abroad will induce more cosmopolitan interests and orientations among students and intellectuals. At the same time, the increasing presence of foreign teachers and students at Chinese universities brings exposure to and sometimes confrontation with the values and expectations of Western academics.

Finally, the "four modernizations" policy had potentially far-reaching effects on the political and social experience component of Chinese socialization. Emphasis on order and discipline, the abolition of revolutionary committees in primary units (and later, in 1979, in local government units), and the reinvigoration of the old mass organizations all pointed toward more structured and regularized forms of participation. The defense of professional and technical authority (especially in factories and schools) coupled with official praise for individual professional achievement seemed likely to encourage sharper awareness of social stratification. Greater use of material incentives and acknowledgment of consumer demands raised further questions about the possible growth of revisionism and materialism in Chinese society. Of special concern is the household responsibility system in agriculture, which has led to much greater disparities of wealth in rural areas, although the regime claims that neither exploitation nor economic polarization is occurring. The revolutionary values discussed at the beginning of this chapter are still affirmed, but the significance of these values in controlling individual behavior and the definitions of the values themselves have shifted enormously from the Cultural Revolution. The new policies as a whole have shifted the thrust of socialization practices away from the highly politicized populism of the Cultural Revolution and toward themes more supportive of social order and discipline, economic performance, and professional-educational advancement and achievement.

We conclude with four observations that summarize, or possibly refine, the preceding discussion. First, there are elements of continuity in PRC socialization policy that counterbalance some of the fluctuations described. In rural China (where over 80 percent of the population resides), the structures of family and village life have been relatively stable since the early 1960s, despite some calls during the Cultural Revolution for radicalization of kinship and production units. The greatest policy innovations at the family level in recent decades have been the household responsibility system and population policy. In terms of socialization, the most important changes have been the gradual development of better rural educational opportunities and communications facilities, deepening the incorporation of rural China into the national educational and communications networks. Post-1976 policies support continued expansion of primary education and continued efforts to modernize the countryside. They continue to support as well the spare-time, part-time schools that are particularly important in the countryside and are pushing new adult education programs. Work experience and practical training have been reduced but not eliminated in the new school curriculum. In short, official socialization policies have maintained a steady emphasis on the needs of rural areas and their integration with the more modern sectors.

Moreover, despite the post-1976 cultivation of the intellectual elite and a shift of emphasis on the "red-expert" scale, the PRC remains a highly politicized and relatively egalitarian society by world standards. Social and economic inequalities existed throughout the Maoist period and may grow in its aftermath. Deviance from official norms was possible before Mao's death and may be more common in the future. Nonetheless, highly politicized official norms still dominate the educational, communications, and organizational networks, exerting strong pressures toward political sensitivity and conformity. The content of these norms has never been static, with changes particularly evident since Mao's death. But there are also core themes— acceptance of party leadership, service to state and society, the illegitimacy of gross inequalities, and emphasis on collective over individual goals and obligations—that are well entrenched in the official political culture that dominates the socialization process.

Second, the Cultural Revolution and its aftermath suggest that cumulative Maoist socialization efforts have had a significant impact on popular political orientations, in terms of mass identification with the national political system, awareness of political issues, and willingness to participate in the politics of primary units. The strength and spontaneity of Red Guard involvement in the Cultural Revolution, largely in affirmation of Maoist values, was testimony to the impact of Maoist socialization on the younger generation educated since 1949. Whatever the degree or motive of participation in that campaign, it represented an open questioning of or assault on political authorities, an experience not likely to be forgotten by any who experienced it. The simmering basic-level politics that followed over the next decade, with unrest in schools and factories and large-scale demonstrations such as the 1976 Tiananmen Incident, indicate active participatory tendencies in Chinese society—tendencies that are not necessarily antiestablishment but that are not necessarily confined to unquestioning support of political elites either. Whether these will endure under a post-Mao leadership that is more hostile toward factionalism and disorder than was Mao remains to be seen, but it is not likely that they will disappear without a trace, without a more direct confrontation between participatory and order themes than has yet taken place.

Third, Chinese socialization processes have produced among the citizenry a mixed subject-participant political culture in the terminology of Almond and Powell, meaning that most citizens fill "subject roles" in which they identify with the national political system and are involved in implementation of its policies, and that some fill "participant roles" of attempting to influence policy making. The emergence of this political culture in a society previously characterized by little popular involvement in politics is the most significant product of post-1949 political socialization. Beyond that, it is difficult to specify the dimension of the mix and, in particular, to assess the frequency and character of participant orientations. A few additional comments are in order, however. First, the subject-participant mix, whatever its configuration, does not guarantee unanimous support for political elites and their policies; broad citizen identification with the system has not precluded diverse kinds of opposition and dissent, ranging from passive resistance to active criticism.[62] Effective opposition is rare, given elite resources, but the spread of subject and participant roles does not produce uniformity of attitudes

[62] For analysis of pre-1976 opposition, see Peter R. Moody, *Opposition and Dissent in Contemporary China* (Stanford, Cal.: Hoover Institution Press, 1977). Dissident activity in Guangzhou is well described in various articles by Stanley Rosen. The personal stories of some well-known dissidents are presented in Liang Heng and Judith Shapiro, *Son of the Revolution*; and Roger Garside, *Coming Alive: China after Mao* (New York: McGraw-Hill, 1981).

toward different leaders and policies. The second point is that participant roles are more common among the urban and better-educated strata, which are the recipients of the most intense forms of political education. The Cultural Revolution was primarily an urban phenomenon,[63] as were most post-1949 episodes of pronounced popular political activism—land reform being a major exception. In assessing the significance of this pattern, we must remember that the spread of education and modernization will increase the proportion of the population exposed to more intense politicization experiences.

It should be remembered that the analysis of popular political roles and attitudes is complicated by the fact that opportunities for participation are concentrated in very small-scale units. For most Chinese, the main arena for political action is a primary unit: production brigade or team, factory or enterprise, office, school, or neighborhood. Participation in the affairs of such units can be highly political and can cement ties to the national political system, but it is also difficult for the analyst to observe this participation systematically. Moreover, these units are defined by nonpolitical functions and are permeated with highly personalized relationships (kinship, neighbor, peer group, small-group leader or follower, etc.), making it difficult to say exactly when and how their activities are "political."

Fourth, the clash of political cultures, that is, the confrontation between different images of what the Chinese political community should be, is unresolved. Despite the bankruptcy of the Gang of Four, it should not be assumed that Cultural Revolution values have been eliminated from Chinese political consciousness. The return of Deng Xiaoping showed the resilience of his values despite vehement attacks; and the values of revolutionary class struggle are undoubtedly harboured by many just as stubbornly. The fact that there is no legitimate opposition in China gives a misleading impression of unanimity. In the meantime, in part as a result of its policies, forces have emerged that pressure the government's position from the right, desiring more bourgeois

[63] Richard Baum, "The Cultural Revolution in the Countryside: Anatomy of a Limited Rebellion," in Thomas W. Robinson, ed., *The Cultural Revolution in China* (Berkeley: University of California Press, 1971), p. 367, passim.

freedoms, less ideological control, and more participatory politics. The regime's middle road of modernization, controlled by orthodoxy, is difficult to define. Its two greatest assets in political socialization will be the length of time it has to educate and influence the Chinese population and the persuasive power of its successes in modernization.

CHAPTER VI

Political Interests, Recruitment, and Conflict

THE CENTRAL PROCESS in every political system can be described as the conversion of demands representing the interests, goals, and desires of individuals or groups within the society into political decisions that are then applied and adjudicated through government structures. This process includes two stages: the first is the *input* stage in which demands are fed into the decision-making structures; the second is the *output* stage, which includes the making and implementation of decisions. Although this description best fits states with distinct legislative and executive organizations, it can also be used to analyze the functioning of Communist systems. This chapter explores the input process of demands on the system, while the following chapter examines the output process of transmitting decisions into governmental action.

Almond and Powell divide the processing of demands into "interest articulation" and "interest aggregation."[1] The former refers to the process by which individuals and groups make demands upon the political decision makers, the latter to the conversion of demands into general policy alternatives. In modern democratic societies, these two functions have relatively distinct structural counterparts. Interest articulation typically finds its

---

[1]Gabriel A. Almond and G. Bingham Powell, Jr., *Comparative Politics: System, Process, and Policy* (Boston: Little, Brown, 1978), chaps. VII and VIII.

most effective channels in the communications media and a variety of more or less organized interest groups, while interest aggregation is performed primarily by political parties. Analysis of political demands in the Chinese system cannot rely on comparable institutional patterns, but the functional distinction between articulation and aggregation leads to an opening generalization about the handling of conflicting interests in China.

In a directive written for the Central Committee in June 1943, Mao Zedong offered a classic statement of the mass line that still stands as the CCP's core conceptualization of how the political process should work:

> In all practical work of our Party, all correct leadership is necessarily "from the masses, to the masses." This means: take the ideas of the masses (scattered and unsystematic ideas) and concentrate them (through study turn them into concentrated and systematic ideas), then go to the masses and propagate and explain these ideas until the masses embrace them as their own, hold fast to them and translate them into action, and test the correctness of these ideas in such action. Then once again concentrate ideas from the masses and once again go to the masses so that the ideas are persevered in and carried through. And so on, over and over again in an endless spiral, with the ideas becoming more correct, more vital and richer each time.[2]

This statement suggests a number of basic principles that are relevant to the analysis in the next two chapters. Of immediate interest is the implicit distinction between interest articulation and aggregation: the masses articulate (express their "scattered and unsystematic ideas"); the party aggregates (turns them into "concentrated and systematic ideas"). As this core concept developed over the years, the CCP established a set of techniques and institutions designed to implement it. Prominent among these are discussion groups, mass movements and meetings, representative bodies, mass organizations, mass media, and a party leadership style emphasizing accessibility and investigation, all seen in part as structures for encouraging the expression of popular opinions and demands. The structural channels for articulation are, therefore, extensive, and they carry a large volume of popular

[2]Mao Zedong, "Some Questions Concerning Methods of Leadership," *Selected Works* vol. 3, p. 119.

political opinion and discussion. At the same time, they function in a political context that significantly curtails the scope and effectiveness of the demands they transmit.

One major restriction is that the CCP monopolizes the aggregation function. The party sees expressed interests as "scattered and unsystematic" and intends that they remain so except as they are "concentrated and systematized" by its organization alone into policy alternatives. There are, of course, organizations other than the CCP that have the potential capacity, in terms of their memberships and scale, to aggregate the demands of particular groups in Chinese society, and they do tend to support the interests of their members. These organizations are not autonomous, however. Their leadership is dominated by party members whose job it is to ensure that the organizations in question do not compete with the CCP in formulation of policy proposals or advance demands that are in conflict with the CCP's general line. The official monopoly on communications media reinforces this pattern; even if a group wishes to act in a more autonomous way, it cannot make its position known to a larger public except through media that are subject to close party supervision.

Moreover, the distinctions discussed in Chapter 4 between "people" and "enemies," between nonantagonistic and antagonistic contradictions, have their most forceful practical impact in making vulnerable all expressions of competition in political demands and policy alternatives. Whenever the element of conflict or contradiction is introduced, it brings with it the possibility that one side or the other may be cast into an antagonistic role, meaning not simply loss of the issue in question but exclusion from the political arena. That this practice has a certain legitimacy in Chinese political culture (in the belief that political roles should normally conform to and support the prescriptions of a single source of authority) increases its restrictive effect on the expression of political demands.

In order to understand the logic of CCP's political hegemony, it should be remembered that as a revolutionary Marxist party, its claims to legitimacy are based on its vanguard role vis-à-vis the masses rather than its representational character. Effective leadership requires a concern for the welfare and opinions of the masses, but it also requires organizational and ideological discipline. The party and other public organs are not to be a battle-ground for politicians representing various particular interests and constituencies. Each cadre and party member should be accessible to and solicitous of every individual citizen's needs while advancing the good of the whole society. The good of the whole society should be reflected in current party directives. Openly to promote the interests of one particular group is not permitted if the interests of a part of society are put above the interests of the whole. By contrast, modern multiparty democracies assume that the best policy for society as a whole will emerge from the relatively unrestricted political competition of particular interests.

The articulation of popular interests consists mainly of frag-mented, unsystematic demands that have few resources for effective political organization and communication, or of more organized demands that tend to support known party policy. The effective expression and aggregation of competing demands is largely a function of elites whose position legitimizes their handling of controversial issues and provides some protection against the possibility of exclusion from the political process. Given that effective articulation and aggregation of conflicting interests is normally carried out by elites, this chapter gives particular attention to the recruitment process that determines the composition of political leadership and to major patterns of elite conflict in post-1949 China. However, political conflict exists at all levels of Chinese society and is expressed in certain ways outside elite circles. We turn first, therefore, to a closer consideration of the popular articulation of interests.

POPULAR ARTICULATION OF INTERESTS

Conflict and Stratification in Chinese Society. Despite the prominence in Chinese politics of struggle against antagonistic contradictions in which the "enemy's" position is denied any right or means of expression, a wide range of conflict remains nonantagonistic and hence entitled to airing. Nonantagonistic conflict is also seen in terms of correct and incorrect resolutions, but CCP theory insists that the incorrect position should express itself and be corrected by persuasion rather than repression. The best statement of this principle is, of course, Mao's 1957 speech on contradictions. In that speech, Mao also forthrightly identified some of the class or group dimensions of such conflict:

> In the conditions prevailing in China today, the contradictions among the people comprise the contradictions within the working class, the contradictions within the peasantry, the contradictions within the intelligentsia, the contradictions between the working class and the peasantry, the contradictions between the workers and peasants on the one hand and the intellectuals on the other, the contradictions between the working class and other sections of working people on the one hand and the national bourgeoisie on the other, the contradictions within the national bourgeoisie, and so on. Our People's Government is one that genuinely represents the people's interests, it is a government that serves the people. Nevertheless, there are still certain contradictions between this government and the people. These include the contradictions between the interests of the state and the interests of the collective on the one hand and the interests of the individual on the other, between democracy and centralism, between the leadership and the led, and the contradictions arising from the bureaucratic style of work of some of the state personnel in their relations with the masses.[3]

Omitted from Mao's 1957 speech was a discussion of contradictions within the leadership, but elsewhere he spoke freely of this problem. Thus, in August 1966 at the Eleventh Plenum of the Central Committee, he commented that there were, and always had been, factions within the party.[4] However, the admission that conflict occurred "among the people" was not intended to encourage public conflict. There is no place for public opposition. Those who disagree with a policy express themselves privately or work behind the scenes to reverse policy, but, in public, the appearance of unanimity is maintained.

The CCP's attempt to grapple with the problem of conflict within the accepted classes and structures of socialist society also acknowledges the existence of politically derived stratification. One scholar has reconstructed official statements on stratification before the Cultural Revolution into the following hierarchy:

---

[3]Mao, "On the Correct Handling of Contradictions Among the People," *Selected Works* vol. 5, pp. 385–386.

[4]"Selections from Chairman Mao," *Translations on Communist China*, no. 90, JPRS–49826 (February 12, 1970), pp. 6–7.

I. The ruling elite or "vanguard"
   A. Party cadres
   B. Party members
   C. Communist Youth League members
   D. Nonparty cadres
II. The working class and its allies ("the people")
   A. Workers
   B. Peasants, with "poor and lower-middle peasants" on a par with workers and distinctly above wealthier peasants
   C. Intellectuals and petty bourgeoisie
   D. National bourgeoisie
III. Declassed "enemies of the people"[5]

In contrast to this image of horizontal divisions, another scholar has conceptualized Chinese society in terms of vertical lines between institutional sectors; that is, party, government, and army rule over five major socioeconomic sectors—industry, agriculture, business, schools, and army—or more simply over two great divisions of cities and villages.[6]

Finally, Mao's increasing concern, from the early 1960s on, about the emergence of new bourgeois elements among the people or even within the party, led him to apply old class labels to groups defined by ideology rather than by social background. The result was great flexibility if not confusion in class analysis, since class references were sometimes to official labels, which all Chinese were assigned in the early 1950s, and sometimes to current manifestations of "revolutionary" or "counterrevolutionary" character, which might be different from the original class label.[7]

[5]John W. Lewis, "Political Aspects of Mobility in China's Urban Development," *American Political Science Review*, vol. 60, no. 4 (December 1966): 906–07. We have simplified Lewis' description of the hierarchy.

[6]Franz Schurmann, "The Attack of the Cultural Revolution on Ideology and Organization," in Ping-ti Ho and Tang Tsou, eds., *China in Crisis* (Chicago: University of Chicago Press, 1968), vol. 1, pp. 539–40. Cf. Schurmann's earlier and fuller discussion of classes and contradictions in *Ideology and Organization in Communist China*, 2nd ed. enl. (Berkeley: University of California Press, 1968), pp. 73–104, in which he stresses the bifurcation of elites into "red" and "expert" components, and suggests a basically three-class society of political cadres, intellectuals, and masses.

[7]Richard Curt Kraus, "Class Conflict and the Vocabulary of Social Analysis in China," *China Quarterly*, no. 69 (March 1977): 54–74.

These different perspectives on conflict and stratification suggest the range and variety of potential cleavage in Chinese politics. Among elites, the principal lines of cleavage may lie between different factions or opinion groups on major policy decisions; between governmental sectors, such as party, state, and army and their functional ministries or departments; between regional groupings and units, such as urban and rural or coastal and inland areas, or provinces and cities; between the central government and its subordinate administrative groupings, with the minority areas posing a special problem in the balancing of local autonomy against central direction; and between various elite strata—senior and junior cadres, party and nonparty cadres, "reds" and "experts," and so forth—with differing qualifications and experiences. Roughly comparable lines of cleavage may emerge at the basic level between groups who differ on the wisdom or means of implementing received policy; between local departments and offices; between local units, such as differently endowed or different types of collectives and enterprises; between the masses and local cadres; and between different classes or groups within local units such as regular and seasonal workers in factories, richer and poorer peasants in communes, politically favored and disfavored students in schools, and so forth.

The general pattern of these conflicts is that the prevailing opinion group or faction has an apparent consensus behind its policy. Ideally, it is also responsible for the results of its leadership and is removed if they are unsatisfactory. However, there are many less than ideal outcomes. In some cases, the interest conflict is between inherently unequal groups. For instance, during the Cultural Revolution seasonal factory workers tended to be more radical than regular workers, expressing the frustrations of their inferior status. In other cases, the prevailing group uses its authority to attack and permanently weaken potential opposition. This kind of factional behavior is now condemned by the center, but Deng's insistence in 1984 on total negation of the Cultural Revolution displays a kindred element of factional consolidation. In still other cases, vertical linkages determine the fates of lower-level leaderships. Personal ties or policy identifications can produce ripple effects on lower-level officials when provincial or central leadership is changed.

All of these lines of cleavage, which delineate potential or latent interest groups, have been discussed in official writings and have been involved visibly in the policy process. They have been most evident in crisis periods, which have permitted or even encouraged latent conflicts to express themselves openly, but the potential for group conflict is always present in Chinese politics. To analyze all of these conflicts in detail, tracing their rise and fall over time, would require a volume in itself. The discussion here concentrates on the ways in which popular interests are articulated, stressing the crucial question of organization and offering a few illustrative examples of particular conflicts.

Unorganized Articulation. The CCP's desire to encourage expression of popular demands combines with its hostility toward organized competition or opposition to produce a substantial volume of unorganized, fragmented articulation of interests. By *unorganized* articulation, we mean articulation of interests by individuals or small numbers of people who have little opportunity to link up or communicate with others who might support the same demands. The public to whom these demands are known is normally quite limited, consisting essentially of immediate superiors and other members of the groups from which the demands come. The communications media may publicize them to a wider audience but usually only when higher elites have decided that the expression merits attention as a good or bad model. Selection as a good model may induce visits or communications from other units, but again this happens only with the stamp of official approval. The basic rule is that those expressing the demand have no independent means of expanding their audience and maintaining regular contact with those outside of their own unit who might be interested.

The prevalence of unorganized articulation of interests in Chinese society lends great importance to two political assets: access to decision makers and personal connections. In theory, any citizen can approach a public official with his or her problem, and considerable publicity is given to the mass outreach efforts of the government and party. However, the task of influencing policy often begins with a visit to friends or relatives in power or to friends who have friends in power. This is known pejoratively as using the "back door." The back door is universally resorted to when available because of the vulnerable and powerless situation of the person attempting to influence policy. The role is essentially that of a petitioner attempting to persuade someone in authority; the assertion of individual rights or the threat of electoral action would usually be inappropriate. In seeking to gain power or simply to minimize risks in such a political environment, an individual would be well advised to nurture relationships that would favorably incline officials to his or her interests. In extreme form, the importance of access and connections has led to large structures of patron-client ties, and many careers have been made by climbing the connection network.

The most frequent and effective unorganized articulation occurs precisely where the system provides for it—in the political processes within basic-level government, that is, the level of production teams and brigades (or now simply villages), workshops and factories, and residents' committees.[8] Here, several features encourage the regular expression of popular demands. First, the smallest groupings (production teams or villages in the countryside, work teams in factories, and residents' small groups in cities) have frequent meetings and choose their own group leadership. Second, the masses also have a direct voice in the more inclusive groupings at this sublevel (production brigades, factorywide organization, and residents' committees) through the selection of representatives to managing committees or,

[8]See James R. Townsend, *Political Participation in Communist China* (Berkeley: University of California Press, 1969), chaps. 5 and 6, on pre-Cultural Revolution organization of primary units. More recent studies analyzing Cultural Revolution–era political participation include Marc Blecher, "Leader-Mass Relations in Rural Chinese Communities: Local Politics in a Revolutionary Society" (Ph.D. diss. University of Chicago, 1978); John P. Burns, "The Election of Production Team Cadres in Rural China, 1958–74," *China Quarterly*, no. 74 (June 1978): 273–96; Janet Weitzner Salaff, "Urban Residential Communities in the Wake of the Cultural Revolution," in John Wilson Lewis, ed., *The City in Communist China* (Stanford, Cal.: Stanford University Press, 1971), pp. 289–323; and Victor C. Falkenheim, "Political Participation in China," *Problems of Communism*, vol. 27, no. 3 (May–June 1978): 18–32. The most thorough, up-to-date analysis of rural participation is John P. Burns, *Political Participation in Rural China* (unpublished book manuscript, 1985); for urban areas, see Martin King Whyte and William L. Parish, *Urban Life in Contemporary China* (Chicago: University of Chicago Press, 1984). A fascinating account of political relationships in rural China is Richard Madsen, *Morality and Power in a Chinese Village* (Berkeley: University of California Press, 1984).

again, through meetings of the entire constituency. Selection of leaders and representatives may follow the path of discussion and consensus rather than contested elections and is not likely to produce individuals unacceptable to higher cadres. Nevertheless, those chosen come from within the unit itself and are in constant association with the mass membership; they are ordinary citizens serving in unpaid leadership posts, not cadres assigned to manage these units in the interests of the bureaucracy. In this context, popular interests can and do make themselves heard.

Third, primary units have responsibility for the management or consideration of many matters that are important to their memberships. The responsibilities vary according to the size and types of units but may include the following: allocation of work assignments and arrangements including nomination of candidates for advanced training and education; distribution of unit economic resources (within received guidelines) among worker remuneration, production costs and investment, and reserves for welfare and services, or participation in such decisions; establishment of pay scales and "work point" systems within the unit, again within certain guidelines; approval of household production contracts; management of welfare and service programs for members and families, and participation in the management of attached schools and health care facilities; cooperation with state offices in public security activities and mediation of disputes; consultation with higher levels on planning, budgetary, and developmental decisions for the unit in question; resolution or transmission upward of mass grievances and suggestions concerning all of the above. In none of these activities are primary units free to reject policies or supervision of higher levels, nor can one claim that masses, leader-activists, and cadres are uniformly conscientious in fulfilling the opportunities for popular inputs that this system affords. Nonetheless, participation in primary units encourages regular articulation of popular interests relating to living and working conditions at the grass roots of society.

The articulation process just described has a consensual quality that obscures personal expressions, conflicts, and opposition. Does more individualized articulation occur, especially of an oppositional nature? It certainly does, primarily in the course of frequent meetings and discussions about unit affairs. At this level, given the restrictions on external organization and communications and the administrative guidelines that make serious deviation unlikely, expressions of difference and even opposition pose little threat. The Chinese tendency to report decisions as consensus-building acts—"after thorough discussion and education, all agreed that this was the correct line"—does not mean that real give-and-take has no place in the process. The nature of the primary unit setting ensures a substantial variety of expression among its members.

Beyond this, there are other means of expressing individualized or deviant demands in a focused way. In the more confrontational days of the Cultural Revolution, the writing of big character posters (*dazibao*) was a common means of placing one's views before the unit as a whole. Since 1977, letters to communications media and personal visits to higher-level cadres and offices are encouraged. In rectification campaigns, the masses have a special opportunity to review and criticize the performance of local elites. All of these add to the scope of unorganized articulation but do not escape the restraints imposed by party leadership. The public debate of the winter of 1978–1979 exemplifies this. Emboldened by the new "hundred flowers" atmosphere of 1978 and elite attacks on the Gang's violations of socialist democracy, many citizens began to write letters and posters that questioned the Maoist legacy, criticized aspects of the socialist system, and called for fuller observance of democracy, legality, and human rights in China. Democracy Wall in Peking became a special gathering point for displaying and distributing dissident writings. The public expression of these views, often in full view of Western reporters and accompanied by discussion and rallies in the streets, soon brought official reaction. By the spring of 1979, authorities had arrested some of the leading dissidents, reminded all citizens that public debate must support the party and socialism, and curtailed activities at Democracy Wall. Socialist democracy was not to be confused with bourgeois democracy or to be used as a vehicle for weakening party leadership.

Finally, popular demands may express themselves through acts of noncompliance or resistance, such as absenteeism, slowdowns, concealed violations of regulations, capitalization on loopholes or ambiguities in policy, and so forth. The history of rural collectivization provides an example. The first push to collectivization in the early and mid-1950s saw its share of peasant footdragging, slaughtering of livestock, and withdrawals from cooperatives and collectives. During the commune and retrenchment period, some peasants withheld personal implements from the communes, concealed or misreported harvests, and took advantage of the restoration of private plots and free markets.[9] This mode of articulation, unlike those discussed previously, may have a quick and forceful impact on national elites and may possibly result in policy change; however, it must be very widespread to do so. Resistance to collectivization in the 1950s was noticeable but accomplished little more than short-run delays or adjustments. Resistance to the Great Leap did bring major policy changes but only in combination with a national political and economic crisis. Of far more concern than direct resistance to national policies are acts of opposition toward local policies and leaders. However, the strongly hierarchical structure of Chinese politics makes retribution more likely than success. Individualized noncompliance or resistance, then, also has its limitations and is risky for those who engage in it.

Organized Articulation. Organized articulation occurs when the group making the demand has members drawn from many units or localities and some means of communication with its membership and the larger public. The most powerful and enduring organizations of this kind in China have been elite political structures—the state bureaucracies, the CCP, the PLA, and the Youth League. We are concerned here with the representative organs of the state and organizations of a more popular character such as the Women's Federation, the trade unions, the democratic parties, and so forth. What these organizations have in common is that they provide an institutional interface between the political leadership of the CCP and the various officially acknowledged segments of the masses.

[9]See Kenneth R. Walker, "Collectivisation in Retrospect: The 'Socialist High Tide' of Autumn 1955–Spring 1956," *China Quarterly*, no. 26 (April–June 1966): 1–43, and *Planning in Chinese Agriculture: Socialization and the Private Sector* (Chicago: Aldine, 1965); Peter R. Moody, *Opposition and Dissent in Contemporary China* (Stanford, Cal.: Hoover Institution Press, 1977), provides other examples, detailing the regime's capacity to contain and/or manipulate oppositional tendencies.

There is a basic ambiguity in the political role of these organizations that has led to fluctuations in their salience and even existence. From the founding of the PRC until the anti-rightist campaign of 1957, the CCP was very concerned with giving citizens, including capitalists and intellectuals, a sense of security and contribution to the new regime. The people's congress system established in 1954 and the Chinese People's Political Consultative Conference (CPPCC) were only the most prominent of officially sponsored organizations purporting to represent certain categories of the population. Of course, Mao Zedong had made it clear in his 1949 speech "On the People's Democratic Dictatorship" that a class revolution had taken place and that the party's dictatorship was not to be questioned, but the existence of these groups and the access they provided to the party lent some legitimacy to the particular interests they symbolized. With the anti-rightist campaign, and more emphatically with the Cultural Revolution, proletarian dictatorship was tightened and the party tended to displace all other political and societal organizations. The party represented the interests of the ruling majority class of society as a whole, and it was unnecessary to have quasi-autonomous people's congresses, unions, economic organizations, and so forth. It was not legitimate to represent special interests in society, so such associations could only be justified as special instruments of party control. The post-Mao era, however, has shown a respect for particular interests in society and has allowed a wide variety of organizations to flourish again. The reforms in the people's congress system and the resurrection of the CPPCC described in Chapter 3 are only the most important examples of a trend favoring the proliferation of organizations.

Although the acknowledgement of the complexity of society and the need for various representative groups is stronger in the 1980s than it was in the 1950s, these groups should not be mistaken for their Western interest-group counterparts, although they have cognates in other Communist systems.[10] They do not

[10]See Gordon Skilling, "Interest Groups and Communist Politics Revisited," *World Politics*, vol. 37, no. 1 (October 1984): 1–27; and Robert Furtak, "Interessenpluralismus in den politischen Systemen Osteuropas," *Osteuropa*, vol 24, no. 11–12 (November–December 1974): 779–92.

officially lobby the party on behalf of special interests, and they do not criticize current policies. They have advanced the interest of their members within the political system with regularity and effectiveness only when their demands were compatible with general party policy. Leadership at the provincial and national levels is held closely by party groups within the organizations that are directly responsible to the respective level of CCP leadership. Nevertheless, the organizations are not simply passive sounding boards for the party. They provide important access points between the party and the organized masses, which allow the voicing of special interests in ways that do not threaten party hegemony and yet pressure the shaping of policy.

The general political process within these organizations might be called the building of a targeted consensus. The party provides the target. It sets the agenda, the terms of public discussion, and the general outcome. The party is interested in the reception of its policies and their improvement, but it does not encourage open criticism or autonomous policy formulation. Within the framework set by the party, participants pursue their individual and group interests by reinterpretation, discussion, and proposals. Most of the significant activity is informal and unreported, and conference resolutions are for the most part bland and unanimous. The process benefits the party by establishing an official consensus, although, given the party's agenda monopoly, the consensus can be more apparent than real. The party can also amend its policies and acquire new inputs without facing the conflict of open criticism or competition. The participants benefit through the access they have to party decision makers and through the possibility that their specific requests might be attended to.

Given its constitutional status as the supreme political power in China, it may seem strange to treat the people's congress system in the same category as groups with no constitutional role. However, the elections of the people's congresses and the course of their meetings are more similar to the other groups under discussion than they are to a Western legislature. It is true that the political and even legislative powers of the standing committees of national and provincial people's congresses have been expanded, but the role of normal members and the standards governing elections remain the same.

An election unit for a county-level people's congress is a small and relatively cohesive group: one or several work units or several production brigades. Candidates do not usually campaign openly for election, and they do not endorse political platforms. They run on their status as model citizens, on organizational affiliations, and perhaps on their representativeness as a woman, a minority nationality, a scientist, and so forth. Once elected, a delegate is to keep in touch with his or her constituency and to forward their complaints and suggestions to the government. The relevant government agency is required to respond to such delegate initiatives. At meetings of lower-level people's congresses, discussion of government work reports and budgets provides members with access to important officials and some opportunity to amend government plans, however, there is no legislative agenda. Legislation is passed at the provincial and national congresses, although the passage of the drafts is not in doubt and, as at the lower levels, the importance of the meeting for the delegate is not the power to vote but the opportunity for access and discussion.

The CPPCC occupies an ambiguous halfway position between the citizen-based interest articulation of the people's congress system and the clearly delineated constituencies of other mass organizations.[11] It is the symbol of the united front between the CCP and nonparty groups, which, for patriotic motives, furthers reunification with Taiwan, modernization, and intellectual and cultural affairs. Membership includes non-Communist parties that sided with the CCP in the civil war, representatives of religious and ethnic minorities, large numbers of distinguished personages from various fields, but especially intellectuals, educators, and CCP members involved in United Front work. Meetings of the CPPCC coincide with people's congress meetings, and their members have comparable access to government officials. CPPCC meetings tend to be more lively than their corresponding people's congress meetings, possibly because they have a larger percentage of intellectuals and distinguished figures. Members are permitted to address petitions to government agen-

[11]See Philippe Ardant, "La Conference Consultative Politique du Peuple Chinois," *Revue d'Etudes Comparatives Est-ouest*, vol. 11, no. 1 (March 1980): 7–34.

cies. In general, the CPPCC acts as the main institutional interface between a large number of groups, especially intellectuals, and the party-government decision makers.

Since 1978, there has been an explosion of special interest organizations. Professions, academic disciplines, and even hobbyists such as stamp collectors are establishing organizations at the national, provincial, and municipal levels, holding conferences, and publishing journals. A typical case is the academic discipline of political science, which was abolished in 1952 and revived in 1980. As of 1984, the Chinese Political Science Association had a membership of 1,000, eleven local associations, a research institute with a staff of twenty, and two inhouse journals.[12] The influence of organized articulation of interests in Chinese policy making should grow if these groups continue to proliferate, consolidate, and develop a public voice, but the experience of older organizations is instructive concerning the historical vulnerability and limits of such organizations.

The women's movement, represented organizationally before the Cultural Revolution by the Women's Federation and its official publication *Chinese Women (Zhongguo Funu)*, has probably been the most outspoken and effective articulator of particular interest groups. It alone among the mass organizations has consistently criticized the social position of its membership and demanded that this situation be improved. It has, for example, called for election of more women representatives, advancement of more women into schools and the CCP, better enforcement of the marriage law, and elimination of inequalities between men and women in pay and employment opportunities. The CCP has frequently endorsed these demands, agreeing that women have not attained the full equality promised in the initial reconstruction reforms. To some extent, therefore, the vigor of the women's movement has rested on the support or receptivity of national elites. Nonetheless, elite support has been neither constant nor sufficient to realize the goals in question, so that women's organizations have had to push their demands aggres-

---

[12]Zhao Baoxu, "The Revival of Political Science in China," *PS* (Fall 1984): 745–57. In 1983–1984, the author, a distinguished Chinese political scientist, became the first Chinese professor to teach courses on contemporary Chinese politics at a foreign university.

sively and can claim much credit for gains in their constituents' status since 1949.[13] It is important to note that much of the effectiveness of women's organizations has been at the local level, pursuing their cause on specific policies and cases. Generally, the organized expression of popular demands seems more effective at the local level than the national level, as long as it stays within the guidelines endorsed by the leadership.[14]

The All-China Federation of Trade Unions (ACFTU) offers a different example of the possibilities for organized articulation. Although workers' organizations have also enjoyed generalized elite support and have done much to improve their members' working and living conditions, the ACFTU illustrates the political hazards of explicit defense of group interests. On three occasions since 1949, trade unions have moved toward positions that provoked elite retaliations.[15] The first two in 1951 and 1957 involved demands by ACFTU leaders for some independence from the CCP and for greater attention to worker interests, as opposed to state or managerial interests. In both cases, the CCP removed the principal offenders from their ACFTU positions and reasserted the primacy of its policies as a guide for union action. The third occurred in the winter of 1966–1967, when some workers, encouraged by their union leaders and promises of economic benefits, entered the Cultural Revolution on the side of the Liuists and resisted extension of the revolution into the factories. Subsequently, the ACFTU was dissolved, its publications suspended, and its policies denounced as "economism"

[13]The eclipse of the Women's Federation during the Cultural Revolution and the CCP's tacit toleration of some traditional marital practices (see chap. 5) are evidence of elite vacillation, although neither represents a denial of the principle of female equality. Useful sources on the women's movement in the PRC include: Elisabeth Croll, *The Women's Movement in China: A Selection of Readings* (London: Anglo-Chinese Educational Institute, 1974); Delia Davin, *Woman-Work: Women and the Party in Revolutionary China* (Oxford: Clarendon Press, 1976); Kay Ann Johnson, *Women, the Family and Peasant Revolution in China* (Chicago: University of Chicago Press, 1983); Judith Stacey, *Patriarchy and Socialist Revolution in China* (Berkeley: University of California Press, 1983); and Marilyn B. Young, ed., *Women in China* (Ann Arbor: University of Michigan, Center for Chinese Studies, 1973).

[14]Studies of local government reveal this balancing of central directives and popular interests. See, for example, William Hinton, *Shenfan* (New York: Random House, 1983).

[15]Paul Harper, "The Party and the Unions in Communist China," *China Quarterly*, no. 37 (January–March 1969): 84–119.

in the service of Liu Shaoqi's line. The demise of the ACFTU thus stemmed partly from its tendencies to offer a competing view of workers' interests but mainly from its close identification with the party bureaucracy that existed before the Cultural Revolution—an identification established, ironically, with some union resistance. For the ACFTU, organized articulation of interests that conflicted with CCP policy led to a quick reassertion of party control but not to organizational dismemberment; the latter came only with the unions' apparent entry into CCP factional struggle as an organizational base for one of the competitors. However, when the disgraced faction returned, so did the unions. Since the death of Mao, the unions have broadened their influences and functions within enterprises.

Trade union experience suggests the dilemma that confronts organizations whose demands deviate from CCP policy. If the top leadership says that these demands represent a narrow, selfish interest contrary to the collective interest, the organization has little choice but to give in or to advance a different image of the collective interest. However, the latter course enters the field of aggregation and challenges the CCP's monopoly over the formulation of policy alternatives. Despite the obvious political hazards of this course, nonparty groups have moved toward it on occasion. One example is the "hundred flowers" campaign of 1957, in which a few intellectuals moved beyond complaints about their own role in socialist society to a broader attack on party leadership and line. The critics of 1957 had some of the rudiments of an oppositional organization in the democratic parties and their newspaper, *Enlightenment Daily (Guangming Ribao)*, but entry into interest aggregation—if indeed it really went that far[16]—was bound to fail for lack of any real power base. A much more vigorous and formidable form of organized group conflict emerged in the Cultural Revolution.

Factionalism among mass organizations was a decisive factor in the Cultural Revolution's shift from mass "power seizures" to

[16]Party leaders probably overstated the political aspirations of the 1957 dissidents and may have even deliberately publicized the most extreme criticism to strengthen their hand for the coming counterattack on the rightists; see Richard H. Solomon, *Mao's Revolution and the Chinese Political Culture* (Berkeley: University of California Press, 1971), pp. 314–15.

restoration of order under PLA auspices.[17] That influence alone indicates the importance of organizational conflicts during the campaign, but these conflicts are also of interest for their progression from a relatively narrow articulation of interests to a broader aggregation of multiple interests in competition for local power. From mid-1966 to early 1967, Red Guard and rebel groups proliferated, frequently along discernible economic, political, or institutional lines. That is, they tended to begin as small-scale organizations based on a single school or factory; where organizational divisions emerged within a unit, they were often between regular and seasonal workers, between different classes within a school, or between students of more or less privileged political and economic backgrounds.[18] Conflict centered on which group would lead the movement in its unit, on how to go about ridding the unit of its capitalist-roaders, and on whether students should "make revolution" in factories and enterprises.

However, these early organizational limitations evaporated quickly. As the campaign continued, Red Guard and rebel attention shifted to municipal and provincial offices where the old power holders were still sitting tight. Citywide organizations of students and workers began to emerge, and when the Maoists in Peking authorized power seizures in the winter of 1966–1967, the way was open for the formation of federations of the new mass organizations. In most cities, two major coalitions loosely identifiable as conservatives and radicals (but each claiming support from cadres, workers, students, and peasant groups) came to the fore. Although economic and political interest probably influenced lines of cleavage, each coalition claimed to speak for the revolutionary masses as a whole and wanted to control mass representation on the revolutionary committees that were then being formed. The principal issue was that conservatives tended to accept the trend toward compromise with old cadres, whereas

[17]Philip Bridgham, "Mao's Cultural Revolution in 1967: The Struggle to Seize Power," *China Quarterly*, no. 34 (April–June 1968): 6–37.

[18]See Hong Yung Lee, *The Politics of the Chinese Cultural Revolution* (Berkeley: University of California Press, 1978). For an in-depth study of factionalism within one unit during the Cultural Revolution, see Marc Blecher and Gordon White, *Micropolitics in Contemporary China* (White Plains, N.Y.: M. E. Sharpe, 1979).

radicals held out for a thorough cleansing of the system. In effect, these coalitions were aggregating local interests around the broader issue of consolidating or deepening the Cultural Revolution.[19] This was something the national leaders could not tolerate, and the ultimate victory of consolidation spelled the end for all of the larger-scale mass organizations, conservative and radical alike.

Bureaucratic Articulation. The foregoing discussion indicates that elite control of the articulation process is neither static nor absolute. Unorganized popular input at the lowest levels is substantial. Top elites have controlled organized articulation much more closely but have not prohibited it. Rather, their stance has been to support organized expression of popular demands in principle and then to take corrective action against those perceived as erroneous or antagonistic. They have been unequivocal in their hostility to popular organization that appears to compete for legitimacy as the aggregator of interests. The Cultural Revolution was an extreme manifestation of this pattern in which an extraordinary level of popular political activity was followed by an attack on factionalism and a sharp reduction of organizational opportunities. It is significant, however, that popular demands do enter the political process. Even if mass organizations lack the autonomy and resources to present these demands effectively, elites may consider them and at times champion them in the decision-making process. Bureaucratic articulation of popular interests is, in fact, the key variable in determining their viability and effectiveness.

The importance of bureaucratic articulation stems from the relative security, influence, and access to communications media that higher elites enjoy. Bureaucratic position is by no means invulnerable, as demonstrated by the Cultural Revolution, but its advantages over popularly based organizations and represen-

---

[19]For a close study of how one of these federations, the *Shengwulian* (short for Hunan Provincial Proletarian Revolutionary Great Alliance Committee), set forth a radical political program that challenged even the Maoist orthodoxy, see Klaus Mehnert, *Peking and the New Left: At Home and Abroad* (Berkeley: University of California, Center for Chinese Studies, 1969).

tatives are clear. Citizens have no significant means of pressuring decision makers above the basic level. If they or the organizations accessible to them persist in advancing disfavored demands, they risk political reprisals. Bureaucratic support is normally essential for popular demands to receive a hearing among higher officials. On the other hand, bureaucrats do not need a demonstration of public opinion to advance what they may perceive as popular interest; they may initiate, as well as screen, the articulation of popular demands.

Bureaucrats naturally tend to articulate their own interests, and in authoritarian regimes these interests are especially powerful.[20] It is their responsibility for the proper functioning of some aspect of society that governs their attention to popular interests. For instance, both the Ministry of Agriculture and the masses of peasants would be happy to have a bumper crop. Ideally, then, a plausible proposal from the masses for improving productivity would find an audience in the bureaucracy. From a slightly different angle, part of the proper functioning of society is a smooth and cooperative relationship between party, government, and people. It is somewhat risky for cadres to persist in policies that create widespread dissatisfaction or apathy, and conversely, it is useful to their careers to find policies that unleash the enthusiasm of the masses. Given the many levels of Chinese leadership, it is even possible that a higher bureaucratic level might articulate popular criticism of a lower level. One interpretation of the 1979 reforms of the county-level people's congresses is that the center, which originated the reforms, assumed that its modernization policies were more popular with the people than they were with lower-level functionaries and therefore wanted to increase the avenues for democratic pressure on local government.[21] However, in general, it is to the interest of bureaucracy as an elite and it is consonant with Leninist ideology to maintain the hegemony of the party-state apparatus. Our analysis of the Chinese political process turns logically, therefore, to elite recruitment and conflict.

[20]See Darrell Hammer, *USSR: The Politics of Oligarchy* (Hinsdale, Ill.: Dryden, 1974) for a portrayal of the Soviet Union from this viewpoint.

[21]Brantly Womack, "The 1980 County-Level Elections in China," *Asian Survey*, vol. 22, no. 3 (March 1982): 261–77.

POLITICAL RECRUITMENT

Three core political roles—activist, cadre, and party member—dominate the staffing of the Chinese political system. These roles may overlap (and each has its own important subdivisions), but the differences among them shed light on some basic characteristics of the recruitment process. Activists are ordinary citizens not holding full-time official positions who acquire a special interest, initiative, or responsibility in public affairs. Cadres are those who hold a formal leadership position, normally full-time, in an organization.[22] Party members are, of course, just what the term states.

Activists. Becoming an activist is generally the first step in the political recruitment process, and it is from the ranks of activists that most new cadres and CCP members are drawn. Local party organizations keep close track of activists within their jurisdiction, counting and labeling them as such and turning to them when political campaigns and recruitment are under way. However, in practice there can be no rigid criteria for determining who merits this designation. Virtually every citizen is potentially eligible, the traditional exclusions being the "five bad elements"—landlords, rich peasants, counterrevolutionaries, rightists, and miscellaneous "bad elements"—who have never constituted more than a few percent of the population. There are myriad considerations that may distinguish certain individuals from the mass. Personal qualities and community standing are particularly important, however.

Personal qualities leading to activism include motivational and skill elements. From an official point of view, "correct" motivation is the cardinal ingredient; selfless commitment and the desire to serve is by itself sufficient to establish activism. Some approximation of the ideal motivation no doubt infuses most activists, but personal ambition also enters in and, as elites ruefully acknowledge, may even be the decisive

---

[22]On the origins, definition, and ramifications of the "cadre" concept, see A. Doak Barnett, with a contribution by Ezra Vogel, *Cadres, Bureaucracy, and Political Power in Communist China* (New York: Columbia University Press, 1967), pp. 38–47; John Wilson Lewis, *Leadership in Communist China* (Ithaca, N.Y.: Cornell University Press, 1963), pp. 185–95 passim; and Schurmann, *Ideology and Organization in Communist China*, pp. 162–67. The discussion in this section draws heavily on these works.

motivational factor at times. Young men in rural areas may establish themselves as desirable mates by demonstrating prowess in activist roles, while youths of undistinguished class background sometimes attempt to prove their revolutionary zeal through taking the lead in volunteer activities.[23] Some personal skills or ability are necessary to translate desire into operational activism. Literacy, intelligence, energy, and skill in human relations are obvious assets. For mature activists, standing in the community is important since much of the activist's work involves mobilization of associates. The key factor here is not simply popularity but rather an expectation of informal leadership, a popular willingness to accept the activist's credentials. This may derive from the aforementioned personal qualities or from more generalized institutional considerations. Members of a unit may expect an individual to fill the activist's role because of his or her evident desire and ability, or because the individual is a PLA veteran, a party or league member known to be favored by local cadres, or even a natural leader through age or kinship determinants. A strong group feeling about an individual's fitness for the activist role may compensate for modest motivation or skills.

Local elites are by no means passive observers of this process. The party consciously recruits and even cultivates activists, particularly in the course of mass movements, which are the single most important testing ground for the demonstration of activism, and it has the power to deny political recognition to individual candidates for the role. On balance, however, self-selection, personal ability, and group support tend to determine recruitment of activists, with local officials watching the process closely to veto undesirables and select for more important roles those deemed most promising.

Cadres. Recruitment to cadre status is quite a different matter. At the lowest levels, activist and cadre roles may overlap when an activist is selected for formal leadership

[23] Richard Madsen, "Harnessing the Political Potential of Urban Youth," in David Mozingo and Victor Nee, Eds., *State and Society in Contemporary China* (Ithaca, N.Y.: Cornell University Press, 1983), pp. 244–64); Anita Chan, "Images of China's Social Structure," *World Politics*, vol. 34, no. 3 (April 1982): 295–323.

responsibilities within a primary unit. For example, activists fill many posts in production teams and brigades, and to a lesser extent in commune governments, that carry local cadre status. However, local cadres who receive their salary from the primary unit involved and whose recruitment reflects the considerations described above are a special group within cadre ranks. More influential and typical are the twenty million state cadres who staff state, party, and mass organizational hierarchies above the primary level and receive their salaries from the government. Recruitment to these posts is by appointment from within the bureaucracies through personnel sections of the state and organization departments of the CCP. Since party-member cadres dominate personnel sections within the government, owing to the obvious importance of this function, the CCP tends to control the appointment, promotion, transfer, and dismissal of all cadres above the primary level. Influences from outside enter the process through examination of a prospective appointee's motivation and relations with the masses; opportunities for mass criticism of cadres, especially during rectification campaigns, may also affect personnel decisions. With the shift from activist to cadre roles, however, the critical influence on recruitment shifts from individual motivation and community preferences to decision by party-member cadres within the bureaucracy.

The most serious problem in cadre recruitment is tension between political and professional criteria, the "red-expert" contradiction. Before 1949, party leaders thought of the cadre as a combat leader fighting in the context of guerrilla war. The role demanded direct leadership over and relationships with the masses, a high degree of political consciousness, and an ability to apply central directives flexibly in the course of an acute political struggle. After 1949, many cadres became workers in state institutions and departments, in which job-oriented skills were of critical importance. The definition of a cadre expanded to accommodate the role's new requirements, but the old conception of ideal cadre qualities endured. Cadres were to be "both red and expert"—"red" to ensure the desired style of leadership and "expert" in the work assignments demanded of them. Unfortunately, there were simply not enough red-experts to staff the expanding bureaucracies. But if red and expert qualities could not be combined in each cadre, they could be balanced organizationally through the employment of some reds and some experts. The distinction between party and non-party cadres is obviously relevant here.

Party-member cadres are not always red and lacking in expertise; nonparty cadres are not always experts and lacking in redness. However, the CCP has relied on party-member cadres to maintain the redness of cadre ranks as a whole. That is, it has been willing to employ nonparty experts as cadres so long as party-member cadres occupy the leading positions or retain de facto control in each bureaucratic unit. The goal of "both red and expert" has never been abandoned, but in practice there has been a tendency to accept the priority of expert qualifications in the recruitment of nonparty cadres. For these cadres, insistence on redness shifts from the recruitment stage to their control and education in office. At the same time, the demand for redness in the recruitment of party members becomes more intense, since it is the role that must ensure the primacy of politics in the system as a whole. However, the designation in 1978 of modernization as the party's central task has given expertise an unaccustomed influence within the party. When the content of politics requires expertise, then one must be expert in order to be red.

Party Members. Admission to the CCP is the decisive act of political recruitment. For the activist, politics remains basically an avocation pursued within the primary unit. For the nonparty cadre, politics is a full-time job of broader scope, but the political status attaches to the position, not to the individual, and carries no presumption of permanent or growing political responsibilities; moreover, the nonparty cadre has no access to positions of supreme power and only limited opportunities for upward advancement. Party membership alone implies a life-long commitment to politics, confers a political status independent of work assignment, and provides entrance into a political career with significant opportunities for advancement and power. In 1984, there were 388,000 party members involved in central-level and provincial-level organizations, and 13.5 million were involved at the prefectural and county levels.[24]

[24]*China Daily*, December 24, 1984, p. 1.

Thus, one-third of the party's 40 million members are involved with relatively high governmental levels, and about three-fourths of all state cadres are party members. Of course, party membership is not necessarily permanent and does not lead inevitably to positions of power; members may withdraw or be expelled and many never become cadres. But the presumption of permanence and special political qualities remains, so that the party member is always in a position of relative political prominence. If an ordinary worker, the party member is always a prime candidate for the activist role; among activists, the party member is most likely to be selected as a cadre; and among cadres, the party member is superior in political status and opportunities to nonparty colleagues.

The CCP intends that recruitment to its ranks be carefully controlled and highly selective, admitting only those who are truly red and expert. It alone decides who shall enter its organization, vesting control of recruitment in the party branch subject to approval by higher party committees, although popular opinions on candidates may be solicited. Since competition for membership is keen, party recruitment is really at an advanced level, drawing heavily from the ranks of those who have already attained activist or cadre status. Nonetheless, there is nothing cut and dried about this process. Historically, political recruitment has been a constant source of concern for the CCP, shifting frequently in its intended and unintended consequences for the composition of political leadership. A survey of changing patterns of recruitment, with particular attention to the party itself, will help to clarify this point.

Recruitment Patterns to 1953. The CCP began to grow in the 1920s as an urban-oriented party of intellectuals and workers, but this pattern ended abruptly in 1927. Although the influence of these early years was crucial for the oldest Communists, Chiang Kai-shek's April 12th "coup" virtually eliminated the party's mass membership (see Table VI.1) and drove the remaining members to the countryside. From the late 1920s to the late 1940s, the CCP was a party of peasants and soldiers—the latter also of peasant origin—led by a small number of better-educated revolutionaries and occasionally infused with some idealistic intellectuals. Recruitment was in a real sense self-recruitment.

The CCP tested and screened its own membership, of course, but the very act of association with the revolution was a powerful, prior testing device. Most followers did not join the Communist movement casually for security, material, or opportunistic reasons. Hardship, danger, and the threat of execution by the Nationalists were risks faced by party members and followers alike, and there was little assurance of ultimate victory until very late in the game. A strong element of political commitment was implicit, therefore, in identification with the movement. The CCP, eager to expand and faced with steady losses from death and defection, was able to absorb most of the followers who applied.

Once members of the party, new recruits received a natural socialization in Maoist virtues. Life was frugal and rustic, organization simple and close to the masses, policy implementation decentralized, and the military experience always close-at-hand. Survival alone was almost sufficient to ensure upward mobility as the movement filled the places of departed comrades and tried to extend its influence. In short, environmental factors tended to resolve questions of recruitment and advancement in a way that produced a relatively homogeneous party of dedicated peasant-soldier revolutionaries.

A second pattern began to emerge in the late 1940s and lasted through 1953. This was the period when CCP military power spread rapidly over all of China, when the establishment of a new political structure to consolidate victory and implement reconstruction reforms became necessary, and accordingly, when a burst of recruitment to activist, cadre, and party roles took place. Significantly, it was also a period when many of the earlier situational controls on recruitment disappeared. Although tense political struggle continued, particularly in land reform and suppression of counterrevolutionaries, the movement was now victorious. To join was to cast one's lot with a government in power whose future seemed secure and promising. Those who wanted to join no longer had to live in or travel to the red areas but could seek access to political positions in their own communities—although many were sent to other areas for actual service. The cities became a major source of recruitment for the first time since the 1920s. The CCP recognized that the new circumstances made it easier for opportunists, careerists, and

TABLE VI.1. *Growth of the Chinese Communist Party, 1921–1982*

Period and year	Number of members	Years covered	Average annual increase or decrease
First revolutionary civil war			
1921 (1st Congress)	57	—	—
1922 (2nd Congress)	123	1	66
1923 (3rd Congress)	432	1	309
1925 (4th Congress)	950	2	259
1927 (5th Congress)	57,967	2	28,508
1927 (after "April 12")	10,000	—	—
Second revolutionary civil war			
1928 (6th Congress)	40,000	1	30,000
1930	122,318	2	41,159
1933	300,000	3	59,227
1937 (after the Long March)	40,000	4	−65,000
Anti-Japanese War			
1940	800,000	3	253,333
1941	763,447	1	−36,553
1942	736,151	1	−27,296
1944	853,420	2	58,635
1945 (7th Congress)	1,211,128	1	357,708
Third revolutionary civil war			
1946	1,348,320	1	137,192
1947	2,759,456	1	1,411,136
1948	3,065,533	1	306,077
1949	4,488,080	1	1,422,547
Under the People's Republic of China			
1950	5,821,604	1	1,333,524
1951	5,762,293	1	−59,311
1952	6,001,698	1	239,405
1953	6,612,254	1	610,556
1954	7,859,473	1	1,247,219
1955	9,393,394	1	1,533,921
1956 (8th Congress)	10,734,384	1	1,340,990
1957	12,720,000	1	1,985,616
1959	13,960,000	2	620,000
1961	17,000,000	2	1,520,000
1973 (10th Congress)	28,000,000	12	916,666
1977 (11th Congress)	more than 35,000,000	4	1,750,000
End of 1981	39,657,212	5	1,000,000

Sources: The figures for the years 1927–1961 are reprinted from John Wilson Lewis, *Leadership in Communist China,* pp. 110–111, copyright 1963 by Cornell University, used by permission of the publisher, Cornell

even "class enemies" to acquire political status and was relatively cautious in party recruitment. Although organizational growth was substantial during 1949–1953, it was modest and irregular relative to later years. Rectification campaigns in 1951–1952, designed to weed out the undesirables admitted during this fluid period, even brought a temporary halt to party growth (see Table VI.1).

The need for activists and cadres could not be postponed, however. The great campaigns of 1949-1952 demanded and produced millions of new activists primarily from oppressed and outcast groups in the countryside with large numbers of students also rising to the call. These early rural activists, recruited in often violent campaigns against the old social order, became the foundation of Communist political power in the villages. They probably constitute even now a significant proportion of the local cadres in rural production units. The need for state cadres was no less urgent, and here the CCP was particularly short of talent. Intensive efforts raised the number of state cadres from 720,000 in 1949 to 3,310,000 in 1952; 5,270,000 in 1955; and 7,920,000 in 1958.[25] Of the 2,590,000 cadres recruited between 1949 and 1952, the majority (57.7 percent) were worker and peasant activists from the mass campaigns; 40.1 percent were members of the CCP and PLA or progressive elements among the retained personnel (former Nationalist officials) who had gone through short-term training; and 2.2 percent were graduates of higher schools.[26]

This early period was one of trememdous political mobility, both downward and upward. Most old officials were ruined, and many who stayed on as retained personnel were forced out later when more reliable cadres emerged. Some of the new recruits as

University Press; the 1973 figure, from Zhou Enlai's "Report" to the CCP *Congress of the Communist Party of China* (Documents), (Peking: Foreign Languages Press, 1973), p. 8; and the 1977 figure, from *PR*, no. 35 (August 26, 1977): 6. The 1981 data is from *Zhongquo Gongchandang di shi'er ci quanguo daibiao dahui wenjian huibian* (Collection of documents from the 12th national congress of the CCP), Beijing: Renmin Chubanshe, 1982, pp. 150–151.

[25] Ying-mao Kau, "Patterns of Recruitment and Mobility of Urban Cadres," in Lewis, ed., *The City in Communist China*, pp. 98–106; figures from p. 106.

[26] Ibid., pp. 103–104.

well as old revolutionary cadres failed to pass the test when their qualifications and performance were reviewed in rectification programs. Mainly, however, the period was one of relatively open recruitment and upward mobility in which new activists and cadres entered the political system in its formative years, thereby establishing themselves within it. The CCP could take satisfaction in having met the immediate problem of numbers, but it was acutely aware of qualitative problems arising from the necessarily loose standards of the time. Party strength was still insufficient to supervise thoroughly the work of all offices, many filled with cadres of questionable redness. In addition, the cultural and technical skills of most activists and low-level cadres were quite low; in fact, many were illiterate and totally untrained for administrative work.

Institutionalization of Recruitment, 1954–1965. Between 1954 and 1965, the CCP developed an institutionalized recruitment system that responded to the weakness and irregularities of the earlier period, changed significantly the determinants and composition of party membership, and became an underlying cause of the Cultural Revolution. The central rationale for this transformation was to ensure CCP dominance over the process of socialist construction. If a large bureaucracy liberally staffed with experts was necessary for administering the transition to socialism, the CCP was determined that these experts be red or at least be under red leadership. This in turn required a vigorous expansion of the CCP and its organizational units and a movement of party members into other organizations. Beginning in 1954, the CCP added over 1 million new members in nearly every year until 1961—the last year in which figures were reported before the Cultural Revolution—at which time its membership reached 17 million (see Table VI.1). The number of basic-level party organizations increased from 250,000 in 1951 to 538,000 in 1956 and 1,060,000 in 1959.[27] The dominance of party members within state and mass organizations advanced so rapidly that by the time of the Great Leap, CCP committees were the effective governing bodies within all levels of administration.[28] Mean-

[27]Schurmann, *Ideology and Organization in Communist China*, p. 134.
[28]See Barnett, *Cadres, Bureaucracy and Political Power*, passim.

while, all cadres came under a regularized system of graded ranks and salaries, annual review, and bureaucratic stratification.[29]

The composition of the CCP changed as it grew into its increasingly intimate relationship with government departments. Although a majority of its members continued to come from peasant backgrounds and to work in rural areas (due to the overwhelmingly agrarian society and economy), urban influences increased sharply. By 1957, only 66.8 percent of members came from peasant backgrounds, whereas 14.8 percent were intellectuals, 13.7 percent were workers, and 4.7 percent fell in the "other" category.[30] Sample data on major cities indicate that by 1959 4.4 percent of urban residents were party members, compared to only 2.2 percent of the total national population admitted to membership; urban members probably totaled about 4.4 million in that year, or nearly one-third of all party members.[31] Many of those recorded as working in agriculture—about 58 percent of CCP members in 1956[32]—were local cadres with administrative responsibilities in rural towns.

Where did the CCP find such large numbers of new recruits, and how did it satisfy itself that they were red and expert candidates who could work effectively in state administration and economic construction? Basically, it institutionalized the recruitment process through two organizations, the People's Liberation Army (PLA) and the Communist Youth League (CYL). The PLA historically had been a major supplier and employer of CCP members. From the late 1940s, with the influx of ex-Kuomintang troops and then younger conscripts, and with the increasing civilian orientation of the CCP, the proportion of party members in the army gradually declined. The officer corps retained a heavy concentration of members, who virtually monopolized the senior grades, but members became a minority among the rank and file.[33] On the other hand, as the PLA demobilized from its Korean War strength and entered into

---

[29]Ibid., pp. 41–43; and Ezra F. Vogel, "From Revolutionary to Semi-Bureaucrat: The 'Regularisation' of Cadres," *China Quarterly*, no. 29 (January–March 1967): 36–60.

[30]Lewis, *Leadership in Communist China*, p. 108.

[31]Kau, in Lewis, ed., *The City in Communist China*, p. 109.

[32]Schurmann, *Ideology and Organization in Communist China*, p. 133.

[33]John Gittings, *The Role of the Chinese Army* (London: Oxford University Press, 1967), pp. 110–11.

a conscription system with regular terms of service, it began to feed a steady stream of demobilized soldier into civilian life—nearly 7 million between 1950 and 1958.[34] Supplementing these were much smaller numbers transferred to duties in civilian organizations, usually as cadres, without being released from service. For a variety of reasons, demobilized and transferred soldiers were prime candidates for activist, cadre, and party member roles. Their term of service (according to the 1955 conscription law, three years for the army, four for the air force, and five for the navy) gave them disciplined organizational experience, regular political education, minimal literacy, and, in some cases, special technical skills. Moreover, the PLA's conscripts were an elite group to begin with, since only a fraction of those who reached the conscription age of eighteen were taken. Many were from peasant families, which gave them the added advantages of a favored class background, but they were the pick of China's rural youth.

The Youth League. The Youth League's importance in recruitment is obvious, since it received official recognition (until 1966) as the most appropriate organization in which youth demonstrate and acquire advanced political qualifications. The League's growth in the 1950s was impressive (see Table VI.2). Starting from scratch in 1949, it matched the CCP in size by 1952 and was close to double the size of its parent organization by 1956. Its growth slowed during the Leap and its aftermath, but the CYL remained the largest activist political organization in the People's Republic. Membership apparently remained around the 25 million mark into the early 1960s, when pressures for growth resumed. One scholar estimates that membership rose to around 40 million by 1965, although Communist sources have confirmed only that a great recruitment drive in 1964–1965 brought in 8.5 million new members.[35] The League probably became the leading source of new party members about 1954, the time that the CCP began its own major growth period. Indeed, the CYL's emergence in the early 1950s as a substantial pool of organized, accessible, and presumably reliable activists was

[34]Ibid., p. 305.
[35]Victor Funnell, "The Chinese Communist Youth Movement, 1949–1966," *China Quarterly*, no. 42 (April–June 1970): 105–30, esp. pp. 115–16, 128.

TABLE VI.2 *Communist Youth League Membership, 1949-1959*[a]

Year	Members in millions	Branch units
1949 (April)	0.19	—
1949 (October)	0.50	—
1949 (December)	1.30	—
1950 (June)	3.00	—
1951 (September)	5.18	242,000
1952 (September)	6.00	—
1953 (June)	9.00	380,000
1954 (May)	12.00	520,000
1955 (December)	16.00	600,000
1956 (June)	20.00	700,000
1957 (May)	23.00	920,000
1958 (July)	23.20	—
1959 (May)	25.00	1,000,000

[a]Reprinted by permission of the author and the publisher from Klaus H. Pringsheim, "The Functions of the Chinese Communist Youth Leagues (1920-1949)," *China Quarterly,* no. 12 (October–December 1962): 90–91.

undoubtedly one factor encouraging the CCP to open its recruitment drive. The precise number of League members entering the party is not known. One of the few direct references was a 1957 report that 2.8 million had done so between 1949 and the end of 1956.[36] This represented over 40 percent of CCP growth for the same period; in fact, since the League probably began to provide large numbers of party recruits only from 1954, the figures suggest that by the mid-1950s a solid majority of new party members were Youth Leaguers.[37] The last report on this topic before the Cultural Revolution stated that 600,000 league members joined the party in 1965, which must have been a very high proportion of those entering the CCP in that year.[38]

[36]"What Has Happened to the Youth Corps?" *China News Analysis,* no. 633 (October 21, 1966), p. 2.

[37]In September 1956, CYL leader Hu Yaobang said that 2,150,000 Leaguers had joined the party by that time; if this and the 2.8 million figures are correct, then 650,000 League members joined the CCP in the last three months of 1956, supporting the statement in the text. Se Hu Yaobang's speech in *Eighth National Congress of the Communist Party of China,* vol. 2 (Peking: Foreign Languages Press, 1956), p. 319.

[38]Funnell, "The Chinese Communist Youth Movement," p. 116.

The CYL's centrality in recruitment before the Cultural Revolution is clarified by the distribution of its membership. In effect, the League was the key organizational linkage for China's incipient "new class," the subelite of activists and low-level cadres concentrated in urban settings—among students, industrial workers, and state employees—and in the PLA. A few figures will indicate how organizational membership in the League, with its direct political advantages, overlapped with and reinforced the opportunities of skilled occupational groups. In 1957, League membership was distributed as follows: 16.4 million in villages; 3.6 million in schools; 2.28 million in industry; 1.8 million in the army; 970,000 in government offices; and 680,000 in commerce.[39] Village members constituted only 70 percent of total League membership, a figure well below the rural percentage of China's population and an indicator of the CYL's persistent and acknowledged weakness in the countryside. (As late as 1964, the League had recruited only 13 percent of rural youth between the ages of fifteen and twenty-five and had major organizational gaps in production teams and brigades.) But in 1957 League members constituted major proportions of all the other categories given. Consider the following: 3.6 million in schools, when total secondary and higher school enrollment was about 5.6 million (and many in junior middle schools, the largest group of students in the total, would be underage); 2.28 million in industry, when the total of industrial workers was 7.9 million (and the majority overage for the CYL); 1.8 million in the PLA, when PLA strength was 2.5 million (with many overage); 1.65 million in "government offices" and "commerce," a very high percentage of employees under the age of twenty-five in such categories.[40]

Despite their limitations, these figures leave little doubt about the institutionalized character of recruitment in the

[39]"What Has Happened to the Youth Corps?" *China News Analysis*, p. 2. There is double counting here, as the total of 25.7 million exceeds the announced membership of 23 million at that time; many included as "village" members probably fell into other categories as well.

[40]School enrollment in 1957 from Leo A. Orleans, *Professional Manpower and Education in Communist China* (Washington, D.C.: Government Printing Office, 1961), pp. 35, 66. Industrial workers in 1957 from Nai-Ruenn Chen, ed., *Chinese Economic Statistics* (Chicago: Aldine, 1967), pp. 474–75. PLA strength from Gittings, *The Role of the Chinese Army*; Chen shows 2.88 million employees in "government administration" in 1956 and 3.7 million in "trade enterprises" in 1957, but we do not know if these categories match those referred to in the text.

1954–1965 period. The CCP, seeking red and expert candidates with particular concern about redness, logically focused its search on the CYL, which was its own auxiliary and second only to the party in the assumed political activism and purity of its membership. To the extent that the party also wanted young candidates with somewhat advanced education or training (students and soldiers), or who were already acquiring valued work experience (low-level cadres, state employees, and industrial workers), it was also turning to institutions that were very much a part of the League's organizational domain. The CYL was probably enrolling from 60 to 90 percent of its age group in the PLA, the regular schools, the factories, and government offices. The League was relatively weak in the countryside, but even here it served as the logical provider of rural party recruits because so many of its rural members were village activists and cadres. As early as 1954, an estimated 6 million Leaguers were serving as basic-level officials in the countryside;[41] given a League membership of 12 million and estimating rural members as 70 percent of the total, about 70 percent of rural Leaguers held village cadre positions in 1954.

Standing astride the institutional channels of political recruitment, the League interposed itself as a crucial barrier between the young citizen and higher political status. Yet that citizen's access to the League was often dependent on earlier entry into institutions highly selective in their admissions process (the regular secondary schools and the PLA). Moreover, all was not well with the League from a Maoist point of view. It was a huge bureaucracy, heavily oriented toward the cities and advanced schools, closely tied to the central party Secretariat and Propaganda Department, jealously guarding its power to pass judgment on the political qualifications of candidates, and filled with overage cadres making a career of youth work.[42] The implications were not lost on the political aspirant who

[41]Funnell, "The Chinese Communist Youth Movement," p. 144.

[42]Cf. the previous chapter's discussion of the pre–Cultural Revolution crisis in socialization, and see ibid.; John Gardner, "Educated Youth and Urban-Rural Inequalities, 1958–1966," in Lewis, ed., *The City in Communist China*, pp. 276–86; and James R. Townsend, *The Revolutionization of Chinese Youth* (Berkeley: University of California, Center for Chinese Studies, 1967), esp. pp. 59–71.

recognized the institutional roles of the game that had to be played for the sake of a career.[43]

Finally, we should note that institutionalization of recruitment gave great importance to seniority and made upward mobility difficult for the post-1954 recruit. As shown in the next section, central leadership remained closed to all but the oldest of the party elite. A study of local leadership reveals that cadres recruited before 1949 or during land reform tended to hold on to their posts, steadily advancing the age of *xian* and district cadres in particular and blocking advancement for those at lower levels.[44] The influence of seniority was also evident among top elites at the provincial level who tended to retain their positions or be replaced by cadres of roughly comparable age, having the same result of a rising average age.[45] Reliance on old cadres is particularly important in view of the distribution of party members by date of admission. As early as 1961, only 20 percent were pre-1949 entrants, while those joining after 1953 constituted 70 percent of the party.[46] Those who entered the party after 1953—that is, after the revolutionary wars and reconstruction struggles— probably constituted close to 80 percent of the party by 1965. By 1965, the CCP was an organization of recent recruits lacking revolutionary experience, led by a small stratum of old revolutionary cadres who held most of the responsible positions within it.

Table VI.3 offers a simplified summary of the preceding discussion, emphasizing changes experienced by party organization between 1945 and 1965. Maoists recognized the shift from a revolutionary to a bureaucratic party and tried to combat it.

[43]Michel Oksenberg, "The Ladder of Success on the Eve of the Cultural Revolution," *China Quarterly*, no. 36 (October–December 1968): 61–92.

[44]Michel Oksenberg, "Local Leaders in Rural China, 1962–65: Individual Attributes, Bureaucratic Positions and Political Recruitment," in A. Doak Barnett, ed., *Chinese Communist Politics in Action* (Seattle: University of Washington Press, 1969), pp. 155–215. This article analyzes local leadership and recruitment in detail, bringing out many dimensions of local recruitment not discussed here.

[45]Frederick C. Teiwes, *Provincial Party Personnel in Mainland China, 1955–1966* (New York: Columbia University, East Asian Institute, 1967), pp. 7, 31–33.

[46]Lewis, *Leadership in Communist China*, p. 111–13.

TABLE VI.3 *Contrasts in the Chinese Communist Party of 1945 and 1965*

	1945	1965
Membership	1,211,128	Over 17,000,000
Age of top leaders	Forties	Sixties
Social background		
Percentage rural	Near 100	Over 60
Percentage urban	Near 0	Over 30
Primary work	Peasant or soldier	Cadre or office work
Style of political work	Generalist: mass mobilization and face-to-face relationships	Specialist: administrative in a bureaucratic setting
Remuneration	Nonsalaried	Salaried
Mobility	Open	Closed
Recruitment	Self-recruitment, screened by performance in revolutionary action	Competitive selection, screened by admission to feeder institutions (PLA, schools, Youth League)

There were attempts to reduce cadre numbers in the mid-1950s; initiation of movements to recruit more peasant CCP and CYL members, and repoliticization of the PLA in the late 1950s; socialist education and cultivation of revolutionary successor campaigns in the early 1960s; and a new CYL recruitment drive to add worker-peasant members and rejuvenate League organization in 1964–1965. These measures checked but did not reverse the institutionalization of recruitment. With the exception of the PLA, where Lin Biao's revival of the revolutionary political style had a marked impact,[47] none of the institutions involved turned decisively away from the post-1953 pattern. Maoist pressures simply created ambiguity and uncertainty in recruitment policy, possibly explaining the withholding of data on party and League membership after 1961.

"Fresh Blood" in the Cultural Revolution. The advantage of hindsight makes clear that pressure was building in the early 1960s for a radical rectification of the party. For one thing, the

[47]See Gittings, *The Role of the Chinese Army*, pp. 225–62.

socialist education movement of 1962–1965 was a precursor to the Cultural Revolution in a number of respects.[48] The treatment of local cadres by visiting work teams was extremely harsh compared to earlier rectification campaigns. Political losses and hard feelings caused by this treatment created the base for later Cultural Revolution factionalization. Moreover, the movement clarified the differences between Mao's desires to involve poor peasants in an external criticism of the party and the more Leninist approach of relying on internal party discipline. Mao appeared less critical of local party leaders but more radical in his solution, while the center organization, inspired by a report by Wang Guangmei (Liu Shaoqi's wife), advocated harsh discipline through traditional hierarchical channels. Another event that contributed to radical rectification was the criticism of Soviet revisionism in the 1960s and the consequent commitment to prevent the emergence of revisionism in China. The first of the "five criteria for revolutionary successors" enunciated by Mao in 1964 was that "they must be genuine Marxist-Leninists and not revisionists like Khrushchev wearing the cloak of Marxism-Leninism."[49]

The harshness of the Socialist Education Movement and the ideological leftism of the antirevisionist polemic combined explosively in the Cultural Revolution. Although the party itself was not under attack and the targets were supposed to be limited to the "handful of capitalist-roaders," the Cultural Revolution was replete with real and rhetorical attacks on the established recruitment process. The upsurge of Red Guards and rebels, purges of office holders, and suspension of the CYL cut sharply through existing routines and channels for political advancement. Maoist accounts commended the rise of millions of "previously unknown"

---

[48]Frederick Teiwes, *Politics and Purges in China* (White Plains, N.Y.: M. E. Sharpe, 1979), pp. 493–633; Harry Harding, *Organizing China: The Problem of Bureaucracy 1949–1976* (Stanford, Cal.: Stanford University Press, 1981), pp. 195–234.

[49]*The Problem on the General Line of the International Communist Movement* (Peking: Foreign Languages Press, 1965), pp. 477–79. Each of the other criteria also contrasts the correct behavior of revolutionary successors with the crimes of Khrushchev. The "five criteria" (without the references to Khrushchev) were written into the 1973 party constitution, chapter 2, article 3.

activists who were appearing on the political scene. As the campaign shifted to its consolidation phase in 1968, an important editorial in *Red Flag* forecast a more open and vigorous recruitment policy. Emphasizing the importance of recruitment in determining the future of the revolution, the editorial took its theme from a Mao quotation:

> A human being has arteries and veins through which the heart makes the blood circulate, and he breathes with his lungs, exhaling carbon dioxide and inhaling fresh oxygen, that is, getting rid of the stale and taking in the fresh. A proletarian party must also get rid of the stale and take in the fresh for only thus can it be full of vitality. Without eliminating waste matter and absorbing fresh blood the Party has no vigor.

The editorial continued in explanation:

> "Eliminating waste matter" means resolutely expelling from the Party the proven renegades, enemy agents, all counter-revolutionaries, obdurate capitalist roaders, alien class elements and degenerated elements. As for apathetic persons whose revolutionary will has declined, they should be advised to leave the Party.
>
> "Absorbing fresh blood" consists of two inter-related tasks: Taking into the Party a number of outstanding rebels, primarily advanced elements from among the industrial workers, and selecting outstanding Communist Party members for leading posts in the Party organizations at all levels.[50]

The preference for industrial workers is interesting, but the editorial made it clear that recruitment criteria ought to be political and moral rather than socioeconomic: "boundless loyalty" to Mao; defense of his line during the Cultural Revolution; exercise of power for Mao and the proletariat, not for self-interest; vigorous study and propagation of Mao's thought with no pride, conceit, or halfway revolution; close ties with and service to the masses. The editorial attacked Liu Shaoqi for relying on

---

[50]"Absorb Fresh Blood from the Proletariat—An Important Question in Party Consolidation," *Red Flag*, no. 4 (October 14, 1968), in *PR*, no. 43 (October 25, 1968): 4–7.

the bourgeoisie and bourgeois intellectuals and inveighed against "conventional criteria," "old habits," and "blind faith in elections" as conservative influences used to exclude good comrades. "Direct action by the revolutionary masses" coupled with approval by the leadership was the editorial's approved formula for the constitution of new organs of power.

How far the CCP actually went in absorbing "fresh blood" and procedures is a complicated question to which several answers are possible—all of which are limited by insufficient data. One response is that the Cultural Revolution initiated another spurt of party growth, with membership rising to 28 million by 1973 and over 35 million by August 1977 (see Table VI.1). Assuming that growth must have been slow in the early 1960s, and stopped altogether from 1966 to 1969, the 1970s were as heavy a recruitment period as the mid-1950s. The result was a substantial increase in the ratio of party members to total population, a ratio that rose from 1.72 percent in 1956 to 3.68 percent in 1977 (calculated from Table VI.1 and common population estimates). By the late 1970s, the CCP was almost entirely an organization of post-1949 recruits; about half of them were recruited after the Cultural Revolution.

There was also a substantial radical influence on party recruitment in the first few years after the Cultural Revolution. The constitution adopted at the Ninth Party Congress in 1969 removed an earlier requirement for a year's probation before full membership and added a stipulation that popular opinions be solicited in assessing applicants' qualifications. Scattered reports indicated that admission in this period was simpler and quicker, generally favoring Cultural Revolution activists. It may be assumed that there was strong influence on recruitment by dominant factions within party branches. The strongest evidence that post-1969 recruitment was under radical influence stems from later charges that the Gang of Four were stacking party rolls with their own supporters. In commenting on CCP membership at the Eleventh Party Congress in 1977, Ye Jianying observed, "There is the serious problem of impurity in ideology, organization and style of work among Party members as a result of the rather extensive confusion created by the 'gang of four' who in recent years vitiated the Party's line, undermined the Party's organizational principle and set their own standards for

Party membership."[51] Ye clearly implied that the Gang's "crash admittance" efforts, bringing "political speculators" and "bad types" into the party, were one reason for the restoration of the one-year probation requirement and other disciplinary emphases adopted in the 1977 constitution. In general, the post-1976 assault on the Gang's intraparty activities testifies to the radicalization of recruitment procedures during 1969–1976.

Recruiting for Modernization after Mao. Party recruitment in the post-Mao period has had two overlapping aspects. The first is directed at ridding the party of the factions and leftism of the Cultural Revolution, while restoring earlier organizational patterns. There is a clear preference for a more orderly, disciplined recruitment process. The reactivation of the old mass organizations—especially the Youth League, with its reported 1978 membership of 48 million and with explicit praise for its having "trained large numbers of outstanding cadres for the Party"[52]— provided the screening institutions to implement it. The rise of former CYL leaders Hu Yaobang to General Secretary of the Party and Hu Qili to Permanent Secretary of the CCP Secretariat certainly strengthens its prestige, although the ideological reorientation of the post-Mao period has made the League's function especially difficult. Meanwhile, the party has been engaged in a lengthy effort to root out leftism, factionalism, and corruption. The reinstitution of the discipline inspection committees is the most important institutional reform, but there have also been numerous campaigns against undesirable tendencies in the party. The anti-crime campaign of 1983 included corruption among its targets, and a major part of the 1983–86 rectification campaign is the elimination of three types of party members: followers of the Gang or Lin Biao, factionalists, and persons implicated in violence.[53]

[51] "Report on the Revision of the Party Constitution," *PR*, no. 36 (September 2, 1977): 36. "Radical-moderate" struggles over rehabilitation of cadres attacked during the Cultural Revolution were prominent throughout 1969–1976, suggesting similar conflict over recruitment; see Hong Yung Lee, "The Politics of Cadre Rehabilitation Since the Cultural Revolution," *Asian Survey*, vol. 18, no. 9 (September 1978): 934–55.

[52] *PR*, no. 20 (May 19, 1978): 10.

[53] See David Goodman, "The Second Plenary Session of the 12th CCP Central Committee: Rectification and Reform," *China Quarterly*, no. 97 (March 1984): pp. 84–90.

The second aspect of post-Mao party recruitment is the adaptation of party leadership to the tasks of modernization. The problem of party modernization is closely linked to that of rectification and regularization, but it involves the additional element of reorientation. In order for the party to lead modernization, it must recruit intellectuals, reeducate its existing cadres, and prevent party interference in the proper functioning of state organs. Recruitment of intellectuals is a pressing concern because in 1984 only 17.8 percent of party members had a senior middle school education and only 4 percent were college graduates. Of course, these figures only reflect a general lack of advanced education in China. One in ten senior middle school graduates and one in three college graduates is a party member, compared to less than one in twenty party members in the general population.[54] Nevertheless, it is vital to the party to recruit even more intellectuals because of their key role in modernization. From 1978 to 1984, a total of 580,000 professional and technical people were recruited into the party, approximately 10 percent of total recruitment during that period. Despite some members' resistance to adding so many intellectuals to the party, this recruitment pattern will probably be intensified. Many current party members are being retrained in cadre schools at the central and local levels. The curriculum of these schools previously emphasized ideology but now is being reoriented toward science and management.

In general, post-Mao recruitment has reverted to the pattern of the mid-1950s, except that recruitment now is less class-oriented and even more committed to including intellectuals. The trends since 1977 have been predictable. Given the size of the CCP—surely the world's largest bureaucracy, and one that attempts to maintain close control over every member—the routinism and institutionalization of recruitment must be difficult to resist. When the requirements of the "four modernization" policies are added, the evidence points strongly toward a recruitment process that will favor the more highly skilled and educated sectors of Chinese society, creating closer links between political status and socioeconomic status and fostering tendencies toward the

[54]*People's Daily*, November 20, 1984; comparisons calculated from 1982 census data in *Statistical Yearbook of China 1983*, p. 116.

emergence of a new class of technocratic party elites, a situation already existing in the Soviet Union and many Eastern European countries.[55]

Recruitment to Top Leadership. Much more is known about China's top political elite—commonly identified by membership in the CCP Central Committee (CC)—than about membership in the party generally or in any other stratum of Chinese society. Although information is still limited, it reveals significant facts about recruitment to the highest level of the political system. These data illustrate broad trends in elite composition and more detailed shifts in intraparty struggles; attention here focuses on larger trends, with only a few observations on the relationship between CC composition and factional struggles.

Table VI.4 suggests several important changes in the CC over time. One of the more obvious is that the CC has grown steadily in size, making it less effective as a decision-making body but increasing its potential as a representative body for the party as a whole and strengthening its training and screening function for future Politburo service. Growth also means the CC has had regular infusions of new members; the lowest percentage occurred in 1973 when 31 percent of those elected to the Tenth CC were newcomers. Such figures are important since there are other ways in which elite change and mobility appears highly restricted. Moreover, Table VI.4 points to three major consequences of the Cultural Revolution: first, there was a particularly heavy turnover of membership in the election of the Ninth CC in 1969; second, the campaign sharply increased military representation on the Ninth CC, followed by successive reductions of PLA influence on the Tenth, Eleventh, and Twelfth committees; third, the upheavals of 1966–1969 and the decentralizing policies associated with the Maoist model shifted the balance of power on the CC from those holding positions in central offices in Peking to those with primary responsibilities in the provinces (for example, secretaries of provincial party committees, heads of provincial revolutionary committees, or commanders of regional

---

[55]For a critique of this tendency in European Communist countries, see Georg Konrad and Ivan Szelenyi, *The Intellectuals on the Road to Class Power* (New York: Harcourt, Brace and Jovanovich, 1979).

PLA forces)—a shift that was reversed in the Eleventh and Twelfth CCs; fourth, the mass representatives, who became members of the Central Committee during the Cultural Revolution, had been eliminated by 1982. Those of this category in the Twelfth CC were new members associated with mass organizations such as trade unions. Finally, this table documents the return of rehabilitated cadres to the Tenth and Eleventh CCs, the "reversal of verdicts" on older cadres purged in the Cultural Revolution that was such a potent issue between the radicals and moderates during 1969–1976. The relatively small percentages refer to sixteen returnees in 1973 and twenty more in 1977, representing a substantial component of the former purge victims who were still alive to benefit from this reversal.

The iron grip of the Long March generation (people who had joined the CCP by the time of the epic Long March of 1934–1935) on PRC political power can be seen in the steady rise of the age of CC members. The average age of the CC rose from 46.8 on the Seventh CC elected in 1945 to 56.4 in 1956 and 61.4 in 1969; in other words, despite substantial turnovers of or additions to CC membership over these twenty-five years, most changes came from *within* the same increasingly elderly generation. The average age of the two committees elected in the 1970s continued to increase, although (inevitably) not as rapidly as before. More specifically, 67 of the 77 members of the Seventh CC were reelected to the Eighth in 1956; and even though only 53 of the 193 members of the Eighth CC weathered the Cultural Revolution storm to serve on the Ninth, the Long March group continued to hold 80 percent of the seats. The Long Marchers fell to 63 percent of the Tenth CC but then actually rose to 67 percent on the Eleventh CC elected in 1977.[56] The percentage of post-1949 recruits on the CC rose sharply in 1973 but then fell in 1977, while the percentage of members of 60, and also over 70, rose steadily on the 1969, 1973, and 1977 committees. Although the Long March generation's dominance is obviously about to end, with many of its most prestigious representatives gone, its control of top leadership was still in place thirty years after 1949, even though the CCP had become essentially an organization of post-

[56] Jürgen Domes, "China in 1977: A Reversal of the Verdict," *Asian Survey*, vol. 18, no. 1 (January 1978): 8.

TABLE VI.4 *Changes in Composition of the CCP Central Committee*

	8th Central Committee (1956–1958)		9th Central Committee (1969)		10th Central Committee (1973)		11th Central Committee (1977)		12th Central Committee (1982)
I. Number of members									
Full	97		170		195		201		210
Alternate	96[a]		109		124		132		132
Total	193		279		319		333		348
II. Turnover of members[b]									
Holdover from previous Central Committee									
Committee	40%		19%		64%		56%		39%
Newcomer	60%		81%		31%		38%		61%
Returnee[c]	0%		0%		5%		6%		N/A
III. Occupational background		(entered 9th)		(entered 10th)		(entered 11th)		(entered 12th)	
Cadres	70%	27%	29%	83%	33%	82%	44%	56%	69%
PLA	21%	47%	43%	59%	30%	63%	27%	39%	19%
Masses	0%	0%	28%	94%	37%	44%	27%	18%	11%

IV. Occupational level					
Center	61%	30%	28%	35%	47%
Local	39%	70%	72%	64%	53%
V. Average age of full members at election	56.4	61.4	62.1	64.6	N/A

[a]Twenty-five alternate members were added to the 8th Central Committee at its second plenary session in 1958.

[b]Figures in II, III, and IV represent percentages of total (full and alternate) Central Committee membership.

[c]Returnees are those full and alternate members who were not elected to the immediately previous Central Committee but who were members of an earlier Central Committee.

Sources: For I and III: *Who's Who in Communist China* (Hong Kong: Union Research Institute, 1966), pp. 703–7; Donald W. Klein and Lois B. Hager, "The Ninth Central Committee," *China Quarterly*, no. 45 (January–February 1971): 37–56; Malcolm Lamb, *Directory of Central Officials in the People's Republic of China, 1968–1975* (Canberra: Australian National University, 1976), pp. 5–16; K'ung Te-liang, "An Analysis of the CCP's 10th National Congress," *Issues and Studies*, vol. 10, no. 1 (October 1973): 17–30; Central Intelligence Agency, *China: A Look at the 11th Central Committee* (Rp 77–10276, October 1977).

For III and IV and all 1982 data: Hong Yung Lee, "China's 12th Central Committee: Rehabilitated Cadres and Technocrats," *Asian Survey*, vol. 23, no. 6 (June 1983): 673–91.

For V: Jürgen Domes, "The Ninth CCP Central Committee in Statistical Perspective," *Current Scene*, vol. 9, no. 2 (February 7, 1971): 5–14; Jürgen Domes, "China in 1977: A Reversal of the Verdict," *Asian Survey*, vol. 18, no. 1 (January 1978): 6–9.

1949 recruits. The disappearance of the Long Marchers in the 1980s will be a momentous change, providing both a challenge and an opportunity for the CCP and its younger cohorts.

The Twelfth Central Committee. The combination of succession problems, factional struggles, and organizational reform created a considerable disjunction between the Eleventh and Twelfth CCs.[57] A Central Advisory Committee was created in order to ease old leaders out of active positions, allowing them continued access to decision making but making room for newcomers in the CC. The Central Discipline Inspection Committee, which had been formed in 1979, had become a major party organ under the leadership of Chen Yun. A proposal to make a formal division of powers between the CC and the other two organs was rejected, but the proposal itself was indicative of a trend toward the division and institutionalization of authority.

The membership of the Twelfth CC reflects the victory of Deng Xiaoping and his pragmatist allies over leaders who had been against the Gang of Four but not totally opposed to Cultural Revolution policies. Hua Guofeng was the symbol and, in some respects, the leader of this group, and he went from CCP chairman, premier, and chairman of the party military committee in 1977 to an ordinary member of the CC in 1982. Many of Hua's supporters were either not reappointed to the Twelfth CC or forced into the semiretirement of the Central Advisory Committee. On a more positive note, there was a doubling of the representation of the State Council, from 10 percent in the Eleventh CC to 20 percent in the Twelfth.[58] This reflects the importance of economic issues as well as the growing political clout of the state apparatus.

Table VI.5 displays some of the complexities of political continuity at the CC level from 1977 to 1982. If we ignore transfers to the Central Advisory Committee and examine only the percentage of Eleventh CC members continuing in the Twelfth,

[57]See Hong Yung Lee, "China's 12th Central Committee: Rehabilitated Cadres and Technocrats," *Asian Survey*, vol. 23, no. 6 (June 1983): 673–91; and Lowell Dittmer, "The 12th Congress of the Communist Party of China," *China Quarterly*, no. 93 (March 1983): 108–24. Our analysis in this section does not cover September 1985 changes in Twelfth CC membership that strengthened Deng's position and policies by retiring old cadres and promoting younger leaders.

TABLE VI.5 *Continuity Between the Eleventh and Twelfth CCs*

Eleventh CC:	Full Members	Alternates	Total
Entered Twelfth CC at same level	99 (44%)	18 (14%)	117 (33%)
Promoted to full members	— —	16 (12%)	16 (5%)
Demoted to alternate	6 (3%)	— —	6 (2%)
Transferred to Advisory Committee	52 (23%)	13 (10%)	65 (18%)
Not continued	51 (23%)	80 (61%)	131 (37%)
Died or transferred elsewhere	15 (7%)	5 (4%)	20 (6%)
TOTAL	223 (100%)	132 (101%)	355 (101%)

Source: Hong Yung Lee, "China's 12th Central Committee: Rehabilitated Cadres and Technocrats," (*Asian Survey* vol. 23 no. 6 June 1983): 680. © 1983 by the Regents of the University of California. Reprinted from *Asian Survey*, Vol. 23, No. 6, June 1983, p. 680, by permission of the Regents. We have added the total column and the percentages; rounding yields percentages over 100.

then a very serious purge is evident, more serious than the removal of Gang adherents in 1977 but not as serious as the gutting of the Eighth CC by the Cultural Revolution. One might argue that the Central Advisory Committee is a prestigious, if less active, organization, and, with an average age of 75, many of its members are not being purged but simply transferred to a more appropriate level of activity. However, the matter is not quite so clear, because even relatively young leaders were "kicked upstairs" if they had been promoted rapidly before Deng's ascendency, while the truly powerful figures in the Politburo refused to be retired regardless of their age.[59] Even if transfer to the Central Advisory Committee is considered a lateral transfer, however, the discontinuity between the Eleventh and Twelfth CCs is considerable. It mirrors an important shift in factional strengths and in policy orientation during the post-Mao period.

Changes in the Politburo command special attention, since this body is generally considered the supreme decision-making elite. Recruitment of the Politburo mirrors the CC pattern of age and Long March domination; the average age of seventy-two for full members of the 1982 Politburo (up from sixty-eight in 1977) gives the PRC an extremely elderly top national leadership. Turnover on the Politburo has also been about the same as on

[58]Lee, "Rehabilitated Cadres," p. 687.
[59]Ibid., p. 682–84.

the CC, slightly higher overall due to more deaths but very close to the CC in purge percentages. In other ways, however, Politburo recruitment differs from the CC. Its size has been constant, reflecting the fact that it is a functioning committee, whereas the CC is more a representative assembly. In the Twelfth CC, there is a very strong linkage between the Secretariat and the Politburo. Of the nine new members of the Politburo in 1982, six had been members of the Secretariat.[60]

The current organizational affiliations of Politburo members shown on Table VI.6 indicate the importance of linkage and access at the top of the Chinese political system. Except for the commanders of two important military regions, all of the linkages are with other central organs. This reflects the Politburo's position of being the center of the center. There are ten joint appointments with the military, eight with the State Council, and four with the National People's Congress. The military's overrepresentation in the Politburo began with the Ninth CC in 1969 and continues, somewhat reduced, into the 1980s. The affiliations of the Politburo Standing Committee are a microcosm of those of the Politburo. Of its six members, two are leaders of the Central Military Committee and two are leaders in state organs. There are also linkages to three other key organizations, the Secretariat and party apparatus in general through Hu Yaobang, the Central Advisory Committee (CAC) through Deng Xiaoping, and the Central Discipline Inspection Committee (CDIC) through Chen Yun. The Central Commission for Guiding Party Consolidation (CCGPC) is the task force in charge of party rectification. It is the most important example of a comprehensive, ad hoc organization. It features a blue-ribbon leadership (Hu Yaobang and six other Politburo members) and extensive participation by CAC and CDIC personnel.

A fascinating question is what combination of qualifications and experiences creates access to CCP elitehood, but few solid generalizations can be formulated. By far, the most important criterion for PRC leadership has been membership in the Long March generation plus a capacity to survive physically and politically; those who met these conditions simply *were* the elite prior to the Cultural Revolution. That campaign

---

[60]Dittmer, "The Twelfth Congress," p. 123n.

revealed other considerations, however, with three new criteria emerging as particularly important recruitment assets. One was high military command, which seems to be a prime functional specialty for access to the top. A second was success as a provincial leader, with many new elite recruits capitalizing on their provincial bases; Hua Guofeng was an example, although his Hunan experience was not the only factor in his ascent.[61] Finally, personal support from the highest leaders was a very effective asset, the best example being the Gang of Four who benefitted from Mao's patronage in the late 1960s. These criteria overlap and must blend with other personal and political skills to produce a successful career, but they remain important—not exclusive—paths to the top. Post-1976 priorities suggest that some technocrats, highly skilled in the administration of modernization policies, will join military commanders, provincial leaders, and protégés in the late 1980s as a fourth type of upwardly mobile cadres.

The 1970s transformed what Mao Zedong perceived to be the core problem of political recruitment. Mao was keenly aware of the necessity of "cultivating revolutionary successors" in large numbers to staff the burgeoning Chinese bureaucracies. His search was for cadres like himself who combined revolutionary ideology with intellectual or technical skills. The problem was that Chinese society seemed to offer relatively few recruits with these talents. Initially, there were plenty of reds, but their expertise was limited, whereas the available experts were contaminated by KMT influence or bourgeois education. When Mao saw that the new recruitment processes were not replicating his brand of revolutionary ideology, he began to fear that revisionist influences would overwhelm the party's revolutionary core. Hence his suspicion of the new elite, his promotion of the Cultural Revolution, and his continuing search for "fresh blood" that had escaped or renounced the influence of impure background or education.

By the late 1970s, two developments had changed this perception of the problem. Mao and his closest associates were gone, and although Long Marchers remained influential, the

[61] Michel Oksenberg and Sai-cheung Yeung, "Hua Kuo-feng's Pre-Cultural Revolution Hunan Years, 1949–66," *China Quarterly*, no. 69 (March 1977): 3–53.

TABLE VI.6 *Affiliations of Politburo Members, 1983*

Standing Committee

Chen Yun	1st Secretary, Central Discipline Inspection Committee (CDIC).
Deng Xiaoping	Chair, Central Advisory Committee (CAC); Chair, Central Military Committee (CMC).
Hu Yaobang	General Secretary; Chair, Central Commission for Guiding Party Consolidation (CCGPC).
Li Xiannian	President of the PRC; State Council Standing Comm. (SCSC).
Ye Jianying	Vice-Chair, CMC.
Zhao Ziyang	Premier; Head, Science and Technology Leading Group (S&TLG); Minister in Charge, State Comm. for Restructuring the Economy.

Full Members

Deng Yingchao	Chair, CCPCC[a].	Wan Li	Vice Premier; Vice Chair, CCGPC; SCSC; CC Secr[b]; CAC.
Fang Yi	State Councilor; Deputy Head, S&TLG; Min. in Chg., State State S&T Comm.	Wang Zhen	President, Party School; Adviser, CCGPC.
		Wei Guoqing	Vice Chair, NPC. SC.
Hu Qiaomu	Adviser, CCGPC; Honorary President, Acad. of Soc. Sci.	Xi Zhongxun	Adviser, CCGPC; CC Secr.
		Xu Xiangqian	Vice Chair, CMC.
		Yang Dezhi	Chief of Staff and 1st

Li Desheng	Commander & 1st Sec. Shenyang Military Region.	Yang Shangkun	Party Sec., PLA; CMC. Exec. Vice Chair, CMC; Adviser, CCGPC.
Ni Zhifu	Chair, Trade Union Fed.	Yu Qiuli	Director, Gen Polit Dept. PLA; SCSC; CMC; Vice Chair, CCGPC; CC Secr.
Nie Rongzhen	Vice-Chair, CMC.	Zhang Tingfa	Commander, Air Force.
Peng Zhen	Chair, Standing Comm. of NPC; Sec., Polit. & Legal Comm.		

Alternate Members

Song Renqiong	Adviser, CCGPC.	Chen Muhua	SCSC; Minister, Foreign Econ. Rel. and Trade.
Ulanhu	Vice President, PRC; SCSC.	Qin Jiwei	Commander and 1st sec., Beijing Military Region.
		Yao Yilin	SCSC.

[a]Chinese People's Political Consultative Conference.
[b]CCP Central Committee Secretariat.

Source: Directory of Chinese Officials: National Level Organizations and *Directory of Chinese Officials: Provincial Organizations*, U.S. Central Intelligence Agency, 1983.

CCP was no longer dominated by a desire to replicate old revolutionary cadres. Moreover, the pool of potential recruits had expanded enormously due to increases in the number of activists, middle school graduates, members of mass organizations and the party, and cadres with substantial administrative experience. With this large and diverse body of potential recruits, nearly all of whom were products of socialist society and spread throughout that society, the danger of any particular group of recruits (such as intellectuals) transforming the party seemed small. Or perhaps it would be more accurate to say that the party was *already* transformed so that it could no longer perceive the problem in Mao's terms or with his sense of urgency.

The core recruitment problem for the 1980s, then, seems to be emerging as a mix of managerial and bureaucratic concerns: how to administer a process that requires review and examination of tens of millions of cases; how to balance priorities in the training of various specialties, ranging from rural to nuclear technology, from basic-level activists to computer experts, from foreign language specialists to factory managers, and so forth; and how to prevent political recruitment processes, necessarily based on a great variety of institutional training and election grounds, from producing enclaves of special interests that will breed factions and threaten the CCP's centralized organization and ideology.

ELITE CONFLICT

To summarize the discussion thus far, CCP theory recognizes the existence of multiple interests within Chinese society and maintains that nonantagonistic ones among the people should be expressed politically. The possibly competitive demands so legitimized emanate from a wide range of socioeconomic, institutional, and geographic groups. Popular articulation of demands occurs largely within basic-level government, especially within primary production and residential units, and is typically unorganized and fragmented. Organized articulation by nonparty groups is supervised closely by CCP elites to check competition with the party and to ensure that demands conform to its general line; deviations can and do occur to bring disciplinary and, if necessary, repressive responses from the CCP. Bureaucratic articulation, in which office-holding elites champion selected interests, is the primary means for injecting demands into the decision-making process, hence the importance of recruitment to higher political roles. The CCP hopes that its recruitment process will produce a unified elite of "red-experts" who will rise above partial interests in their aggregation of political demands. In fact, the party never has been monolithic in either ideology or organization. It maintained a relatively high degree of cohesion from the late 1930s into the early 1950s, but with its victory in 1949 it began to undergo major changes. It increased greatly in size; began to accept recruits of more varied motivation, skills, and backgrounds; expanded its control over, and then direct management of, the administrative processes of government; and bureaucratized its organization to cope with these new conditions. In the process, the CCP absorbed the basic contradictions of Chinese society, and its organization became an arena for conflict between the demands of different strata, regions, generations, and institutions.

The resulting political process bears some similarity to the bureaucratic politics of traditional China as discussed in Chapter 2, but it operates in a much more encompassing and complicated governmental structure that opens the process to a greater variety of institutional and societal pressures. Closer to the mark is Rigby's concept of "crypto-politics," in which state direction of a tremendous range of activities creates an elaborate set of political institutions without permitting truly open, competitive politics in any of them; political conflict tends to be carried on in secretive or guarded ways throughout the governmental structure, in executive and administrative as well as nominally political institutions.[62] The Chinese brand of crypto-politics is a volatile one that has encouraged a good deal of guided conflict resolution at the mass level and at times opened elite conflict to public view and even participation. In general, however, the definition and resolution of major political issues is the responsibility of party officials, whose conflicts are fought inside the bureaucracies in which they serve and are seldom exposed fully to public view. The political criticisms that appear in the media are usually case analyses of a particular failing such as factionalism, or more

[62]T. H. Rigby, "Crypto-Politics," *Survey*, no. 50 (January 1964): 183–94.

general critiques with unspecified targets. Political attacks are never openly and directly rebutted. Opposition is shown through inattention or reinterpretation of the attack, or through emphasis on some countervailing political principle. The process is political, but it does not lend itself to easy distinctions between articulation and aggregation, between decision making and administration.

As Frederick Teiwes has pointed out in an insightful review of political conflict in China, there are official "rules of the game" for intraparty conflict.[63] These include such principles as collective leadership and democratic centralism, and contain provisions for dissenting minorities to reserve their opinions on particular policies as long as they do not obstruct implementation. However, the organizational norms are heavily weighted in favor of authority. The room for legitimate opposition is narrow, ill-defined, and shifting; dissent is treated as a disciplinary problem. Organized opposition is forbidden. Under such rules, opposition and conflict are risky in the best of times. During the Maoist period, these rules were often violated.

Since opposition is so disadvantaged in the official arena of Chinese politics, it is not surprising that informal patterns of elite politics are common. A major source of information about informal patterns are the frequent criticisms of them in the press. Leftism, feudalism, factionalism, localism, and departmentalism are all known to be serious problems through official denunciations. However, it is impossible to know the extent to which each of these influences Chinese politics. Moreover, some oppositional patterns are based on policy differences (leftism, for example), some are based on individual loyalties and have no policy content (feudal patron-client relations), while others may involve a mixture of policy and personal commitments (departmentalism and localism). Factionalism, in particular, is

---

[63]Frederick Teiwes, "'Rules of the Game' in Chinese Politics," *Problems of Communism*, vol. 28, no. 5–6 (September–December 1979): 67–76.

[64]For a lively discussion of the limits of factional analysis, see Tang Tsou, "Prolegomenon to the Study of Informal Groups in CCP Politics," *China Quarterly*, no. 65 (March 1976): 98–114. Tsou's article is a critique of Andrew Nathan, "A Factionalism Model for CCP Politics," *China Quarterly*, no. 53 (January–March 1973): 34–66.

an ambiguous problem, both as a term of analysis and as a term of abuse.[64]

Because of the evident importance of informal patterns of elite conflict and the opacity of Chinese decision making, a number of explanatory models of elite conflict have been formulated. One of the most prominent is Lucian Pye's factionalism model, which utilizes his theories of Chinese political culture to argue that Chinese politics is based on the conflict and accommodation of hierarchical clusters of personal relationships.[65] A faction may promote a certain policy in order to advance its interests, but basic to the faction is the cluster of personal relationships. Although some scholars would dispute Pye's political culture explanation for factionalism,[66] all would agree that factionalism has played a very serious part in Chinese politics at least since 1966. Proof of this is that the party rectification campaign has as a major goal the elimination of factions, and yet there are complaints that the campaign itself has been manipulated by factions.[67] It is not easy to separate personal factional ties and policy commitments. It may seem reasonable to distinguish conceptually between opportunistic "factions" and policy-oriented "opinion groups," but they are much more difficult to distinguish in reality, and, in any case, Leninist party discipline disapproves of both. A faction might promote a policy for its own advancement and then find that its policy stake requires other, congruent policies. At this point, the opportunistic faction has a policy platform that it cannot abandon without costs. If we start from the policy end of the analysis, a group of cadres passionately devoted to a particular policy but who had no prior personal relationship would find it to their policy-oriented, political interests to develop personal contacts and be concerned for one another's weal or woe. This indistinguishable interplay of personal and policy interests can be seen in the behavior of political groups in every political system.

[64]Lucian Pye, *The Dynamics of Chinese Politics* (Cambridge, Mass.: Oelgeschlager, Gunn & Hain, 1981). An earlier version was published as *The Dynamics of Factions and Consensus in Chinese Politics: A Model and Some Propositions* (Santa Monica, Cal.: Rand Corporation, 1980).

[66]See, for instance, Chalmers Johnson, "What's Wrong with Chinese Political Studies?" *Asian Survey*, vol. 22, no. 6 (October 1982): 922–23.

[67]*People's Daily*, November 13, 1984, p. 5.

A pattern of elite conflict somewhat more unique to China is the Cultural Revolution concept of the "struggle between two lines," an alleged long-term, mortal conflict within the party between the true revolutionaries, led by Mao, and the revisionists, headed by Liu Shaoqi.[68] Although the leftists made every effort to show that Liu had always been a counterrevolutionary, "two-line struggle" as historical analysis was for the most part invidious interpretation and slander. The actual policy differences between Liu and Mao will be discussed below, but the political function of "two-line struggle" was to brand the party establishment as class enemies and as targets for mass attack. The ideological terrorism implicit in two-line struggle raised the stakes of political conflict for both elite and masses.

The greater institutional pluralism of the post-Mao period may lead to a phenomenon much discussed in Soviet and Eastern European politics, namely the emergence of political interest groups.[69] Chinese mass organizations were discussed earlier in this chapter, but one must be cautious about calling them "political interest groups," and other organizations would appear to have even less claim to the designation. There are surely group interests, but it is difficult to prove that interest groups exist as a regular means of advancing them. Critics of the interest group approach in the Soviet and East European studies have argued that these groups have little legitimacy or autonomy within their systems. This caution applies with great force to China, where the struggles of the 1960s and 1970s revealed not only the existence of factions but also their vulnerability to charges of illegitimacy. Further research may delineate more sharply the kinds of interest groups that operate and endure in the Chinese political process, or possibly what kinds will emerge in the more institutionalized system that is taking shape, but the question remains a controversial one.

As the discussion of "two-line struggle" and interest group politics implies, the patterns of elite conflict have changed considerably over time. The relative balance of consensus and conflict

[68]The best analysis is Lowell Dittmer, "'Line Struggle' in Theory and Practice: The Origins of the Cultural Revolution Reconsidered," *China Quarterly*, no. 72 (December 1977): 675–712.

[69]For a review of the literature on Soviet interest groups, see H. Gordon Skilling, "Interest Groups and Communist Politics Revisited," *World Politics*, vol. 37, no. 1 (October 1984), pp. 1–27.

within the party, the salience of official norms for conflict management, and the prevalence of factionalism have all responded to the existing political situation. Therefore, we must look for phases of development in patterns of elite conflict.

Contained Conflict in the 1950s. Earlier discussions of radical-conservative and Maoist-bureaucratic conflicts have outlined the major issues of post-1949 politics. We now explore the changing patterns of elite cleavage produced by these issues. From 1949 to 1957, the CCP maintained a relatively high degree of cohesion without repressing intraparty differences or resorting to extensive purges. The crucial decisions—those that marked the shift from the First Five-Year Plan (FFYP) to the Great Leap—emerged from a vigorous debate that addressed itself directly to issues and avoided open, personalized attacks on top leaders. Conservatives stated their positions, accepted their defeats, and continued to serve. Radicals, too, accepted temporary setbacks without turning vindictively on colleagues who opposed them. Opinion group politics was thus the dominant mode of conflict. Leaders were able to differ on policy issues without forming permanently antagonistic groups. As new issues or stages arose, individuals might shift their positions or find themselves aligned with a new opinion group. Generally, elites were willing to maintain the appearance of unity in support of majority decisions.

Party cadres experienced significant consolidations and disciplinary movements during the first half of the 1950s, but, in general, party discipline confirmed the official organizational norms. The special demands on party members were offset by special consideration in disciplinary matters. Although disputes were not carried into the public media, there is evidence that party members spoke their minds without retaliation. There were relatively few ideological campaigns during this period, and their targets were usually bourgeois intellectuals.

The only major factional crisis among the elite was the 1954 purge of Gao Gang (Kao Kang) and Rao Shushi (Jao Shu-shih).[70]

---

[70]The "Gao-Rao Affair" is described in detail by Frederick Teiwes, *Politics and Purges in China: Rectification and the Decline of Party Norms, 1950–1965* (White Plains, N.Y.: M. E. Sharpe, 1979), pp. 166–210.

Gao was a Politburo member, the party leader of Northeast China, a vice-chairman of the PRC, and head of the State Planning Commission; Rao was a leader in the East China region and director of the CC's Organization Department. The Gao-Rao clique was a faction aimed at controlling succession after Mao, not simply an opinion group taking a distinctive stand on certain issues. Although Gao represented a Soviet-style approach (particularly in factory management) that was in conflict with Mao's, his group's fatal error was an attempt to capture control of the central apparatus using its organizational position as a base and trying to recruit additional followers within the CC. The specific accusations were that they opposed Liu Shaoqi and Zhou Enlai in order to become vice-chairman of the party and premier, that they engaged in activities designed to split the party, and that Gao Gang enlisted Soviet help in these activities and gave inner-party secrets to the Soviets.[71] This factional power play was smashed in February 1954, although it was not made public until 1955. The Gao-Rao affair was the exception that proved the rule of moderate elite conflict in the mid-1950s, because Gao and Rao were punished for the breaches of organizational norms. After 1966, such factional behavior seemed almost normal, and Lin Biao's attempt to seize power in 1971 was a logical outgrowth of a changed elite environment.

The Sharpening of Conflict, 1957–1966. The anti-rightist campaign that concluded the brief experiment with open criticism in the hundred flowers campaign introduced a new level of coercion and ideological harshness into Chinese politics. However, at this point in 1957 the victims were still primarily bourgeois intellectuals—teachers, students, merchants and non-Communist political figures.[72] Remaining rightists had their labels

[71]These charges are mentioned by Liao Gailong, "Lishi di jingyan he women di fazhan daolu" (Historical experience and our developmental path), a speech given on October 25, 1980 to the Conference on Party Historiography of the national party school system. The speech was not publicly released, but it was reprinted in the Taiwanese *Zhonggong yanjiu (Research on Chinese Communism)*, vol. 15, no. 19 (September 15, 1981): 108–177. The Gao-Rao reference is on p. 119.

[72]According to Teiwes, *Politics and Purges*, p. 291, 8.5 percent of the teachers at Fudan University and 6.6 percent of the China Democratic League were declared rightists, in comparison with 1.9 percent of party members in Chongqing (Chungking).

removed in 1979; however, in its 1982 official history, the party declared the campaign excessive but justified.[73] The major goal of the antirightist campaign was that of consolidating the party's ideological and political leadership, but the methods of "merciless criticism" that it introduced were shortly to be applied within the party.

The strains placed on China's leadership structure by the Great Leap Forward and its failure led to harsh treatment of local cadres and a major purge of top leaders. This was the August 1959 purge of Peng Dehuai, minister of defense and Politburo member; Huang Kecheng (Huang K'o-ch'eng), PLA Chief of Staff; Zhang Wentian (Chang Wen-t'ien), vice-minister of foreign affairs and an alternate member of the Politburo; and Zhou Xiaozhou (Chou Hsiao-chou), first secretary of the Hunan Provincial Party Committee.[74] Peng's removal was a questionable decision in terms of the opinion group-faction distinction, as he and his associates ostensibly were promoting a debate on Great Leap economic policies. They did this mainly within organizational channels, in closed session, and without attacking Mao's leadership directly. There were two arguments for designating Peng's activities as factional and hence legitimizing his purge. First was his and Huang's powerful military position, their known dissatisfaction with Maoist pressures against military professionalism, and the possibility that Peng had communicated his unhappiness to Soviet Premier Khrushchev; the threat of organizational opposition was formidable even if the debate was cast in terms of policy issues. Beyond this, Mao apparently regarded the attack as a challenge to his own policies, which had already been debated and approved; Peng was violating discipline and indulging in "right opportunism" by questioning Mao's leadership at a critical juncture and raising issues that he could have raised earlier.[75] These considerations were sufficient to

[73] "Resolution on Certain Questions in the History of Our Party Since the Founding of the PRC," adopted by the Sixth Plenum of the Eleventh Party Congress, *BR*, vol. 24, no. 27 (July 6, 1981): 19.

[74] Teiwes, "The Evolution of Leadership Purges in Communist China," pp. 126–29; David A. Charles, "The Dismissal of Marshall Peng Teh-huai," *China Quarterly*, no. 8 (October–December 1961): 63–76; and *The Case of Peng Teh-huai, 1959–1968* (Hong Kong: Union Research Institute, 1968).

[75] See Mao's statement at the Lushan (Eighth Plenum) meeting in *Chinese Law and Government*, vol. 1, no. 4 (Winter 1968–1969): 25–51, 60–63, and esp. 45–46.

secure Peng's dismissal as defense minister but not wholly persuasive. He was not denounced by name; he retained his seat on the CC; and he was even a candidate (albeit unsuccessful) for reinstatement in 1962. The unsettled status of Peng reflected the marginal nature of his guilt as seen by many on the CC and was a harbinger of the more open and divisive conflicts of the 1960s.

Open Conflict in the 1960s. Just as the debate over the FFYP and Great Leap lines dominated the 1950s, so the Cultural Revolution dominated the politics of the 1960s. The former contained intraparty conflict in shifting opinion groups, which blurred lines of cleavage and made political liquidation of opponents the exception rather than the rule. The latter opened conflict to public view, revealing hardened cleavages that led to sweeping purges. Factions in the earlier period were weak and vulnerable to a majority consensus against that style of politics. They grew stronger in the 1960s, providing protection for their members and serving as building blocks in the formation of coalitions of power. Behind this shift lay an intensification of conflict over fundamental issues, represented by the "struggle between two lines" of the two most powerful leaders, Mao Zedong and Liu Shaoqi.

It is not possible to review here the full range of differences between two men so deeply involved for so long in leadership of the Communist revolution. The record is not complete and has been distorted by the vilification of Liu that accompanied the Cultural Revolution. Still, the differences between Mao and Liu were real, particularly in their general views of the worker-peasant relationship; of the relationship among party organization, leader, and masses; and of the proper attitude toward the Soviet Union and its example.[76] Liu tended toward a more orthodox Marxist admiration for the industrial worker and suspicion of the peasant's potential, whereas Mao had tremendous faith in the peasant's capacity for self-initiated political and economic advance. This difference found expression in Liu's skepticism

[76]See the summary in Stuart R. Schram, "Mao Tse-tung and Liu Shao-ch'i, 1939–1969," *Asian Survey*, vol. 12, no. 4 (April 1972): 275–93. The most thorough analysis is Lowell Dittmer, *Liu Shao-ch'i and the Chinese Cultural Revolution* (Berkeley: University of California Press, 1974).

about rapid agricultural collectivization and his belief that it ought to follow mechanization, industrialization, and close state guidance. Mao, in contrast, was the foremost advocate of rapid collectivization, arguing that it could foster and even precede mechanization and industrialization and that the peasants could carry this out largely on their own.

Differences on the industrial-agricultural relationship spilled over into questions of organizational leadership. Liu was at heart an organization man, dedicated to the principle of party above leader and to the maintenance of organizational discipline and authority. Although sensitive to the evils of bureaucracy, he saw no substitute for orderly, hierarchical administration and was inclined to defend higher cadres, including "experts," against what he saw as excessive mass democracy. Mao recognized the virtues of organization but placed his primary faith in the authority of the highest leader coupled with mass support and action; he was thus less inclined to defend the sanctity of the organization against the unsettling effects of mass movements and found it intolerable to subordinate his own views to those of his colleagues.[77] Finally, Liu was more inclined than Mao to see the Soviet Union as a positive model for China and possibly less inclined to see it as a real military threat.

Neither Mao nor Liu was totally consistent in articulation of these differences. Both tried at times to accommodate the other's views, or at least to conceal their divergence. The fascinating question is why their conflict, contained in the 1950s, should acquire sufficient virulence to split the party openly in the 1960s. The change was due partly to a natural hardening of views with age and experience. With each new round of debate, each probably became more familiar with the other's arguments and more persuaded of his own correctness. With advancing age and Liu's apparent grip on the succession to Mao (he had already replaced Mao as chairman of the PRC and was second in command within the party), resolution of the struggle acquired more urgency. Moreover, there were several trends in the Chinese governmental process that contribute to an understanding of the split and why it took the factionalized form that it did. These

[77]See Stuart R. Schram, "The Party in Chinese Communist Ideology," *China Quarterly*, no. 38 (April–June 1969): 1–26.

trends underscore the point that political conflict in China pervades executive and administrative processes as well as articulation and aggregation. They are noted briefly here, with a fuller discussion reserved for the succeeding chapter.

Mao's declining role in the decision-making process was one trend that exacerbated his struggle with Liu Shaoqi. During the 1950s, Mao's vigor and prestige were usually sufficient to build a consensus on major decisions. As late as 1959, he was able to induce at least temporary and surface unity on the controversial dismissal of Peng Dehuai. However, at some point in the 1950s Mao had agreed to a division of the highest leadership into a first and second front, placing himself in the second front and thus removing himself from direct supervision of party and government operations. His relinquishment of the chairmanship of the PRC in late 1958 reinforced his isolation from administrative processes. Moreover, his refusal to retreat on such pivotal issues as the Great Leap and the Sino-Soviet conflict strained his relationship with some of his senior colleagues. By the early 1960s, Mao had lost his decisive authority within the top leadership, although his public stature was undiminished. This weakening of the authoritative voice of party consensus encouraged a growth of factionalism in which Mao himself participated.

Lines of potential cleavage also were expanded and complicated by the party's increasing assumption of governmental responsibilities, the differentiation of governmental structure, and the 1957 decentralization that strengthened the powers of provincial-level governments. The CCP's top elite no doubt retained their memories of more homogeneous experiences, but their contemporary roles had become distinctly heterogeneous. By the late 1960s, most had acquired responsibility for leadership in functionally defined governmental and party systems or in geographic units of administration. Inevitably, they became preoccupied with their immediate responsibilities and sensitive to the interests of their constituencies. Inevitably, too, they acquired potential power bases in the bureaucracies they supervised.

How far this compartmentalization of power had progressed by the time of the Cultural Revolution is uncertain, but it had at least created a situation in which no unitary bloc could control the party. Factions or potential factions were too numerous to be isolated and repressed by a unified majority. Power required a coalition of forces and invited coalition tactics on the part of opponents. The struggle that Mao forced on the CCP in 1965–1966 could not be contained, simply because the adversaries were too evenly matched and too well defended by their own institutional resources. Mao reestablished his leadership only by forging a coalition and mobilizing mass support for a public attack on his entrenched opponents. For the first time in post-1949 history, a purge was initiated and made public before the CC had worked out its own consensus decision.

No simple description does justice to the intricate factional maneuverings—demonstrable and alleged—that characterized elite behavior between 1965 and 1969. In simplest terms, Mao defeated the Liu-Deng revisionists by seizing the initiative in coalition politics and playing it with great skill. His opponents were probably a majority of the top leadership, judging from what is known of CC meetings in 1965–1966 and from the extent of later purges, but they never succeeded in building a unified defense against the onslaught; their bases protected them for a time, but their fragmented organization was a fatal weakness. Mao, on the other hand, established early a coalition that gradually destroyed his opponents and emerged supreme at the Ninth Party Congress in 1969. This coalition was held together by a personal commitment to Mao's leadership and varying degrees of sympathy for his political stance, but it consisted of at least three factions. The most distinct of these was a radical faction, which favored a thoroughgoing Maoist position as enunciated early in the Cultural Revolution and which had its organizational base in the CC's Cultural Revolution Group as reconstituted in the summer of 1966. Its leaders were Chen Boda (Ch'en Po-ta), Kang Sheng (K'ang Sheng), and Jiang Qing, supported by other radical propagandists serving in the Cultural Revolution Group. It was close to Mao in personal terms, in that it included his wife, Jiang Qing, and his reputed son-in-law, Yao Wenyuan; Chen and Kang also had histories of intimate association with Mao. Furthermore, it had a powerful regional base in Shanghai, where Jiang and Yao were active and had gained the support of Zhang Chunqiao, who rose to leadership in Shanghai during that city's January Revolution of 1967. Finally, the radical faction had a mass base in the Red Guards, who looked to members of this group for authoritative indications of Mao's wishes. For obvious reasons, then, it held the initiative during the early part of the Cultural Revolution.

The second faction was associated with Lin Biao, whose strength rested on the PLA and his designation in the summer of 1966 as Mao's "closest comrade-in-arms" and heir apparent. The Lin faction was by no means coterminous with the PLA, which had its own internal divisions, but rested largely on military officers closely associated with its leader. Still, Lin's post as defense minister gave his faction tremendous leverage within the organization that became the de facto government during much of the Cultural Revolution. Premier Zhou Enlai headed a third group of high-level cadres who survived the first year's purges. The most defensive and least distinct of these three groups, it was perhaps a faction by default, a residual category of leaders who held on due to Zhou's protection and the need for some continuity in administrative leadership.

Tension within the Maoist coalition became evident as early as the summer of 1967, when the slogan "drag out the handful of capitalist-roaders in the army" was put forth.[78] Authority for this slogan came from a Mao directive of May 16, 1966, which had included the PLA among those institutions that had to be purged of their capitalist-roaders—one of the few such references to the PLA, which otherwise was accorded the privilege of conducting internal rectification of its own. Those behind this attempt to turn the campaign on the army and perhaps other leaders became known, from the date of the directive, as the May 16 Group (or 516 Group). More accurately, only some of them were so labeled, because the slogan initially had widespread support particularly from the Cultural Revolution Group. The anti-PLA campaign peaked during the Cultural Revolution's most threatening military confrontation in Wuhan in July–August 1967.[79] In the aftermath of the Wuhan incident, however, a reaction set in. The top leadership retreated from the "drag out a handful" theme and laid the blame on the May 16

[78]On these events, see Barry Burton, "The Cultural Revolution's Ultraleft Conspiracy: The 'May 16 Group,'" *Asian Survey*, vol. 11, no. 11 (November 1971): 1029–53.

[79]Thomas W. Robinson, "The Wuhan Incident: Local Strife and Provincial Rebellion During the Cultural Revolution," *China Quarterly*, no. 47 (July–September 1971): 413–38. The Wuhan Incident was a complicated affair, but it centered on the fact that Chen Zaidao (Ch'en Tsai-tao), Commander of the

Group, now indentified as an "ultraleft conspiracy" aimed at Zhou Enlai as well as military figures. Purged as core elements of May 16 were Wang Li, Qi Benyu (Ch'i Pen-yü), Guan Feng (Kuan Feng), Mu Xin (Mu Hsin), Zhao Yiya (Chao I-ya), and Lin Jie (Lin Chieh)—all members of the Cultural Revolution Group and the leading writers and propagandists of the early stages of the campaign. Although none of the radical faction's most prominent members was implicated at the time, the purge of the May 16 Group marked a sharp decline of its influence within the Maoist coalition. Moreover, the May 16 incident was to surface again in elite conflict after the Cultural Revolution.

Factional Conflict in the 1970s. Elite conflict in the 1970s combined elements of both earlier period. Generally, leaders tried to contain conflict, to avoid open charges and full-scale mass mobilization in their struggles, and to keep purges secret until after the event; the two key purges, of Lin Biao and the Gang, brought mass criticism campaigns only after the victors had acted against their targets. On the other hand, factional groupings made use of organizational bases, communications media, and popular activities—especially demonstrations and the writing of posters—in a way that belied any idea of elite consensus. Two-line struggle was at best a loose conceptualization of the resulting tensions. Hua Guofeng's group claimed adherence to Mao's revolutionary line, initially branding Lin and the Gang as successors to Liu's rightist line; the travesty of this effort to continue using two-line analysis was obvious when Deng later insisted on an ultraleftist label for the Gang. Closer to the mark was the radical-moderate interpretation that the Gang was the successor to Cultural Revolution radicalism, with Zhou, Hua, and Deng successors to earlier revisionists. However, the

---

Wuhan Military Region, was backing a rebel federation labeled "conservative" by Peking rather than the opposing Red Guard and rebel organizations that Peking deemed "correct." When Xie Fuzhi (Hsieh Fu-chih) and Wang Li (sent by Peking to mediate the dispute) affirmed the central view, the Wuhan command and their "conservative" allies arrested the emissaries and took control of the city. Peking's dispatch of Zhou Enlai and loyal troops to the area reestablished its authority, but not without a very tense confrontation that involved some fighting between loyalist and regional forces.

Gang was in some ways more Maoist than Mao, and the moderates continued many policies associated with Mao. In other words, the radical-moderate cleavage of the 1970s was not identical to the Mao-Liu cleavage of the mid-1960s in either style of substance.

The Maoist coalition—consisting of radicals, Lin Biao's faction, and Zhou En-lai's supporters—began to disintegrate shortly after the Ninth CCP Congress of 1969. Chen Boda, the highest ranking radical, disappeared from public view in August 1970; subsequent attacks on his "careerism" and on the May 16 Group indicated that his group was on the defensive for some of its campaign excesses. Lin Biao fell shortly thereafter, accused of planning a coup against Mao.[80] The official version had Lin conspiring with Chen to seize power, planning the coup when his efforts were obstructed, and dying in an airplane crash in Mongolia, on September 13, 1971, when his attempt to assassinate Mao failed. Many observers doubted this story, but Lin had clearly split the coalition with his ambitions and probably his opposition to some policies favored by Mao and Zhou, such as rapprochement with the United States. The incident eliminated the Lin faction—five military members of the Politburo and several other CC and provincial figures fell with him—and led to a general decline of the administrative power acquired by the PLA during the Cultural Revolution.

By 1982, Zhou was the active governmental leader, as Mao increasingly withdrew from public life. The next four years were full of tense debates as Zhou tried to institutionalize a new development program, while the radicals (now led by Jiang Qing, Zhang Chunqiao, Yao Wenyuan, and their young Shanghai protégé Wang Hongwen) tried to weaken or dislodge him. Inhibited from overt attacks on the Gang by their close association with Mao, Zhou relied on his organizational base in the establishment, which he strengthened by sponsoring the rehabilitation of many experienced cadres purged in the Cultural Revolution.

The Gang engaged in more overt factional activities, capitalizing on their strongholds in the communications network, some universities and factories, and the Shanghai region. Through

---

[80]See the analysis and documents in Michael Y. M. Kau, *The Lin Piao Affair* (White Plains, N.Y.: International Arts and Sciences Press, 1975).

the media, they urged militant struggle against the continuing threat of capitalist restoration, using several campaigns of the 1972–1976 years as thinly veiled offensives against the moderates; particularly striking was their publication in Shanghai, beginning in September 1973, of a new theoretical journal titled *Study and Criticism (Xuexi yu Pipan)* to carry more extreme attacks than those in the official CC publications in Peking, over which they also had considerable control.[81] They mobilized mass support to criticize industrial and educational cadres who were modifying Cultural Revolution reforms, giving national publicity to a few individuals willing to "go against the tide" with such criticism. Shanghai was a locale for organization of a model urban workers' militia that lent paramilitary support to their position.[82]

Zhou's death in January 1976 exposed the complexity and volatility of elite alignments.[83] The Gang struck quickly, with Mao's support, to open criticism of Deng Xiaoping (who had essentially taken over Zhou's duties during the premier's illness) and to block Deng's accession to the premiership. But others, possibly also including Mao, opposed radical claims to the post, resulting in a compromise choice of Hua Guofeng as acting premier. Growing tension in Peking climaxed with the Tiananmen Incident of April 5, in which popular protest against removal of memorial wreaths for Zhou from the great public square turned into an unruly demonstration of some 100,000 people, many expressing antiradical slogans and demands. Peking authorities finally broke up the demonstration late in the day, calling it a counterrevolutionary action staged by Deng's supporters. Politburo directives named Hua full premier, dismissed Deng from all his posts (but left him a party member),

---

[81]Ting Wang, "Propaganda and Political Struggle: A Preliminary Case Study of *Hsüeh-hsi yü P'i-p'an,*" *Issues and Studies,* vol. 13, no. 6 (June 1977): 1–14.

[82]James C. F. Wang, "The Urban Militia as a Political Instrument in the Power Contest in China in 1976," *Asian Survey,* vol. 18, no. 6 (June 1978): 541–59.

[83]For detailed accounts of events of this period and of the complex factions and interests involved, see Jürgen Domes, "The 'Gang of Four'—and Hua Kuo-feng: Analysis of Political Events in 1966–76," *China Quarterly,* no. 71 (September 1977): 473–97; and John Bryan Starr, "From the 10th Party Congress to the Premiership of Hua Kuo-feng: The Significance of the Colour of the Cat," ibid., no. 67 (September 1976): pp. 457–88.

and defined his contradiction as "antagonistic." Hua's position was not solid, however, despite profuse claims that he was Mao's personal choice. The Maoist umbrella now seemed to cover several actors (the Gang, Mao himself, Hua, and some military and security leaders), while the moderate spectrum included some cadres going along with Hua and others working for Deng's restoration. Great confusion marked the debates of the next several months, with Tiananmen-type incidents occurring in many provincial cities, while the leftist-controlled media seethed with anti-Deng polemics.

Hua's purge of the Gang soon after Mao's death in September 1976 rested on a broad coalition, with prominent support from the military-security apparatus, that necessarily included many who had taken different positions on events surrounding the Tiananmen Incident. Hua initially continued the criticism of Deng, but he was faced with powerful pressures—publicized, like most conflicts of the 1970s, in both elite communications and popular posters—which favored Deng's second restoration as CCP vice-chairman and vice-premier of the government. Deng was restored to these positions at the Eleventh CCP Congress in September 1977. For roughly a year, Hua and Deng maintained a working relationship, mediated by Ye Jianying as senior leader of the military cadres, in advancing the four modernizations policies. There were evident differences between them, however, with Deng less inclined to invoke Maoist symbols and more emphatic about the need for economic, scientific, and technical revolution.[84]

Deng and his supporters became more aggressive in 1978, pushing for further diminution of Mao's stature and demotion of several Politburo members associated with Deng's 1976 setback. The year began with an announcement of a campaign to criticize the Gang's ultra-leftist system of thought, and, in May, Deng's supporters launched the slogan, "Practice is the only criterion for determining truth." This slogan was important because it provided a basis for breaking away from policies endorsed by

---

[84]The texts of speeches given by Hua Guofeng and Deng Xiaoping at the National Science Conference in 1978 can be compared as a "case study" of their different approaches. For Deng's speech, see *BR*, vol. 21, no. 12 (March 24, 1978): 9–18; for Hua's, *BR*, vol. 21, no. 13 (March 31, 1978): 6–14.

Mao before his death. The impact of the slogan was that Mao's directives could be questioned, a position opposed by the remaining leftists in the government. These leftists were now attacked for being "imprisoned by the system of thought of the Gang and Lin Biao." In October, this pressure brought dismissal of Wu De (Wu Teh) who, as mayor of Peking, had led the suppression of the Tiananmen demonstration and subsequent criticism of Deng. Other Politburo targets of Pro-Deng posters were Chen Xilian (Ch'en Hsi-Lien), commander of the Peking military region, Ji Dengkui (Chi Teng-k'uei), commissar of the Peking region and Wang Dongxing (Wang Tung-hsing), member of the Politburo Standing Committee and head of the security establishment. Since removal of these men would strip Hua of much of his Politburo support, the wall poster campaign suggested that Deng might be seeking Hua's positions for himself. Deng's supporters were increasingly open, too, in their insistence that the classification of the Tiananmen Incident as counterrevolutionary be reversed and that its suppression be investigated, and they openly repudiated the Cultural Revolution. In attacking the 1965 article by Yao Wenyuan that began the great campaign, they were very close to a repudiation of Mao's entire post-1965 career. These themes were also very threatening to Hua, whose own position rested very heavily on Mao's endorsement and the Tiananmen affair. The news reports on all these posters, articles, events, and rumored events included some references to physical violence in mass debates over the issues.

The Third Plenum of the Eleventh CC, held in December 1978, confirmed Deng's political ascendancy and began a major new phase of Chinese politics.[85] In addition to endorsing many demands associated with him—reversal of the Tiananmen verdict, continued rehabilitation of veteran cadres, the stronger criticism of the Cultural Revolution—the Plenum added several of Deng's supporters to the Politburo and to other high state and party posts. There was compromise, too, as Hua initially retained his leading positions and considerable Politburo support; however, the victory of Deng, rather than the compromise with Hua,

[85]See "Communiqué of the Third Plenary Session of the 11th Central Committee of the Communist Party of China," *PR*, no. 52 (December 29, 1978): 6–16.

turned out to be the lasting result of the Third Plenum. There were posthumous rehabilitations of remaining victims of leftism, including Peng Dehuai and Liu Shaoqi. Public commentary on the Cultural Revolution and on Mao's leadership after 1957 became increasingly harsh, culminating in an official reinterpretation of party history adopted in the summer of 1981.[86] In addition to voicing a total condemnation of the Cultural Revolution, the reinterpretation criticized Hua Guofeng for leadership errors. This marked the final stages of Hua Guofeng's decline in power. He ceded the premiership to Zhao Ziyang in 1980. In 1982, the post of party chairman was abolished, and Hua lost his Politburo seat (although as of 1985, he still retained a seat on the Central Committee).

The struggle between Hua Guofeng and Deng Xiaoping is a very interesting and complex case of elite conflict. First, there was a strong influence of personal factionalism. Except for his post as chairman of the Military Affairs Commission (announced in June 1981), Deng has not held a top position since his rehabilitation in 1977. However, his personal prestige and connections have made his power irrefutable. Much of his support came from other rehabilitated leaders, as we have seen in the personnel changes in the Central Committee. By contrast, Hua initially held the top positions of party chairman, premier, and chairman of the Military Affairs Commission, but lacked the depth of personal relations with other leaders. Hua had come to the top as a compromise candidate, which meant that he lacked the solid personal and ideological support networks that Deng had developed. Moreover, as a compromise candidate, he found it difficult to exclude Deng, since Deng had allies within Hua's initial coalition. Finally, the coalition was unstable because Hua's more pragmatic supporters could find more effective leadership with Deng, and his leftist supporters were a defensive minority. As Hua's position eroded, he sided more openly with his leftist supporters. It would be a mistake, however, to see the conflict only as the struggle of personal factions. Hua's political stance was necessarily between Maoism and modernization. He both praised the Cultural Revolution and announced a "new

[86]"Resolution on Certain Questions in the History of Our Party," *BR*, vol. 24, no. 27 (July 26, 1981): 10–39.

era" of the four modernizations. But the Cultural Revolution was deeply unpopular, and Deng Xiaoping was a national symbol of opposition to leftism. Deng's proteges were referred to as the "practice faction" because of his slogan that "practice is the only criterion for determining truth," while Hua's supporters were known as the "whatever faction" because of a statement he made in early 1977 that "whatever Mao said must be followed." With these contrasting policy stances, Deng attracted the support of all those who hoped for a modern future for China, while Hua was left with those who had prospered during the Cultural Revolution. Moreover, some of Hua's potential leftist support was alienated by his overthrow of the Gang. In sum, Hua's high positions but weak personal and ideological support networks were no match for the connections and prestige of the initially ostracized Deng.

With power consolidation, Deng began to move into a middle position ideologically, while at the same time promoting boldly innovative economic policies. Deng began to move against the dissidents at Democracy Wall in early 1979, although he had welcomed their support against Hua a few months earlier. In March 1979, he enunciated the "four fundamental principles" that became the test for political heresy, and, by 1981, the remainder of the dissident movement had been sent to labor reeducation camps or been driven underground. Restraint was placed on the expression of negativism in literature by the criticism in 1981 of the screenplay for *Unrequited Love* by the PLA writer Bai Hua. The most extreme attack on new tendencies in literature and culture occurred in 1983 with the campaign to oppose spiritual pollution, but this campaign ran into high-level opposition and was aborted. Deng's moves against the right after the Third Plenum did not mean a reconciliation with the left. On the contrary, attacks on the left have become steadily harsher, culminating in a campaign in late 1984 to "totally reject the Cultural Revolution." The regime is trying to define an acceptable middle ground in Chinese politics by engaging in what it calls "a struggle on two fronts."[87]

[87]See Tang Tsou, "Political Change and Reform: The Middle Course," in Tsou, *After the Cultural Revolution, a Historic Change in Direction: The Chinese Communist Movement and Regime in Historical Perspective* (Chicago: University of Chicago Press, 1985).

Of course, elite conflict did not end with Deng's consolidation of power. Differences over new decisions produce new conflicts, and problems of succession create personal opportunities. Within Deng's camp, some have been more conservative ideologically and in economic policy, while others have been more daring. Party General Secretary Hu Yaobang and Premier Zhao Ziyang are both considered among the more daring, while Chen Yun, the chairman of the Central Commission for Discipline Inspection, and Deng Liqun, director of the Propaganda Department, are considered more conservative. In 1984, Deng himself claimed to have withdrawn from active decision making, but these claims may be interpreted as an attempt to strengthen the prestige of Hu and Zhao and to prevent any succession problems. Clearly, Chinese politics remains in the mid-1980s an inextricable mesh of positions, policies, and personalities. The evolution of institutions, the success or failure of policies, and the death of a personality such as Deng (witness the aftermaths of the deaths of Zhou and Mao) will upset any existing equilibrium. As with political contests anywhere, the results cannot be predicted confidently.

CHAPTER VII

The Governmental Process

THE CHINESE GOVERNMENTAL PROCESS, through which authoritative decisions are translated into action, involves all the institutions discussed in earlier chapters. This chapter identifies
several principles and problems that are prominent in the process
without attempting to explore them in detail;[1] it is more in the
nature of an essay, trying to bring together themes and material
that have, for the most part, been introduced earlier. We begin
with an overview of the governmental process and then turn to
salient aspects of decision making, administration, the enforcement and adjudication of rules, and external influences on the
process.

OVERVIEW OF THE PROCESS

Party leadership and mass line are the dominant principles of
the Chinese governmental process. Although not inherently in
conflict, they tend, in practice, to produce contradictory impulses
that account for much of the complexity and instability of

---

[1] The most thorough analyses of governmental institutions and processes for
the pre-Cultural Revolution period are: A. Doak Barnett, *Cadres, Bureaucracy
and Political Power in Communist China* (New York: Columbia University
Press, 1967); and Franz Schurmann, *Ideology and Organization in Communist
China*, 2nd ed. enl. (Berkeley: University of California Press, 1968). The best
recent books for a general overview are Harry Harding, *Organizing China: The
Problem of Bureaucracy, 1949–1976* (Stanford, Cal.: Stanford University Press,
1981); and Frederick Teiwes, *Politics and Purges in China* (White Plains, N.Y.:
M. E. Sharpe, 1979).

Chinese politics. The struggle to maintain a working balance between them has been perhaps the most persistent problem of the post-1949 government.

Party Leadership. The principle of party leadership has a decisive impact on the organization and operation of formal government. It requires, above all, that authoritative leadership at the center be in the hands of the CCP. It thus ensures at least a minimal degree of ideological conformity and organizational continuity at the core of the political process. Elites may differ in their interpretation of the ideology, and the leading organization may undergo changes in composition and style, but there is no possibility, short of an overthrow of the system, that national elites will be chosen except through internal party processes or that any other political organization will capture control of the government. On the other hand, the party considers it part of its leadership mission to cooperate with nonparty forces and to absorb new personnel and policy directions, whether they be mass organizations, as in the Cultural Revolution, or intellectuals, as in the post-Mao period.

The CCP itself is a centralized organization whose internal processes are essentially closed to and largely concealed from outsiders. Ordinary citizens may influence initial decisions on recruitment into the organization but from that point on have no significant participatory roles in CCP decisions. Even during the Cultural Revolution, when activists outside the party challenged some of its policies, procedures, and personnel, it was the surviving organizational leadership that made final decisions on the reconstitution of its membership and structure. Important meetings of the organization are closed affairs, frequently unannounced and unreported, their publicized results limited to those that the leadership wishes to disclose. Provisions for internal party democracy may encourage open discussion at meetings and result in infrequent, formalized elections of hierarchies of committees, but lower levels of the organization have no real control over higher levels; it is higher-level committees and organs, culminating in the Politburo, that can prescribe and overrule the actions of lower committees. The party secretary and other members of his or her (usually his) leading group are by far the most powerful people at any level of the hierarchy, although formally they are subject to election and recall and to the will of the majority at committee meetings. Instances of the abuse of power by party officials are common in the Chinese media.

Although very concerned with preventing abuses of party power and facilitating modernization, the reforms of the 1980s have only slightly modified the role of the party. Like its predecessors, the 1982 party constitution reaffirms the political, ideological, and organizational leadership of the party.[2] All CCP committees and branches are to play a leading role at their respective levels, a role that all nonparty organizations are to accept. In practice, the extent to which leadership constitutes direct control of governmental processes varies at different levels. At the center, the party elite monopolizes decision-making power and the controlling positions in state, party, and military bureaucracies that implement its decisions. At intermediate levels, the proportion of party members in leading positions is sufficient to ensure CCP dominance of governmental organs. At the basic level, party members may or may not constitute majorities on committees; their role becomes that of a "leading core," which must realize CCP policy through persuasive cooperation with nonparty cadres and committee members. Within the smallest primary units, the CCP may have little representation. The extent of party leadership has also varied significantly over time, being most complete during the Great Leap and weakest during 1966–1968, and it sometimes differs among comparable administrative units in different geographic areas.

Of course, party organs are not to dictate their orders to governmental and other organizations. To do so would be "commandism," a violation of the mass line. A major focus of party reform in the post-Mao period has been the restriction of inappropriate or arbitrary party control, especially at the basic level. The economic reforms of the 1980s will probably have the effect of weakening party control, because the responsibilities and discretion of rural households and enterprise management have been increased. The attempts to strengthen party discipline, most notably the reinstitution of the discipline inspection

[2]"Constitution of the Communist Party of China," *BR*, vol. 25, no. 38 (September 20, 1982): 10.

commissions and the 1983–1986 party rectification, are aimed in part at reducing and punishing the arbitrary power of party cadres. On a broader level, the party and state constitutions of 1982 both proclaimed that the party is subject to the constitution and laws of the PRC. The constraint to act within the law is largely symbolic, given the interpenetration of party and state organs, however, it does indicate a promise of more regular and institutionally responsible party behavior.

These self-restrictions notwithstanding, the primary locus of decision making in the Chinese system is the CCP, which establishes policy on the basis of alternatives and demands made known to it. At higher levels, administrative acceptance of party decisions is virtually automatic due to overlapping roles. At lower levels, where CCP members may not dominate governmental organs numerically, the members' role as a leadership core and the power of higher party-controlled bodies are normally sufficient to ensure compliance with CCP decisions. In general, then, the decision-making structure is a narrow one based on party committees acting in closed session. Although the amount of law-making activity has increased dramatically since 1978, the legislative process remains one of the circulation of drafts for comment among impacted organizations. The situation is well described in a Chinese legal manual: "The general method is that party organs produce legal drafts after investigation, research and the collection of experiences. After approval by the party center they are sent to legislative organs for discussion and revision, then they are either proclaimed publicly or simply implemented internally."[3] There is no media coverage as yet of contending proposals or of unofficial drafts, although Peng Zhen, the chairman of the NPC Standing Committee, suggested in 1984 that the media might report such things.[4] Decisions tend to take the form of generalized statements on policy or doctrine, or emerge as administrative directives and regulations.[5]

[3]Chen Xuan, ed., *Gongmin falu guwen* (The citizen's legal advisor), Harbin: Heilongjiang Renmin chubanshe, 1983, p. 66.

[4]*People's Daily,* May 12, 1984, p. 5.

[5]There is nonetheless great variety and subtlety in the directives and other communications that move through the Chinese bureaucracy; see Kenneth Lieberthal, *Central Documents and Politburo Politics in China* (Ann Arbor: University of Michigan, Center for Chinese Studies, 1978), esp. pp. 5–19; and Michel Oksenberg, "Methods of Communication Within the Chinese Bureaucracy," *China Quarterly,* no. 57 (January–March 1974): 1–39.

The CCP elite's monopoly of central decision making does not translate into a comparable monopoly of policy implementation; that is, the Politburo's power vis-à-vis the formulation of national goals and policies presents a misleading image of its control over the governmental structure. One reason for this is that the central government itself is a structure of considerable differentiation and complexity. Diverse interests are represented initially in Politburo decisions, through the involvement of provincial party secretaries, vice-premiers of the functional sectors of the State Council, and directors of CC departments. These are elites who themselves head major bureaucratic structures, replete with their own conflicts and interests and fully capable of defending their positions. Moreover, it is these units that develop the actual targets and directives that represent the central will. Feedback and bargaining are unavoidable features of the process, if not in the formal decision then at least in the drafting of implemental rules.[6]

Once central decisions have been cast as central directives in a process already somewhat removed from the collective wisdom of the Politburo, the influence of decentralization and the mass line comes into play. Lower units may be permitted to draft their own rules or at least to interpret central directives flexibly with reference to their own circumstances, with much of the ultimate meaning of governmental outputs left to the actions of basic-level institutions. The actual capacity of central elites to control governmental performance was probably at its peak in the 1955–1958 period but declined thereafter.

The Mass Line. As noted at the outset of Chapter 6, Mao conceptualized the policy process as a dynamic pattern of reciprocating communication between leaders and followers. If we define the mass line in these general terms rather than in terms of the activities of mass organizations during the Cultural Revolution, the mass line has been a fundamental aspect of the party's political style since 1942. In Mao's formulation, it assigns the masses a continuous role in presenting their ideas to the party and in carrying out decisions rendered from above; the masses

[6]On the way in which the central bureaucracy and its functional sectors may influence the policy process, see Barnett, *Cadres, Bureaucracy and Political Power*, pp. 6–7, 71–84, 431–32.

are to initiate as well as implement policy. Even in ideal form, the principle reserves for the party decision-making power and the right to distinguish between "correct" and "incorrect" ideas. Moreover, PRC institutions provide few opportunities, except within primary units, for direct popular influence on political decisions. But the mass line has a significant broadening effect on the postdecisional process, which leaves room for considerable local initiative, relies on popular action in the implementation of policy, and provides opportunities for feedback on cadre performance and policy effectiveness.

The mass line's influence on the policy process is closely related to and reinforced by the CCP's willingness to decentralize management responsibilities in many areas. Decentralization, discussed in greater detail later, does not necessarily broaden the popular role in administration, nor is it always justified by the mass line concept. Nonetheless, when decentralization extends to primary units that are organized for member participation, encouraging them to embark on projects of their own and to assist in the operation of schools, health facilities, and other social services, it provides the institutional opportunity for practice of the mass line's basic tenet: the people must accept party policies as their own and demonstrate them in political action. There is, at least in Mao's view of decentralization, a direct link between the transferral of responsibilities to the lowest feasible level and the mass line's emphasis on direct popular action rather than bureaucratic administration.

The Mass Movement.   On many domestic problems, Chinese leaders have turned to the mass movement as a means of informing the population about policy objectives, of soliciting broad-based acceptance of the policy, and of mobilizing local units for action on central plans. As these movements have unfolded, the structures activated have moved in an ever-widening progression from party and state organs, through the communications media and experimental projects, and on into basic-level organizations, meetings, rallies, and discussion groups. There has been an intimate connection between the mass line and mass movements since their origination in the base areas, but the destructive effects of large-scale mobilization in the Great Leap Forward and the Cultural Revolution have led to the rejection of disruptive

mass movements since 1979. Nevertheless, there are strong traces
of the campaign-style approach in current Chinese politics. The
law and order campaign of 1983, in which thousands of criminals
were executed, some of them publicly, and the spiritual pollution
campaign of 1983 are the two most obvious examples. The
influence can also be seen in campaigns to study the constitution,
to plant trees, to promote socialist ethics month, or to engage in
any other activity that the leadership perceives as urgent. In
contrast to Western governments, which tend to reach for the
wallet when faced with urgent tasks, the Chinese will often reach
for the megaphone.

One of the consequences of this frequent reliance on mass
movements has been irregularity in the pace and results of policy
implementation. Local areas have varied in the speed with
which they have carried out their preliminary organizing and
testing as well as their extension of the campaign on a general
scale. Different models have sometimes appeared in the course of
a campaign, producing discrepancies between the results of its
earlier and later stages. A policy applied through a mass movement simply does not follow a precise timetable or lend itself to a
detailed set of regulations of uniform applicability. National
elites may set target dates for completion of campaign stages, but
they cannot be sure that targets will be met; they may establish
guidelines for expected results, but they cannot be sure that a
process relying so heavily on local performance will produce
uniform results. Under these circumstances, it becomes difficult
to say precisely what a policy is, when it has gone into effect, and
what its operative consequences are. These answers may be clear
only when the campaign is over. One need only examine the
general outlines of land reform, agricultural collectivization and
communization, and the Cultural Revolution to recognize that
the governmental process in China has a highly fluid and
open-ended quality that is incompatible with a legalistic style of
administration.

Experimentalism in Decisions. How can we reconcile the
principle of party leadership with the flexibility that characterizes
policy implementation? Part of the answer lies in a strong
element of experimentalism in the Chinese elite's view of the
policy process. Although the government issues some legalistic

rules, implying implementation at a certain point in time with procedures to enforce compliance, its decisions on many important issues have an experimental quality. They are cast in the form of general statements, indicating models to be followed or goals to be attained but not specifying exact procedures, forms, and relationships. The meaning of such a decision emerges only in practice as lower levels carry out their preliminary work and begin to develop concrete responses to the tasks demanded of them. In the midst of this process, higher levels will begin to review and investigate the early results. On the basis of these reports, central organs may accelerate or decelerate the process, publicize new models, or even issue new directives that alter the initial thrust of the policy. Party elites seem to regard the attendant shifts and variations as healthy or at least necessary for the development of viable policies. It is their way of practicing the mass line, of testing mass consciousness and local conditions, and of refining their views through practical experience.

The role of models in Chinese policy making cannot be over-estimated. They are the primary source of facts upon which policy is made and modified. If a village or enterprise is successful and innovative in a particular experiment, its case may be studied in great detail and reported to the highest leadership. Visits to the site may ensue, which, if publicized, already indicate a certain amount of approval of the model. The innovation may then be copied by other units, usually advanced units where conditions promise success. Finally, the innovator might be generally advertised as a model, thereby becoming the paradigm for an emulation campaign or at least an example of an approved policy alternative.

The factual basis of policy making by models tends to be exemplary rather than typical; instead of being based on what would probably succeed in the average unit, policy tends to be based on what has succeeded in the unusual unit. Once a unit becomes a model, there is considerable pressure to maintain and even exaggerate its accomplishments. The most famous model of the PRC was the Dazhai Brigade of Shanxi Province. A very poor brigade in a mountainous area, Dazhai had become fabulously successful through good leadership and collective effort. When Mao penned the words, "In agriculture study Dazhai," it rose to dizzying heights of national emulation. The brigade chairman eventually became a member of the Politburo. But the fall of Dazhai was more rapid than its rise. First, articles appeared claiming that the spirit of Dazhai was worth emulating but not necessarily all the details of the model. Next, the brigade chairman fell from power and accusations appeared concerning misrepresentations of Dazhai's accomplishments. It is now claimed that the brigade is doing much better with different leadership and more individualistic policies.[7]

Experimentalism in policy making does not necessarily weaken party leadership. It reduces the specificity and permanence of central decisions and increases the responsibilities of lower-level committees, but neither of these outcomes implies an abdication of the organization's leading role. It raises the possibility of deviation from central wishes, but only in the Cultural Revolution—and then only with the Maoist's initial blessing—did local actions take the form of outright defiance of CCP organizational authority. Probably the most important consequence of a reliance on mass movements and experimentalism is a tendency to blur the distinction between state and party organization. By attaching so much importance to the actions of lower levels, it leads the party to strengthen its leadership over local government. In its extreme form, as during the Great Leap, the phenomenon of party as government may mean the virtual displacement of state administration. Of course, such phenomena have led the post-Mao leadership to strong assertions of the autonomy of state organs, and occurrences of local party leaders riding roughshod over other organizations now provoke criticism. Nonetheless, the CCP retains overall leadership and with it the constant temptation to intervene in state administration.

A significant challenge to local party leadership in the 1980s is posed by the fact that the major campaigns are economic, and the active agents in these campaigns are households and enterprises. To a large extent, these are not mass campaigns that require party leadership, but dispersions of economic decision

[7]Of the voluminous literature on Dazhai, we especially recommend Tang Tsou, Marc Blecher, and Mitch Meisner, "Policy Change at the National Summit and Institutional Transformation at the Local Level: The Case of Tachai and Hsiyang in the Post-Mao Era," in Tsou, ed., *Select Papers from the Center for Far Eastern Studies* (Chicago: University of Chicago, 1981), pp. 249–392.

making that require noninterference from the party. Such campaigns confuse even the exemplary role of the party member: should he or she continue to work selflessly for the common good or take the lead in pioneering new ways to personal profit? At this point the policies are too novel and the information too sketchy to predict the effect on local party leadership.

We turn now to a closer look at some of the problems suggested by these introductory comments. A section on decision making examines the central institutional framework, the role of Mao, and some enduring questions about the effectiveness of the process. Bureaucracy, political controls over it, and decentralization are discussed under the rubric of administration. The section on rule enforcement and adjudication deals with the formal legal system, coercion and voluntarism, and mechanisms of social control. A concluding section discusses briefly the importance of external influences on the governmental process.

DECISION MAKING

Institutional Considerations.   Supreme decision-making power resides in the CCP Politburo and its Standing Committee. Politburo members are the core leadership of all major CCP meetings, and there is no regular mechanism by which other organs can overrule the Politburo's decisions. The decline of Politburo authority in the early part of the Cultural Revolution was made possible by a deep internal split within the body, not by an assertion of external control over it. Nonetheless, the Politburo does not monopolize decision making in the sense of excluding other elites and groupings from participation in the process. It is the authoritative locus of policy decisions; but if we look at decisions as inseparable from the policy-making process that accompanies them, then it is clear that the Politburo does not act alone. The history of the PRC indicates that top elites have regularly convened a great variety of larger and more representative meetings to assist in the formulation of national policies.[8]

[8] Kenneth Lieberthal, *A Research Guide to Central Party and Governmental Meetings in China, 1949–1975* (White Plains, N.Y.: International Arts and Sciences Press, 1976).

The Central Committee, contrary to what one might expect, has not been a particularly important part of this expanded policy-making process. The CC was most active in 1956 to 1962 when it met in ten plenums; even so, these meetings were relatively brief and usually announced policies thrashed out in less formal gatherings preceding the plenums. The Eighth CC met only twice more after its Tenth Plenum of September 1962 before it was succeeded by the Ninth CC elected in 1969. The Ninth CC had only two plenums in its 1969 to 1973 span, the Tenth CC only three in its 1973 to 1977 tenure. The CC, then, has not been a regular instrument of policy making but rather a forum for ratifying and publicizing decisions reached elsewhere.

In contrast to the Central Committee, which has great formal authority but participates infrequently as a body in decision making, the Secretariat has been extremely influential in the 1980s. Formally, its duty is "to attend to the day-to-day work of the Central Committee under the direction of the Politburo and its Standing Committee,"[9] but, in fact, the advanced age of the top leadership and the strong ties of the Secretariat to Deng Xiaoping and Hu Yaobang have given it a very powerful decision-shaping function. Its counterpart in the state apparatus is the Standing Committee of the State Council under Zhao Ziyang. The younger and more active membership of these two groups now constitutes the "first line" of central decision making, according to a 1984 interview with Zhao Ziyang.[10]

The substantive policy-making meetings have been diverse, ranging from slightly enlarged Politburo meetings; through middle-range gatherings of selected party, state, PLA and provincial elites; and including some conferences of several thousand participants, with even low-level cadres in attendance. The most significant conferences have been those of Politburo members with selected leaders of various functional and geographic hierarchies. Before 1966, there were several variations on these conferences. One was the Central Work Conference, common in the 1960s, that convened around a hundred people representing the Politburo and its administrative departments, the State Council,

[9]"Constitution of the CCP," article 21.
[10]A. Doak Barnett, "A Peek at China's Foreign Policy Process," *New York Times*, August 13, 1984.

regional party organs, and the PLA. Another was the Supreme State Conference, a loose governmental advisory body authorized by the 1954 state constitution, that both Mao and Liu used in their capacity as chairman of the government. As party chairman, Mao also convened several meetings of provincial party secretaries or mixed groups of central and provincial party elites. The Cultural Revolution and its factionalized aftermath upset this pattern of informal but somewhat institutionalized working conferences. Of 298 identified meetings of central party and state organs held between 1949 and 1975, 271 occurred before August 1966, with the remaining 27 stretched out between August 1966 and January 1975.[11] While some of the difference in frequency of identified meetings may be due to nonreporting in the 1966 to 1975 period, it seems fair to conclude that the latter period saw a decline in the Politburo's convocation of consultative conferences.

The secrecy referred to above is an important aspect of the policy-making process. Only about 10 percent of the 298 meetings in question—and only 1–2 percent if CC plenums and party congresses are excluded—were given substantial coverage in Chinese media when they occurred.[12] In general, both the format and substance of key policy meetings remain closed to public view until well after the event, if indeed they are ever announced. Finally, we should note that the informal and even ad hoc convocation of diversified conferences for policy debate and formulation has mixed implications for decision-making effectiveness. It injects far more variety, deliberation, and political give-and-take into the process than the formal structure shows. Precisely because it is irregular and informal, however, it may still leave information gaps, be manipulated by elites who want to exclude other positions, or succumb to the paralyzing effects of factional struggle within the Politburo.[13]

The Role of Mao. Mao Zedong was the central figure in the policy-making process for most of PRC history. That fact alone justifies reflection on his influence, which has clearly posed

[11]Lieberthal, *Research Guide.*
[12]Ibid., p. 7.
[13]Ibid., pp. 10–13; and Lieberthal, *Central Documents*, pp. 79–82.

continuing problems for his successors. Mao's roles between 1949 and 1966 were multiple, including initiating, deciding, and legitimating many of the most important policies adopted by the CCP. As initiator, he was the most vigorous and forceful advocate of new measures, presenting to his colleagues proposals that forced the decision-making process into action. His role as initiator included a willingness to promote his views before wider audiences—such as the provincial secretaries in the mid-1950s or the general public in the Cultural Revolution—thereby adding political pressure to the intrinsic force of his views. As decision maker, he was first among equals within the small group that bore ultimate responsibility for the direction of national affairs; more than any other individual, he was able to swing the judgment of his colleagues toward the decisions he favored. As legitimator, he served as a symbol of both elite and national unity, the figure whose support for a policy placed on it the stamp of authoritative approval.

Underlying these roles was a tremendous reservoir of personal ability, power, and prestige. Whatever his limitations, Mao displayed exceptional political capacities. His knowledge of personalities and issues, his self-confidence and determination, his persuasive abilities, and his sensitivity to both tactical and strategic maneuver made him a formidable politician. As party chairman, he occupied a position that gave him ample power to influence the procedural and institutional context of elite politics. His personal identification with the success of the revolution and the guidance of postrevolutionary construction made him virtually invulnerable to removal. His policies were criticized, resisted, or altered at times, but direct challenges to his leadership were doomed to failure. How far Peng Dehuai, Liu Shaoqi, and Lin Biao truly wanted to go or might have gone in their opposition to Mao may never be known. What is clear is that Mao's definition of the conflict as a choice between him and his antagonist always brought a reaffirmation of his leadership.

Although Mao had a great influence on the policy-making process, he never shaped it wholly to his wishes. His overall impact was a function of several variables, the most important of which seem to have been his own assertiveness, his relationship with his senior colleagues, the capacity of the party center to control the governmental structure, and the capacity of the system generally to realize centrally determined objectives.[14] The first two are discussed more thoroughly below. The basic point is that Mao was erratic in exercising his leadership potential, owing to his changing perceptions of political priorities and, perhaps, to variations in his health and vigor, and that his authority among his senior colleagues was much more fluid than his relatively constant popular prestige would indicate. The latter points are also discussed in subsequent sections but require some comment here.

Perhaps the most fundamental restraint on Mao's and other elites' policy-making power has been the system's finite resources and capacities. Vagaries of weather, harvest, and popular morale, and the necessity for making hard choices among competing claims on scarce resources, have intruded constantly on the formulation of national goals. At times, as during the Great Leap, elite decisions have seemingly defied these limitations, but the realities of system capabilities have always been close at hand, forcing compromise and modification on the predispositions of the leadership. Combined with China's size and complexity, the scarcity of resources makes total central power a practical impossibility, although the Chinese media have sometimes conveyed the opposite impression.

When these variables are considered, the relativity and changeability of Mao's influence over the policy process become clearer. Mao alluded to this frequently in reference to policies that he did or did not approve and to his general command of governmental operations. His most revealing comment was at a Central Work Conference in October 1966, when he stated that he had approved division of the leadership into a first echelon and a second echelon, with himself in the second echelon and hence removed from supervision of the daily work of the government.[15] Mao identified the duration of the two echelons as seventeen years,

---

[14]This discussion draws liberally on Michel C. Oksenberg, "Policy Making Under Mao, 1949–68: An Overview," in John M. H. Lindbeck, ed., *China: Management of a Revolutionary Society* (Seattle: University of Washington Press, 1971), esp. pp. 80–88. See also Parris H. Chang, "Research Notes on the Changing Loci of Decision in the Chinese Communist Party," *China Quarterly*, no. 44 (October–December 1970): 169–94.

[15]"Talk at the Central Work Conference" (October 25, 1966), in Stuart

presumably from 1949 to the Eleventh Plenum of August 1966. The precision of this reference is questionable, since Mao's second-echelon status was not rigorously observed throughout the 1949–1966 period; the years between 1959 and 1965 seem to mark his clearest performance of a second-line role. Nonetheless, the statement affirms Mao's willingness to restrict the scope of his political involvement, a willingness based, he said, on a desire to cultivate other leaders and to avoid the Stalin pattern of rule.[16]

More concretely, Mao's involvement in the 1949–1958 period was quite flexible. On the one hand, his political visibility was relatively low. He was absent from some key conferences,[17] let Liu and Deng take the lead at the Eighth National Congress of the CCP in 1956, and accepted the absence of reference to himself in the 1956 constitution. He was quite active, however, in the initiation and promotion of three crucial policies: accelerated collectivization in 1955; the hundred flowers episode of 1957; and the adoption of rectification, decentralization, and Great Leap policies in 1957–1958. In all three cases, Mao was able to secure favorable decisions and prompt governmental implementation. The mix of these variables permitted Mao to act with considerable freedom and effectiveness without assuming a dictatorial role.

However, as the Leap ran into difficulties, the mix shifted against Mao. In adopting decentralization and the Great Leap approach, the central leadership had stimulated local initiative and the mass movement but had also relinquished some of its control over governmental performance; its decisions became more controversial, less informed of local conditions, and more difficult to implement. Resource limitations, such as lowered output and popular morale, began to circumscribe the options

---

Schram, ed., *Chairman Mao Talks to the People* (New York: Pantheon, 1974), pp. 270–74.

[16]Ibid., p. 270. In another reference, Mao also cited his health as a reason for the two fronts; ibid., p. 266.

[17]For example, Mao was absent from the Fourth Plenum of the Seventh CC in February 1954, which heard Politburo accusations against Gao Gang and Rao Shushi, and from a September 1957 conference that preceded and prepared for the Third Plenum of the Eighth CC; Chang, "Research Notes," 183–86.

open to decision makers. Mao stepped down as chairman of the PRC, accepted some criticism of the Leap and his role in promoting it, but threatened to form a new revolutionary movement if his colleagues repudiated him.[18] Subsequently, Mao's policy-making influence fell to its lowest ebb. Although his colleagues bolstered his public image with campaigns against the "rightists" of 1959 and in support of the wisdom of his "thought," their respect for his counsel seems to have declined. The veiled criticism of Mao that appeared in Peking publications in 1961–1962 was an accurate indication of his reduced prestige at the center.[19] Retrenchment policies, oriented to restoration of governmental controls and accommodation of overstrained resources, left Mao little room for maneuver or initiative. When he began to assert his views again at the Tenth Plenum of September 1962, he found state and party bureaucracies much more resistant to compliance with his policies than in the 1950s.

Mao broke through in the Cultural Revolution, ending the two echelons and assuming undisputed leadership in central decision making. Once the Liu-Deng revisionists were purged, he seemed to hold more unqualified support from participants in the political process at all levels than ever before. Both the tone and substance of ensuing policy formulations reflected his ideas. But the political reality of China was one of chaos, and even Mao's unquestioned dominance did not translate easily into governmental action. Over four years passed (January 1967 to August 1971) before revolutionary committees and new provincial party committees were established. The formalities of the state structure remained unsettled, despite repeated allusions to a forthcoming National People's Congress and the adoption of a new draft state constitution at the Second Plenum in August–September 1970. Efforts to reopen schools and establish Maoist

[18]See Mao's speech at the Eighth (Lushan) Plenum in July 1959, in *Chinese Law and Government*, vol. 1, no. 4 (Winter 1968–69): 27–44.

[19]We refer primarily to the writings of Wu Han ("The Dismissal of Hai Rui" and "Hai Rui Scolds the Emperor"), Deng Tuo (Teng T'o) ("Evening Talks at Yenshan"), and Wu, Deng, and Liao Mo-sha ("Notes from a Three Family Village"). These literary efforts by prominent Peking officials became the initial target of the Maoists in the late 1965–early 1966 beginnings of the Cultural Revolution. For a discussion of these writings and a survey of literary dissent in 1961–1962, see Merle Goldman, "The Unique 'Blooming and Contending' of 1961–62," *China Quarterly*, no. 37 (January–March 1969): 54–83.

educational reforms began as early as 1967 but had little visible effect for several years thereafter. The contrast with the 1950s, when central decisions brought relatively prompt and thorough compliance throughout the country, was striking.

In any case, by the early 1970s Mao had entered the personal and political decline leading to his death. The "cult of Mao" receded as he moved into the background, leaving administrative leadership to Zhou Enlai and, as Zhou's health also failed, to the rehabilitated Deng Xiaoping. Deng's rapid rise in 1973–1975 was a prime indicator of Mao's declining capacity to control the process, as was his inability to resolve the debilitating factional conflict of this period. Yet his symbolic authority as legitimator held firm, and his support was crucial for some of the key decisions of his last years, such as rapprochement with the United States and the second purge of Deng in 1976. The power of Mao's symbolic authority was evident after his death, as Hua and Deng used it to legitimize the four modernizations. It was also a source of conflict, however, since Hua used it to bolster his leadership, whereas Deng seemed intent on repudiating Mao's last decade—and necessarily reducing Mao's overall stature in the process—to serve Deng's personal and policy goals. It may be a long time before Chinese elites resolve the question of how to deal with Mao's substantive and symbolic legacy.

In the 1980s, Deng Xiaoping is dealing with some of the same problems of personal leadership that beset Mao in his last decades. Deng would like to establish a smooth transition between his rule and his handpicked successors, Hu Yaobang and Zhao Ziyang. Therefore, he allows the Secretariat and the Standing Committee of the State Council to function as a first echelon of leadership, while he takes a more leisurely place on the second echelon. However, he cannot refrain from interfering in policy. The knowledge of his power and the strength of his convictions compels him to step in. But interference can lead to quite complex political situations. In the case of the 1983 campaign against spiritual pollution, Deng almost certainly was instrumental in approving the campaign, against the hesitations of Hu and Zhao; however after its failure, he disclaimed any responsibility.[20] It might seem that Deng was dumping the

---

[20]For an excellent analysis of the campaign, see Stuart Schram, "'Economics in Command?': Ideology and Policy Since the Third Plenum, 1978–84," *China*

responsibility for the failure on his subordinates, but, ironically, his disclaimer was instead a belated expression of support for their opposition. Even the most astute politicians find graceful retirement difficult, and there are few precedents within the Communist or Chinese imperial traditions.

The Legacy of Maoist Decision Making. The death of Mao Zedong and the overthrow of the Gang of Four ended twenty years of leftist policy-making, but the post-Mao leadership had to tackle the problems and habits that those years had created. Three problems merit discussion: the role of ideology in policy, the "red-expert" dichotomy, and the institutional weakness of popular participation. It is unfair to consider these as problems created by Mao; in part, they are endemic to Communist regimes, and, in part, they are the collective responsibility of the party. Regardless of where the fault lies, however, these problems have set major reform tasks for the post-Mao regime that it is now in the process of fulfilling.

The problem of the role of ideological commitments has several aspects. The most obvious is expressed in the Maoist slogan that "Politics takes command." Every problem was scrutinized for ideological dimensions, and discussion of these dimensions often forced out more practical deliberation. Obsession with ideology did not preclude debate—ideology is rarely univocal—but it certainly skewed discussion toward questions of dogma. Perhaps a more serious hazard of the role of ideology was the political risks it created for cadres. Ideology tended to define policy debate as class conflict, so one side or the other was in danger of being labeled an enemy class, whereupon its supporters became targets for the harsh struggle reserved for antagonistic contradiction. Lastly, the ideological commitment to Mao's personal writings and directives restricted policy options in important areas. The overall effect of the role of ideology was to rigidify and restrict political discussion, while introducing great personal risk and instability for cadres.

In 1978, Deng scored a spectacular victory on the problem of ideological commitments, but the problem could not disappear

Quarterly, no. 99 (September 1984): 417–61; see Deng's speech to the Central Advisory Commission on October 22, 1984 for his disclaimer of responsibility, *People's Daily*, January 1, 1985, p. 1.

easily. His campaign on the slogan that "practice is the only criterion for determining truth" solved, in principle, the dogmatic allegiance to Mao's policy preferences, and the decision of the Third Plenum to take economics as the chief problem turned attention toward practical dimensions of policy. "Hats" and "clubs" were condemned as weapons of the Gang. However, after assuming power in 1979, Deng has found it necessary to impose his own ideological commitments. This has included an emphasis on his own writings as a source for authoritative ideology. The hat and club problem has certainly been less serious in the 1980s than it was in the Maoist period, but it has not disappeared. The 1982 party constitution contains the ominous message that "class struggle will continue to exist within certain limits for a long time, and may even sharpen under certain conditions."[21] The function of this statement is to justify antagonistic struggles against selected targets in the future. There have been important changes in the role and content of ideological orthodoxy; however, in some respects, the Maoist mold has yet to be broken.

The second question involves the role of expertise in decision making and leadership, a problem aptly summarized in the "red-expert" dichotomy. During the Maoist period, the call to be "both red and expert" expressed a suspicion of intellectuals and the monopolization of all decisions by party cadres, and it reinforced the precedence of ideological over practical criteria. In general, the CCP has denied that the expertise of intellectuals and technical specialists implied any claim to political authority. However, this approach has not precluded utilization of their services and advice. Most senior CCP decision makers have had ample access to staff experts, in addition to personal experience in one or more of the specialized administrative hierarchies.[22] On the other hand, those of the top elite have probably underutilized the intellectual resources available to them, mainly because the "red-expert" issue has been so vulnerable to extreme interpretation. In both the Great Leap and the period after the Cultural Revolution, hostility toward experts encouraged some

[21]"Constitution of the CCP," p. 9.

[22]See Lieberthal, *Central Documents*, pp. 26–49, for description of the extensive consultation, including technical review, that goes into the drafting of central documents, and for case studies of the process.

ill-conceived policy experiments or caused a decline in the quality of specialized training. The devastation caused to the Chinese educational system, especially higher education, was described in Chapter 5.

This has been an area of great reform for the post-Mao regime. Deng announced at the First National Science Conference in 1978 that intellectuals were workers, thereby undercutting the class grounds for the suspicion of intellectuals. They have been recognized as a key force in modernization and have been treated accordingly. Funds have been poured into higher education and research, and academic control over educational institutions has been strengthened. The encouragement given to overseas study shows a confidence in intellectuals that is not often found in communist countries. Within the party, the recruitment of intellectuals has been stressed, and the curricula of party schools has been adjusted to include more science and management courses. Understandably, there has been considerable resistance and resentment of these changes among party members, and implementation has been gradual. The excesses of the campaign against spiritual pollution revealed a latent constituency for anti-intellectual (and possibly antiforeign) activities within the party that will not quickly dissipate.

Finally, the Maoist period left institutions of popular influence on government in a shambles, despite the large amount of mass participation in movements and in basic-level politics. The weakness of popular representation at higher levels and the absence of independent communications media led to an information gap, so that elites were poorly informed on how policies would be or have been received at the grass roots. This was and remains a real danger, since decision makers rely for their information largely on bureaucratic hierarchies, and what reaches the top is a very indirect and selective representation of the grass roots situation; as in all bureaucracies, tendencies to report data acceptable to superiors or data enhancing the position of the reporter are strong. There were spectacular misjudgments, for example, about the consequences of the hundred flowers experiment, the Leap, and the mobilization of the Red Guards. The basic problem of distorted popular feedback is due to structural problems inherent in Communist political systems, but it was exacerbated by the scale and novelty of Mao's policy interventions. The structure of the Leninist state assumes that party leadership is correct and that there is no serious problem of information concerning popular interests. The effect of these assumptions can be seen in the weakness of the people's congress system, the control of the media, and the absence of any loyal opposition on major issues. To some extent, Chinese politics has compensated for these problems by various mass line techniques, including experimentalism. The post-Mao regime has improved the situation somewhat by strengthening the people's congress system and election mechanisms, allowing various voluntary associations, and encouraging diversity and expansion in the media. But the basic situation is still one where, as Deng Xiaoping himself complained, the fate of a policy may well depend on the preferences and attention span of a top leader.[23]

If we review the results of Chinese decision making over the first thirty-odd years of the PRC, the impressions are paradoxical. There were spectacular policy failures and yet cumulative successes that are no less impressive. There were requirements of ideological conformity and yet flexibility in policy implementation and modification. Technological feats such as the production of nuclear weapons have been accomplished, but intellectuals as a group have been politically and sometimes socially ostracized. The failures were no doubt induced in part by the inexperience of the leadership and the novelty of its goals; successes in some cases probably occurred despite the decisions made. The political reforms of Deng Xiaoping constitute an important structural reform of the Maoist legacy, probably the most important reforms in the history of the PRC. But Chinese decision making does not promise to change rapidly.

ADMINISTRATION

Bureaucracy. the Chinese political system entrusts the application of its rules to a variety of structures, including: state, party, and army bureaucracies and the communications systems that they control; the management organs of primary units; and a multitude of popular committees, organizations, and meetings that mobilize the population for direct action on governmental

---

[23]Deng as quoted in Peng Zhen's speech reported in *People's Daily*, May 12, 1984, p. 5.

programs. The national bureaucracies dominate the administrative process that brings central decisions to the local level. They are complex hierarchies, containing both territorial and functional divisions, but they share a common subordination to the authority of the central CCP leadership. They are staffed by full-time career cadres, appointed and assigned through internal processes. Their performance, too, is directed and supervised largely from within by party members in leading positions and by higher levels of their organizations. Since there is very little interorganizational mobility, state cadres tend to identify with their organizational location rather than with their profession. For example, someone doing economic work for the Ministry of Education would consider himself a ministry official specializing in economics rather than an economist working for the Ministry of Education. Institutionally speaking, state cadres have a high degree of autonomy from society, being organized as agents of central decision-making organs.

There are important qualifications in this picture, however, because the Chinese Communists have made serious efforts to restrain the exercise of bureaucratic power. Although they accept the necessity of centrally directed organizational hierarchies that will implement the CCP's monopoly of political power, they have tried to ensure bureaucracy's responsiveness to political controls and to keep its structure relatively simple and efficient. As a result, the history of bureaucracy in post-1949 China has been one of recurring tendencies to expand and institutionalize, matched by counterpressures to limit and modify its role.[24]

Bureaucratic institutions were not prominent in the pre-1949 movement. Environmental factors inhibited the growth of large-scale territorial units or of functionally sophisticated governmental departments. The major exception to this rule came in Yanan in the early 1940s, when United Front policies, assumption of a more complete governmental role, and an influx of intellectuals encouraged bureaucratization. But the base area simply could not afford a large central organization, and the tendency was resisted by the rectification, "crack troops and simple administration," and "to-the-village" campaigns of

[24]See Harding, *Organizing China.*

1942–1944.[25] After 1949, pressures for bureaucratization became much more formidable. The implementation of socialist reforms throughout the country not only required a governmental structure significantly larger and more complex than any the CCP had previously known, but it also encouraged co-optation of many cadres who had not experienced the socializing effects of the revolutionary movement. Despite sporadic campaigns against bureaucratism, the path was opened for a flow of more traditional bureaucratic influences into the new government. The initiation of the Soviet-style economic plan, with its centralization of power in the state ministries, brought the rapid growth of an administrative structure that was almost a direct antithesis of the CCP's earlier organizational model.

The mid-1950s probably marked the peak of bureaucratic power in post-1949 China, but the new structure was not yet highly institutionalized. It proved vulnerable to the growing reaction against it, which culminated in the Great Leap Forward. For a few years, an antibureaucratic tide was in ascendancy, only to give way in the early 1960s to a reassertion of official authority and prerogatives. The governmental system of 1961–1965 was less centralized and, in terms of its actual control over society, probably less powerful than that of the mid-1950s. On the other hand, it was more institutionalized, and it seemed to be creating a new establishment that made routinized concessions to mass lines principles but was increasingly the preserve of bureaucratic interests and specialized skill groups. Its capacity to deflect and then resist the early thrusts of the Cultural Revolution was evidence of its strength and autonomy, even though it ultimately disintegrated under the Maoist attack.

Actually, the Cultural Revolution did not eliminate bureaucracy but rather replaced some bureaucratic sectors with others. The old state and party organs held on to their power until the winter of 1966–1967. It was only in the seizure of power stage that the country entered a period in which no bureaucratic apparatus seemed capable of providing effective government. Before long, however, the PLA began to fill this gap by taking over the basic administrative functions. The Maoists regarded

[25] Mark Selden, *The Yenan Way in Revolutionary China* (Cambridge, Mass.: Harvard University Press, 1971), pp. 188–229.

the PLA as a "revolutionary" organization, owing to Lin Biao's reforms of the early 1960s, and had encouraged it to expand its political role as early as 1963–1965.[26] But even though the PLA entered the political arena under Maoist auspices, it was still a bureaucratic organization that displayed little enthusiasm for sharing its administrative duties with the radical mass organizations; the provincial revolutionary committees whose formation it supervised were dominated by military figures and included many former cadres.[27] With the reconstruction of the CCP after 1969, military administration gradually began to give way to the reviving civilian bureaucracies, controlled by party cadres though with a facade of mass participation.[28]

As noted repeatedly, the years between 1969 and 1976 brought intense struggle between administrative priorities oriented toward stabilization and economic development, and radical pressures for continuing revolutionization of the system. The post-1976 leadership resolved this debate with a forthright assertion of administrative prerogatives, stressing the need for central planning and controls, for technically competent management, and for regulations and labor discipline to ensure attainment of production targets. One lesson to be drawn from the Cultural Revolution experiment, therefore, is that bureaucratic administration is a given feature of Chinese politics, one that cannot be sacrificed even for goals that might have higher rhetorical priority. However, it is also important to recognize the Chinese efforts to curb "bureaucratism," if not bureaucracy, in an effort to control what are seen as the negative aspects of the institutions they cannot do without. These efforts have been most evident in two principles—politicization of bureaucracy and decentralization—which were advanced vigorously in the Maoist period and which, with important changes, continue to influence post-Mao administration.

Politicization of Bureaucracy. The Chinese Communists' attitude toward bureaucracy is two-sided. Some view bureaucracy

[26]Ellis Joffe, "The Chinese Army Under Lin Piao: Prelude to Intervention," in Lindbeck, ed., *Management of a Revolutionary Society*, esp. pp. 353–66.

[27]Ellis Joffe, "The Chinese Army in the Cultural Revolution: The Politics of Intervention," *Current Scene*, vol. 8, no. 18 (December 7, 1970): 1–25.

[28]David Goodman, "The Provincial Revolutionary Committee in the PRC, 1967–1979: An Obituary," *China Quarterly*, no. 85 (March 1981): 49–79.

in negative terms as a nonproductive superstructure that is divorced from the front line of political struggle; they seek to reduce the scope of bureaucracy and to transfer administrative powers to the lowest feasible level. Others accept some degree of bureaucratization as inevitable and potentially even positive in its provision of correct models and leadership; they focus on the politicization of bureaucracy to ensure its subordination to political leadership and its acceptance of a mass line style of behavior. To use Harry Harding's terminology, these viewpoints correspond to the radical and the rationalistic approaches to bureaucracy.[29] In reality, few leaders and few policies were thoroughly radical or thoroughly rationalistic; these were polar positions between which normal Chinese politics oscillated. Because of its successful experience in the base areas, the top CCP leaders have tended to be hostile toward bureaucratic elitism and conservatism, appreciative of a strong relationship to the masses and of decentralized government, and searching in fairly innovative ways for administrative relationships that will promote the all-round development of Chinese society. No Chinese leadership has doubted that political control of the bureaucracy was necessary. The contentious issues have been the relationship of the party hierarchy to the administrative hierarchy and methods of the political control of cadres.

One of the crucial issues in the politicization of bureaucracy is the relationship between the CCP and the state structure. Party and state have never been separated sharply in terms of personnel, due to the high proportion of party members serving in state organs. The very first step in establishing CCP rule was the placement of its members in controlling positions in the government. Since the party had only one-third of the trained cadres it needed to fill state posts,[30] a fair number of nonparty officials were retained in the early years, although their proportional representation fell steadily. By the late 1950s, party-member domination of state organs was complete. Nonetheless, the CCP insisted that the two hierarchies were functionally and organizationally distinct; the state was responsible for administration of policy, especially in the economic realm, whereas the party was

[29]Harding, *Organizing China*, pp. 329–60.
[30]Ibid., p. 35.

responsible for political and ideological affairs. Initially at least, the CCP tried to observe the distinction, so that its organizational control did not necessarily follow the placement of party members in governmental positions.

From the early 1950s to the Cultural Revolution, the Chinese leadership addressed this problem in terms of a choice between "vertical rule" and "dual rule."[31] Both types of rule assumed the existence of two parallel organizational hierarchies: the first, a bureaucratized network of branch agencies of the central ministries extending downward through subnational governments; the other, a less-bureaucratized hierarchy of party committees at each administrative level. Under vertical rule, which prevailed during the early part of the FFYP, the functional departments of local government were responsible to corresponding departments at higher levels leading up to the appropriate ministry in Peking. This system maximized central ministerial control over administration and encouraged the development of specialized bureaus at lower levels; however, it also inhibited coordination across departmental lines within governmental levels and made local departments resistant to supervision by local party committees. The alternative of dual rule, which was endorsed by the Eighth Party Congress of 1956, strengthened local control by making departments responsible to local committees as well as to their higher administrative counterparts.

Dual rule, which came into its own with the decentralization of 1957 and the ensuing Leap, greatly increased the involvement of party committees in state administration. Indeed, for a brief period in the late 1950s, the central ministries simply lost much of their former control over lower levels. Local decisions were made by party committees, which became the effective agencies of subnational government. The phenomenon of party as government threatened to obliterate the distinction between state and party. However, the state regained some of its authority in the retrenchment period, and an approximation of dual rule resumed. The adoption of dual rule was a decisive step in asserting the primacy of politics, through the medium of CCP committees throughout the bureaucracy. As Harding points

[31]See detailed analysis in Schurmann, *Ideology and Organization*, esp. pp. 188–219.

out, "By the early 1960s the party had created a network of functional departments that paralleled the functional bureaus of the government and enabled the party to play an extensive role in policymaking at all levels of Chinese society."[32] But success in politicizing bureaucracy had the unforeseen side effect of bureaucratizing politics. That is, as CCP organs intervened in the daily work of government departments, they began to absorb some of the interests and concerns of those departments. Nominally, the organizational and functional distinction between state and party remained; however, in practice, the two came closer together. The contrast between the antibureaucratic impulse of 1955–1958 and that of the Cultural Revolution is instructive. The former viewed the state as the prime base of bureaucratic evils and sought a solution through increased party penetration of administrative functions; the latter saw the CCP itself as a stronghold of bureaucratism and turned to nonparty elements for assistance in rectifying it.

Following the Cultural Revolution, the CCP experimented briefly with the principle of "unified leadership," combining administrative and political tasks in a single organ—the revolutionary committee—which relied on the leadership of party members within it. Ultimately, however, the organizational distinction between administrative and party organs returned, although the party's domination was even more marked than it had been earlier. Administrators were responsible for meeting goals set from above in the bureaucratic hierarchy, but they also operated under the close supervision of the party committee within their own level or unit. Given the concentration of power within the party, the party secretary was in an extremely powerful position. In effect, everyone working at his level was his subordinate. This situation created opportunities for the abuse of power that did not pass unnoticed and also weakened the administrative coordination of the state.

Since 1976, reforms affecting the role of the party in administration have been made in a number of directions. Attempts have been made to reduce the unnecessary and arbitrary interference of party cadres, to improve their technical and managerial competence, and to improve party discipline, all in the name of

[32]Harding, *Organizing China*, p. 284.

strengthening party leadership. The formal authority structure of work units has been strengthened at the expense of their party structure.[33] A system of dual rule still prevails, but the reorientation toward modernization has greatly strengthened the state-expert role.

The other major aspect of politicization of the bureaucracy has been the political orientation and control of the individual cadre. There can be little doubt that the message of "serve the people" has penetrated the Chinese bureaucracy, and yet there is probably no area of Chinese political life where the contradictions are stronger. On the one hand, cadres work in highly bureaucratized settings subject to complicated regulations and controls, have fixed pay scales and ranks that make them a privileged stratum, and hold considerable power over citizens with little access to the inner workings of the system.[34] The tradition of bureaucratic rule and authoritarian social relationships still reinforces these features. On the other hand, there are the normative ideals and expectations of the regime concerning closeness to the masses. Exhortations to live up to the pre-1949 traditions of revolutionary populism are common, as are examples of exemplary behavior by officials. Mao's conviction that the strength of a regime lies in its popular support has become an axiom of CCP ideology, and the citizenry is encouraged to develop high expectations about cadre responsiveness to mass needs and criticism. The tensions between the opportunities of authority and the norms of service are impossible to resolve, but one can contrast Mao's and Deng's methods of coping with the problem of bureaucratism.

Mao viewed bureaucratism as a problem of political style. The bureaucrat who sought his own comfort was out of touch with the masses and under the influence of bourgeois values. Typically, Maoist methods of correction were: requirements that cadres do a certain amount of productive labor; May Seventh cadre schools emphasizing labor and ideological study; criticism of cadres by the masses; and emphasis on political criteria for

---

[33] "Decision on Reforming the Economic Structure," (3rd Plenum of the 12th Central Committee), *BR*, vol. 27, no. 44 (October 29, 1984): i–xvi.

[34] Barnett, *Cadres, Bureaucracy and Political Power*, passim.

promotion.[35] All of these methods attempted to sustain or recreate the base area experience of close mass-cadre relations, and they used episodic rather than constant measures to put personal pressure on the cadre to behave correctly.

By contrast, the approach characteristic of the post-Mao period views bureaucracy as an organizational defect. An organization that is not doing its job of service to the people, whose officials are allowed to be lazy and aloof, is a poorly designed and disciplined organization. Its problem is not too much capitalism but too much feudalism. With this idea of the problem, the solutions are the clear specification of organizational and individual responsibilities, efficient disciplinary procedures, proper training for officials, and intraorganizational democracy. These reforms do not attempt to recreate the base area experience in order to transform the outlook of the individual official. Instead, they attempt to structure the organization permanently in such a way that desirable, functional behavior is encouraged, and undesirable, dysfunctional behavior is discouraged. Institutionalization is used as a weapon against bureaucratism.

Decentralization. The relationship between national and subnational administrative units is one of the most complex problems of the Chinese political system.[36] The system is highly centralized in its formal allocation of political authority. Central organs may assign certain functions and powers to lower levels but retain the authority to reclaim them or to intervene in their implementation; decentralization does not guarantee lower levels the right to exercise their powers permanently or autonomously. Yet decentralization is a principle of real operational importance that seems to be well established. Despite its theoretical subordination to the principle of centralism, it has gradually emerged since the late 1950s as one of the PRC's primary administrative

[35]The most typical period for Maoist administrative reforms was not the Cultural Revolution but the measures for administrative revitalization of 1967–1969. See Harding, *Organizing China*, pp. 267–95.

[36]For general discussion, see Schurmann, *Ideology and Organization*, passim; and the contrasting views of Parris Chang and Victor Falkenheim in "Peking and the Provinces," *Problems of Communism*, vol. 21, no. 4 (July–August 1972): p. 67–83.

characteristics. Decentralization has been part of both the Maoist and post-Mao administrative programs, but for very different reasons.

The influences that have prompted decentralization are diverse. They include desires to restrict the power of central bureaucracy and thereby to give local units enough political space to develop their own internal resources. Underlying this view is the conviction that creation of a new political culture requires opportunities for local action that cannot be realized under a highly centralized system. More pragmatic considerations include efforts to rationalize the economic system by encouraging diversification and regional growth, cutting transport and distribution costs, and reducing the red tape and expense of a centralized planning apparatus. The size of the country and its uneven economic development provide powerful arguments for experimentation with decentralization. Decentralization may be, in part, a response to pressure from subnational elites or at least a product of bargaining between central and local authorities. As noted earlier, Mao mobilized provincial support for his advocacy of the Great Leap, and, in recent years, decentralization has drawn support from influence acquired by subnational governments during the Cultural Revolution. Questions of national security and defense also affect elite thinking on some aspects of decentralization, particularly economic diversification and the development of regional or local self-sufficiency.

Decentralization impulses have taken the form of bureaucratic simplification and administrative decentralization. The former is that recurring wish, found in most political systems, to reduce the size and complexity of governmental structure. Motivated by desires for economy and efficiency, and by an innate suspicion that bureaucracies are always overweight, advocates of bureaucratic simplification try to eliminate excess staff and departments. The CCP embarked on its first simplification campaign as early as 1941, in the context of its Yanan rectification movements.[37] Attempts at a repeat performance began as early as 1950. By 1956, Mao had proposed a two-thirds cut in party and government organizations to correct "structural obesity."[38] Although his

---

[37]Selden, *The Yenan Way*, pp. 212–16.
[38]"On the Ten Great Relationships," *Selected Works*, vol. 5, pp. 284–307.

goal was unrealistic, a substantial reduction of administrative personnel and some simplification of lower-level administrative units took place over the next two years. However, the CCP's greatest assault on bureaucratic proliferation came with the Cultural Revolution. According to one report, the forty ministries, eleven commissions, and twenty-one special agencies of the 1965 State Council had been reduced to seventeen ministries, three commissions, and fifteen special agencies in 1972.[39] The Shanghai Municipal Statistical Bureau had a staff of 200 before the Cultural Revolution; it was abolished, and statistical work was carried on by four persons.[40] The 1969 party constitution indicated that central CCP organization would be much less complicated than in the past. Model revolutionary committees were also noteworthy for their simplicity of administrative structure and staff. There can be little doubt that the governmental apparatus of 1972 was significantly smaller and less top-heavy than it had been in 1965. But bureaucratization then resumed, so that by the late 1970s the general size and complexity of administration was not greatly different from the pattern before the Cultural Revolution. Perhaps the most that can be said is that Chinese leaders are sensitive to the problem of bureaucratic proliferation and that they can be expected to mount recurring attacks on it.

Administrative decentralization refers to a reordering of responsibilities within the government in which powers as well as personnel are shifted to lower levels. CCP historical experience was mainly with decentralized modes of government, a pattern continued in the 1949–1954 administrative system, which gave a major role to regional units. Rapid centralization accompanied the FFYP; however, in late 1957, the CCP adopted a decentralization policy that remained in effect, albeit with many twists and turns, through the 1970s. The initial 1957 decisions shifted control over many industrial and commercial enterprises, as well as financial resources, from the central ministries to provincial authorities.[41] This action, combined with dual rule, resulted in a marked increase in the powers of provincial party committees.

[39]*Current Scene*, vol. 10, no. 7 (July 1972): 12.

[40]World Bank, *China: Socialist Economic Development* (Washington, D.C.: World Bank, 1983), vol. 1, p. 226.

[41]The following discussion draws on Schurmann, *Ideology and Organization*, pp. 175–78, 195–210.

Subsequently, a reverse process occurred in the countryside, as control over agriculture was pushed upward from the cooperatives to the rural communes. The Great Leap was marked, therefore, by a concentration of power in the middle (provincial and commune) levels at the expense of the center and basic production units.

A different pattern emerged as Leap policies yielded to retrenchment policies. Further decentralization occurred at lower levels as the communes were reduced in size and as rural production teams and individual enterprises acquired more autonomy. At higher levels, provincial dominance lessened with renewed emphasis on central planning and the reestablishment of regional party bureaus to oversee provincial activities. On the eve of the Cultural Revolution, the Chinese administrative system was thus highly differentiated. The central ministries retained direct control over some enterprises—largely those of most importance for national defense and heavy industry—and responsibility for overall planning of the economy. Provincial and municipal authorities managed the bulk of nonagricultural economic activities, subject to coordination with central plans. However, basic-level units also operated a variety of small-scale enterprises, and agricultural management essentially was decentralized to production units within the communes. Throughout this system, individual production units had some leeway in managing their activities either through negotiation with higher planning authorities or through setting their own targets and distribution arrangements.[42]

The Cultural Revolution brought little formal change in this system, but the balance shifted toward decentralization. The weakening of CCP organization and the preoccupation with resolution of political disputes apparently gave units at all levels greater room for maneuver in performance of their routine activities. Second, decentralization took on a broader political significance due to the expansion of mass participation in basic-level decisions; powers that initially devolved to local elites were partially shared with more representative bodies. Finally, the

[42]On pre–Cultural Revolution industrial organization and management, see Barry M. Richman, *Industrial Society in Communist China* (New York: Random House, 1969), esp. chaps. 8 and 9.

objectives of local development, self-reliance, and self-sufficiency received greater emphasis in the Cultural Revolution. Administrative units of all sizes were urged to be small but complete, that is, to be able to take care of all their own needs. All provinces were urged to become self-sufficient in grain, and all counties were urged to produce their own walking tractors (one small enough to be operated by a person on foot).

Administrative politics since 1976 have seen an alteration of centralizing and decentralizing tendencies. Many Chinese leaders assumed that modernization would be according to the Soviet model of a high rate of investment, economic decision making concentrated in the central ministries, and a number of expensive key projects directly controlled by the center. This would represent a return to the policies of the mid-1950s, a time of rapid economic growth for China. Other leaders were persuaded by the economists and theorists of the Chinese Academy of Social Sciences to embark on much more innovative and decentralized economic initiatives. Before he became premier, Zhao Ziyang had been very successful with such policies in Sichuan, and after he assumed national power, they became increasingly widespread. Among the most important post-Mao decentralizing policies are the household contracting and specialized household systems in rural areas; the expansion of enterprise control over personnel, investment, and production in urban areas; and the facilitation of direct contact with foreign capital, including special economic zones and grants of decision-making authority to various provinces and cities. These major policies have required, in turn, numerous other adjustments in economic policies and structures, including a greater priority for the production of consumer goods, restriction on party interference in enterprise management, development of economic law and courts, and so forth. Altogether, the devolution of economic power in the 1980s is so extensive that it is difficult to predict its political effects. In a fairly short time, the Chinese political economy has moved from leftist ideological experimentation to the most advanced experiments in market socialism in the Communist world.

It appears paradoxical that decentralization could be a policy of both the left and the right in China. The answer to the paradox is that Maoist decentralization is very different in motivation and policies from current efforts. Before discussing that difference, it is important to recall some features of the general ecology of decentralization in China. First, some degree of decentralization is inevitable in China. The size of the population, the ruggedness of the territory, and the weakness of communications and central resources require that many decisions be made outside of Peking. Second, the political tradition of China is emphatically unitary, and this is reinforced by the ethnic homogeneity of the population as well as by the Leninist party-state. The ethnically based federalism and separatism of Yugoslavia are not problems in China, nor are minority questions as significant as they are in the Soviet Union. Third, decentralization is costly in terms of central information and control. To the extent that the hundreds of thousands of Chinese enterprises really make their own decisions, the state will be less knowledgeable about what is happening, less able to guide decisions, and less able to coordinate general development. These problems may be counterbalanced by an increase in productivity, but they remain problems. Attempts to improve information and control generate centralizing tendencies. Fourth, decentralization is attractive to the CCP because of its rural revolutionary experience. The CCP has always felt confident of its relationship to the peasants and of the potential of local initiative. This is in great contrast to the Soviet Union, where mutual mistrust between the peasantry and the urban Bolshevik leadership contributed to many tragic (and centralizing) policies. These four factors imply that any Chinese Communist regime would be decentralized to some degree, but probably not in a federal manner, and that the central leadership would be attracted to but at the same time inconvenienced by decentralization policies. There is much room for ideological and policy differences within this framework.

Self-sufficiency, egalitarianism, and communal mobilization were the key features of Maoist decentralization. The norm of self-sufficiency meant that each unit of society should try to take care of its own basic needs. For example, a village in Mongolia should try to raise enough grain to feed itself even if conditions were not favorable for grain growing, rather than exclusively raising sheep and then using the profits from sheep raising to buy grain. Egalitarianism encouraged decentralization by favoring the distribution of resources rather than their concentration. In health services, for instance, extensive and rather unregulated programs such as the barefoot doctors were preferred to the more centralized urban hospitals. Lastly, decentralization was intended to encourage initiative, but not individual initiative. Building socialism meant increasing collective activities and rewards and decreasing or eliminating private activities and rewards. The Great Leap Forward is a good example because, at the same time that central controls were relaxed, the key unit of rural organization was moved from the cooperative to the much larger commune. Moreover, decentralization relied on communal mobilization within a campaign cycle, implying a later consolidation phase with centralizing tendencies. Politically, Maoist decentralization encouraged an egalitarian, communal, and small-scale society, responding to and controlled by his own charismatic leadership. There are strong rural and traditional elements in this vision. It is a poor peasant's dream of middle-class peasant security and independence transposed into a socialist framework.

Decentralization under Zhao Ziyang emphasizes the opposite virtues of commodity production, maximum growth, and individualism. In the 1980s, villages and families are allowed to make their own production decisions based on profitability rather than self-sufficiency. Peasants are encouraged to engage in commodity production rather than producing for their own needs. Peasants are freer to produce what they want, but they are more dependent on markets and other producers. Maximum growth, rather than egalitarianism, is the criteria by which policy success is measured. Sometimes, this leads to concentration and centralization of resources in areas of maximum return, but this tendency is counterbalanced somewhat by the conviction that enterprise leadership and lower-level administration should have more decision making discretion. Moreover, maximum growth also means that innovators can justify their irregular behavior by favorable economic results. Although maximum growth has its own inherent flaws as a policy criterion, it is less constraining than egalitarianism. The emphasis on individual initiative and reward is one of the most amazing aspects of post-Mao policy. The principle behind it is that individual benefit is legitimate if society is benefitted as well. In rural areas, it has led to a decollectivization of resources and decision making. At this level, twenty-five years of Maoist collectivism has been reversed. Decollectivization is not presented as part of a campaign, but as a long-term policy backed up by fifteen-year and twenty-year contracts. In general, what lies behind this approach to decentralization is a modern commitment to efficiency and rationalization, in which the front line of producers should have discretion with commensurate risks and rewards, backed up by stable and nonintrusive political-administrative coordination. The two approaches to decentralization presented here have been simplified and somewhat stereotyped for purposes of contrast, but it is important to note that the same general policy direction can have such different ideals and policy content.

RULE ENFORCEMENT AND ADJUDICATION

The Chinese attitude toward conflict, the role of law and the role of legitimate violence in society is quite different from that of developed Western countries, but increasing social complexity and the negative experience of the Cultural Revolution have led to reforms that emphasize "socialist legality," a concept very similar to legal reforms in European Communist countries and much closer to modern Western ideals than previous Chinese approaches. But the practice of conflict resolution does not change as rapidly as its theory, so the legal reality of the 1980s is a mixture of recent reforms with a system of social control that has evolved over thirty years of Communist rule.

Social Control. Despite the tension and outbreaks of violence that have accompanied political mobilizations, social life in the PRC has been relatively orderly. One reason for this is the lack of geographic mobility in Chinese society. Even in cities, people tend to live in the same place for decades, forming tight little neighborhoods in which strangers are noticed. Another reason is the government's success in reducing opportunities and temptations to violate its prescriptions. Chinese socialism, with its egalitarianism and austerity, is a factor here. Basic economic needs are met with few gross differentials in income and little conspicuous affluence. People know, in a general way, what others around them earn and the rationale behind income differentials. There are few opportunities to increase one's income except by publicly known changes in employment status. In other words, perceptions of economic inequity are low, and illegal income is difficult to conceal and dangerous to display.

Strict regulation of possession of firearms, rationing of scarce goods, controls on marketing activities, and close supervision of residence and travel present further obstacles to the commission of crimes and the evasion of authority.[43]

Moreover, the Chinese pattern of social organization leaves little space for individual privacy. Basic-level cadres and activists are close to the people and are able to engage in frequent face-to-face contact with the citizens whom they lead. Primary units are organized in small groups, each with an internal leadership structure that is necessarily familiar with individual activities and problems. The fact that many of these units are both work and residential groups adds to the fullness of knowledge that members have about each other. Group meetings and discussions provide a forum for direct solicitation and exchange of information about members' thoughts and behavior. Nor are officials free from supervision by subordinates, peers, and superiors, since the checks, reports, and discussion meetings required for cadres are more intense than those for ordinary citizens. Cadres are better able to manipulate the system to their advantage than are the masses, but the government makes serious efforts to counter the abuse of official position.

These conditions and controls cannot eliminate the possibility of deviant behavior. They are less effective in large cities than they are in towns and villages, and their effectiveness has varied with the intensity of changes demanded by the government, with economic conditions, and with the stability of political authority. For example, there was considerable noncompliance with the marriage law and collectivization directives. The economic crises of 1959–1961 led to hoarding, black marketeering, and a revival of official corruption. Crimes of violence increased during 1967–1968, although it was difficult to distinguish in

[43]On rationing and residence controls and the control aspects of education and job assignments, see Lynn T. White, III, "Deviance, Modernization, Rations, and Household Registers in Urban China," in Amy Auerbacher Wilson, et al., eds., *Deviance and Social Control in Chinese Society* (New York: Praeger, 1977), pp. 151–72; and Lynn T. White, III, *Careers in Shanghai: The Social Guidance of Personal Energies in a Developing Chinese City, 1949–1966* (Berkeley: University of California Press, 1978). White's analysis of the way in which diverse government controls serve as positive guides to careers and community involvements, as well as deterrents to deviant behavior, is relevant to much of the following discussion.

those years between organized political violence and random criminal acts. Post-1976 criticism of the Gang's activities and influence involved many allegations about criminal behavior, profiteering, embezzlement, and so forth in 1974–1976. In 1978–1979, the press reported many current examples of crime and corruption to dramatize the need for stricter observance of law. In 1983, it was felt that a major anticrime campaign was necessary. Despite these variations in degrees of compliance, however, the Chinese pattern of control and supervision has been relatively effective in limiting rule violations.

The preceding comments have referred to controls that seek to minimize the use of coercive measures by denying opportunities for offenses or by making their consequences risky or unrewarding. We should also note the more positive and voluntaristic aspects of social control at the basic level in the PRC. Two phenomena of particular importance are popular participation in rule enforcement and adjudication, and the effects of political socialization.

The popular role in rule enforcement and adjudication includes some participation in formal legal organs.[44] The people's tribunals established early in PRC history the principle of mass participation in trials in both participant-observer and judicial roles. When state organs were formalized in 1954, a system of people's assessors was provided to continue this practice. People's assessors are mass representatives who sit with judges and theoretically participate equally with them in the hearing and deciding of a case. Popular exposure to court proceedings contributes to a better understanding of the judicial system and possibly lessens traditional fears of litigation; it may also inject some popular notions of equity into court decisions. However, the modest role of the courts and their general subordination to police and party organs limit the significance of this kind of participation.

Much more important as a means of involving the population are the security and defense committees and mediation committees that are organized within basic-level units. The former were, before the Cultural Revolution, the lowest arm of the public

[44] James R. Townsend, *Political Participation in Communist China* (Berkeley: University of California Press, 1967), pp. 137–42.

security system, operating under close police supervision. Their primary responsibilities were to watch for and report on illegal or suspicious activities, and to maintain surveillance over the "five bad elements" and other offenders sentenced to supervised labor in their home locale. Following attacks on police and the public security system during the Cultural Revolution, security committees evolved more diverse organizational arrangements with broader and possibly more autonomous law enforcement functions within their units.[45]

Mediation committees come close to representing the Chinese ideal of dispute resolution. As elected bodies, they add to the popular role in the local governmental process. As localized institutions composed of activists rather than full-time cadres, they are decentralized and nonbureaucratic in character. And in their mission of mediation, they display the Chinese preference for informal, persuasive, and voluntary modes of settlement over formal litigation and adjudication. Mediation is a preferred course of action for courts as well, with judges frequently advising disputants to work out settlements on their own or through intermediaries. Police, women's and labor organizations, cadres and activists, friends and relatives may also play mediating roles. But it is the mediation committees—which are charged with educating their fellow citizens about their social obligations and anticipating possible conflicts as well as mediating actual disputes—that perhaps symbolize best the ideal of a self-regulating society.[46] Although security and mediation committees are largely the domain of activists in close touch with political superiors, they shift much responsibility for social control from the state apparatus to mass-based community organizations. In 1983, there were more than 927,000 mediation committees, with 5.5 million members. In the five years of 1979–1983 they settled 33

[45] See Ezra F. Vogel, "Preserving Order in the Cities," in John Wilson Lewis, ed., *The City in Communist China* (Stanford, Cal.: Stanford University Press, 1971) pp. 87–88; and Janet Weitzner Salaff, "Urban Residential Communities in the Wake of the Cultural Revolution," in ibid., pp. 307–12.

[46] For a discussion of the organization and philosophy of mediation, noting its linkages with traditional modes of dispute settlement, see Stanley Lubman, "Mao and Mediation: Politics and Dispute Resolution in Communist China," *California Law Review*, vol. 55, no. 5 (November 1967): 128–59; see also Jerome Alan Cohen, "Drafting People's Mediation Rules," in Lewis, ed., *The City in Communist China*, pp. 29–50.

million disputes, approximately ten times the number of civil cases tried by China's basic-level people's courts.[47]

Political socialization extends the development of voluntary social control to the entire population. As noted in Chapter 5, socialization in the PRC stresses the citizen's obligation to serve the community and creates multiple opportunities for the practice of this obligation in daily life. Participation in political study and discussion, in mass movements, in the management of primary unit affairs, in *xiafang* and other forms of productive labor are all multifunctional activities. In them, the citizen gains a better understanding of the system's policies and norms and simultaneously takes part in their realization. Insistence on practice is of utmost importance, partly because it reinforces learning and individual commitment and partly because it creates a social milieu of collective effort toward attainment of community goals. Governmental pressures for compliance are intensified by the example of one's peers and by pressures for group conformity. Although the strength of these pressures has lessened since the end of the Cultural Revolution, they are still a major reality of Chinese life. There is nothing automatic about either group or individual acceptance of the system's prescriptions, but the CCP continues to push for the development of a social ethic in which compliance with the demands of the political community is recognized as a legitimate obligation of every citizen.

The Formal Legal System. It is important to note that there is very little involvement of the formal legal system in the pattern of social control described previously. Conflict and deviant behavior is not a private matter to be brought to court by the involved parties, but a public concern of families, neighbors, fellow workers, and superiors. What would certainly be viewed as meddling in a more individualistic society is seen as social duty. Most petty conflicts and transgressions are dealt with by basic-level social units rather than by the specialized legal system. The problems and offenses of party members are generally handled within the party. Victor Li aptly describes the Chinese

---

[47]*Zhongguo fazhi bao* (Chinese Legal News), September 21, 1984, p. 3.

system as "law without lawyers."[48] The role of the formal legal system is more or less limited to special cases, irreconcilable conflicts, and transgressions requiring stiffer legal penalties.

The sharply limited social role of the PRC's formal legal system reflects its turbulent and tragic history. In the base areas and in rural areas after 1949, legal decisions were made by mass meetings or by local cadres. The lawyers and legal system that the PRC inherited were disdained for their bourgeois origins. By the mid-1950s, however, the regularity and control promised by an established legal system produced a short-lived spurt of legal institutionalization. Work began on law codes, and lawyers and judges were trained. It was thought that the period of irregular, spontaneous mass justice was over.[49] However, the antirightist campaign of 1957 quickly brought down the fledgling institutions. It was claimed that they showed insufficient class consciousness and restricted the enthusiasm of the masses. Lawyers who had defended criminals were criticized for unscrupulous behavior. A pattern evolved of unrestricted mass struggle against class enemies during campaigns and decisions by the political-legal secretary of the relevant party committee in other matters.[50] The duties of the procuratorate were left to the security organs, a procedure that was formalized in the 1975 constitution.[51] The legal system was inseparable from the political system, which in turn was identical with the party. Under these circumstances, judicial training and legal services were unnecessary.

The rehabilitation of the formal legal system began in 1978. Its destruction was blamed on Lin Biao and the Gang of Four (although in fact it had been ineffective since 1957), and its restoration was linked to the restoration of socialist democracy.[52] Law schools began to be rehabilitated, and working groups were

[48]Victor Li, *Law Without Lawyers* (Boulder, Colo.: Westview Press, 1978).

[49]Speech by Dong Biwu on March 18, 1957, reprinted in *People's Daily*, October 19, 1978.

[50]Shao-Chuan Leng, "Criminal Justice in Post-Mao China," *China Quarterly*, no. 87 (September 1981): 440–69.

[51]Chen Xuan, ed., *Gongmin falu guwen*, p. 105.

[52]See *People's Daily*, Special Commentator, "Democracy and the Legal System," *Chinese Law and Government*, vol. 15, no. 3–4 (Fall–Winter 1982–1983): 51–59.

formed by the party center to review and amend the draft legal codes that had been aborted in the 1950s. The Second Session of the Fifth National People's Congress passed a battery of new organic laws and codes in July 1979, including China's first official criminal code. The legal committees of the party and the people's congress system continue to be very active, and many new laws have been promulgated, including a patent law designed with international advice. Judicial autonomy has been emphasized, and, since 1979, the power of judicial decision making has been taken from party political-legal secretaries and given back to the judges. The new importance assigned to law and the courts has put an unbearable strain on China's meager and atrophied legal resources. In 1957, there were 2,500 full-time lawyers in China; in 1982, there were approximately the same number, or less than one two-hundredth of the number of lawyers in the United States.[53]

The recent reforms in the Chinese legal system are intended to eliminate the excesses of mass movements and to substitute the "rule of law" for the "rule of persons." One legal manual describes the latter problem as follows:

> The proletarian rule of law requires the creation of a comprehensive constitution and a comprehensive legal code so that in every area of work there will be laws to rely on and regulations to follow. It requires that all party organs and social organizations, all working officials and individual citizens act strictly according to the law. It requires that the law be concrete and stable, continuous and authoritative. No leader whatsoever should be able to change it arbitrarily.
>
> The rule of persons is the opposite. Law is viewed as a restriction of one's activities; if there are party directives there are no need for laws. Laws are viewed as mere reference guides for work; individual authority should be greater than law, the will of the leader should be higher than law. Business should be done according to persons rather than according to law, relying on words rather than on law. The "creative spirit of the masses" can be higher than law, and a mass movement could throw the laws to one side like waste paper. These theories, views and thoughts which opposed law and emphasized the rule of persons were once popular.

[53]Liao Junchang and Xu Jingcun, *Lushi gongzuo zhishi* (Information concerning legal work), Chengdu: Sichuan Renmin Chubanshe, 1983, pp. 6–7.

> Currently, legal and theoretical circles have not yet come to a unified opinion on the question of the rule of law and the rule of persons.[54]

As the last line of this passage suggests, it is easier to introduce laws than it is to change behavior. Changing cadre behavior is one of the goals of the 1983–1986 party rectification campaign, and changing mass behavior is the goal of the 1985–1990 legal education campaign.

Recent legal reforms are not supposed to change the class base of the regime or the hegemony of the party; instead, they are intended to regularize the regime and prevent excesses. Therefore, authors emphasize and even overemphasize the difference between socialist legality and bourgeois legality. And indeed there are important differences between the two. The PRC has an explicit class base of the working class and its allies; these comprise the "people." Although even class enemies are considered citizens and have the rights and duties of citizens, they will be treated as political enemies by the state. Although the current definition of the "people" is very broad—"all those classes strata and social groups who approve support and participate in construction of modernization"[55]—it is flexible enough to be manipulated by officials. As far as the hegemony of the party is concerned, legal reform is not a challenge to party leadership, but it is a limitation of its direct ruling and administrative activities.[56] It represents the self-restriction of the party to regulated behavior. However, the party can violate this self-restriction only with the loss of prestige and popular confidence.

Perhaps the current trend of legal reform is more challenging to the idea of the Leninist party-state than its proponents would care to admit. There is a latent tension between a strong, comprehensive legal system and the class basis of the state, because the former guarantees equal rights to all citizens and the latter presumes an internal war against enemies who are citizens. Some accommodation can be made—class-based legislation, for example—but the procedural principles are contradictory. This

---

[54]Chen Xuan, *Gongmin falu guwen*, p. 63.

[55]Ibid., p. 3.

[56]See, for instance, Wu Jialin, ed., *Xianfa xue* (The study of constitutional law), Beijing: Qunzhong Chubanshe, 1983, p. 157.

problem and the decline of exploiting classes led Khrushchev, in the early 1960s, to discard the notion of the "dictatorship of the proletariat" and declare the Soviet Union a "state of the whole people." Another hidden problem is the relationship of current reforms to Western models. Quite obviously, a major reason for current legal reforms is the disastrous consequences brought on by the haughty disdain of legal institutions and procedures. Notions such as constitutionalism, judicial autonomy, and the rule of law should not be necessary according to Marxist-Leninist ideology, but they have proven necessary for China. Rather than question the ideology, however, most reformers pretend that what they are proposing has little to do with inferior, Western models. A more satisfying approach would be to view problems of the rule of law and of some aspects of constitutional structure (such as the basic criteria for effective elections) as problems faced by any large, modern country rather than as capitalist or socialist problems. If there were common problems of modernity, it might be expected that ideas for coping with them might be borrowed from different systems.[57]

Coercion and Voluntarism. Rule enforcement in the PRC emphasizes prevention of violations, through voluntary compliance or other deterrents, rather than legal processing and punishment of offenders. This has been described as an "internal" model of compliance because of its concern for ideological and moral rectitude, in contrast to the familiar, Western "external" model that identifies certain actions as crimes and then punishes violations.[58] Even in the post-Mao period when the role of law has been emphasized, formal legal action has been mainly a last resort or a means of publicizing model cases for deterrent or educational purposes. Moreover, the penal system has a strong emphasis on the reeducation and rehabilitation of criminals. Jobs are found for released criminals with their old units or with new units, and the claimed level of recidivism is low. Control of deviance thus shifts away from formal legal institutions toward

[57] An analysis of this sort is done by Xu Chongde in Wu Jialin, ed., ibid., pp. 401–04.

[58] Victor H. Li, "The Evolution and Development of the Chinese Legal System," in Lindbeck, ed., *Management of a Revolutionary Society*, pp. 221–55.

a great variety of other social institutions and pressures.[59] The emphasis on voluntarism does not, however, apply to class enemies, nor does it obviate the need for coercive instruments, which are an important part of the legal system.

The PRC's coercive apparatus is extensive. It centers on the state public security system, which is tightly controlled by the CCP and is particularly influential within local governments.[60] Public security organs are resourceful and powerful. They include administrative cadres, police, and secret police; they maintain extensive files based on both regular police reports and the numerous activities over which they have some supervisory powers (for example, rationing, census, travel, and the work of popular security and mediation committees); and they have de facto power to arrest, investigate, adjudicate, and sentence in many cases that never reach the courts or are subject to only nominal review and ratification by other arms of the legal structure. The police presence is not an oppressive one in terms of numbers or display of force and arms; however, it is backed by the militia and ultimately the PLA, which leaves little doubt about its capacity to employ force when it chooses to do so.

In cases of acute class struggle, the coercive apparatus has also included certain structures of a quasi-legal or extralegal nature, which have acted episodically but with telling effect. The most prominent of these were the "struggle" and "speak bitterness" meetings, people's tribunals, and mass trials of the reconstruction era, which meted out so-called revolutionary justice to landlords, counterrevolutionaries, and other enemies of the new regime. These instruments operated under varying degrees of governmental authority and supervision. For example, peasants' associations had legal authorization to redistribute land; the people's tribunals, to try counterrevolutionaries. All of the localized coercive measures of the early years had general party approval and leadership. At the same time, the party encouraged a degree of spontaneity and popular participation in their operations that

---

[59]An excellent introduction is Victor H. Li, *Law Without Lawyers.*

[60]On the organization and activities of public security organs, see Barnett, *Cadres, Bureaucracy and Political Power,* pp. 194–97, 219–41, 389–94; and Victor H. Li, "The Public Security Bureau and Political-Legal Work in Huiyang, 1952–1964," in Lewis, ed., *The City in Communist China,* pp. 51–74.

blurred the lines of government control and made uniform standards and procedures impossible to maintain. The ad hoc measures of 1950–1952 have not been repeated on a comparable scale, but mass struggle meetings in campaigns have continued the policy of allowing extralegal institutions to bring real or threatened force to bear on political deviants. Red Guard activities, which had generalized support but not direct guidance from Maoist officials, included widespread acts of violence and property confiscation against suspected bourgeois or revisionist elements. During land reform, the objects of mass coercion were clearly identifiable as members of the former exploiting classes, and so there was a natural limit to the targets, if not the level, of violence. In the Cultural Revolution, however, the label of class enemy was much more arbitrary, and mass coercion intended by Mao degenerated into violent factional struggle. The chaos that ensued induced the post-Mao regime to abandon categorically the use of mass coercion.

The sanctions imposed by the rule enforcement apparatus itself can be divided into "administrative" sanctions, with "informal" and "formal" varieties, and "criminal" sanctions.[61] "Informal" sanctions are those imposed by what we have called quasi-legal or extralegal structures. During the land reform in 1950–1952, they included severe penalties up to and including summary execution, but their normal range is varying degrees of criticism by local cadres and peers. The more moderate forms of criticism are constructive and nonthreatening, but the struggle meetings at the other end of the scale may include verbal abuse, physical intimidation, and physical attack. "Administrative" sanctions of a "formal" nature are those imposed by public security organs without recourse to court proceedings. They include warnings, modest fines, and brief detention; "supervised labor," in which the offender remains in society but is subject to special supervision, indoctrination, and stigma; and "labor reeducation" or "rehabilitation," in which the offender is sent to a labor camp for an indefinite period. "Criminal" sanctions are those imposed by the courts, including "labor reform" (sentence

[61] Jerome Alan Cohen, "The Criminal Process in China," in Donald Treadgold, ed., *Soviet and Chinese Communism: Similarities and Differences* (Seattle: University of Washington Press, 1967), pp. 121–23.

to labor for a fixed period, considered a more severe sentence than "labor reeducation"), imprisonment, and death.[62] A unique example of the Chinese dedication to moral reform is the probated death sentence, which allows the condemned criminal two years in which to show internal transformation and then receive a life sentence. Several members of the Gang of Four, including Jiang Qing, Mao's wife, received probated death sentences. However, especially during the 1983 anticrime campaign, the post-Mao regime has been very free with normal death sentences, and the number of those executed ranges well into the thousands.

The extent and effect of these coercive sanctions is difficult to gauge with precision (statistics are not available on such matters), but they have occurred on a scale sufficient to make a deep impression on the population. Those killed during land reform and suppression of counterrevolutionaries campaigns probably numbered in the millions, and virtually all Chinese are familiar with struggle meetings and the various kinds of labor reform that have been the most common sanctions since the reconstruction period. The threat and use of coercion must serve as a significant deterrent to resistance to or violation of state policies. It could not be otherwise for a regime that emerged from a bloody civil war, carried out a radical redistribution of wealth and status, sought to change many traditional social norms, and was to undergo serious internal upheavals in the postrevolutionary period. Opposition and noncompliance was inevitable, as was the impulse to attack it with force. That coercive sanctions were severe and arbitrary in the early years and have remained a ready response to serious deviations, particularly those of a political nature, is not surprising. It is disappointing, however, to see the post-Mao regime increase the severity of formal sanctions, while discontinuing the use of mass coercion. The Cultural Revolution proved that mass coercion was counterproductive for regime stability; it may well be true in a less dramatic fashion that sending large numbers of unemployed youths and dissidents to labor reeducation camps and executing thousands of persons

---

[62]On Chinese labor camps, see Martin King Whyte, "Corrective Labor Camps in China," *Asian Survey*, vol. 13, no. 3 (March 1973): 253–69; and one inmate's story in Bao Ruo-wang (Jean Pasqualina) and Rudolph Chelminski, *Prisoner of Mao* (New York: Penguin, 1976).

is detrimental to modernization or, at least, to a "high level of socialist spiritual civilization."

Nonetheless, coercion is not the primary mechanism of social control in the PRC. There is no single mechanism that dominates the rule enforcement process, but there is a general approach that casts its influence over the entire process. Simply put, it is the view that citizens should be led to a voluntary acceptance of the system's goals and norms, that they should enforce them through their own actions, and that deviations should be corrected through education rather than punishment.[63] The ideal of voluntarism is not attained in practice, hence the need for the coercive appratus. Still, the ideal is operative even within that appratus. Trials seem to be valued more for their educational impact on the public than their punitive effect on the offender, and those on whom sanctions are imposed (whether "administratively" or "criminally") are told that the objective is reeducation rather than punishment. Without denying the harsh realities of labor reform, which is a form of penal servitude, we should note that the regime does try to realize reform as well as labor in its administration of this sanction. Voluntarism manifests itself most concretely, however, in forms of social control that encourage citizens to avoid offenses in the first instance and to develop cooperative orientations toward compliance with governmental rules.

EXTERNAL INFLUENCES ON THE PROCESS

One of the most striking changes brought about by the Chinese revolution is an altered relationship between state and society. The imperial political system, with its orientation toward maintenance of the status quo, accepted a certain isolation from society. It exchanged some of its capacity to mobilize the population in return for a high degree of autonomy from societal influences. The Communist system extends its influence and initiative to the mass level, magnifying greatly its capacity to mobilize social resources. In doing so, it opens the political process to diverse societal pressures and demands that intrude constantly on the calculations of political elites. The welfare and

---

[63]See Ezra F. Vogel, "Voluntarism and Social Control," in Treadgold, ed., *Soviet and Chinese Communism*, pp. 168–84.

morale of the population, the structure and leadership qualities of primary social units, the willingness of the population to comply with national programs, the distribution of resources among different regions and population groups all constitute restraints as well as opportunities within the political process. In expanding the scope of governmental competence, the CCP also has expanded the range of societal influences that it must somehow accommodate. This point has, of course, been the subject of recurring analysis throughout our study.

A somewhat analogous change, which has not yet been discussed directly, has occurred in the system's external relations. Although foreign policy and relations fall outside the scope of this volume, a few observations on the impact of the external environment are in order. We begin with a brief review of changes in China's international role.

Changes in China's International Role. The PRC's early history was marked by a limited role in international affairs. The imperial political system—at least in Qing times—had been relatively aloof from the non-Asian world, preserving in its foreign relations a degree of autonomy and self-sufficiency that more than matched its internal autonomy. There was little tradition of active participation in a system of nation-states. Western and, later, Japanese imperialism shattered China's isolationism, forcing late Qing and republican statesmen to enter into extensive contact and negotiation with representatives of foreign governments. China began to develop a foreign policy apparatus and to engage in a variety of international activities. However, the formalities of this shift were misleading, simply because China's foreign policy focused largely on internal problems. China's international role was that of a subject country whose demands on other countries dealt primarily with the power and privileges that those countries exercised within China. What its role might be after attainment of national independence and unification was an open question.

The CCP was in no position to reverse this role dramatically when it first came to power. Its own experience with other systems rested largely on its relationships with the Nationalists, Japanese, and Russians. Its immediate concerns were predominantly domestic, for obvious reasons, and it faced a Western world already caught up in cold war hostility to Communism. The PRC's intervention in the Korean War sealed an American policy of containment and isolation, which, for two decades, placed American power behind efforts to restrict China's international role. For a few years after 1949, therefore, China's foreign contacts were mainly with other Communist systems.

In the mid-1950s, under the guidance of Zhou Enlai's "peaceful coexistence" policy, the PRC began to diversify its contacts with non-Communist countries, especially in Asia. Still, its foreign relations remained skewed toward the socialist bloc until the Sino-Soviet dispute initiated a fundamental shift, the evolution and consequences of which were to dominate PRC foreign policy (and to some extent domestic policy) throughout the 1960s and 1970s. China's adaptation to the schism was extraordinarily tortuous, but it can be divided into two general phases.

The first phase of the 1960s rested on strong opposition to both the United States and the USSR. In taking this stance, which placed it outside the two great global alliance systems, the PRC necessarily assumed a somewhat isolationist role. The Cultural Revolution reinforced this tendency by radical questioning of the foreign ministry—bringing the temporary recall of most PRC ambassadors at one point—and by creating a number of provocative incidents at home and abroad that strained bilateral relations with a number of countries. The effect was to exaggerate images of China as an outlaw country, intent on isolationist self-reliance. In fact, Mao's strategy was not isolationist at all, but rather a search for new allies to bolster China's exceedingly hazardous position as the world's only serious enemy of both nuclear superpowers.

The search began with an effort to win over the socialist bloc, an effort that split the bloc but failed to create significant support for China. Among Communist states, only Albania became a real ally, the others remained tied to the USSR or, as in the case of North Korea and North Vietnam, maintained a shifting middle ground between the two rivals. Many pro-Chinese splinter groups formed in left-wing parties not in power, but again the results were mixed and gave the Chinese little real leverage. The PRC could not compete successfully with the Soviet Union for leadership of the world Communist parties.

Increasingly, then, Chinese opposition to the superpowers turned to the larger Third World arena. Portraying itself as the champion of resistance to colonialism and neocolonialism, and particularly of Third World liberation movements, the PRC adopted a militant posture on global revolution and channeled limited political and military aid to selected liberation movements. The combination of aid and rhetorical support, plus China's credentials as a Third World country, gave this strategy some substance; however, as the 1960s wore on, Vietnam became its key testing ground. As that conflict escalated and then moved toward North Vietnamese victory, the Chinese realized that American imperialism was in decline and therefore a lesser threat than was the Soviet Union, whose border clashes with China in 1969 had raised the spector of a Sino-Soviet war, and that even in a country as close to China as Vietnam, the Russians could supply more material aid than could the PRC. The prospect of Soviet influence moving into Southeast Asia underscored China's fundamental military and economic weakness relative to the superpowers, a weakness that no amount of revolutionary rhetoric or Third World sympathy could counteract. In short, the strategy of the 1960s was an inadequate answer to the Soviet threat, and its anti-American rationale was dissipating as the United States absorbed its own bitter lessons from Vietnam and began to reconsider its long-standing containment policy.

With the 1970s, therefore, a new Chinese strategy took shape, one of building a global united front against Russian "social imperialism" with heavy reliance on cooperation with capitalist countries and a muting—although not an abandonment—of emphasis on world revolution. The crucial political event initiating the new phase was Sino-American rapprochement, signaled in July 1971 by Henry Kissinger's secret visit to Peking; followed by PRC admission to the United Nations later in the year, with tacit American support; and confirmed in February 1972 by Nixon's visit and the signing of the Shanghai Communiqué that opened the way for greatly improved relations between the two countries. Accompanying the breakthrough in United States-China relations was a sharp increase in diplomatic contacts with other countries, with the November 1972 normalization of Sino-Japanese relations perhaps the most significant development, and the beginnings of a marked expansion of foreign trade. Post-1976 policies accelerated China's economic ties with capitalist countries and made more explicit the desire to rally Western Europe, Japan, and the United States in common opposition to the Soviet Union. While China's relationship with these countries fell far short of a formal united front, resting largely on bilateral economic and cultural exchange, the Chinese openly advocated a strong anti-Soviet military posture for capitalist countries and were obviously deriving military benefits from their high-technology trade with them. Since 1979, China has continued to develop political and economic ties to the West, but the emphasis on a united front against the Soviet Union has diminished. The Vietnamese invasion of Cambodia in 1978 and the Soviet invasion of Afghanistan in 1979 continue to justify Chinese hostility toward the Soviet Union, although in 1979 the Chinese ceased calling the Soviets "revisionists" and seemed to be moving toward better relations until the invasion of Afghanistan. There were considerable increases in trade and diplomatic contacts with the Soviet Union and Eastern Europe in 1984. Possibly as a result of disenchantment with the United States over the Taiwan Relations Act (1979) and the pro-Taiwan posture of the Reagan presidential campaign in 1980, the Chinese seem to be moving toward open but autonomous relations with both cold war camps—a development that has occurred alongside a continual expansion of contacts with the West.

This brief survey underscores two major changes in the PRC's international role. The first has been in international alignments, with the PRC moving from reliance on the Sino-Soviet alliance in the 1950s (an alliance resting on mutual opposition to the United States as the primary enemy), to a united front strategy against the Soviet Union in the 1970s (involving close economic relations—and some shared military-security concerns—with Japan, Western Europe, and the United States), and finally to a more neutral position. In the middle of this great reversal was a period of militant self-reliance and championship of Third World liberation movements, which represented the Maoist response to China's precarious position between the superpowers. Yet the 1960s appear in retrospect as a transitional period in which economic movement toward the capitalist world was already underway. Whereas China's trade during the 1950s was mainly with Communist countries, especially the USSR, non-Communist countries moved into the lead as early as 1963 and increased their share steadily thereafter (see Appendix D). Japan became China's leading trade partner in 1965 and has held that position ever since; in 1966 the PRC's other leading partners, in order after Japan, were Hong Kong, the USSR, West Germany, Canada, the United Kingdom, and France.[64] Although the most significant growth in trade began about 1972 (still well before Mao's death), the shift toward trade with capitalist countries occurred much earlier. The direction of trade remains overwhelmingly Western-oriented in the post-Mao period, and, more importantly, the role of trade in China's economic development has taken a qualitative leap.

The second change has been increasing involvement in the international system. The PRC was never truly isolated, securing diplomatic recognition from many European and Asian states—as well as all Communist states—soon after 1949. It maintained modest economic and cultural relations with a variety of countries around the world throughout its first two decades. Nonetheless, Chinese and American policies combined to limit the PRC's international contacts. As late as July 1971, the PRC held diplomatic recognition from only 54 countries, compared to 63 for the Republic of China (ROC) on Taiwan. Then the situation changed dramatically. By 1979, recognition had shifted to 118 for the PRC and 21 for the ROC; in 1984, the PRC had diplomatic relations with 129 countries. China's foreign trade increased sharply from $6.3 billion (U.S. dollars) in 1972 to $44 billion in 1982 (see Appendix D). After its 1971 entrance to the United Nations, the PRC steadily expanded its participation in UN activities and other international meetings. Post-1976 policies led not only to accelerated growth of foreign trade, but also to increased tourism and cultural exchange, a Sino-Japanese peace treaty in 1978 that brought the two countries into a very close relationship, and extensive negotiations concerning capitalist investment in and loans to China. The diplomatic offensive of the 1970s culminated in normalization of diplomatic relations

---

[64]Nai-ruenn Chen, "China's Foreign Trade, 1950–1974," in U.S. Congress, Joint Economic Committee, *China: A Reassessment of the Economy* (Washington, D.C.: Government Printing Office, 1975), pp. 648–50.

between the United States and the PRC in January 1979. In turn, normalization has ushered in a new era of international openness that would have been unimaginable twenty or even ten years earlier.

National Security and Economic Development. These changing international roles reflect enduring problems of national security and economic development that have exerted a strong influence on domestic politics. Decades of foreign penetration and economic distress had given China's elite a sense of urgency about issues of security and development. This urgency intensified in the post-1949 international environment. Within its first year, the PRC became involved in the Korean War, which was fought close to its borders and threatened attacks on China itself. From then on, it faced an arc of American military power deployed around its eastern and southern perimeter and avowedly maintained to contain and isolate it; the threat of nuclear attack was explicit. The United States supported and defended the rival Nationalist government on Taiwan, which declared its intent to reconquer the mainland. While the PRC had little fear of the Nationalist government as such, its existence perpetuated the civil war and the possibility of military action that might attract American participation. In the 1960s, Vietnam raised the specter of another Korea-type confrontation with the United States, while the Sino-Soviet conflict created new military tension, again including nuclear threats, on the northern border. American pressure finally eased in the 1970s, but the Russians, with their pronounced military and technological superiority and their new influence in Southeast Asia, loomed as a closer and possibly less predictable adversary than the United States had been.

For much of PRC history, security concerns justified and reinforced the Maoist approach. They supported PLA political influence, the value of military virtues, and the idea of militia service for large portions of the population. They encouraged new applications of CCP historical experience with decentralized administration and dispersed production facilities. Especially during the Maoist period, when China confronted both superpowers, they buttressed the emphasis on self-sufficiency and self-reliance. Military encirclement, foreign intelligence activities, and the nearby presence of the ROC lent urgency to mobilization campaigns, intensified the secretive and coercive side of CCP rule, and heightened the tendency to view political opposition as "national betrayal" or "antagonistic contradiction." Perceptions of a hostile international environment helped to legitimize the ethic of austerity, sacrifice, and service for the national cause. In short, Maoism, as practiced in 1958–1976, had strong support from and roots in the "war preparedness" themes of those years.

China's international position also placed sharp limits on its foreign policy options, reserving major commitments for border issues that were, from a Chinese point of view, inseparably linked to domestic affairs and internal security. PRC military ventures since 1949 have included the conquest of Tibet in 1950; the Korean intervention; intermittent hostilities in the Taiwan Straits in the 1950s; brief border wars or skirmishes with India and the Soviet Union; military and construction aid to Vietnam throughout that long war, followed by a brief war on the Sino-Vietnamese border in 1979 and intermittent skirmishes; and the occupation of the Paracel—*Xisha* (Hsisha)—Islands in the South China Sea in 1974. Without accepting the Chinese version of these disputes, it is evident that the PRC has reserved its military risk taking for issues that involved what its leaders perceived to be Chinese territory and to which they had at least some historical claim or to efforts to keep hostile powers away from sensitive border areas.[65]

This is not to minimize the PRC's other international involvements, which have included military and economic aid to a number of Communist states and other Third World countries and, of course, a program of political support and some military aid to Third World liberation movements.[66] These efforts have

[65] For contrasting analyses of these events and the general context of China's foreign relations, see A. Doak Barnett, *China and the Major Powers in East Asia* (Washington, D.C.: Brookings, 1977); John Gittings, *The World and China, 1922–1972* (New York: Harper and Row, 1974); and Harold C. Hinton, *China's Turbulent Quest*, rev. ed. (New York: Macmillan, 1972). The Chinese invasion of Vietnam in February 1979 may challenge this generalization, since the PRC defined its action, in part, as "punishment" for the Vietnamese invasion of Cambodia. Nonetheless, some border territory was in dispute, and Peking's underlying concern was probably intensifying Soviet pressure on its southern flank through the medium of a Soviet-Vietnamese alliance.

[66] See Peter Van Ness, *Revolution and Chinese Foreign Policy: Peking's Support for Wars of National Liberation* (Berkeley: University of California Press, 1970); and Carol H. Fogarty, "China's Economic Relations with the Third World," in *China: A Reassessment of the Economy*, pp. 730–37.

been modest compared to those of the United States and the USSR, and have not taken a large share of Chinese resources; however, for a country with extraordinary economic needs of its own, they have represented a significant commitment. Yet they have been chosen with great care to minimize risks and maximize publicity, have ranked below frontier and territorial issues in priority, and have frequently involved more rhetoric than substance. The primary commitments of Chinese leaders, including Mao, have been to the security of the Chinese revolution rather than to world proletarian revolution, and many of their actions in alleged support of the latter have been designed to preserve the former.[67] The PRC's dealings with countries such as Pakistan and Iran, its opposition to almost every pro-Soviet movement or government from 1960 to 1980, and its growing cooperation with capitalist countries all reflect the heavy influence of security considerations on the Chinese policy line.

The external environment has its greatest domestic impact on economic development policies and the competition for scarce resources. Although the Chinese military establishment has been relatively lowcost—due to its technological backwardness and its self-supporting or productive economic roles—it has still claimed 5–10 percent of the GNP.[68] The development of nuclear capabilities, which the PRC undertook on its own after the rupture with the Soviet Union, has been a serious strain on national economic and technological resources. Yet direct military costs are only the most obvious indicator of international pressures on development priorities.

In 1949, the CCP faced a fundamental dilemma: long-term economic development, national security, and restoration of international power all required a program of rapid industrialization, but the base economy was too weak to generate easily the investment capital necessary for it. There were three possible responses to this dilemma. One was gradualism, to compromise on the goal of rapid development; historical, ideological, and security considerations opposed this option, which in fact has never had significant support in the PRC—fantasies about Mao's

[67]John Gittings, "The Statesman," in Dick Wilson, ed., *Mao Tse-tung in the Scales of History* (Cambridge: Cambridge University Press, 1977), pp. 246–71.
[68]See National Foreign Assessment Center, *Chinese Defense Spending, 1965–1979* (Central Intelligence Agency, July 1980), p. 2.

"anti-modernism" notwithstanding. A second was full-scale Stalinism, a forced-march industrialization based on coercive extractions, especially from the rural sector; although Chinese development has had elements of this approach, the lower margin of surplus in China—as compared to postrevolutionary Russia— and the CCP's stronger commitment to popular livelihood made it unacceptable. The third was to seek foreign capital and technical assistance to get industrialization underway; this was the course chosen, with the USSR the only logical provider in the cold war era. From the outset, then, as seen in the FFYP, PRC development strategy reflected strong external influences. Generally, the plan worked to get industrialization started, although the PRC had to make major concessions to the Russians to obtain their aid.[69] It also revealed the dangers of dependence on a single foreign power, especially one whose national interests increasingly diverged from those of China.

The Sino-Soviet conflict forced the Chinese to choose again, this time under even greater constraints since there were no realistic foreign sources of aid and since Mao had become highly suspicious of the Soviet model as a whole. The Maoist self-reliance extolled during 1958–1976 was an effort to continue rapid industrialization and simultaneously to strengthen the rural sector, in both production and provision of social services, by relying on fuller mobilization of domestic resources. It succeeded in maintaining strong industrial growth rates, in keeping agricultural growth abreast of population growth and in raising popular living standards. Yet it, too, had to adapt to international realities in two important respects. Self-reliance was qualified from the first by increasing trade with capitalist countries for grain and industrial equipment imports, which in turn required maintenance of export markets, especially those in Hong Kong, Singapore, and other areas of Southeast Asia. Foreign trade remained low as a percentage of GNP, but its substance was crucial to China's development, and it forced the PRC to moderate, or compromise, some of its professed principles in order to get what it needed from the global economy.

---

[69]For a cost-benefit analysis of Sino-Soviet economic relations in the 1950s, see Alexander Eckstein, *Communist China's Economic Growth and Foreign Trade* (New York: McGraw-Hill, 1966), esp. chap. 5.

The other and ultimately decisive liability of the Maoist approach was that it retarded technological development, preventing a breakthrough in agriculture and compromising long-term defense and security prospects. It is, of course, an open question as to whether this was really a consequence of Maoist development or of the factional difficulties that beset it. On this question, as on all issues discussed in this section, domestic politics interacted with external pressures in ways that obscure simple cause-and-effect relationships. What is clear is that some CCP elites realized that China was losing ground to the advanced countries—most importantly the Soviet Union—and that something like the four modernizations approach, with emphasis on science and technology, was essential if China were ever to secure its place as a major world power. Mao apparently shared some of these convictions, as seen in his doubts about Cultural Revolution extremism and his desire to improve relations with the United States and other capitalist countries, but he was too closely identified with the earlier pattern to permit its reversal.

It is not an exaggeration to say that a new era in Chinese international economic policy began in 1978. Policies have been abandoned or modified that hitherto had been considered basic to Chinese policy. In every respect, China is more open to Western contact, influence, and investment than at any previous time in PRC history. Moreover, every year since 1978 has seen the adoption of progressively more open policies. Foreign involvement in the economy has moved from the purchase of whole plants in the early 1970s to joint ventures (1978), special economic zones (1980), designated cities authorized to deal directly in international economic concerns (1983), selling bonds on the Tokyo bond market (1984), and the hiring of foreign management personnel by Chinese firms (1985). Credit financing and even international aid have been accepted as legitimate. There have been few hesitations in the onward march of liberalizing policies, and they have been facilitated by corresponding administrative and legal changes. Perhaps most importantly, a patent law, which protects transfers of technology, went into effect in April 1985. The full import of the new "open door" on the Chinese economy, politics, and society will be known only with time, but it certainly is a far-reaching initiative to which Deng, Hu, and Zhao have irrevocably committed themselves.

The changes in China's international economic policy since the death of Mao have been so spectacular that it is worthwhile to reflect on its continuities with previous policies. First, it should be remembered that the diplomatic prerequisite of stable economic relations is political normalization. The process of normalization with the United States and its allies began under Mao in 1971; it was an option that was not really available to China in the 1950s and 1960s. Second, the 1980s are not the first time that China has adopted a path to modernization that depends on external inputs. Soviet advice and assistance played a major role in modernization in the 1950s, and later Chinese emphasis on self-sufficiency can be explained in part as an adjustment to the unavailability of such aid. Third, China will inevitably remain an internally oriented nation. Size of population, sufficiency of major resources, and a strongly Sino-centric culture dictate that domestic politics generally will have a greater reality and saliency than foreign politics. The current "open door" is tied to a strong, popular leadership and to domestic policies that have been very successful, but observers of Chinese foreign policy would be well advised to keep in mind the domestic context of policy and policy makers.

CONCLUSION

The description of Chinese political processes in the last two chapters shows some of the strengths and weaknesses of the input/output model described at the beginning of Chapter 6. On the one hand, Chinese politics can be meaningfully analyzed in these terms. We have described activities and institutional arrangements approximating interest articulation and aggregation and also have described changes in Chinese policy that have affected the volume and content of political input. It is much easier to describe the output side of Chinese politics, although the role of the mass line and decentralization imply concrete limits on the ability of government simply to execute its will. On the other hand, the analytical distinction between input and output has cut across the major institutions and processes of Chinese politics. The principles of mass line and party leadership have featured prominently in both input and output functions, and the distinction has led to a rather artificial division between conflict within the CCP and its decision-making functions.

Even institutions that are essentially on the input side (e.g., mass organizations) have been found also to have output functions of policy propagandizing; and the quintessential output institution, the administration of law, contains important aspects of mass participation.

It should be recalled that input and output functions are not fully separate in Western politics. Bureaucracies often formulate policy, and legislators become involved in the executive process. However, the analytical distinction does correspond to a major institutional cleavage in parliamentary regimes between legislative and executive institutions or between policy-forming and policy-implementing processes. The division has its origin in the early Middle Ages and has been nearly universal in the West since the French Revolution. In China, for a variety of reasons, the institutional cleavage does not exist. There is no tradition of such a distinction in imperial China, and the distinction has been rejected in Marxist-Leninist theory ever since Marx praised the Paris Commune for unifying executive and legislative functions in 1871. It may well be argued that China is being analyzed and, to some extent, judged by alien criteria. To examine China from the perspective of parliamentary regimes necessarily produces some distortions.

It is therefore worthwhile to consider briefly the advantages and disadvantages of other, non-Western approaches to Chinese politics. Two such approaches are especially inviting: first, the PRC as part of the tradition of Chinese government; and second, the PRC as a Marxist-Leninist regime.

The first approach would have the advantage of highlighting continuities in Chinese behavior and culture. The imperial aspects of the rule of Mao Zedong and Deng Xiaoping, the rather limited role of law and formal procedures, and the importance of personal access and connections have not been absent from our discussion, but they would be central to this alternative approach. Such an approach would probably be truer to the ambiance of Chinese politics at the personal level. However, the discontinuities of imperial and PRC politics are as important as their continuities, and these would tend to be slighted in an approach based on Chinese tradition. Behavior within the party may well have traditional overtones, but the party as an institution, the content of policy since 1949, and the strength and pervasiveness of politics are all radically new.

A second alternative approach would be to view the PRC from the perspective of comparative Communism. This approach has much to recommend it, primarily because the politics and government of the PRC have been explicitly modeled on the Soviet Union. For example, it would certainly be easier to understand the role of the people's congress system in terms of the system of soviets in the Soviet Union than in terms of legislatures in the West. The role of the party, the centralization of political and economic power, and the ideology of class struggle are perhaps best understood in their relationship to similar phenomena in other Communist countries. The problem with this approach is a subtle but very important one; namely, the actual role of Communist institutions and ideology in China has been determined by the experience of the Chinese themselves. Chinese politics appears more similar to Soviet politics than it actually is. This fact has contributed to consistent misinterpretations of Chinese politics by the Soviet Union, and vice versa. The success of Mao Zedong was an enigma to Stalin, and to some extent Sino-Soviet hostility has been based on misunderstandings concealed or exacerbated by a common ideological heritage.

A particularly interesting question from the comparative Communist perspective would be the orthodoxy of current reforms. The somewhat naïve claim that China is giving up on Communism and turning toward capitalism can be clarified by observing that, in some respects, China is simply catching up with European Communist reforms of the 1960s. In other respects, however, China has jumped to the lead in the reform of Communist political economies and presents a considerable ideological challenge to the others.[70] This challenge consists not of the abandonment of party hegemony and public ownership of the means of production, but of demonstrating the flexibility possible within a Communist system. In this respect, China should be a

---

[70]It is very interesting in this regard to compare the well-known economic historian Alec Nove's criticisms of Communist economics to the reforms currently being adopted in China. See his *Feasible Socialism* (London: Allen & Unwin, 1983).

lesson to both Eastern and Western observers, who are both overly burdened with the Stalinist stereotype.

The point of the preceding discussion has been to clarify for the reader the limits of our analysis by reviewing the strengths and weaknesses of alternative approaches. The advantage of the Western approach is that it is more familiar to most readers and that it highlights those aspects of Chinese politics that are shared by other modern governments, regardless of political system. This may be an especially advantageous approach for the appreciation of post-Mao reforms because of the boldness of the regime in pursuing modernization.

CHAPTER VIII

From Maoism to Modernization: Socialism With Chinese Characteristics

---

THE DEATH OF MAO ZEDONG was a turning point in Chinese politics, marking the end of the revolutionary era and initiating a transition to a new modernization model. By the end of 1984, that new model was in place as the guiding spirit of Deng Xiaoping's reforms. "Socialism with Chinese characteristics" remained an elusive phrase that often came across as defensive insistence that China had not abandoned socialism, yet it also suggested a growing confidence that the PRC had carved out a different developmental path that deserved a different label.

The particulars of the modernization model and the process by which it evolved have been discussed in detail. In concluding, we will raise some larger questions that surround the passing of China's revolutionary era. One set of questions deals with the fate of the Maoist model. Has it been decisively rejected in favor of a different model? What continuities or precedents link the two models and periods? And is the Maoist model still of any interest, or can it be discarded as an outdated set of policies or principles? A second set of questions concerns assessment of China's revolutionary era. If it is really over, can we now tally its successes and failures, or produce a balance sheet of its accomplishments? Finally, what issues are emerging in the 1980s that demand attention from the student of Chinese politics, either because they threaten the stability of the present course or because they suggest consequences that may follow its continuation? Although there are no definitive answers to such broad questions, it is important to consider their significance and some of the ways they might be answered.

THE FATE OF THE MAOIST MODEL

Socialism with Chinese Characteristics. By the mid-1980s, "building socialism with Chinese characteristics" was a primary theme in definitions of the CCP's task, displacing—although not eliminating—the "readjustment" emphasis of the early 1980s and the "four modernizations" slogan of the late 1970s. If CCP history is a guide, this theme will yield in a few years to a new slogan deemed more appropriate for its time. Socialism with Chinese characteristics is nonetheless an extremely important political symbol, one whose significance far exceeds its predictably short life span as a slogan or the first vague Chinese efforts to specify its content. It is a symbol of China's separation from its recent past and of its future hopes. Reserving questions about the future for later discussion, let us examine what the symbol suggests about the Maoist past.

There is no doubt that socialism with Chinese characteristics symbolizes a decisive shift from Maoist to modernization models. The stress on socialism reveals the reformers' determination to maintain their ideological legitimacy, which might be taken as evidence of their inability to separate themselves from the Maoist path. Many foreign observers have emphasized the obstacles to reform that seemed to slow its process in the early 1980s and to restrict the extent of actual change in the system.[1] They suggested that a combination of ideological rigidity, bureaucratic inertia, and residual leftism blocked a real breakthrough, so that Deng's legacy might be a failed or half-hearted reform effort, or even might indicate some backsliding toward Maoism. These cautions must be taken seriously as the obstacles are real and powerful. Nonetheless, the reforms have moved ahead, especially with the dramatic decisions of 1984 to expand the opening to foreign

[1] See, for example, Ronald A. Morse, ed., *The Limits of Reform in China* (Boulder, Colo.: Westview, 1983).

economic interests and to relax central bureaucratic controls over the urban and industrial economies. Of course, there may be reversals in the future (that is always a possibility in Chinese politics), but the policies and rhetoric that constitute socialism with Chinese characteristics mark it as a confirmed, significant departure from the Maoist model. The transition is over, with the old model discarded and the new one in place.

At the center of the new order is the idea of "integrating the basic tenets of Marxism with actual conditions in China." Like all such formulations, it permits endless variation in the proper mix of universal tenets and particular conditions. What counts is the political context and understanding of the phrase, which is unmistakable: it is a mandate for sweeping policy changes and redefinition of what socialism in contemporary China entails. The policies are those associated with the modernization model: the shift from ideological to material and market incentives; the dismantling of the commune system with a return to household farming; the expansion of opportunities for entrepreneurial activities; the freeing of some market transactions from bureaucratic controls; the new status and opportunities for intellectuals and professionals; the ever-widening opening to the international system; the ambivalent, modest, but still significant relaxation of dictatorial party controls in legal, academic, and other institutional spheres; and other related policies discussed throughout this book. These policies have overcome initial resistance, weathered a series of critical debates and compromises, and gradually acquired a measure of stability and ideological legitimacy. They are neither secure nor sacrosanct, but they have become the new orthodoxy. Future changes of whatever sort will have to deal with them on their own terms, that is, on the terms that the modernization model has prescribed as appropriate for the times, not on terms prescribed by the Maoist model.

Continuities and Precedents. It is one thing to say that the modernization model differs from Maoism and has freed itself from the unwanted ideological restraints of its predecessor. It is quite another thing to assume it is wholly new. In fact, the modernization model is *not* wholly new, for it displays many continuities with and precedents in the Maoist period. Initially, during Hua's neo-Maoist interlude and for a few years thereafter, these links seemed quite restrictive, even inescapable. They represented policies and principles that party leaders could defy openly only at great political risk. Today, it is different. Deng and his colleagues have made their break with Maoism and have considerable latitude to accept or reject elements of the immediate past depending on their fit with the new orthodoxy. Yet, in making their choices, the current leaders have maintained some strong lines of continuity with Maoism and have drawn heavily for guidance and legitimacy on precedents from earlier periods.

Just as "socialism with Chinese characteristics" symbolizes the break with the Maoist period, so the "four principles" symbolize the link. In emphasizing the CCP's continuing adherence to the socialist road, the people's democratic dictatorship, party leadership, and Marxism-Leninism-Mao Zedong Thought, the reformers have demonstrated their determination to locate themselves in the mainstream of the Communist Revolution, including its Maoist component, and excluding only those aspects of Maoism now regarded as serious errors—still said to be far outweighed by Mao's overall contribution to the revolution. In keeping with this commitment, perhaps the strongest continuity is in the structure of political leadership where senior party elites hold a virtual monopoly of power over a vast bureaucratic machine that effectively determines the general direction of policy throughout the country. Neither party dictatorship nor the bureaucracy is likely to suffer more than modest dimunition of power in any current or contemplated reforms, although there may be significant shifts of power and responsibility within the system. Also continued from the Maoist period are two important qualifications about the system's supposedly monolithic character. One is the factional nature of elite politics, far less virulent now than it was during the Cultural Revolution but still a fact of life, which means that major political debates and decisions are carried out through behind-the-scenes maneuvering among high-level factions. The other is an element of decentralization and particularism that allows flexibility and slippage in central policies through policy modification, noncompliance, and various forms of personal favoritism at lower levels.

A second area of continuity is in the political system's tolerance of internal conflict and opposition. Top elites are very suspicious and erratic in their attitude toward this penomenon, yet the party's history, especially the ramifications of the mass line, has encouraged episodic eruptions of more or less open political conflict. Although the Gang of Four is now characterized as authoritarian or "fascist" in style, the Cultural Revolution included a remarkable outburst of popular participation in higher-level political struggles. No other ruling Communist party has encouraged or experienced such a dramatic opening of elite politics to mass intervention. The democratic reforms of more recent years are quite different in style from the violent struggles and uncontrolled movements of 1966–1976 (although there have been spontaneous popular demonstrations since 1976 as well), but they are still an institutionalized expression of the mass line. We do not know how far the democratic reforms will go or how durable they will be, but they reflect an element in CCP style that is closely associated with Mao's thinking.

Finally, the post-1978 period continues to emphasize Chinese self-reliance, even as it violates the Cultural Revolution meaning of that phrase. At issue here is what "self-reliance" means. For Deng, it does not mean sharp restrictions on international exchanges, as it did during the 1960s; the open foreign policy has reversed that aspect of the concept. But "socialism with Chinese characteristics" is above all an assertion of Chinese independence within the Marxist-Leninist tradition, an insistence that China must follow its own socialist road that integrates Marxism with Chinese conditions. The most prominent advocate of that position was Mao Zedong, of course, in his celebrated "sinification of Marxism" in the 1930s and 1940s.[2] Moreover, Deng advocates Maoist self-reliance in a second sense—the idea that China is an independent power—not dependent on either superpower and not tied to either of their blocs. The two themes join in an image common to both leaders of a strong, independent, socialist China pursuing its own unique developmental model.

These continuities should not be surprising given the composition of the post-Mao leadership. Although many of the current leaders were out of office for some or most of the Cultural Revolution decade, the group as a whole is very much a part of

[2]On the "Sinification of Marxism," see Stuart R. Schram, *The Political Thought of Mao Tse-tung*, rev. and enl. ed. (New York: Praeger, 1969), esp. pp. 110–17.

the post-1949 mainstream Chinese elite. Many worked in close association with Mao for substantial periods of time; others were too junior for that association but administered Maoist policies throughout the Cultural Revolution. Of course, there is great variety in the career paths and degree of closeness to Maoist policies among these people. The point is that the post-1978 leadership is obviously not a revolutionary group or even a sharply distinguished anti-Maoist opposition faction within the broader post-1949 party elite. It is a group that largely opposed or grudgingly accepted Cultural Revolution policies; however, its rise to power was neither a revolt from below nor a coup by counterelites excluded from the ruling organization. It is legitimately called a "reformist" group, one that seeks to correct what it perceives as serious defects in the system but has no interest in overturning the system as a whole.

Given the reformers' roots in the preceding order, one would expect their policies to draw heavily on earlier precedents. This is precisely the case, with many of the policies in question modeled on those of three earlier episodes. The first was 1971–1974, when Zhou Enlai presided over rapprochement with the United States, a rapid expansion of international contacts including trade and capital-intensive imports, and a variety of measures aimed at restoring and developing the economy. These policies provided the foundation for the "four modernizations" slogan that ushered in the post-Mao era. A second fertile source of precedents for reform was the post-Leap retrenchment of the early 1960s, which brought extensive use of material incentives, experiments with household production contracts that foreshadowed the current rural responsibility system, and a number of political debates on themes resurrected after 1976. The third period was the mid-1950s, when the emphasis on modernization, institutionalization, legalization, and expanding international contacts (including substantial Soviet aid and training of tens of thousands of Chinese students and technicians) provided numerous precedents for the recent reforms. If one were to extend this search into the pre-Communist period, there would be further precedents in the early decades of the twentieth century, a time when China learned from abroad by sending large numbers of students to Japan and the West and when the importation of foreign goods, capital, technology, and ideas was advancing rapidly. It is obvious from references in their debates that the reformers are well aware of these pre-1949 precedents, just as they are of the more recent ones. In this light, the current reform is hardly new, although it differs from Cultural Revolution Maoism and contains some novel elements.

Significance of the Maoist Model. What can we conclude about the significance of the Maoist model? That depends on what we mean by "Maoism," which is a complicated, controversial concept. At least five versions can be considered. One refers to the entire body of Mao's writings and actions throughout his career. Another refers to his revolutionary strategy and the extent of its differences from orthodox Marxism-Leninism. A third version (used frequently in this book) concentrates on the theory, concepts, and policy proposals that Mao advanced during what we have called the Maoist period of 1958–1976. A variation of this identifies Maoism with its most radical manifestations during the Cultural Revolution. A final version is the set of principles deduced from various Maoist statements and translated into a logically consistent developmental model that contrasts with more conventional ideas about development.

Most foreign references to the "Maoist model" have followed the last usage, seeing Maoism as a frontal challenge to both capitalist (or Western) and Soviet developmental models. In this view, the Maoist model emphasizes national independence and self-reliance over dependence on foreign aid, trade, and technology; it advances the idea of "walking on two legs"—that is, utilizing indigenous as well as foreign methods, traditional as well as modern methods—to compensate for the abstention from full-scale modernism. It emphasizes all-around development, particularly of the rural sector, over the specialized development of the heavy industrial, urban sector; its image of development is a push from the bottom, raising backward sectors and bringing local forces into play, rather than a pull from the top in which the leading sector forges ahead and benefits trickle down to the rest of society; its test of performance is the elimination of poverty and the wider distribution of social services rather than growth rates and increases in per capita income. It emphasizes mobilization of the population, with campaign attacks on national problems and decentralized encouragement of local initiative over stability of bureaucratic controls and institutions. And it calls for "politics in command" in preference to "planning in command," an insistence that ideological purity and continuing revolution take precedence over technical or purely economic considerations.

The appeal of this version rested on its clear challenge to concepts that dominated global thinking about development for two decades after World War II, but then came under increasing attack. During the 1960s, there was a growing realization among students of development that the gap between advanced and underdeveloped countries was growing, that the passing of colonialism had not ended Third World economic dependence on or subordination to the core capitalist powers, that economic development was lagging in much of the world, and that even substantial gains in GNP and per capita income might conceal increasing impoverishment for large sectors of the population. The burgeoning critique of standard development ideas, with new stress on problems of poverty and dependence and calls for a new international economic order, coincided with the Cultural Revolution and its forceful presentation of the Maoist model. In effect, the critics seized on Maoism as a countermodel of self-reliant, equitable growth and took the Cultural Revolution as evidence that it could be put into practice. Needless to say, post-Mao reforms and criticism of the Cultural Revolution have left this version of Maoism in disarray.

The simplest resolution would be to say that the model failed, that it caused China great damage and that it was rejected by the Chinese, who have now committed themselves enthusiastically to development through interdependence with the capitalist world. The problem with this conclusion is that the Maoist model, as described, was a distorted representation of Mao's ideas and even further removed from the realities of Cultural Revolution China. In other words, this version of the model was not really practiced in China, so there is no way to say if it succeeded or failed. It remains useful as an abstract concept of self-reliant development, which can draw on Chinese experience and Mao's writings for illustrations of how elements in the model might be debated or practiced in a specific case. The most important lesson, however, seems to be that complex issues of national security, bureaucratic power, social conflict, and the like would make it difficult for any state to pursue this pure form of the Maoist model.

The other versions of the model all have empirical reference points in Mao's works or contemporary Chinese history and hence are more appropriate subjects for judgments about significance. The verdict on Cultural Revolution Maoism, the actual practice of policies associated with Mao's name in that turbulent decade, is clear: it was, on balance, a damaging episode that has been condemned by the Chinese leadership and cannot really be viewed as a model at all because it was a product of such disparate and spontaneous political phenomena. It is the first three versions of Maoism that constitute the heart of the issue in searching for its significance. Although the passage of time and the accumulation of new data and scholarship are making possible a fuller appreciation of Mao's career and its historical significance, it is impossible to fully explain here.[3] However, one general observation on the Maoist model of 1958–1976, which has been the primary reference in this study, can be made.

Whether or not the 1958–1976 model was a success or failure depends on one's perspectives and expectations. Despite the disruptions, there was considerable national development in these two decades. Rates of growth were less than in Japan, South Korea, or Taiwan, for example, but higher than in most Third World countries. Growth was strongest in the industrial sector, while the rural standard of living stagnated (note the contrast to the foreign image of the model); yet there were important advances in agricultural production and modernization. Distribution was less egalitarian than many observers claimed; yet Chinese society was relatively egalitarian, extremely so in some respects. In evaluating such issues, of which these are only a small sample, we must ask what the alternatives and trade-offs were. The decisions facing Mao in 1958 were different from those faced by elites elsewhere at the time, or those faced by Deng in 1978. Before establishing the significance of the Maoist model, we must set it in its historical context and ask what problems it addressed. This is still no simple matter, and there is

[3] For a stimulating review of new scholarship and evidence on Mao's career and thought, identifying issues for future research and debate, see Stuart R. Schram, "Mao Studies: Retrospect and Prospect," *The China Quarterly*, no. 97 (March 1984): 95–129.

one aspect of the model's context that demands particular attention.

We suggest that the Maoist model is best viewed as a strategy for sustaining socialist development, while establishing China's economic, political, and strategic independence from the Soviet Union. By the mid-1950s, the PRC was developing rapidly in close association with the USSR. Although not a satellite, as were many of the Eastern European states, it relied heavily on Soviet trade, technology, and strategic protection, and it was subordinate politically to Soviet leadership of the socialist camp. By 1976, China had established full independence from the Soviet Union, had maintained a socialist system with relatively high growth rates, and had developed vastly improved relations with capitalist countries. Severe problems emerged in the course of this transition, which discredited some (not all) features of the model. But what were the alternatives? Should China have kept its semidependent relationship with the USSR, hoping that it would not sacrifice Chinese to Russian interests? Should it have made an abrupt shift to the other side, risking Soviet reprisals or intervention? Should it have attempted something like the modernization model at a time when it had support from *neither* bloc and very few resources of its own to mount a self-reliant rapid modernization drive? Or should it have pushed for self-reliant development that seemed to capitalize on what the CCP regarded as its strengths—which is what Mao thought his model was doing? However one answers such questions, it was in fact the Maoist model that guided China through this transition, and that tells us a great deal about the questions that must be asked in evaluating its significance

ASSESSING THE REVOLUTIONARY ERA

Viewing the Maoist model as a strategy for negotiating the transition from semidependence on the Soviet Union to autonomous growth based on an independent place in the global order leads to a larger set of questions. If abandonment of that model signified transition to international equality as well as the end of the revolutionary era, can we say the revolution has accomplished its mission? To what extent have the revolutionary objectives described in Chapter 2 been attained? This section assesses some accomplishments and shortcomings of CCP efforts to realize national independence and unification, economic and social development, and national integration.

National Independence and Unification. Challenges to the national independence and unification of modern China have taken three forms: foreign influence in Chinese affairs; the removal of Chinese territory from the control of the central government; and the existence within the political system of rival claimants to political authority. At issue here is state building in its most fundamental sense, that is, maintaining unchallenged central control over what is regarded as national territory. Chinese governments from the mid-nineteenth century through the 1940s were unable to accomplish this task. The defeat of Japan and CCP victory in the Civil war of 1946–1949 gave the new Communist government a greater measure of national control than had prevailed for several decades. Nonetheless, a vigorous expansion of its power was required to complete and secure its gains.

The defeat of Japan, postwar weakness of Europe, and American preoccupation with cold war issues facilitated the PRC's eradication of foreign penetration. Only the Soviet Union retained significant influence in Chinese affairs. Its aid program brought Soviet advisers into the Chinese government, established Russian language study and books in Chinese schools, and created a substantial Chinese debt to and economic dependence on the Soviet Union. The PRC also granted the Russians special privileges in Manchuria and Xinjiang (Sinkiang) that bore strong similarities to the foreign concessions extracted from China in earlier decades. However, the privileges were relinquished in the mid-1950s, aid ended in 1960, and the debt was repaid a few years later. There was a strong revival of foreign contacts in the late 1970s, with a resumption of foreign economic activity in and loans to China, but these contacts were diversified among a large number of countries, none likely to match earlier Soviet influence. The PRC entered into these relationships on its own terms, with much greater resources than in the past for resisting foreign pressure. As emphasized in our discussion of the Maoist model, the goal of independence has been fully attained.

The unification of national territory has proved to be a more enduring problem. The new central government quickly incorporated all significant areas of the mainland, occupying Tibet and erasing the last serious KMT resistance by the end of 1950. Territorial issues remained, however, in border areas, foreign colonies, and islands off the China coast. The key border disputes were with India and the USSR, and more recently with Vietnam. All involved armed clashes, demonstrating their seriousness in terms of PRC national security, but the areas in question are not integral to China's sense of national identity and unity. The two remaining colonies are Portuguese Macao and British Hong Kong, both being small areas that were part of Guangdong province before their seizure in the sixteenth (Macao) and mid-nineteenth (Hong Kong) centuries. Macao has been under de facto Chinese control since 1967, and a 1984 Sino-British Joint Declaration specifies that Hong Kong will revert to Chinese sovereignty in 1997, while maintaining for fifty years after that date its current economic and social system and autonomous status within the PRC as a Special Administrative Region—this being a special provision of the 1982 constitution designed expressly to allow the reincorporation of Hong Kong and Tai-wan.[4] Many questions remain about the implementation of this agreement. Some observers doubt that Hong Kong will be able to maintain its present character, including its international role as a free port and commercial/financial center, once it passes under PRC sovereignty. Nonetheless, the Joint Declaration appears to resolve the unification issue from the PRC point of view. The island claims are groups in the East and South China Seas, with many countries of the region advancing competing claims. Like the border issues, these claims carry the potential for international conflict and should not be taken lightly—possible oil reserves and control of shipping lanes make the islands very important—but their removal from PRC control is not really a problem of territorial unity.

The major problem, of course, is Taiwan. In one sense, Taiwan, too, is peripheral to the territorial integrity of China. The island has never been well integrated into the mainland system, despite formal administrative ties before the Japanese annexation of 1895 and during a brief period of rule from Nanjing (Nanking)

---

[4]For text of the agreement and supporting documents, see "Sino-British Joint Declaration on the Question of Hong Kong," *BR*, vol. 27, no. 40 (October 1, 1984), supplement: I–XX.

during 1945–1949; there is no loss of established relationships in its separation from the mainland. However, that perspective overlooks the multiple political considerations that make Taiwan the last major obstacle to complete national unification. Both governments regard the island as Chinese territory and reject the possibility of an independent Taiwan. The population, save for a few aborigines, is wholly Chinese ethnically, culturally, and linguistically. The Taiwanese, who constitute around 80 percent of the total population (about 19 million in 1984), are Chinese who emigrated from the southeastern provinces of the mainland over the past three centuries. Although distinct as a social group from the mainlanders who came to Taiwan with the Nationalist government in the postwar period, they are no less Chinese than those mainlanders or other distinctive groups among the Han Chinese under PRC control. Moreover, Taiwan received international recognition as Chinese territory during World War II and probably would have fallen to a Communist invasion in the early 1950s had not American intervention prevented the attempt.

Taiwan's role as an obstacle to unification is heightened by the Nationalists' claim to be the government of China. This is not simply a case of national territory removed from central control but a direct challenge as well to the PRC's authority over the mainland. In recent years, the PRC has mounted a persistent diplomatic campaign, with occasional veiled threats, to persuade the Republic of China on Taiwan to give up its claims to be the government of China and accept Peking's sovereignty, in return for autonomous status much like that now offered Hong Kong. Although PRC offers have specified greater autonomy for Taiwan than for Hong Kong under this "one country, two systems" formula, including maintenance of internal security forces and some de facto foreign relations under Taipei's control, the authorities on Taiwan have consistently rejected the offer and refused to negotiate. At present, there are essentially no incentives for Taiwan to accept mainland offers, whereas powerful incentives exist for the PRC to avoid damaging its open foreign policy by resorting to force. Hence there is no immediate prospect of resolving this last major barrier to China's unification. Taiwan's unusual political status is not easily maintained, however, so there is some possibility that internal political changes in the future might encourage a different response to mainland overtures. Moreover, reunification has been designated as one of the PRC's three major tasks for the 1980s, so the Taiwan question might grow in urgency as the decade progresses.

There have been other internal threats to national unity since 1949, but none has produced a rival claimant for political authority. The most serious of the scattered, localized uprisings that have occurred in the PRC was the Tibetan Revolt of 1959, which was crushed promptly and thoroughly—although there was some guerrilla-type resistance both before and after 1959. The Tibetan rebels, like their counterparts in a few other minority areas, offered no challenge at all to the existence of the national government. Their maximum hope—futile at that—was to secure greater autonomy from Peking within their areas. The Cultural Revolution raised the specter of civil war and a revival of warlordism, but none of the competing groups offered itself as an alternative to or sought separation from the central government.

The PRC's creation and maintenance of national independence and unity marks a crucial developmental step for modern China. It is easy to take this step for granted, but one has only to consider the number of governments that have not made it or have had to retrace it to realize its significance. The Communist government's ability to establish its control over the full territorial extent of mainland China was direct evidence of capabilities that its predecessors had not possessed. Once in control of a unified and independent country, it gained access to resources denied to previous governments and could devote a much larger proportion of these resources to constructive purposes. In other words, attainment of this goal not only transformed China's international status but also established a better foundation for progress toward other revolutionary objectives.

Economic and Social Development. Details of PRC economic and social development have been analyzed at several points in the text and are summarized in the appendices. What follows is a general assessment, coupled with a few reflections on the political correlates of this development. PRC socioeconomic development has been erratic but cumulatively impressive, establishing one of the better records among Third World countries. The primary beneficiary has been the state, which has strengthened greatly its internal power and international status. In keeping with state interests, development has been most rapid in heavy industry, military and space technology, and the infrastructure serving these sectors. Agriculture and light industry have also advanced, although much less impressively than heavy industry in the three decades prior to 1978. Before that date, gains in agricultural production were only slightly ahead of population growth, whereas light industrial development fell far short of satisfying consumer needs or rapid export expansion. There were some gains in living standards, primarily in the cities where state subsidies kept housing, food, and transportation costs quite low. Rural areas paid the bill for state extraction, which largely served urbanites and the state itself, with little increase in rural income after the mid-1950s. The economic crisis that followed the Great Leap brought extreme hardship and some famine to the countryside; other campaigns or natural disasters caused more localized difficulties. Since 1978, the rural responsibility system has brought dramatic increases in rural income. Production and availability of consumer goods has also expanded significantly in the same period, so the population has finally begun to claim a greater share of the growing national product.

The social change that has accompanied economic development has mixed ramifications. To some extent, it has compensated for the imbalance in economic distribution by expanded delivery of social services, principally education and health care. There are many shortcomings in these services; however, for the country as a whole, they are greatly improved over 1949 and very impressive for a country with limited resources. Revolutionary movements to equalize social status, to expropriate concentrated wealth, and to establish minimal income and services for the dispossessed have provided social opportunity and psychic gains for the poor, women, youth, and some minorities, while reducing the gap between the very rich and the very poor. Even though the social revolution has fallen short of its goals with respect to all these population groups, it has brought some improvements in their social status. On the other hand, policies and campaigns associated with the social revolution have had severe consequences for many Chinese citizens, particularly those identified as its enemies. New forms of stratification have emerged, leaving the bulk of the population in a distinctly lower-class status. In any case, the harsh realities of economics have made it impossible to provide equal economic benefits and social opportunities for different strata and regions.

The overall picture is thus a complicated one. If one compares the Chinese socioeconomic revolution with the development of other revolutionary and nonrevolutionary systems and includes the consumer gains of the post-Mao period, the Chinese record looks comparatively good. However, this is a detached judgment that ignores the political correlates of the revolution, which emerge more clearly if two questions are posed. One such question is: are the people, or different social groups, satisfied with the changes the socioeconomic revolution has brought them? A reasonable generalization might be that the public acknowledges substantial socioeconomic progress but believes it could have been stronger, fairer, or freer. In fact, whenever there has been an opening in Chinese public life for expression of grievances—in the mid-1950s, the early 1960s, 1966–1967 (and episodically throughout the Cultural Revolution decade), 1978–1979, and to a lesser extent to the present—various groups have made known their displeasure with some aspects of PRC development. Intellectuals and poor peasants, disaffected youth and demobilized soldiers, women and factory workers, religious groups and minorities, local cadres and politically labelled "enemies"— virtually all major social strata have found ways, on rare occasion to be sure, to challenge or resist the course of the revolution. Because most such demands could not be met by Mao's continuing revolution, they now generate even stronger demands on the modernization model. We return to this issue in a later section.

The second question deals directly with the problem of political development: to what extent has the revolution developed China's political capacity to provide for the needs and desires of its people? In general, it has greatly expanded state capabilities ("state" referring to the complex of party, state, and military institutions), whereas its record in expanding popular political resources and benefits is mixed. The expansion of state capabilities was most noticeable in the 1950s, as the new institutional order steadily increased its regulatory and extractive activities, developed new symbolic appeals, and carried out a major redistribution of national resources. The Maoist period placed even greater emphasis on symbolic and distributive powers, while further advancing state penetration of all social organizations, but the effort produced virulent conflicts that ultimately sapped the state's morale and its capacity to control the processes it had set in motion. The post-Mao state has shifted to a new form of state building that emphasizes legal regulation, institutionalization, development of new modernization-oriented symbolic appeals, and broader distribution based on market mechanisms. Overall, especially in light of this renewed state development after the Cultural Revolution, the record of state development is a strong one.

Unfortunately, at times, state development has been politically expensive to the people, because the authoritarian system and the disruptive, threatening consequences of campaigns have denied citizens significant influence over the state, while exposing them directly to its extractive powers and its erratically oppressive actions. This is not to deny that there has been some development of popular political resources. PRC institutions have increased opportunities for political participation, relative to the past, and have expanded the educational and ideological supports for such participation. For some groups, at some times, the political system has dispensed justice that was lacking in the past, has brought greater regularity and security, and has stimulated feelings of national or communal pride. The problem is obvious from the analysis of preceding chapters: these indicators of political development have been at the mercy of an arbitrary and erratic performance by the state, which has often denied or subverted its own institutions for providing political goods to its people. This, too, is an issue that calls for further analysis.

National Integration. The unification of modern China required not simply the consolidation of rival forces into a unitary national government but also the reintegration of society and polity. Once the revolution had begun, reintegration could only be on terms that would, in effect, create a new form of political community within the Chinese tradition. The leaders of the Communist movement understood well the integrative requirements of national unification. They came to power determined to break down the barriers that divided Chinese society within itself and the political system from society as a whole. Their objective was the creation of a modern, socialist nation-state that would eliminate cleavages between nationalities, communal groups, and classes and establish a national community based on primary identification with the political system. Progress toward this objective has been substantial, although key problems remain in each of the areas mentioned.

The PRC is a multinational state overwhelmingly dominated by the Han or Chinese people, who are said to constitute about 94 percent of the population. Chinese sources identify some fifty-five minority nationalities, of which thirteen have an estimated population in excess of one million.[5] Most reside in frontier or isolated areas, that today tend to be designated as "autonomous" administrative units, that will encourage preservation of the cultural tradition of the minorities who inhabit them. Historically, most were poorly integrated into the Chinese system, although there were great variations among the minorities in their degree of contact with and assimilation into Han society. Minority membership is, in a sense, peripheral to creation of a Chinese political community, but the CCP is understandably concerned that the territories they inhabit be securely held by the central government. Moreover, it asserts emphatically that all citizens of the PRC—not just the dominant Han—must share in and contribute to the new Chinese political identity.

Since 1949, the integration of minority peoples and areas has been proceeding at a much more rapid rate than in the past. Han migration and resettlement threatens to overwhelm some minorities in their own areas, particularly those of strategic importance (Xinjiang and Inner Mongolia, for example). Economic and social change, new lines of transportation and communication, and the spread of educational themes approved by Peking are breaking down some of the barriers of the past. There has been a periodic resistance to this process, but none of the minorities has any realistic hope of stemming the tide. The real question is whether the process will ultimately lead to a total assimilation by the Han or whether the minorities will be able—as the CCP promises—to retain their national identities even as they become members of the new political community. It would be a mistake to assume that national identities will disappear simply because

[5] For thorough analysis of minority policy and problems, see June Teufel Dreyer, *China's Forty Millions* (Cambridge, Mass.: Harvard University Press, 1976).

Chinese pressures for integration are so great and the current prospects for resistance so futile. Modernization probably will bring the minority nationalities ever more firmly into the Chinese system, and yet it may also encourage or revive a strong sense of community among them. Separatism is a doubtful alternative now or in the future, but the terms of integration will remain open and fluid for decades to come.

Communal cleavages are those within the major nationalities or ethnic groups. Our concern here is with subethnic groupings among the Han, the vertical lines of cleavage that have for centuries divided Chinese society into myriad smaller communities. The pattern of communal differentiation in pre-Communist society was rich and varied, but three general types of community were particularly important. One was the kinship group, which identified itself on lines of descent from common ancestors. Best known, of course, were the great clans and lineages, particularly dominant in southeastern China, which were social organizations of considerable power in local settings.

Second, local territorial communities, based on an economic unit that tended to supply most of its residents' needs and to mark the effective limits of their activities and concerns, were extremely important throughout China. Exactly what this unit most commonly was and what determined its extent is a difficult question. Some have assumed that it was the natural village, others that it was a supravillage marketing area.[6] Almost all Chinese had strong community attachments to a local territorial unit centered on the cellular network of peasant villages and market towns. They also might identify with the larger territorial units in which they lived or from which they came—county, large city, province, region—but the intensity or identification tended to decline with increasing size of the unit. Finally, there were distinct linguistic and cultural groupings among the Han Chinese, which surpassed both kinship and territorial communities in scale. Most commonly identified by their different spoken dialects (Cantonese, Hakka, Hokkien, Shanghai, provincial variants of Mandarin, and so forth), they frequently produced

[6]G. William Skinner, "Marketing and Social Structure in Rural China," *Journal of Asian Studies*, vol. 24, nos. 1–3 (November 1964, February 1965, May 1965).

sharp economic, social, and cultural rivalry when brought into contact with each other.

These various communal cleavages were a source of much suspicion, prejudice, rivalry, and even violent conflict in Qing China, and they tended to focus individual loyalties on localized or distinctive segments of the larger society. Nationalism had no significant claim on the population in this context, except for those elites whose activities and ambitions brought them into direct association with the imperial political system. One of the most fascinating problems of modern China is the way in which foreign penetration, economic change, and revolutionary movements began to disrupt these communities, bring them into closer contact with each other, and create new lines of cleavage and identification.

Chinese Communism has accelerated this redefinition of community, trying to eradicate the inherited lines of division and to create a universal sense of membership in a national community defined in political terms. It has assaulted directly some of the organizational supports for traditional communalism, most notably in its destruction of lineage organization and property holdings. Through its formal educational system and its multiple instruments of socialization, it has made Mandarin or *putonghua* a national language[7] and has promoted new orientations toward the political system. Increased travel and mobility and a more extensive communication system have spread knowledge about the country as a whole among its citizens. Economic modernization has enlarged the basic territorial communities, bringing rural areas into the sphere of larger towns and creating new metropolitan and regional systems.

Although these efforts have not eradicated the old particularism—the preference for association with insiders of one's own group and the suspicion or resentment of outsiders—China has developed a vigorous and growing mass nationalism. Limiting the growth of nationalism is the fact that most Chinese experience political activity mainly within their primary units. So long as this is the case, it will be difficult to tell exactly how

[7] Efforts to establish Mandarin as a national language began well before the Communists came to power; for non-Mandarin-speaking areas, it is a second language that does not replace the native dialect.

the development of loyalties to the national system affects orientations toward local communities. Localism has been a recurring problem in the PRC, usually identified with cadres who are, after all, the only ones in a position to show much effective favoritism for their own kin, locality, or dialect group. How problems of localism will be affected by recent reforms is not clear. The dismantling of communes, creation of new elected county and township governments, and expansion of rural marketing all support fragmentation of existing local communities and the emergence of new, possibly larger ones. Yet the reforms also throw households back on their own resources and permit traditional forms of organization (e.g., kinship groups) to reassert their role. In fact, there is evidence that the reforms have encouraged revival of many pre-socialist ties—religious groups as well as lineages—while weakening organizations based on the state-defined collective.

Traditional China's third main kind of social cleavage, along with nationality and communal divisions, was of a class character.[8] The basic horizontal division of society was between elites and masses, between the gentry (in the broadest sense) and the peasantry. We will not attempt to unravel the question of whether class or community was the most powerful determinant of social conflict in imperial China. Both found modes of expression, and their interrelationship was exceedingly complex. Suffice it to say that the Chinese Communists made class cleavage their initial point of attack and that they succeeded in destroying the social and economic base of the pre-Communist elite. The question that concerns us is whether the PRC has developed new lines of class distinction and, if so, what implications that has for the integration of society and polity.

In general, contemporary Chinese society is not marked by powerful class distinctions. There are, of course, differences in income, social status, and political influence among different strata of the population, but they have a relatively moderate character. Yet class is by no means a dead issue in the PRC. The retention throughout the Maoist period of old class labels assigned during the 1950s, and the insistence that the basic conflict within

[8] See Richard Kraus, *Class Conflict in Chinese Socialism* (New York: Columbia University Press, 1981).

society and party alike was that between proletarian and bourgeois forces, made class analysis and labeling a potent weapon in Chinese politics. There was a tendency to exaggerate or even manufacture class distinctions in interpreting social conflict.

This sensitivity to class relationships will become more important in the course of modernization. During the Maoist period, the political leadership—itself the PRC's closest approximation of an elite class—deflected class struggle toward intellectuals, experts, and defeated factional leaders, insisting on its vanguard relationship with the working classes and promoting the PRC's image as a relatively egalitarian, if not literally classless, society. Since 1976, three important changes have occurred. One is the denial of a class distinction between mental and manual labor. Now, the regime insists that intellectuals and technicians are really workers whose different occupations represent no more than a necessary division of labor within socialist society. It has also removed most of the old class labels from landlords, rich peasants, and rightists. In effect, CCP doctrine no longer identifies large categories of the population as enemy or suspect classes. A second change is in policy toward material gain, with the state now endorsing desires to "get rich" and acknowledging that some will get rich quicker than others. The effect of this, in combination with the removal of political labels from many who are well placed to take advantage of new economic opportunities, is to encourage the emergence of *real* economic classes in place of the former *politically defined* classes.

The third change is the CCP's post-1978 effort to merge intellectual and political elitehood by recruiting experts into the party and insisting on more expertise from party cadres. The creation of a new technocratic elite is underway, an elite that is indeed "both red and expert" but hardly in the Maoist sense. If the old class labels weaken, if mental labor as such has no class character, and if class analysis continues to dominate Chinese political discourse, it is difficult to see how the emerging political-technocratic elite can escape identification as a politically defined new class. In contrast to ethnic and communal cleavages, which may gradually yield to a new national identity, class cleavages are likely to intensify as Chinese look anew at the distribution of power and privilege in their modernizing society.

EMERGING ISSUES

The preceding discussion has identified a number of problems that have emerged in the transition from Maoist to modernization models. Although it would be foolish to attempt to predict the future course of Chinese politics, it appears that three issues will become increasingly important as China's modernization proceeds. One is the relationship between socioeconomic modernization and political participation, in particular the question of how new patterns of social stratification will affect political conflict. Another is the problem of political succession and its impact on the character of Chinese socialism. The third issue is the international implications of China's modernization.

Stratification and Political Participation. The initial thrust of Deng's reforms suggests three lines of cleavage in Chinese society that may have particular political significance in the future. The first is the primary economic division between poor individuals and those who are able to capitalize on reform policies to propel themselves into relative affluence. Although there will be an urban component to the lower class, it will be overwhelmingly rural, consisting largely of peasant families that do not have sufficient labor power, agricultural resources, or entrepreneurial skills to make a success of the responsibility system. The upper class will be urban professionals and entrepreneurs, plus many rural families that have become rich peasant families or that have succeeded as nonagricultural "specialized households."

The second division is between richer and poorer regions; the former will be largely centered on the eastern cities, especially those that have been opened for foreign trade and investment and designated as core areas for regional economic development. The gulf between regions such as greater Shanghai and the hinterland of an inland province is already immense and will become wider (see Appendix A.2). The socioeconomic gap between such regions will increasingly be one of culture as well, as the modernizing cities will be centers of interaction with foreign cultures and always in the forefront of new commercial and industrial developments. The third division is between the political elite and its co-opted intellectual/technical supporters on the one hand and, on the other, those educated and/or politically active people who cannot or will not work within the system. There are many other potential sources of social conflict, of course, such as lineage disputes in the countryside, Han-minority rivalry in the autonomous regions, and tension between low-salaried employees and the new bourgeoisie in the cites. It is the first three, however, that seem most likely to become national issues productive of open political debate and conflict. What are the chances this might happen?

As far as elite politics are concerned, these issues are certain to cause conflict. They constitute part of the fundamental problematic of Deng's policies, with arguments already joined in inner-party debate on their merits. In considering the possibility that these debates might attract extra-party participants, we should note the legacy of Maoist patterns of participation. First, it expanded popular participation in the affairs of primary units, usually, but not always, limiting it to activities supportive of elite positions. Second, it encouraged elite factional conflict, thereby opening differences to public view and expanding the political arena; however, it denied the legitimacy of political opposition so that factional struggles became high-risk enterprises in which losers might be charged with antagonistic contradictions. Third, through the first two characteristics, it linked elite and popular participation as leaders tried to mobilize popular support for their factional battles; the result was to draw some citizens into higher-level conflicts, occasionally in support of issues not necessarily favored by their elite patrons. These characteristics gave participation in Maoist China a volatile quality not found in other Communist systems. Moreover, although Deng has repudiated the Maoist style, he has supported more institutionalized forms of socialist democracy. Consequently, it appears that popular political participation will indeed be a limited but significant outlet for socioeconomic tensions arising in the course of modernization. The question remains as to how the limits might shape public debate on the issues identified.

The conflict between rich and poor is not likely to enter the public arena as an open argument between proponents of each side, because the character of the Chinese media precludes such conflicts. It is true that tensions and conflicts over such issues in Chinese society already appear in the Chinese press under the rubric of ultraegalitarian resistance to the new policies. The newly rich in the countryside are sometimes pressured into buying expensive items for the village; sometimes their property is vandalized; sometimes local party leaders tear up valid contracts. Such behavior is decried in press accounts, but the accounts suggest it is not uncommon. Nevertheless, such acts of protest are likely to remain localized under normal conditions. If a segment of the party took the side of resisting peasants, it would be challenging the principle of democratic centralism as well as an important policy. CCP elites have no interest in acknowledging publicly that such a fundamental conflict exists in socialist society. In a sense, they are on the side of the rich, which is where state interests currently lie, although from the beginning the effect of the responsibility system on poor households has been a matter of attention and concern. Therefore, CCP leaders will want to confine debate within inner-party circles, while taking the public position that the issue is not a fundamentally divisive one. However, if a situation of acute factionalization already existed in the party, then it might be to the advantage of one group to articulate and stir up the dissatisfactions and tensions caused by modernization. As in the case of the Cultural Revolution, uncovering such tensions would be more likely to lead to chaos among mass factions than to clear-cut support for one elite faction; however, if articulation of potentially divisive interests is not permitted within the system, then it remains potential support for a radical faction.

Debate over the distribution of resources between richer and poorer regions is more likely to become public, appearing in the press and at local congresses. In this case, acknowledgment of the issue is not quite so damaging to the top elite, and local elites in underprivileged regions have a clear interest in mobilizing popular support behind demands for equity. Counterposed to the pressure for equity from regional constituencies is the political and economic power and capacity of Peking, Shanghai, and the more developed provinces. The center's natural proclivity is to favor the more developed areas, because their success proves the wisdom of modernization policies. Much of this conflict will be expressed in competitive regional boosterism, but the nativist aspect of the issue—inland Chinese resentment of foreign-influenced coastal cities—should not be discounted, because it is so obvious a point of attack for the hinterland. Here, then, is an issue that might generate popular political activity in the course of normal politics.

The third issue is one between dissidents and the establishment. In substance, it may range across all the controversial topics mentioned here, but its cutting edge will be argument over the meaning of socialist democracy. What is "socialist" expression (political and artistic), and what are the proper roles governing its institutions and processes? There have been three main periods of open intellectual debate on this question in PRC history—the hundred flowers of 1957, the early part of the Cultural Revolution, and the democratic movement (Democracy Wall) of 1978–1979— and there will certainly be more. The majority of Chinese intellectuals will probably continue to work within the system, avoiding risk of censure or imprisonment; however, the pattern of recurring intellectual dissent is well established. Dissenters can only be encouraged by expansion of socialist democracy and the open foreign policy and hence are likely to become more active, and possibly bolder, as time goes by. The sociological background of dissidents has been quite diverse and will probably become more so. The Cultural Revolution generation is fertile ground because they were deprived of the opportunity to acquire the technical skills that are now being rewarded, and they were socialized into a radical egalitarian ideology whose warnings about revisionism seem to be borne out by current developments. On the other side, exposure to the West may induce political opposition from an increasingly self-confident technical elite, as it has in the Soviet Union. However, dissidents will probably remain numerically insignificant with very little if any mass following, and the authorities will continue to suppress them, as in the past, when their activities begin to show signs of an organized movement. If the first division provides some potential for mass factionalism in abnormal times, and the second is most likely to become part of normal politics, this third one is likely to take the form of episodic fringe activities that attract little mass support, and are easily suppressed, but which play an important role as a latent opposition with some access to influential people.

Succession and Chinese Socialism. Although pressures for popular political participation are likely to increase under the modernization model, and to find both sanctioned and unsanctioned modes of expression, the PRC will remain essentially a party dictatorship. The CCP top elite will continue to decide all major policy issues, and its character will determine the general direction of Chinese socialism. How long Deng's leadership will last and who will succeed him are questions of utmost importance. Unfortunately, we cannot answer them, although we can suggest a few of the broader alternatives.

Despite many cautious reminders by foreign observers that Deng's reforms might be defeated by either leftist or conservative bureaucratic forces, his leadership weathered all the challenges of the early 1980s. By the end of 1984, the reforms were firmly in place, and it seemed that Hu Yaobang's and Zhao Ziyang's positions were secure enough to guarantee that Deng's immediate successors would continue his policies. In Deng Xiaoping's personal opinion, expressed in late 1984,[9] the new direction of Chinese politics will hold for the indefinite future, "into the third, fourth and fifth echelons," because the policies are popular and successful. He also expects that successful modernization will bring greater stability and unity to Chinese politics. Certainly, success in modernization will establish a momentum favoring the continuation of current policies, but just as certainly the societal impact of modernization will be diverse and will gradually give rise to new strains and forces in Chinese politics. Therefore, although the distant future is obscure, in the short-term we will probably see a continuation of the reform program.

One alternative to a reformist succession is a revival of radical or leftist influence, but this prospect is steadily decreasing. Despite the fact that about half the party members are Cultural Revolution recruits, there is no reason to assume that this category is actually a cohesive group. Even if it were, it has lost its leaders at the top, is heir to an extremely unpopular set of policies, and has been the recipient of heavy doctrinal criticism and organizational pressure from the reformers. It is implausible to see these putative Maoists regaining command of the CCP, except under two conditions. First, there would have to be a serious political or economic crisis, with renewed factional conflict of a profound,

[9]"A Talk by Deng Xiaoping at the Third Plenary Session of the Central Advisory Committee on October 22, 1984," *People's Daily*, January 1, 1984, p. 1.

even violent character. Second, the radicals would have to formulate a new program, such as an appeal to the lower classes that combined some nostalgic revolutionary themes with a focus on contemporary issues. Short of these conditions, which could only develop gradually and which would produce a new radical movement rather than a true Maoist revival, the intraparty left will remain a declining rear guard action against the mainstream party leadership.

Within that mainstream, which will remain committed to some variant of the modernization model, there appear to be two broad alternatives. One is a conservative version that retains the current emphasis on economic construction but calls a halt to economic and political liberalization and experimentation. These leaders would represent the Chinese military-industrial complex, the old-style vested interests of the Chinese bureaucracy and command economy. They would favor continuing economic, scientific, and technological development with more emphasis on heavy industry and state controls and less emphasis on consumer demands, market mechanisms, and the open foreign policy. Chinese socialism under their leadership would resemble Soviet socialism.

The other alternative is continuation of Deng's reformist version of modernization. The most striking fact about this alternative is that we do not yet know its limits. The reforms are still evolving, pushing against what were once thought to be their most liberal boundaries. Caution and political logic suggest they cannot go much further without encountering too much resistance from conservatives. For that reason, the most likely course of Chinese politics in the succession period is not a decisive triumph for either of these two approaches but rather a series of shifting compromises between them that will continue down the modernization road.

Even if a conservative reaction were to come to the fore, the PRC would continue to modernize along lines reminiscent of Soviet and Eastern European experience. If reformers remain in command and continue to push the policies introduced in the early 1980s, the Chinese political system will appear more singular. Its leaders will continue to refer to "socialism with Chinese characteristics," but to many observers (socialist and nonsocialist alike) those characteristics may seem more Chinese than socialist. Whatever the name, it will be a system that underscores the unique features of the Chinese revolution and the independent path now emerging in the postrevolutionary era.

International Implications. Some of the international implications of China's shift to the modernization model are already apparent. From an external perspective, the most positive are greatly expanded international contacts flowing from the open foreign policy and a general reduction of tension in the East Asian area as a result of the PRC's evident need for a peaceful environment in which to concentrate on economic development. The open foreign policy means new markets for foreign goods and capital, and new opportunities for tourism and cultural exchange. Despite many difficulties in forging these new relationships, due partly to Chinese inexperience and partly to the unrealistic expectations of her new partners, they have been welcomed by the international community. On the security front, military tension in the Taiwan straits is at low ebb, Sino-Soviet relations are slowly warming, and the PRC seems to be exerting some moderating influence on the level of hostility between the two Koreas. None of these tendencies is secure from reversal; however, in general, it seems that China's modernization drive has had a calming influence on the area.

There are exceptions, of course, to this benign view of China's new course. Commitment to modernization is no guarantee that the PRC will refrain from force, as its 1979 invasion of Vietnam indicates. For Vietnam, China's normalization of relations with the United States simply gave it the security to intervene militarily in its dispute with its southern neighbor. Neither Vietnam nor its Soviet ally can be reassured by this message and the prospect of growing Chinese strength, although apprehension in the Soviet case is mitigated by China's clear desire to lessen Sino-Soviet tension. Taiwan also sees negative implications in Deng's policies, which reduce the short-term military threat but increase diplomatic pressures on the Nationalist government to strike an accommodation with the Communists. Growing international participation by the PRC—in trade, formal relations, and representation in international organizations—inevitably reduces the Republic of China's diplomatic contacts, forcing it to rely mainly on unofficial missions to maintain trade and other international business. As China's growing importance to other states increases its leverage on the Taiwan issue, even those unofficial relations may be difficult for Taipei to maintain. Hong Kong may be the most poignant example of the mixed consequences of China's new policies. The PRC has long had the power to take Hong Kong but in the past refrained from doing so because of the economic benefits it derived through that territory; it was unthinkable then to retake the territory and allow it to continue its capitalist ways. With the advent of the modernization model, relations between Hong Kong and the mainland became more intimate than ever, and the prospect of Hong Kong passing to PRC control became less disturbing to the British and most other observers than it had been in the Maoist era. Most importantly, with the opening to market mechanisms and foreign investment within China itself, it became possible to imagine a Hong Kong that was part of the PRC but still a capitalist enclave. Paradoxically, China's adoption of policies quite favorable to and welcome in Hong Kong opened the door to a formal reassertion of sovereignty over Hong Kong—an outcome less clearly welcomed by most of the territory's residents.

Looking further ahead, much depends on the relative success of China's domestic modernization drive. If it fails, if an economic or political crisis ensues, China might enter a period of turmoil with very uncertain foreign policy consequences. Although foreign adventures would not necessarily follow, there might be strong pressures or incentives for Soviet intervention, and hopes for stability in Korea would be shaken. The open foreign policy would almost certainly be a casualty of political upheaval, with substantial losses for those who have banked on its long-term durability. The general conclusion of this study, however, is that the modernization model is not likely to collapse. Although its prospects are uncertain, the basic features seem likely to continue, sooner or later projecting China into a much more powerful economic, political, and military position in world affairs.

Will the emergence of China as a world power early in the twenty-first century pose a threat to its neighbors or to regional or global peace? That is the ultimate question, although it cannot be answered simply. Threats to the international community are not the responsibility of single parties, and there is plenty of time for other parties to work out their response to and relations with a newly powerful China. However, there is no denying that successful modernization in China raises some troubling questions for others. In the first place, it will mark the definitive transformation of the old world of the superpowers. The strictly bipolar world was transformed long ago by the emergence of competing economic centers in Japan and Europe, but these were not new military powers that challenged the dominance of the United States and the USSR. The ascendance of the PRC will mark the arrival of the first true candidate for third superpower status, even though China will lag behind the others in technological development for the foreseeable future. Strategic doctrine, global bargaining, and management of the world economy will be transformed.

More specifically, there will be a sharp challenge to many countries that have close or competitive relations with the PRC. Two areas of particular concern stand out, one being Japan's response. More than any other country, Japan will face a fundamental strategic choice on the cooperation-competition spectrum. It can pursue both, to be sure—witness Japanese-American relations—but the dangers of miscalculation are great. If it appears for any reason that cooperation will not work, or that competition may get out of hand, the pressures on Japan for rearmament will be intense. On the other hand, if cooperation *is* to work and competition be kept within healthy limits, the relationship requires of Japan a high level of foresight, commitment, and diplomatic skill.

The other area of special concern is China's economic impact on other East Asian countries. Already the "four little dragons" of Singapore, Hong Kong, Taiwan, and South Korea are attempting to move up the product-cycle ladder, as Chinese exports begin to swamp the lower rungs. There is good reason for these smaller economies to fear the effects of a massive, cheap labor export drive by the Chinese. The solution lies in continued technological advance and the maintenance of cooperative relations with China, but it will not be easy. The situation in

Southeast Asia is compounded by the presence of many economically powerful overseas Chinese, some of whom already have active economic interests in China. The rise of China as an economic power will have a very different impact on its "sphere of influence" than was the case with the Soviet Union. The latter's hegemony over Eastern Europe, resting on crude military and political power, is no model for the future Chinese relationship with Southeast Asia, which is likely to revolve around close economic ties in which the overseas Chinese commercial and financial network plays an important role. If China maintains its open foreign policy, it may some day begin to reverse the flow of technology and capital, or at least begin to balance the import of overseas Chinese talent and money with more exports along the same network. This is an extremely complicated and provocative question of legitimate concern to Southeast Asian leaders. Given the peculiar overseas Chinese position of economic strength and political subordination in the region as a whole—conditions vary in different countries, of course—it is clear that an expanding Chinese economy already linked to overseas Chinese economic interests will pose delicate political issues. We are not predicting a crisis in PRC-Southeast Asian relations but rather pointing to the complexity of the relationship. Just as Chinese socialism shows unique characteristics at home, so it may abroad. Socialism with Chinese characteristics may include a foreign economic policy that most observers do not associate with socialist countries.

There remains the fundamental issue of aggressive tendencies, so often associated with the rise of a new power on the world scene. Little is gained by asking this question abstractly: will China be an expansionist power bent on foreign conquest? One could list certain assumptions derived from state practice in general, China's imperial past, or the history of PRC foreign policy to argue both sides of this question. In practice, however, China's foreign policy decisions will address specific cases based on analysis of their security costs and benefits. For example, no matter how active and vigorous its foreign policy becomes, it will not launch an unprovoked assault on the USSR or attempt to conquer the Southeast Asian mainland. The risks of aggression lie in limited foreign policy objectives, where the use of force may advance highly prized goals with relatively little danger of serious damage to China. In such cases, force is rightly feared, and the Sino-Vietnamese border war points immediately to one area where that possibility remains high. As Chinese power increases, the temptation to bully Vietnam will also increase and, with it, the risk of military hostilities. So, too, with Taiwan, where we cannot discount the possibility that a future Chinese government, discouraged with rejection of all its overtures and pressed against its own announced timetable of a reunification accord in the 1980s, will bring stronger pressure to bear through economic isolation, military harassment, and the like. In these two cases, Chinese action will be restrained by its estimate of superpower reaction, so there are still limits to how far it will go. It is this kind of restraint, coupled with the PRC's long-term commitment to the peaceful environment that supports economic development and modernization, that will discourage more generalized Chinese militancy or expansionism. Nonetheless, successful modernization will increase Chinese military power and the temptation to use it when the risks seem minimal.

Whatever the merits of these speculative comments on various aspects of China's emerging international position, China's modernization will seal a global shift of power from the Atlantic to the Pacific. The further that modernization proceeds, the clearer it becomes that the twenty-first century will indeed be the "Pacific century"—provided, of course, that the world avoids self-destruction. China's place in that Pacific-centered order will be a major one, so that Chinese may once again look upon their country as at least one of the world's central kingdoms.

APPENDIX A:

Provincial-Level Units

1. Area and Population

Province	Capital	1970 area (thousand square miles)	Population (in thousands)*				1982 urban population	% urban
			1953	1965	1976	1982		
NORTH								
Beijing [Peking]	—	6.6	4,591	7,730	8,490	9,190	5,960	64
Tianjin [Tientsin]	—	1.2	4,622	6,386	7,226	7,780	5,320	68
Hebei [Hopeh]	Shijiazhuang	75	33,181	41,428	55,193	53,560	7,400	13
Shanxi [Shansi]	Taiyuan	61	14,314	18,349	23,000	25,460	5,410	21
Nei Menggu [Inner Mongolia]	Hohhot	225	3,532	5,778	8,500	19,370	5,640	29
NORTHEAST								
Liaoning	Shenyang	90	22,269	32,403	44,474	35,920	15,090	42
Jilin [Kirin]	Changchun	110	12,609	17,177	23,000	22,580	8,940	39
Heilongjiang [Heilungkiang]	Haerbin	280	12,681	21,320	32,000	32,810	13,090	39
EAST								
Shanghai	—	2.2	8,808	10,966	12,312	11,810	6,960	58
Jiangsu [Kiangsu]	Nanjing	40	38,329	48,523	61,504	60,890	9,540	15
Zhejiang [Chekiang]	Hangzhou	39	22,866	28,918	36,000	39,240	10,000	25
Anhui [Anhwei]	Hefei	54	30,663	37,442	45,000	50,160	7,210	14
Fujian [Fukien]	Fuzhou	48	13,143	17,823	24,000	26,040	5,480	21
Jiangxi [Kiangsi]	Nanchang	64	16,773	22,271	29,400	33,480	6,430	19
Shandong [Shantung]	Jinan	60	50,134	63,257	78,478	74,940	14,360	19

SOUTH CENTRAL								
Henan [Honan]	Zhengzhou	65	43,911	54,829	67,468	75,200	10,250	13
Hubei [Hupeh]	Wuhan	72	27,790	35,221	43,848	48,010	8,490	17
Hunan	Changsha	81	33,227	40,563	49,018	54,520	8,180	15
Guandong [Kwangtung]	Guangzhou	83	34,770	42,684	54,100	59,870	11,070	18
Guangxi [Kwangsi]	Nanning	91	19,561	24,776	31,300	36,840	4,510	12
SOUTHWEST								
Sichuan [Szechwan]	Chengdu	220	65,685	81,634	100,080	100,220	14,281	14
Guizhou [Kweichow]	Guiyang	67	15,037	19,302	24,000	28,750	5,420	18
Yunnan	Kunming	168	17,473	22,120	28,000	32,830	4,110	12
Xizang [Tibet]	Lhasa	470	1,274	1,458	1,700	1,890	240	12
NORTHWEST								
Shaanxi [Shensi]	Xian	76	15,881	20,800	26,000	29,040	5,480	18
Gansu [Kansu]	Lanzhou	190	11,291	15,200	19,795	19,750	3,130	15
Qinghai [Tsinghai]	Xining	280	1,677	2,644	3,858	3,930	800	20
Ningxia [Ningsia]	Yinchuan	40	1,637	2,253	3,000	3,930	766	22
Xinjiang [Sinkiang]	Urumqi	640	4,874	7,119	10,000	13,160	3,750	28
TOTALS		3,700	582,603	750,394	950,744	1,015,410	210,154	21

*Provincial population estimates before 1982 are CIA estimates. In 1979, territory from five adjoining provinces was added to Nei Menggu, affecting population comparability.

Sources: Zhongguo Tongji Nianjian 1983 (Chinese Statistical Yearbook 1983), p. 106; Central Intelligence Agency, China: Economic Indicators (ER 77–10508, October 1977), p. 9; Theodore Shabad, China's Changing Map (New York: Praeger, 1972), p. 34.

2. Selected Development Indicators, 1982

Province	Output value (billion yuan)	Output per capita	% value indust.	Agric. output per rural resident	% increase in agric. output since 1979*	Agric. horsepower per rural resident	Senior Middle sch. grads %	Illit. & semi-illit., % of adults	Life expect., 1973–75
NORTH									
Beijing [Peking]	25.0	2716	91.6	648	165	1.01	17.6	10.4	69.5
Tianjin [Tientsin]	23.3	2994	90.9	857	155	1.40	13.4	12.8	70.9
Hebei [Hopeh]	36.5	681	62.9	293	144	.39	7.4	13.2	68.6
Shanxi [Shansi]	19.7	774	67.7	317	162	.40	7.3	14.5	66.6
Nei Menggu [Inner Mongolia]	11.7	604	58.5	353	169	.39	7.3	15.5	66.3
NORTHEAST									
Liaoning	56.7	1577	84.0	433	163	.40	9.1	11.0	69.7
Jilin [Kirin]	20.5	906	70.3	444	164	.39	10.7	14.6	65.8
Heilongjiang [Heilungkiang]	36.4	1109	73.7	485	160	.56	9.4	14.2	70.4
EAST									
Shanghai	67.5	5718	94.2	797	164	.63	20.5	11.2	72.0
Jiangsu [Kiangsu]	73.7	1210	68.2	455	167	.34	6.8	15.9	67.2
Zhejiang [Chekiang]	36.8	938	62.6	470	167	.29	5.1	26.8	68.4
Anhui [Anhwei]	27.0	538	53.8	290	183	.22	3.9	22.8	65.7
Fujian [Fukien]	15.0	575	58.4	303	163	.19	5.7	22.0	67.3
Jiangxi [Kiangsi]	18.4	550	52.7	322	164	.18	5.3	16.5	67.3
Shandong [Shantung]	59.4	791	61.9	372	182	.37	5.8	22.3	63.2

SOUTH CENTRAL									
Henan [Honan]	38.7	514	56.4	259	163	.28	6.2	17.3	66.9
Hubei [Hupeh]	41.0	853	66.5	347	145	.27	7.5	13.9	—
Hunan	34.0	622	56.6	317	156	.20	6.5	12.1	62.5
Guandong [Kwangtung]	41.5	693	65.5	292	175	.22	7.8	13.5	—
Guangxi [Kwangsi]	17.4	471	51.0	263	176	.17	6.5	13.3	—
SOUTHWEST									
Sichuan [Szechwan]	53.5	533	56.3	270	176	.11	3.9	18.5	60.1
Guizhou [Kweichow]	10.2	354	51.5	211	172	.08	2.9	37.3	59.3
Yunnan	14.5	441	55.0	227	170	.15	2.8	22.4	60.6
Xizang [Tibet]	.7	392	16.4	375	151	.22	0.8	30.9	61.3
NORTHWEST									
Shaanxi [Shensi]	17.6	606	64.4	266	156	.30	7.6	15.0	64.6
Gansu [Kansu]	11.3	570	71.6	192	146	.30	6.2	15.3	—
Qinghai [Tsinghai]	2.3	582	61.6	280	152	.29	4.9	14.3	61.3
Ningxia [Ningsia]	2.2	556	64.9	251	166	.41	4.9	18.8	62.3
Xinjiang [Sinkiang]	8.3	633	55.6	392	172	.40	6.1	17.7	62.5

*The 1982 data is based on 1980 prices, the 1979 data on 1970 prices. This inflates the growth rate but should not affect interprovincial comparisons.

Sources: Economic statistics from *Chinese Statistical Yearbook 1983*; 1979 output data and life expectancy data from *China: Socialist Economic Development* (World Bank, 1983); educational statistics calculated from *Zongguo 1982 nian renkou pucha 10% chouyang ziliao* (10% sampling tabulation on the 1982 population census of the PRC), Beijing: Zhongguo Tongji She, 1983.

431

APPENDIX B:

National Economic Indicators

1. General Indices and Rates of Growth

Item	1952	1957	1965	1978	1982	1982 as % of 1952	1982 as % of 1978	Average annual increase	
								1953–82	1978–82
Population (mil.)*	574.8	646.5	725.4	962.6	1,015.1	176.6	105.5	1.9	1.3
Number of workers (mil.).	207.3	237.7	286.7	398.6	447.1	215.7	112.2	2.6	2.9
Total social product index	100.0	170.9	258.2	725.8	969.7	969.7	133.6	7.9	7.5
National income index	100.0	153.0	197.5	453.2	579.1	579.1	127.8	6.0	6.3
Retail price index	100.0	108.5	120.4	121.6	137.2	137.2	—	—	—
Consumer price index	100.0	109.6	120.3	125.3	143.4	143.4	—	—	—
Agr. output index	100.0	124.8	137.1	229.6	306.6	306.6	133.5	3.8	7.5
Grain (mil. tons)	163.9	195.1	194.5	304.8	353.4	215.6	116.0	2.6	3.8
Cotton (mil. tons)	1.3	1.6	2.1	2.2	3.6	275.9	166.0	3.4	13.5
Meat (mil. tons)	3.4	4.0	5.5	8.6	13.5	399.1	157.8	4.7	12.1
Indust. output index	100.0	228.6	452.6	1,598.6	2,115.6	2,115.6	132.3	10.7	7.2
Light indust. index	100.0	183.2	344.5	968.1	1,515.0	1,515.0	156.5	9.5	11.8
Heavy indust. index	100.0	310.7	650.6	2,777.7	3,177.1	3,177.1	114.4	12.2	3.4
Cloth (bil. meters)	3.8	5.1	6.3	11.0	15.4	400.8	139.2	4.7	8.6
Bicycles (100,000)	.8	8.1	18.4	85.4	242.0	30,250.0	283.4	21.0	29.7
Crude oil (100,000 tons)	4.4	14.6	113.1	1,040.5	1,021.2	23,209.1	98.1	19.9	−0.5
Steel (100,000 tons)	13.5	53.5	122.3	317.8	371.6	2,752.6	116.9	11.7	4.0
Cement (100,000 tons)	28.6	68.6	163.4	652.4	952.0	3,328.7	145.9	12.4	9.9
Freight (bil. ton-k)	76.2	181.0	346.3	982.9	1,240.3	1,627.7	126.2	9.7	6.0
Passengers (bil. pers-k)	24.8	49.6	69.7	174.3	274.4	1,104.7	157.4	8.3	12.0

*Official year-end population.
Source: Chinese Statistical Yearbook, 1983, pp. 6–11.

2. Selected Annual Economic Indices

Year	Population (mil.)*	Population % increase	Total soc. product (bil. yuan)	Soc. proc. % increase	Same, adjusted prices**	Foodgrain (mil tons)	Foodgrain per cap (lb.)	Foodgrain per cap, % increase
1949	541.67		55.7			113.1	417	
1950	551.96	1.89	68.3	22.6	132.1		478	14.5
1951	563.00	2.00	82.0	20.0	20.1	143.6	510	6.6
1952	574.82	2.09	101.5	23.7	25.9	163.9	570	11.7
1953	587.96	2.28	124.1	22.2	18.7	166.8	567	-0.4
1954	602.66	2.50	134.6	8.4	8.5	169.5	562	-0.8
1955	614.65	1.98	141.5	5.1	6.1	183.9	598	6.3
1956	628.28	2.21	163.9	15.8	17.9	192.7	613	2.5
1957	646.53	2.90	160.6	-2.0	6.1	195.0	603	-1.6
1958	659.94	2.07	213.8	33.1	32.7	200.0	606	0.4
1959	672.07	1.83	254.8	19.1	18.0	170.0	505	-16.5
1960	662.07	-1.48	267.9	5.1	4.7	143.5	433	-14.3
1961	658.59	-0.52	197.8	-26.1	-33.5	147.5	447	3.3
1962	672.95	2.18	180.0	-8.9	-10.0	160.0	475	6.1
1963	691.72	2.78	195.6	8.6	10.2	170.0	491	3.3
1964	704.99	1.91	226.8	15.9	17.5	187.5	531	8.2
1965	725.38	2.89	269.5	18.8	19.0	194.5	536	0.8
1966	745.42	2.76	306.2	13.6	16.9	214.0	574	7.0
1967	763.68	2.44	277.4	-9.4	-9.9	217.8	570	-0.6
1968	785.34	2.83	264.8	-4.5	-4.7	209.0	532	-6.6

Year								
1969	806.71	2.72	318.4	20.2	25.3	210.9	523	-1.7
1970	829.92	2.87	380.0	19.3	24.1	239.9	578	10.5
1971	852.29	2.69	420.3	10.6	10.4	250.1	586	1.5
1972	871.77	2.28	439.6	4.5	4.4	240.4	551	-6.0
1973	892.11	2.33	477.6	8.6	8.6	264.9	593	7.6
1974	908.59	1.84	485.9	1.7	1.9	275.2	605	2.0
1975	924.20	1.71	537.9	10.7	11.5	284.5	615	1.6
1976	937.17	1.40	543.3	1.0	1.4	286.3	611	-0.7
1977	949.74	1.34	600.3	10.4	10.3	282.7	595	-2.5
1978	962.59	1.35	684.6	14.0	13.1	304.7	633	6.3
1979	975.42	1.33	764.2	11.6	8.5	332.1	680	7.5
1980	987.05	1.19	849.6	11.1	7.9	320.5	649	-4.6
1981	1000.72	1.38	904.8	6.4	4.7	325.0	649	0.0
1982	1015.41	1.46	989.4	9.3	9.0	353.4	696	7.1
1983	1024.95	0.93	1105.2	11.7	10.0	387.3	755	8.5
1984	1036.04	1.08	1283.5	16.1	13.0	407.1	785	3.9

*Official year-end population.

**Total Social Product and the first column of percentage increases are given in current prices; the second column of percentage increases is in terms of adjusted comparable prices. Total Social Product is the sum of the output of industry, agriculture, construction, transportation, and commerce; unlike Gross National Product it does not include the value of service activities.

Sources: Chinese Statistical Yearbook 1983, pp. 13, 103, 158; State Statistical Bureau, "Communiqué on Fulfilment of China's 1983 National Economic Plan," BR vol. 27, no. 20 (May 14, 1984): I–IX; "Communiqué on Fulfilment of China's 1984 Economic and Social Development Plan," BR vol. 28, no. 12 (March 25, 1985): I–VIII.

3. *Selected International Comparisons*

Country	Mid-1982 Population	% urban	1982 GNP per capita*	1960–1982 Average % annual growth	Life expect. 1982	1982 infant mortality	1980 population per doctor	1981 middle school enrol. % age group
China	1008.2	21	310	5.0	67	67	1,810	44
India	717.0	24	260	1.3	55	94	3,690	30
Pakistan	87.1	29	380	2.8	50	121	3480	17
Indonesia	152.6	22	580	4.2	53	102	11,530	30
Thailand	48.5	17	790	4.5	63	51	7,100	29
Nigeria	90.6	21	860	3.3	50	109	10,750	16
Brazil	126.8	69	2,240	4.8	64	73	—	32
Hungary	10.7	55	2,270	6.3	71	20	400	42
Yugoslavia	22.6	44	2,800	4.9	71	34	550	83
United States	231.5	78	13,160	2.2	75	11	520	97
Sweden	8.3	88	14,040	2.4	77	7	490	85

*In current U.S. dollars.

Source: World Bank, *World Development Report 1984* (New York: Oxford University Press, 1984), pp. 218–67.

APPENDIX C:

Consumer and Welfare Indicators

1. General

	1952	1957	1962	1965	1978	1982
Consumption level (yuan/person)	76	102	117	125	175	266
rural	62	79	88	100	132	212
urban	148	205	226	237	383	501
Consumption level index*	100	122.9	103.9	132.4	177.0	233.5
rural	100	117.1	98.8	124.8	157.5	217.7
urban	100	126.3	96.6	136.8	212.9	243.8
Consumption (lb. per person)						
cotton	4.6	5.2	2.3	5.9	4.5	7.1
meat	11.9	12.5	5.8	15.4	17.9	26.8
aquatic products	5.9	9.8	6.8	8.3	9.7	10.2
Students per 10,000 persons						
college level	3.3	6.8	12.3	9.3	8.9	11.4
middle school	55	110	124	197	693	465
primary school	889	994	1,029	1,602	1,489	1,382
Telephones (1,000)						
rural	58.4	200.0	852.6	492.2	733.9	803.8
urban	295.3	464.5	699.5	771.1	1,191.5	1,538.7

Restaurants (1,000)	—	470	256(1963)		117	628
Books						
new titles (1,000)	7.9	18.7	8.3	12.4	11.9	23.4
billion pages	1.70	3.44	3.07	5.62	13.46	21.92
Magazine titles	354	634	483	790	930	3,100
copies per issue (100,000)	119.4	191.1	126.7	288.3	620.0	1,388.5
Newspaper titles	296	364	273	343	186	277
billion copies per issue	73.7	113.1	115.9	247.7	428.0	807.4
Hospital beds (100,000)	1.6	2.9	6.9	7.7	18.6	20.5
Doctors (100,000)	4.3	5.5	6.9	7.6	10.3	13.1

*Consumption level (disposable income) is in current prices; the index is in comparable prices.
Source: Chinese Statistical Yearbook 1983, pp. 184, 320, 398, 484, 511, 529–31.

2. *Rural-Urban Differences, 1978 and 1982*

	1978				1982			
	National	*Urban*	*Rural*	*(R/U%)*	*National*	*Urban*	*Rural*	*(R/U%)*
Consumer goods, 10,000 units								
sewing machines	3,396	1,478	1,918	(27)	6,667	2,839	3,828	(32)
wrist watches	8,206	5,036	3,170	(14)	19,111	10,707	8,404	(18)
bicycles	7,426	4,012	3,414	(18)	13,314	6,510	6,804	(24)
radios	7,546	3,475	4,071	(25)	18,746	6,301	12,175	(44)
televisions	304	226	78	(8)	2,761	1,950	811	(10)
Goods per 100 persons								
sewing machines	3.5	8.6	2.4	(27)	6.6	14.8	4.7	(32)
wrist watches	8.5	29.3	4.0	(14)	18.8	55.8	10.2	(18)
bicycles	7.7	23.3	4.3	(18)	13.1	33.9	8.3	(24)
radios	7.8	20.2	5.1	(25)	18.2	32.8	14.8	(44)
televisions	0.3	1.3	0.1	(8)	2.7	10.2	1.0	(10)
Daily nutrition								
calories	2,311	2,715	2,224	(82)	2,779	3,088	2,707	(88)
protein (grams)	70.8	81.6	68.5	(84)	80.5	85.8	79.5	(93)
fat (grams)	29.9	49.0	25.7	(52)	44.4	70.6	38.3	(54)

Source: *Chinese Statistical Yearbook 1983*, pp. 508–09.

APPENDIX D:

Foreign Trade

1. Growth, Balance, and Composition of Trade

Commodity composition**

Year	Total trade ($bil.)*	Annual % incr.	Exports ($bil.)	Imports ($bil.)	Trade balance ($bil.)	Export Industry and mining	Export Processed agric. products	Export Agricultural products	Import Production goods	Import Consumption goods
1950	1.13		0.55	0.58	-0.03	9.3	33.2	57.5	83.4	16.6
1951	1.96	73.4	0.76	1.20	-0.44	14.0	31.4	54.6	81.3	18.7
1952	1.94	-1.0	0.82	1.12	-0.30	17.9	22.8	59.3	89.4	10.6
1953	2.37	22.1	1.02	1.35	-0.33	18.4	25.9	55.7	92.1	7.9
1954	2.44	2.9	1.15	1.29	-0.14	24.0	27.7	48.3	92.3	7.7
1955	3.14	28.6	1.41	1.73	-0.32	25.5	28.4	46.1	93.8	6.2
1956	3.21	2.2	1.65	1.56	0.09	26.1	31.3	42.6	91.5	8.5
1957	3.11	-3.1	1.60	1.51	0.09	28.4	31.5	40.1	92.0	8.0
1958	3.87	24.4	1.98	1.89	0.09	27.5	37.0	35.5	93.1	6.9
1959	4.38	13.1	2.26	2.12	0.14	23.7	38.7	37.6	95.7	4.3
1960	3.81	-13.0	1.86	1.95	-0.09	26.7	42.3	31.0	95.4	4.6
1961	2.94	-22.8	1.49	1.45	0.04	33.4	45.9	20.7	61.9	38.1
1962	2.66	-9.5	1.49	1.17	0.32	34.7	45.9	19.4	55.2	44.8

1963	2.92	9.7	1.65	1.27	0.38	32.9	42.9	24.2	56.0	44.0
1964	3.47	18.8	1.92	1.55	0.37	32.9	39.1	28.0	55.5	44.5
1965	4.25	22.4	2.23	2.02	0.21	30.9	36.0	33.1	66.5	33.5
1966	4.62	8.7	2.37	2.25	0.12	26.6	37.5	35.9	72.2	27.8
1967	4.16	-9.9	2.14	2.02	0.12	24.4	36.3	39.3	76.0	24.0
1968	4.05	-2.6	2.10	1.95	0.15	21.8	38.2	40.0	77.2	22.8
1969	4.03	-0.4	2.20	1.83	0.37	23.5	39.1	37.4	82.4	17.6
1970	4.59	13.8	2.26	2.33	-0.07	25.6	37.7	36.7	82.7	17.3
1971	4.85	5.6	2.64	2.21	0.43	28.9	34.9	36.2	83.9	16.1
1972	6.30	29.8	3.44	2.86	0.58	27.7	41.0	31.3	79.4	20.6
1973	10.98	74.2	5.82	5.16	0.66	24.7	39.5	35.8	76.4	23.6
1974	14.57	32.6	6.95	7.62	-0.67	33.8	29.8	36.4	75.7	24.3
1975	14.75	1.2	7.26	7.49	-0.23	39.3	31.1	29.6	85.4	14.6
1976	13.44	-8.8	6.86	6.58	0.28	38.9	32.7	28.4	86.8	13.2
1977	14.80	10.1	7.59	7.21	0.38	38.5	33.9	27.6	76.1	23.9
1978	20.64	39.4	9.75	10.89	-1.14	37.4	35.0	27.6	81.4	18.6
1979	29.33	42.1	13.66	15.67	-2.01	44.0	32.9	23.1	81.3	18.7
1980	37.82	28.9	18.27	19.55	-1.28	51.8	29.5	18.7	78.9	21.1
1981	40.37	6.7	20.89	19.48	1.41	56.8	26.1	17.6	72.8	27.2
1982	39.30	-2.6	21.82	17.48	4.34	60.5	24.6	14.9	70.8	29.2

*Current U.S. dollars.

**Figures are percentage shares of either exports or imports.

Source: Chinese Statistical Yearbook 1983, pp. 420–21.

2. Selected Commodities

	1952	1957	1962	1965	1970	1975	1978	1982
Grain								
Exports (10,000 tons)	152.88	209.26	103.09	241.65	211.91	280.61	187.72	125.12
Imports (10,000 tons)	.01	16.68	492.30	640.52	535.96	373.50	883.25	1,611.69
Other exports								
Cotton cloth (million m)	16	350	549	803	696	1,072	1,096	1,124
Polyester blend (mil. m)	—	—	—	1.52	13.16	70.97	133.44	491.02
Quality rugs (1000 sq m)	—	79.8	257.4	152.9	214.0	328.4	740.2	1,011.7
Fireworks (10,000 cases)	—	3	10	28	36	93	136	269
Bicycles (10,000)	—	.38	2.30	16.32	21.51	44.17	30.28	109.13
Coal (10,000 tons)	29	188	260	336	227	300	312	644
Crude oil (10,000 tons)	—	—	6.28	19.64	19.15	987.79	1,131.15	1,520.37
Refined oil (10,000 tons)	—	—	2.71	10.22	19.32	210.06	217.41	527.20
Other imports								
Steel (10,000 tons)	45.99	69.59	23.01	75.86	266.70	400.65	863.76	413.70
Chem. fertilizer (10,000 tons)	21.7	121.65	124.07	273.49	641.86	493.52	733.33	1,110.82
Phosphate (10,000 tons)	—	4.54	59.38	81.4	98.27	33.81	41.24	41.62
Cotton (10,000 cubic m)	7.68	4.77	3.69	19.94	8.12	17.70	50.95	47.40
Granulated sugar (10,000 tons)	5.28	11.93	99.56	70.79	50.92	36.12	129.90	217.72
Wood (10,000 cubic m)	1.17	2.78	29.64	156.77	8.13	28.13	53.40	482.71

Source: Chinese Statistical Yearbook 1983, pp. 420–39.

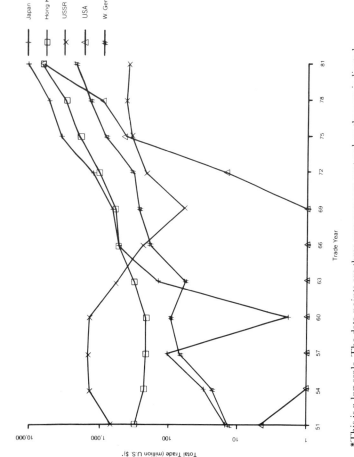

3. *Trade with Selected Countries*

*This is a log scale. The data points are three-year averages centered on the year indicated.
Source: Chinese Statistical Yearbook 1983.

3. Trade with Selected Countries

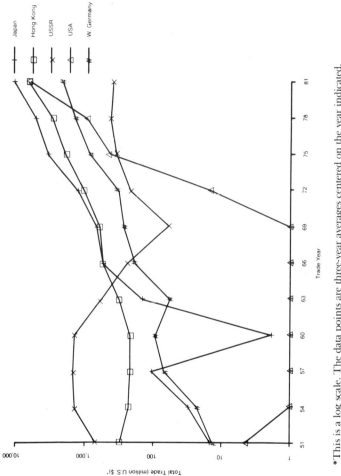

Japan
Hong Kong
USSR
USA
W Germany

Total Trade (million U.S. $).

Trade Year

*This is a log scale. The data points are three-year averages centered on the year indicated.
Source: Chinese Statistical Yearbook 1983.

Subject Index

447

Name Index*

*All names appearing in italics refer to authors mentioned in notes. Complete citations of their works can be found by looking up page reference.